The Foundations of Jurisprudence

The Classical Shīʿah Library

VOLUME 1

THE SHIʿAH INSTITUTE

The titles published in this series are listed at *brill.com/csl*

The Foundations of Jurisprudence

An Introduction to Imāmī Shīʿī Legal Theory

مبادئ الوصول
إلى علم الأصول

By

Jamāl al-Dīn Abū Manṣūr al-Ḥasan ibn Sadīd al-Dīn Yūsuf ibn Zayn al-Dīn ʿAlī ibn al-Muṭahhar al-Ḥillī (d. 726 AH/1325 CE)

Known as

al-ʿAllāmah al-Ḥillī

Introduction, Translation, and Arabic Critical Edition by

Sayyid Amjad H. Shah Naqavi

TUTA SUB AEGIDE PALLAS · 1683 ·

BRILL

LEIDEN | BOSTON

The Library of Congress Cataloging-in-Publication Data is available online at http://catalog.loc.gov
LC record available at http://lccn.loc.gov/2016956691

Typeface for the Latin, Greek, and Cyrillic scripts: "Brill". See and download: brill.com/brill-typeface.

ISBN 978-90-04-31171-8 (hardback)
ISBN 978-90-04-31173-2 (paperback)
ISBN 978-90-04-31177-0 (e-book)

This book is printed on acid-free paper.

To Aun, the helper, and Askary, the soldier;
both veritable reflections of
their respective names

قَالَ الرِّضَا عَلَيْهِ السَّلَامُ

عَلَيْنَا إِلْقَاءُ الأُصُولِ وعَلَيْكُمُ التَّفْرِيعُ

Contents

Foreword

The last decade or so has witnessed a remarkable growth of interest in the unique traditions and intellectual history of Shīʿah Islam, both within Western academia and among a wider community who are curious about the Imāmī Shīʿah tradition, often in light of the vicissitudes of contemporary politics in the Middle East. As it stands, many of the classical works which constitute the intellectual foundations of this extraordinarily diverse tradition—whether they are selections of Prophetic and Imāmic sayings, or works of classical Shīʿah literature, jurisprudential theory, philosophy, or spirituality—have yet to be adequately translated for an English-speaking readership, which may be unfamiliar with the source language in which these texts were written. Accurate, unabridged, and nuanced translations of these classical Imāmī Shīʿī texts are therefore essential, both in order that the tradition of Shīʿah Islam may be allowed to speak for itself—without mediation—and also to foster greater understanding of this tradition in academia and amongst those communities interested in the study thereof. It is, therefore, our great privilege to present the inaugural volume in the Classical Shīʿah Library: an ongoing series, which aims to publish seminal works from the Shīʿah tradition. Many of the titles in this series will be produced as dual-language Arabic-English editions, for ease of comparison with the original, along with contextual and explanatory annotations.

To this end, we are proud to present the first volume in the Classical Shīʿah Library: *The Foundations of Jurisprudence: An Introduction to Imāmī Shīʿī Legal Theory*, a translation of the *Mabādiʾ al-wuṣūl ilā ʿilm al-uṣūl* by al-ʿAllāmah al-Ḥillī (d. 726 AH /1325 CE). This edition is a dual-language Arabic–English text based on the earliest and most authoritative manuscripts of *Mabādiʾ al-wuṣūl ilā ʿilm al-uṣūl* extant from the life of the author, as well as later manuscripts. The work itself is an important text of Imāmī jurisprudence (*uṣūl al-fiqh*), a field of knowledge, which, along with law (*fiqh*), theology (*kalām*), and philosophy (*falsafah*), represents the pinnacle of erudition in the world of Shīʿī scholarship. In this short text, al-ʿAllāmah al-Ḥillī, provides a typically lucid and pithy overview of the principle areas of discussion pertaining to jurisprudence.

Altogether this constitutes the first time that a classical work of Imāmī Shīʿī jurisprudence has been translated into English. As such, this volume will be of inestimable benefit to all those who are engaged in the study of al-ʿAllāmah al-Ḥillī's jurisprudence (*uṣūl al-fiqh*). It is our hope that *The Foundations of Jurisprudence* will encourage further scholarly interest in this subject, and that the following volumes in the Classical Shīʿah Library series will also contribute to a deeper understanding of the intellectual heritage and traditions of the Shīʿah.

Saiyad Nizamuddin Ahmad
Series Editor, Classical Shīʿah Library
Bloomsbury, London
ʿĪd al-Mubāhalah 1437 AH/ 26th September 2016

Preface

For the last millennia or so the scholars of the Imāmī Shīʿah community have been engaged in the erudite study of the complex discipline known as jurisprudence (*uṣūl al-fiqh*). This intellectual endeavour has resulted in a highly sophisticated corpus of literature on legal methodology; one which attests that, whilst for the greater part of the Muslim world 'the door of *ijtihād*' may have been slammed shut a long time ago, it has, nonetheless, remained somewhat ajar for the Shīʿah.

It is from this corpus of Imāmī Shīʿī literature that we are honoured to present the following volume, entitled *The Foundations of Jurisprudence: An Introduction to Imāmī Shīʿī Legal Theory*; a translation and critical Arabic edition of the *Mabādiʾ al-wuṣūl ilā ʿilm al-uṣūl* of Jamāl al-Dīn Abū Manṣūr al-Ḥasan b. Yūsuf b. ʿAlī b. al-Muṭahhar al-Ḥillī (d. 726 AH/1325 CE), known to posterity as al-ʿAllāmah al-Ḥillī. His *Mabādiʾ* is a veritable *summa* of jurisprudence that offers a concise, and highly condensed, overview of the entire subject of jurisprudence (*uṣūl al-fiqh*), as well as a vista from which to fully survey the state of jurisprudential theory in both the era of the author and in that leading up to it.

The writings of al-ʿAllāmah al-Ḥillī mark a pivotal milestone in the intellectual history of Imāmī Shīʿī jurisprudence (*uṣūl al-fiqh*), which have hitherto defined its course across the intervening centuries. However great the distance may seem between al-ʿAllāmah al-Ḥillī's time and our own, a close study of his works remains indispensable for all those who wish to sincerely engage, on either a theoretical or practical level, with the manifold intricacies of Shīʿī jurisprudence (*uṣūl al-fiqh*). In *Nihāyat,* our sage characterises this subject as an investigation into the methods of law, which largely refer to the Qurʾān and *Sunnah*. As such, the matters succinctly encapsulated and deftly handled by al-ʿAllāmah al-Ḥillī in the *Mabādiʾ*, ranging from linguistical matters to the issues pertaining to juristic reasoning, are as pertinent now as they were then.

To date, very little has been written on the subject of Imāmī Shīʿī jurisprudence in Western academia, and of that which has been published on this subject there is not much which does justice to the nuances of this scholarly tradition. It is unfortunate, for instance, to find the sophistication of the epistemological theory which underpins so much of this jurisprudence (*uṣūl al-fiqh*) crudely misconstrued: one emblematic instance of which is the misleading substitution of the manifestly distinct concept of *wahm* for *ẓann* in a recent doctoral dissertation and other published titles. It is also disappointing to discover the terminology of Imāmī jurisprudence treated with such laxity in published works on Shīʿah Islam; for instance *ijtihād* has been translated as 'personal interpretation', or words to that effect, and *taqlīd* as 'imitation' or 'emulation', when in fact neither of these alleged translations adequately captures the technical, or legal, meanings of these particular terms in the finely-wrought nomenclature of jurisprudence. Moreover, the fledgling research made into this area in Western academia has greatly suffered from the imposition of external theoretical frameworks, and laboured hypotheses, onto a millennia's worth of intellectual inquiry, which has yet to be sagaciously presented in itself—Shīʿī jurisprudence *qua* Shīʿī jurisprudence—as though seeking to 'frame' a picture before the artist had finished applying the paint to the canvas.

It is also the case that, in the light of recent political developments, some studies of jurisprudence (*uṣūl al-fiqh*) have inappropriately imbricated the concepts appertaining to this discipline in a contemporary political context to which they do not belong and from which they did not emerge. This, arguably, compromises the disinterested spirit of inquiry which should be the hallmark of good scholarship—an interpretative decision, which, although perhaps a reflection of certain institutional pressures, nonetheless greatly de-contextualises the thinkers, concepts, and thematics, which comprise the long history of Imāmī Shīʿī jurisprudence.

In sum, the effect of such undertakings has presented, for instance, the epistemological inquiry that leads to a *probable* understanding of scriptural evidence to be wrongly configured as though a millennia's theorisation culminates only in 'doubt'. Moreover it has bestowed upon those who are not well-versed in the original sources, or in any case do not have access to them, a somewhat distorted impression of what is—as the work presented below makes abundantly clear—an intricate and highly-technical tradition of jurisprudential thought.

This work attempts to bring the quiddities of Shīʿī jurisprudence to the fore, by attending to the nuances of the terms within which it operates, and by endeavouring, as far as possible, to adequately reflect this terminology in the target language. This edition has been undertaken with the intention of introducing an Anglophone readership—which is increasingly keen to learn about such matters—to the concepts of Imāmī Shīʿī jurisprudence (*uṣūl al-fiqh*), and, moreover, to present Shīʿī jurisprudence *qua* Shīʿī jurisprudence. The introduction to this volume has therefore been offered with a minimum of commentary; instead it provides an explanatory and referential guide through the discussions of al-ʿAllāmah al-Ḥillī's *Mabādiʾ*, which situates each of the pithy statements made therein, in relation to their thoroughgoing analysis and discussion elsewhere in the author's comprehensive and comparative treatment of the subject, entitled: *Nihāyat al-wuṣūl ilā ʿilm al-uṣūl*.

This introduction has been designed to aid the advanced reader in their exploration of this work. However, as will be seen, a comprehensive consideration of al-ʿAllāmah al-Ḥillī's jurisprudential thought demands a work of much greater scope than the brief introduction presented below, and thus we aim for this volume to be followed by our monograph-length study, devoted to an in-depth analysis of the legal theories of al-ʿAllāmah al-Ḥillī, entitled: *The Jurisprudence of al-ʿAllāmah al-Ḥillī.*

The following dual Arabic-English text is without precedent insofar as it constitutes the first time an English translation has been made of a classical work of Imāmī Shīʿī jurisprudence alongside an annotated critical edition of the Arabic text, one based upon all the extant, and endorsed, manuscripts dating from the life of the author. It is our hope that this work will serve as a conduit for further research in, and stimulate new inquiries into, the tradition of Shīʿī jurisprudence (*uṣūl al-fiqh*) as well as the paramount contribution of al-ʿAllāmah al-Ḥillī therein.

*

My interest in the works of al-ʿAllāmah al-Ḥillī stretches back over twenty years, to my first encounter with the *Mabādiʾ al-wuṣūl ilā ʿilm al-uṣūl* when visiting the shrine city of Qum on a research trip, whilst studying for my PhD under the supervision of my late supervisor Dr I. K. A. Howard at the University of Edinburgh. It has only been in the last ten months or so, that I have begun work on this project in earnest—translating it whilst also immersed in the preparation of numerous other publications and projects at the Shīʿah Institute.

This edition has entailed a tremendous exertion of effort in order to come to fruition in such a short duration of time. Of course I cannot help wishing that fate had afforded us more hours to further refine what is presented herein. In any case, thanks are here due to the friends of the Shīʿah Institute, for their kindness and support, as well as to our publisher, Brill, for their sheer patience and commitment to this volume and the Classical Shīʿah Library series it inaugurates. I would also like to thank Sayed Hussain Murtaza, and the following libraries and their staff, for making digital scans of the various manuscripts of *Mabādiʾ al-wuṣūl ilā ʿilm al-uṣūl* available: Astānah-yi Quds-i Raḍawī, Mashhad; the British Library, London; the Kāshif al-Ghiṭāʾ Foundation, Najaf; and the Marʿashī Library, Qum.

The published dual-text, would not have seen the light of day were it not for the combined and sustained labour of our in-house team of researchers, scholars, and editors at the Shīʿah Institute, who have my unreserved gratitude for their kind endeavours; in particular to Sayed Aun Kazemi, for his untiring research and support, to George MacBeth, for his learned editorial input, and to Saiyad Nizamuddin Ahmad, whose tremendous erudition and scholarly precision were of indelible help in bringing the project to completion. Needless to say, any shortcomings present in the volume are entirely my own.

The love, kindness, and support of my parents is beyond what mere thanks can repay; I am forever grateful for the education they availed me, in particular to my late mother, for whose love I am forever indebted. Last but not least, all my humble gratitude is due to my ancestors the *Ahl al-Bayt*, peace be upon them, and to my forebear, Pīr-i Ṭarīqat, Jalāl Ganj, Mīr Surkh, Mīr Buzurg, Sher Shāh, Quṭb al-Aqṭāb, Jalāl Aʿẓam Ḥaydar-i Ṣānī Haẓrat Sayyid Jalāl al-Dīn Ḥaydar, Surkh Pōsh, Naqavī al-Bukhārī (595–690 AH/1198–1291 CE), the grand master of the Lofty Ḥusaynī Murtaẓawī Shāhī order of Bukhara (*silsilah ʿaliyyah ḥusayniyyah murtaẓawiyyah shāhiyyah bukhāriyyah*) and the founder of the Jalālī order (*silsilah jalāliyyah*), and his descendants, my forefathers, for their continuous guidance, *ʿināyat*, and grace.

بندہ شیرخدا
Sayyid Amjad H. Shah Naqavi
Bloomsbury, London
ʿĪd al-Ghadīr 1437 AH/ 20th September 2016

Introduction

قال العلّامة الحلّي رحمه الله: وفائدة تصنيف الكتب مع موت مصنّفها
استفادة طريقة الإجتهاد من تصرّفهم في الحوادث وكيفية بناء بعضها
على البعض ومعرفة المجمع عليه من المختلف فيه.

Said al-ʿAllāmah al-Ḥillī, may God have mercy upon him: 'The benefit of composing books, although the author's referenced therein have long since passed away, is to: reap the benefit of the juristic reasoning that they practiced regarding various cases; [to understand] how each layer of the methodology of juristic reasoning is based upon another; and to gain knowledge of what is agreed upon from that which is disputed'.[1]

1 Part One

1.1 *The Life and Times of al-ʿAllāmah al-Ḥillī*

Jamāl al-Dīn Abū Manṣūr al-Ḥasan b. Sadīd al-Dīn Yūsuf b. Zayn al-Dīn ʿAlī b. al-Muṭahhar al-Ḥillī—subsequently known in Shīʿī scholarship by the honorific title *al-ʿAllāmah*, which can be translated as *Doctor Maximus* (hereafter referred to as ʿAllāmah)—was born on the evening of Friday (*laylat al-jumuʿah*) on the twenty-ninth of Ramaḍān al-Mubārak in 648 AH/1250 CE into a distinguished scholarly family in the Iraqi town of al-Ḥillah, which is situated on the outskirts of the ancient city of Babylon.[2] His father, Sadīd al-Dīn Yūsuf b. ʿAlī b. al-Muṭahhar al-Ḥillī, was a man of formidable erudition, who, although his achievements were to be somewhat eclipsed by those of his prodigious son, was nonetheless clearly a scholar of high standing. ʿAllāmah's maternal uncle was Najm al-Dīn Jaʿfar b. al-Ḥasan b. Abī Zakariyyā Yaḥyā b. al-Ḥasan b. Saʿīd

---

1 Al-ʿAllāmah al-Ḥillī, *Nihāyat al-wuṣūl ilā ʿil al-uṣūl*, 5 vols., ed. Ibrāhīm al-Bahādurī, Qum, 1425 AH/2004, vol. V, p. 249.

2 For the life and times of ʿAllāmah see the following primary Arabic sources: Sayyid Muḥsin al-Amīn, *Aʿyān al-shīʿah*, Beirut, 1420 AH/2000, vol. IX, pp. 14–33; Mīrza ʿAbd Allāh Afandī, *Riyāḍ al-ʿulamāʾ wa ḥiyāḍ al-fuḍalāʾ*, Qum, 1403 AH/1982, vol. IV, pp. 358–90; and, Mīrza Muḥammad Khwānsārī, *Rawḍāt al-jannāt fī aḥwāl al-ʿulamāʾ wa al-sādāt*, Beirut, 1431 AH/2010, vol. II, pp. 269–86. Afandī notes ʿAllāmah's birth date as the twenty-seventh of Ramaḍān 648 AH/1250 CE.

 | DOI 10.1163/9789004311770_002

al-Ḥillī (d. 676 AH/1277 CE), known as *al-Muḥaqqiq* (the Verifier),[3] a prolific scholar who is regarded alongside ʿAllāmah as one of the great Imāmī figures of the age. He was also honoured with the privilege of learning from the two Sayyid brothers Jamāl al-Dīn Aḥmad b. Ṭāwūs (d. 673 AH/1274 CE) and Raḍī al-Dīn ʿAlī b. Ṭāwūs (d. 664 AH/1266 CE); as well as the notable commentator on the *Nahj al-Balāghah,* Kamāl al-Dīn Mītham al-Baḥrānī (d. 699 AH/1300 CE).[4] Whilst none of the extant historical sources confirm his presence in the city of Maragha—home to the observatory of the great Shīʿī philosopher, astronomer and theologian Naṣīr al-Dīn al-Ṭūsī (d. 672 AH/1274 CE)[5]—it would not be an unwarranted conclusion to infer that it was indeed there that he studied with Naṣīr al-Dīn al-Ṭūṣī and Najm al-Dīn al-Kātibī al-Qazwīnī (d. 675 AH/1277 CE) inasmuch as he explicitly mentions both having been his teachers in his *al-Ijāzah al-kabīrah li banī Zuhrah,* which he composed on the fifteenth of Shaʿbān 723 AH/1323 CE. Thus it could be concluded that it was at Maragha that he studied theology and the natural sciences.[6] If that were the case he would have probably left Maragha around the time of Naṣīr al-Dīn's death. For the next thirty odd years ʿAllāmah continued to study, and to teach, between his hometown of Ḥillah and nearby Baghdad.

A turning point in ʿAllāmah's career came at the beginning of the fourteenth century, when he arrived at the court of the Mongol ruler Uljaytū (Öljeitü) Khān (r. 704–716 AH/1304–1316 CE). At around the same time as ʿAllāmah's arrival, Uljaytū converted from Sunnī to Imāmī Shīʿī Islam. It is not known for certain whether ʿAllāmah played any role in the Khān's conversion, though many later Shīʿī accounts do assert that this was the case, contending that ʿAllāmah was summoned to court to adjudicate on a

3 Jaʿfar b. al-Ḥasan b. Abī Zakariyyā Yaḥyā b. al-Ḥasan b. Saʿīd al-Ḥillī, Abū al-Qāsim Najm al-Dīn, known as al-Muḥaqqiq al-Ḥillī (d. 676 AH/1277 CE), was a very prominent and erudite Imāmī jurist, who authored *Maʿārij al-uṣūl.* See Sayyid Muḥsin al-Amīn, *Aʿyān al-shīʿah* vol. VI, p. 128.

4 For an extensive list of ʿAllāmah's teachers and students, see *Aʿyān al-shīʿah*, vol. IX, pp. 22–24; Mīrza ʿAbd Allāh Afandī, *Riyāḍ al-ʿulamāʾ wa ḥiyāḍ al-fuḍalāʾ*, vol. IV, pp. 358–90; and Mīrza Muḥammad Khwānsārī, *Rawḍāt al-jannāt fī awḥwāl al-ʿulamāʾ wa al-sādāt*, vol. II, pp. 269–286.

5 Muḥammad b. Muḥammad b. al-Ḥasan al-Ṭūsī, Abū Jaʿfar Naṣīr al-Dīn, known variously as Naṣīr al-Dīn al-Ṭūsī, Khwājah Naṣīr, and al-Muḥaqqiq al-Ṭūsī (d. 672 AH/1273 CE), is buried in al-Kāẓimayn. He is among the most renowned Imāmī Shīʿī scholars in history, a man of encyclopaedic erudition, who participated, and made indelible contributions to, all the fields of knowledge in his time, including: theology, philosophy, astronomy, astrology, mathematics, mysticism, and literature. See *Aʿyān al-shīʿah* vol. XIV, pp. 242–50.

6 Muḥammad Baqir Majlisī, *Bihār al-anwār*, Beirut, 1403 AH/1983, vol. CVII, pp. 60, 137 at p. 62 and p. 66.

legal problem troubling Uljaytū which none of his courtiers could solve, and that the Khān was so impressed by the Imāmī scholar that he embraced his school of thought. Regardless of the origins of the situation, what is certain is that ʿAllāmah found himself at the court of a patron more sympathetic to, and more powerful than, any Imāmī scholar could have hitherto expected. ʿAllāmah authored several treatises in response to questions raised by Uljaytū, and was part of the 'travelling school' (*al-madrasah al-sayyārah*), a group of trusted scholars appointed to accompany the Khān and provide him with their religious expertise wherever he went. In addition to his usual scholarly activities, at the court ʿAllāmah also had the opportunity to engage in public debates with adherents of different schools of thought, an arena in which he excelled.

Despite this favourable environment, towards the end of his life ʿAllāmah chose to take his leave of the Khān and to depart from Uljaytū's new capital Sulṭāniyah, returning to his native Ḥillah, where he primarily devoted his time to teaching.

ʿAllāmah was a prolific writer and more than a hundred and twenty odd works have been ascribed to him on an astounding range of subjects: theology (*al-kalām*), philosophy (*al-falsafah*), logic (*al-manṭiq*), law (*al-fiqh*), jurisprudence (*uṣūl al-fiqh*), prophetic tradition (*ḥadīth*), biographies of the transmitters (*ʿilm al-rijāl*), grammar (*naḥw*), Qur'ānic exegesis (*tafsīr*), and perhaps even a work on theoretical mysticism.[7]

In addition to his many erudite writings, ʿAllāmah's students included: his son, Fakhr al-Muḥaqqiqīn al-Ḥillī (d. 771 AH/1370 CE), his nephews, al-Sayyid ʿAmīd al-Dīn (d. 754 AH/1353 CE) and al-Sayyid Ḍiyā' al-Dīn (d. after 740 AH/1339-40 CE), Muḥammad b. ʿAlī al-Jurjānī, al-Shaykh Quṭb al-Dīn Muḥammad b. al-Rāzī (d. 766 AH/1365 CE), and al-Shakyh Taqī al-Dīn Ibrāhīm b. Muḥammad al-Baṣrī.

ʿAllāmah passed away in his hometown of Ḥillah on Saturday the twenty-first of Muḥarram in the year 726 AH/1325 CE, by which time he had become the most influential Ithnā ʿAsharī Shīʿī scholar of his day, exerting his unparalleled influence up to the present through his intellectual legacy. His remains were transferred and interred, befitting his status and religious rank, in a chamber located adjacent to, and to the left of, the feet of the tomb of Imām ʿAlī b. Abī Ṭālib in the sacred shrine of al-Najaf al-Ashraf.[8]

---

7 Interestingly, ʿAbd al-ʿAzīz al-Ṭabaṭabā'ī lists a work entitled *Sharḥ ḥikmat al-ishrāq* on p. 132 of his *Maktabat al-ʿAllāmah al-Ḥillī*, Qum, 1416 AH/1995, however, the entry is left blank. For a recent work on the theology of al-ʿAllāmah al-Ḥillī, see: ʿAlī al-Madan, *Taṭawwur ʿilm al-kalām al-imāmī*, Baghdad, 1431 AH/2010

8 For a complete picture of the life and times of ʿAllāmah al-Ḥillī, see: al-ʿAllāmah al-Ḥillī,

1.2 *The School of Ḥillah*

ʿAllāmah represents the pinnacle of a wider revival of Imāmī Shīʿī thought, particularly in the area of jurisprudence, which occurred during the later twelfth and thirteenth centuries; one which is often associated with his hometown of Ḥillah. The first flowering of Imāmī law came about during the lives of Imām al-Bāqir and Imām al-Ṣādiq in the second Hijrī century, which corresponds to the seventh and eighth centuries of the Common Era, The historical sources attesting to this are the biographical encyclopedias and indexes which record the names of various companions of the Imāms who authored treatises on jurisprudence, the most prominent of whom are: Hishām b. al-Ḥakam, companion of Imām al-Ṣādiq; Yūnus b. ʿAbd al-Raḥmān, companion of Imām al-Kāẓim and Imām al-Riḍā; Dārim b. Qabīsah, a companion of Imām al-Riḍā; Abū Sahl al-Nawbakhtī, who lived in the era of the Lesser Occultation; and Muḥammad b. Aḥmad b. al-Junayd, the teacher of al-Shaykh al-Mufīd (d. 413 AH/1032 CE).[9] Thereafter, in the tenth and eleventh centuries of the Common Era, Baghdad was ruled by the Shīʿī Buwayhid dynasty. By and large, the Buwayhid amīrs were tolerant rulers under whose reign the Imāmiyyah flourished, with scholars such as: Muḥammad b. Bābawayh (d. 381 AH/991 CE),[10] Muḥammad b. Muḥammad al-Mufīd, al-Sharīf al-Murtaḍā (d. 436 AH/1044 CE),[11] Sālār al-Daylamī (d. 448 AH/1056 CE or 463 AH/1071 CE),[12] and Muḥammad b. al-Ḥasan

---

Irshād al-adhhān ilā aḥkām al-īmān, ed. al-Shaykh Fāris al-Ḥassūn, 2 vols., Qum, 1410 AH/ 1989-90, vol. I, pp. 23–18; al-ʿAllāmah al-Ḥillī, *Īḍāḥ al-ishtibāh,* ed. al-Shaykh Muḥammad al-Ḥassūn, Qum, 1411 AH/1990-91, pp. 29–75. Together these two works provide a very extensive overview of the life of al-ʿAllāmah and have been extremely well-organised by their respective editors, systematically detailing many matters pertaining to the life of our author.

9 Muḥammad b. Muḥammad b. al-Nuʿmān, Abū ʿAbd Allāh al-Baghdādī al-Karkhī, known as al-Shaykh al-Mufīd (d. 413 AH/1022 CE), was the most eminent Imāmī Shīʿī scholar of his era. He authored more than one hundred and fifty works, his complete writings have been published in fourteen volumes. See al-Khwānsārī, *Rawḍāt al-jannāt*, vol. VI, pp. 153–78.

10 Muḥammad b. Abī al-Ḥasan ʿAlī b. al-Ḥusayn al-Qummī, known as Ibn Bābawayh and al-Shaykh al-Ṣadūq (d. 381 AH/991–2 CE), was one of the most important early Imāmī Shīʿī *ḥadīth* scholars. He compiled the second of the 'Four Books' (*al-kutub al-arbʿah*), namely, *Kitāb Man lā yaḥḍuruhu al-faqīh.* See *Aʿyān al-shīʿah* vol. XIV, pp. 320–22.

11 ʿAlī b. al-Ḥusayn al-Mūsawī, Abū al-Qāsim, known variously as al-Sharīf al-Murtaḍā, al-Sayyid al-Murtaḍā, or ʿAlam al-Hudā (d. 436 AH/1044 CE). He is generally regarded as the successor to al-Shaykh al-Mufīd, and thereby inherited the mantle of the most prominent jurist and theologian of the Shīʿah Imāmiyyah in his time. He was also one of the teachers of Shaykh al-Ṭāʾifah. See al-Khwānsārī, *Rawḍāt al-jannāt*, vol. IV, pp. 294–312.

12 Ḥamzah b. ʿAbd al-ʿAzīz, al-Shaykh Abū Yaʿlā al-Daylamī al-Ṭabaristānī, known as Sālār al-Daylamī (d. 448 AH/1056 CE or 463 AH/1071 CE), was a theologian, master of juris-

al-Ṭūsī (d. 460 AH/1067 CE), known as Shaykh al-Ṭā'ifah,[13] each of whom, with the exception of Ibn Bābawayh, elaborated upon the principles of Imāmī jurisprudence. The son and student of Shaykh al-Ṭā'ifah, al-Shaykh Abū ʿAlī al-Ṭūsī (d. after 515 AH/1121 CE), is attested to have also been a teacher of the developing Imāmī legal tradition in his own right, his students included: Sadīd al-Dīn al-Ḥimṣī al-Rāzī (d. after 583 AH/1187 CE) and Abū Manṣūr Muḥammad b. Ḥasan Manṣūr al-Naqqāsh al-Mawṣilī; the latter of whom is included among the teachers of al-Sayyid Abū al-Makārim Ḥamzah b. ʿAlī b. Zuhrah al-Ḥalabī (d. 585 AH/1189-90 CE), better known as Ibn Zuhrah.[14] This period of Imāmī Shīʿī scholarship on jurisprudence in Baghdad was, to some extent, interrupted by political events. In 447 AH/1055 CE the Seljuqs, signalling the end of Buwayhid power, captured Baghdad. In contrast to their predecessors, the Seljuqs were staunch adherents of Sunnī Islam, a position much reflected in their governance. Thus, shortly after their arrival, Shaykh al-Ṭā'ifah, fleeing escalating anti-Shīʿī sentiment in Baghdad, left the capital for the city of al-Najaf al-Ashraf, wherein he founded a college (*hawzah*) which has remained a bastion of Imāmī scholarship up to the present day, despite the vicissitudes of time. Shaykh al-Ṭā'ifah's departure from Baghdad, in essence, marked the withdrawal of Shīʿah scholarship from the centre of power, an exclusion which cannot have been without a role in the subsequent waning of some of the ambition and vibrancy which had hitherto characterised Imāmī legal writing during the previous century. Indeed, the century following Shaykh al-Ṭā'ifah is often characterised as a period of decline.

This picture of the later eleventh and early twelfth centuries of the Common Era comes, in no small measure, from the writings of the Imāmī scholar Muḥammad b. Manṣūr b. Aḥmad b. Idrīs al-Ḥillī, commonly known as Ibn Idrīs, (d. 598 AH/1202 CE),[15] who begins his work, *Kitāb al-Sarā'ir*

prudence, jurist and grammarian, prolific amongst the scholars of his day as one of the most talented students of al-Shaykh al-Mufīd and al-Sayyid al-Murtaḍā. He authored the jurisprudential work *al-Marāsim al-ʿalawiyyah fī al–aḥkām al-nabawiyyah*, and was a notable teacher of al-Shaykh Abū ʿAlī al-Ṭūsī, son of Shaykh al-Ṭā'ifah. See *Aʿyān al-shīʿah* vol. XI, pp. 109–112.

13 Muḥammad b. al-Ḥasan al-Ṭūsī, known as Shaykh al-Ṭā'ifah (d. 460 AH/1067 CE). This epithet reflects not only his pre-eminent authority among the scholars of his day, but also the enduring significance his work holds for posterity. He authored seminal works in *ḥadīth*, of which two constitute the third and fourth works of the so-called 'Four Books' (*al-kutub al-arbʿah*), as well as other works in law, jurisprudence, biography, bibliography, and Qur'ānic exegesis. See al-Khwānsārī, *Rawḍāt al-jannāt*, vol. VI, pp. 216–49.

14 See *Aʿyān al-shīʿah*, vol IX, p. 534.

15 Muḥammad b. Manṣūr b. Aḥmad b. Idrīs, Abū Jaʿfar, known as Ibn Idrīs al-Ḥillī (d. 598 AH/1202 CE), was the author of *Kitāb al-Sarā'ir al-ḥāwī li taḥrīr al-fatāwī*. See al-Khwānsārī, *Rawḍāt al-jannāt*, vol. VI, pp. 274–90.

al-ḥāwī li-taḥrīr al-fatawī, with a lament upon the deplorable lack of scholarship among his fellows on matters pertaining to the divine law (*sharīʿah*).[16] The teachers of Ibn Idrīs include: al-Shaykh Hibat Allāh al-Sūrāwī;[17] al-Sharīf Abū al-Ḥasan ʿAlī b. Ibrāhīm al-ʿAlawī al-ʿUrayḍī; [18] Ibn Zuhrah; and Abū ʿAlī al-Ṭūsī, the son of Shaykh al-Ṭāʾifah. Despite this, he was strongly critical of his contemporaries mere reliance on the works of previous scholars, such as Shaykh al-Ṭāʾifah, without their placing a greater emphasis on legal methodology, and, indeed, he went so far as to suggest that Shaykh al-Ṭāʾifah himself, never truly espoused an exclusive reliance of this kind.[19] In neither of these contentions was Ibn Idrīs the first to take such a position. Shaykh al-Ṭāʾifah's own teacher al-Sharīf al-Murtaḍā had favoured a more rationalistic approach—he is frequently cited by Ibn Idrīs in corroboration of his own views—and, even among his contemporaries, Ibn Idrīs was not alone in maintaining such a stance towards the understanding of law.[20] The significance of Ibn Idrīs' writings is not only due to the verdict which they give on his predecessors, but also, and perhaps more importantly, down to the reception which they met with in the hands of his successors. The criticisms of Ibn Idrīs provided the impetus for the next few generations of Imāmī legal scholars to develop many ideas which have exercised a profound and formative influence on Shīʿī law ever since.

The end of Seljuq power came emphatically with the Mongols' sack of Baghdad in 656 AH/1258 CE. Sweeping away much of the political status quo which had hitherto defined the Near East for the preceding few centuries, the Mongol invasions nonetheless represented something of an opportunity for the Imāmī intelligentsia. We have already seen how Uljaytū Khān's reign was especially advantageous to ʿAllāmah, however Uljaytū's predecessors, in their at best whimsical disinterest in Islam, were also often an improvement on the Seljuq sultans from the point of view of non-Sunnīs. Indeed, Uljaytū's brother and immediate predecessor, Ghāzān Khān (r. 694–713 AH/1295–1304 CE), was the first Mongol ruler to convert to Islam, and in any case this was not accompanied by any favouring of particular groups at the expense of others. In this context we may understand the inspiration behind the Imāmī scholar

16 See Ibn Idrīs al-Ḥillī, *Kitāb al-Sarāʾir al-ḥāwī li-taḥrīr al-fatāwī*, Qum, 1410 AH/1989, vol. I, pp. 41–46.

17 Al-Shaykh Jamāl al-Dīn Abū ʿAbd Allāh al-Ḥasan b. al-Shaykh Jamāl al-Dīn Hibat Allāh b. Ruṭbah al-Sūrāwī (alive in 560 AH/1164–5 CE). See *Aʿyān al-shīʿah* vol. IX, p. 5.

18 *Aʿyān al-shīʿah* vol. XII, p. 179.

19 See Ibn Idrīs al-Ḥillī, *Kitāb al-Sarāʾir al-ḥāwī li-taḥrīr al-fatāwī*, vol. I, pp. 46–54.

20 See the works of al-Sayyid ʿIzz al-Dīn Ḥamzah b. ʿAlī al-Ḥusaynī al-Ḥalabī (d. 585 AH/1189 CE).

ʿAlī b. Mūsā b. Ṭāwūs's (d. 664 AH/1266 CE) edict that a just non-Muslim ruler is preferable to an unjust Muslim ruler.[21]

Teaching, as he was, almost a century before these events, Ibn Idrīs did not stand to gain from such developments, and his writings bear witness to the fact that Seljuq power only had an initial, temporary, effect on Imāmī thought. This new era of relative tolerance was far more advantageous for his successors. Many of the most influential scholars of the thirteenth and fourteenth centuries, including ʿAllāmah, originated from Ibn Idrīs' own home town of Ḥillah, where the seat of learning was established by him as it had previously been in Aleppo (*al-ḥalab*) during the time of Ibn Zuhrah, and hence this period of Imāmī scholarship has come to be known as 'The School of Ḥillah'. Ibn Idrīs' own students included: al-Sayyid Muḥammad b. ʿAbd Allāh b. Zuhrah al-Ḥusaynī al-Ḥalabī; al-Shaykh Najm al-Dīn Abū Ibrāhīm Muḥammad b. Nimā al-Ḥalabī (d. 645 AH/1248 CE); Aḥmad b. Masʿūd al-Asadī al-Ḥillī,[22] al-Shaykh Abū al-Ḥasan ʿAlī b. Yaḥyā b. ʿAlī al-Khayyāṭ;[23] al-Sayyid Abū ʿAlī Fikhār b. Maʿadd b. Fikhār al-Mūsawī al-Ḥā'irī (d. 603 AH/1206–07 CE);[24] and Ḥasan b. Yaḥyā b. Saʿīd al-Ḥillī,[25] the father and teacher of ʿAllāmah's maternal uncle al-Muḥaqqiq al-Ḥillī. Indeed, all of al-Muḥaqqiq al-Ḥillī's teachers were also students of Ibn Idrīs.

During the Mongol period, al-Muḥaqqiq al-Ḥillī became the first great scholar of the School of Ḥillah. He is regarded as a great systematiser, who was compelled by the critique of Ibn Idrīs to extensively develop and refine the methodology of Shaykh al-Ṭā'ifah, whilst defending and justifying the views of the latter against the observations of Ibn Idrīs.[26] Al-Muḥaqqiq al-Ḥillī's jurisprudential views, which are ordinarily analysed in comparison to those of al-Sayyid al-Murtaḍā and al-Shaykh al-Ṭūsī, are best summarised as follows: He considers the form of the command (*ṣīghat al-amr*) to be veritative in respect to obligation (*al-wujūb*), and does not accept the view of Abū Hāshim[27] that the form *ifʿal* is veritative in regard to approvedness (*al-nudb*),

---

21 See Muḥammad b. ʿAlī b. al-Ṭiqṭaqā, *al-Fakhr fī al-adab al-sulṭāniyyah wa al-duwal al-islāmiyyah*, n.p., 1927, p. 11.

22 *Aʿyān al-shīʿah* vol. IV, p. 555.

23 *Aʿyān al-shīʿah* vol. XIII, p. 24.

24 *Aʿyān al-shīʿah* vol. XIII, p. 56–7.

25 *Aʿyān al-shīʿah* vol. IX, p. 8.

26 For his defence of al-Ṭūsī, see his *Nukat al-nihāyah*, which takes the form of a commentary on al-Ṭūsī's manual of law, *al-Nihāyah fī mujarrad al-fiqh wa al-fatāwā*. See also al-Muḥaqqiq al-Ḥillī and Shaykh al-Ṭā'ifah al-Ṭūsī, *al-Nihāyah wa nukatuhā*, Qum, 1417 AH/1996.

27 ʿAbd al-Salām b. Muḥammad b. ʿAbd al-Wahhāb, known as Abū Hāshim al-Jubbā'ī (d. 321 AH/933 CE), was one of the founders of Muʿtazilī *uṣūl al-fiqh*. His adherents became known as the Bahshamiyyah, derived from his *kunyah* Abū Hāshim. None of his works

or the view of al-Sayyid al-Murtaḍā that it is common between obligation and approvedness. He does not consider the command to signify expedition (*al-fawr*) nor postponement (*al-tarākhī*), because at times it has been employed to denote both of these, thus, according to him, the command is assigned for the veritative regarding the common extent between expedition and postponement. He considers the prohibition (*al-nahy*), with respect to ritual acts of worship (*al-ʿibādāt*), as signifying the unsoundness (*al-fasād*) of that which is prohibited, and, as far as social interactions (*al-muʿāmalāt*) are concerned, he does not consider the prohibition to signify unsoundness. With respect to the discussion of the utterances of generality (*alfāẓ al-ʿumūm*), al-Muḥaqqiq al-Ḥillī accepts the opinion of Shaykh al-Ṭāʾifah, and maintains that the utterances assigned for generality are not to be found. This is contrary to the view of al-Sayyid al-Murtaḍā, who maintains that such utterances are the common extent between generality and specificity (*al-ʿumūm wa al-khuṣūṣ*). Furthermore, al-Muḥaqqiq al-Ḥillī expounded the discussion on the solitary narration (*khabar al-wāḥid*) by re-examining the subject in detail. According to him, action in accordance with the solitary narration is permissible on the basis of intellection; an opinion which is shared by both al-Sayyid al-Murtaḍā and Shaykh al-Ṭāʾifah.

It is unclear what al-Muḥaqqiq al-Ḥillī's view is with respect to the following of the solitary narration on the basis of the divine law. Although he accepts the solitary narrations which have been reported by the companions of the Imāms, and compiled in the books of narrations, along with the specific conditions, such as justness, faith and so forth, and considers action that is congruous with such traditions to be allowed: at the same time, he criticises those who put forward reported and intellective evidences for the occurrence of legally following the solitary narrations, and considers them thereby marred (*makhdūshah*). He also claims that Shaykh al-Ṭāʾifah maintains the permissibility of acting in accordance with the solitary narration of a just person, but only that which has been reported from Imāmī companions and recorded in their works; to wit, Shaykh al-Ṭāʾifah does not maintain the permissibility of acting in accordance with the solitary narration of a just person in absolute terms. Additionally al-Muḥaqqiq al-Ḥillī does not consider the skilled practitioner of juristic reasoning (*al-mujtaḥid*) to always be correct in regards to the unveiling of a legal ruling, rather, as is the tenet of the Imāmiyyah, he states that the skilled practitioner could sometimes err in his juristic reasoning and thus not arrive at the ruling, and hence be excused in

survive. See Khayr al-Dīn Ziriklī, *al-Aʿlām*, 11 vols., supplement, Beirut, 1389 AH/1969, vol. IV, pp. 130–31.

respect to that. Lastly, al-Muḥaqqiq al-Ḥillī also introduces a new nomenclature (*iṣṭilāḥ*) for the concept of juristic reasoning in jurisprudence.[28]

The jurisprudential writings of ʿAllāmah may largely be seen as a continuation of his maternal uncle's project. ʿAllāmah further refines the undertaking of Shaykh al-Ṭāʾifah, applying various rational, systematic ideas to Shaykh al-Ṭāʾifah's own engagement with the texts. In such developments we see the fruits of ʿAllāmah's polymathic education; he applies mathematical principles to problems such as the division of inheritance and the calculation of the times of prayer.[29] He also introduced to Shīʿī law a new system for classifying the reliability of traditions, dividing them into true (*ṣaḥīḥ*), good (*ḥasan*), reliable (*muwaththaq*), and weak (*ḍaʿīf*), drawing on terminology only previously found in other schools of legal theory.[30]

Such an adaptation of new vocabularies to the discussion of jurisprudential problems constituted an important part of al-Muḥaqqiq al-Ḥillī and ʿAllāmah's revivification and expansion of Shaykh al-Ṭāʾifah's legacy. Perhaps the most significant instance of this adjustment is to be found in regards to the relationship of qualified legal scholars to the law itself, on the one hand, and to the unqualified masses, on the other. Whilst acknowledging the need for one who makes edicts (*mufti*) to provide legal opinions for those who are ignorant of the law, Shaykh al-Ṭāʾifah retains the early Imāmī wariness of juristic reasoning (*ijtihād*), included as it is among a group of other terms—most notably personal opinion (*raʾy*), and analogical reasoning (*qiyās*)—which, in the early Imāmī *ḥadīth* corpus, are denounced as representing the ill-advised, arbitrary hubris of relying on fallible human reason to determine God's will, rather than the inspired guidance of the divinely-appointed infallible Imām.[31] There is, thus, an affirmation of the necessity of hierarchies of knowledge and the leadership of the community by qualified scholars (*al-ʿulamāʾ*), accompanied nonetheless by a suspicion of the nomenclature which other schools of thought apply to this reality. In the writings of al-Muḥaqqiq al-Ḥillī and ʿAllāmah this terminological deadlock is broken, and we find the normative structure of authority in Shīʿī law elaborated for

---

28 See, al-Ḥillī, al-Muḥaqqiq, Najm al-Dīn Abū al-Qāsim Jaʿfār b. al-Ḥasan, *Maʿārij al-uṣūl*, ed. Muḥammad Ḥusayn al-Raḍawī, Qum, 1403 AH/1983, pp. 64–65, 77, 140–48, 179–81.

29 See Hossein Modarressi Tabātabāʾī, *An Introduction to Shīʿī Law*, London, 1984, p. 48.

30 To our knowledge only two of ʿAllāmah's works on the sciences of *ḥadīth* are extant, *Īḍāḥ mukhālafat al-sunnah*, and *Al-Durr wa al-marjān fī al-aḥādīth al-ṣiḥāḥ wa al-ḥisān*. See ʿAbd al-ʿAzīz al-Ṭabaṭabāʾī, *Maktabat al-ʿAllāmah al-Ḥillī*, p. 62, p. 128. ʿAllāmah's classification of the *ḥadīth* in turn made him a prime target of the Akhbārīs; See: Muḥammad Amīn Astarābādī, *al-Fawāʾid al-madaniyyah*, lithograph, Tehran, 1321 AH/1904.

31 See Muḥammad b. al-Ḥasan al-Ṭūsī, *al-ʿUddah fī uṣūl al-fiqh*, Qum, 1376 SH/1997, pp. 723–32.

the first time in the language in which it has been discussed ever since: that in order to be an authority on law one must be a skilled practitioner of juristic reasoning (*mujtahid*), possessing the necessary qualifications and all that entails to independently deduce the law of God from the appropriate sources, and, in the absence of such qualifications, to resort to and comply with the conclusion in such matters that the qualified practitioner of juristic reasoning puts forth. The latter are therefore obliged to comply with the conclusions of the skilled practitioner of juristic reasoning (*taqlīd*) and those of whomsoever is the most learned (*al-aʿlam*) in any given epoch, provided that this can be readily discerned; for rulings given in the past by a now deceased skilled practitioner of juristic reasoning are not to be relied upon, as they cannot take into account the affairs and circumstances of the here-and-now.[32] The ideas of Muḥammad b. al-Ḥasan al-Ṭūsī were thus further systematised, and in the process Imāmī jurisprudence thereby took ownership of a terminology that had long been monopolised by the literature of rival groups and expressed by itself, albeit in somewhat different terms.[33]

This fruitful engagement with other schools of thought is emblematic of how Imāmī thought took full advantage of the opportunities presented by Mongol rule. As we have seen, the sages of the School of Ḥillah, ʿAllāmah perhaps more than any, greatly profited from the new political landscape. It was not the case, however, that a sympathetic ruler, even a Shīʿī one, initiated a Shīʿī intellectual dominance in the region, nor does the success of ʿAllāmah and his peers reflect such a dominance. Rather, what we see in the writings of the school of Ḥillah can also be observed in the writings of the Buwayhid scholars two centuries earlier: not the complacency of political supremacy but the vibrancy of a teeming polemical context. The blessing of the reign of Uljaytū was that it allowed Shīʿī scholars to co-exist side by side with scholars from other schools of thought, as part of a cosmopolitan environment which both provided the ongoing impetus for Imāmī scholars to clearly and coherently define and defend their positions against those of other Muslims, whilst also supplying a diverse context of ideas and concepts from which they could draw inspiration.

Some have alleged that the teachings of the School of Ḥillah were responsible for a momentous shift of emphasis in the Imāmī tradition towards the law, and away from philosophical and mystical currents of thought. However

32 See al-Muḥaqqiq al-Ḥillī, *Maʿārij al-uṣūl*, pp. 179–82, pp. 197–202; al-ʿAllāmah al-Ḥillī, *Tahdhīb al-wuṣūl ilā ʿilm al-uṣūl*, lithograph, Tehran, 1308 AH/1890–91, pp. 100–10.

33 See al-Sharīf al-Murtaḍā, *al-Rasāʾil*, Qum, 1405 AH/1984. See also Ahmad Kazemi Moussavi, *Religious Authority in Shiʾite Islam: From the Office of the Mufti to the Institution of Marjaʿ*, Kuala Lumpur, 1996, pp. 7–85.

this conclusion is far too broad insofar as it constructs a false dichotomy regarding matters which are, in reality, considerably more complex.[34] In this connection one may note that jurisprudence (*uṣūl al-fiqh*) was in fact the *last* subject which ʿAllāmah undertook to write about. In the introduction to his *Ghāyat al-wuṣūl wa īḍāḥ al-subul fī sharḥ mukhtaṣar al-suʾāl wa al-amal,* he states that, having completed works on theology and philosophy, he now saw fit to address the subject of jurisprudence.[35] This work was completed on 12 Rajab 697 AH/1286 CE.[36] Furthermore, in the section on preliminary matters in his *Nihāyat al-wuṣūl ilā ʿilm al-uṣūl,* he makes a similar statement that all other subjects such as theology—even though it is the highest of the sciences—language, and syntax, are antecedents to the study of jurisprudence (*uṣūl al-fiqh*).[37] With this in mind, we may view the legal sciences, as understood by ʿAllāmah and his fellow scholars, not as something that sweeps away other branches of knowledge, but rather as their culmination. As we have seen, ʿAllāmah's legal thought incorporates the other sciences in his repertoire; a development that, far from diminishing their status, only makes them more indispensable.

1.3 *Al-ʿAllāmah al-Ḥillī's Jurisprudence*

The flourishing of the Imāmī intellectual tradition in this context of confrontation and exchange is fully reflected in the prodigious breadth of ʿAllāmah's scholarly oeuvre, and, though he was far from being the last of the sages of Ḥillah—he was followed, among others, by his own son—he certainly embodies this period of Imāmī scholarship at its height. His works on Jurisprudence are no exception to this. As with his writings in other disciplines, these jurisprudential works not only expound his own views of the topic at hand but also provide an encyclopaedic, even-handed, treatment of the opinions of other

---

34 See, for instance, Mohammad-Ali Amir-Moezzi, *The Divine Guide in Early Shiʿism: The Sources of Esotericism in Islam*, trans. David Streight, Albany, 1994, pp. 138–9.

35 ʿAllāmah al-Ḥillī, *Ghāyat al-wuṣūl wa īḍāḥ al-subul fī sharḥ mukhtaṣar al-suʾāl wa al-amal*, Ms. British Library, Or. 3970, fol. 2b.

36 Āghā Buzurg Tihrānī, *al-Dharīʿah ilā taṣānīf al-shīʿah*, Beirut, 1983–88, vol. XVI, pp. 24–5.

37 Al-ʿAllāmah al-Ḥillī, *Nihāyat al-wuṣūl ilā ʿilm al-uṣūl*, 5 vols., ed. Ibrāhīm al-Bahādurī, Qum, 1425 AH/2004, vol. I, pp. 71–3. Unfortunantly this is the only published edition and it suffers from certain infelicities in both Arabic style and convention, namely erratic punctuation and random paragraphing. To make matters worse each of the five volumes is prefaced by lengthy prolegomena, which by reasonable standards should have been combined into a single coherent prolegomena heading the first volume only, such a procedure not only disrupts the flow of the original work but also makes it rather cumbersome to navigate.

schools of thought, varying from polemics to constructive and sustained critical engagements with the views of other scholars.

ʿAllāmah composed a number of works on jurisprudence, both commentaries on previous works and manuals of his own. As noted above, his first work on this topic was *Ghāyat al-wuṣūl wa īḍāḥ al-subul fī sharḥ mukhtaṣar al-suʾāl wa al-amal*, a commentary on a work by ʿUthmān b. ʿUmar b. al-Ḥājib (d. 646 AH/1249 CE).[38] He also composed two prodigious surveys of the topic, which survive, *Nihāyat al-wuṣūl ilā ʿilm al-uṣūl*, and the smaller *Tahdhīb al-wuṣūl ilā ʿilm al-uṣūl*. In addition to this there is his *Muntahā al-wuṣūl ilā ʿilmay al-kalām wa-al-uṣūl*, which is half given over to jurisprudence—the other half being concerned with theology—and a further two works, *al-Nukat al-badīʿah fī taḥrīr al-dharīʿah* and *Nahj al-wuṣūl ilā ʿilm al-uṣūl*, which are no longer extant. Finally, there is the introductory text, *Mabādiʾ al-wuṣūl ilā ʿilm al-uṣūl*.[39]

1.4 *Mabādiʾ al-Wuṣūl ilā ʿIlm al-Uṣūl*

'The Foundations of Jurisprudence' is, as its title implies, a brief work, providing only the skeletal outline of concepts, which are elsewhere given their full and voluminous treatment in ʿAllāmah's other works of jurisprudence. His smallest work in the field, *Mabādiʾ* nonetheless provides both a survey of many key arguments, which shaped the thought of ʿAllāmah and his successors, and a microcosm of the intellectual richness of the period from which his scholarship comes. As well as outlining the Imāmī position on each topic, the work also functions as a concise textbook for the opinions held by other schools of thought, which are each dissected and appraised as the context demands.

The book was written at the request of ʿAllāmah's student Taqī al-Dīn Ibrāhīm b. Muḥammad al-Baṣrī.[40] ʿAbd al-Ḥusayn Muḥammad ʿAlī al-Baqqāl, the editor of the only extant Arabic published version—hereafter referred to as the Baqqāl version—who states that it is modelled on the *Minhāj al-wuṣūl ilā maʿrifat al-uṣūl* of ʿAbd Allāh b. ʿUmar b. Muḥammad al-Bayḍāwī (d. 685 AH/1286 CE),[41] though he does not provide a source to substantiate this claim.

38 Uthmān b. ʿUmar b. Yūnus, Abū ʿAmr Jamāl al-Dīn, known as Ibn al-Ḥājib, (d. 646 AH/1249 CE) was a prominent Mālikī scholar of Qurʾānic recitation, Arabic grammar, law, and jurisprudence. See Mīrzā Muḥammad Bāqir al-Mūsawī al-Khwānsārī, *Rawḍāt al-jannāt*, vol. V, pp. 184–88.

39 *Aʿyān al-shīʿah*, vol. IX, p. 27.

40 This request for the composition of the book is noted by Āghā Buzurg Tihrānī, *al-Dharīʿah ilā taṣānīf al-shīʿah*, vol. XIX, pp. 43–4.

41 ʿAbd Allāh b. ʿUmar b. Muḥammad al-Bayḍāwī, Abū al-Khayr or Abū Saʿīd Nāṣir al-Dīn al-Shīrāzī, known as al-Qāḍī al-Bayḍāwī (d. 685 AH/1286 CE), was a Shāfiʿī scholar of the Arabic language, exegesis, *ḥadīth*, law, theology and jurisprudence. See the introduction

To this and other matters of the Baqqāl version we shall have cause to return to below.[42] As a scholar well-versed in Shāfiʿī jurisprudence, ʿAllāmah would most likely have been familiar with the work of Bayḍāwī. The main thing that both books share in common, however, is that each represents a *summa* of the legal methodology of their respective schools, although the topics which ʿAllāmah covers are rather different in many cases. As will become clear below, ʿAllāmah cites a great number of authorities from numerous schools of thought. Not only is he is well-versed in the theology and jurisprudence of his predecessors and their works from the Imāmiyyah but he is also well acquainted with the various other contributions to these subjects by other theological and jurisprudential schools. Although these ideas sometimes converge with ʿAllāmah's own position there are also many areas of divergence. To represent the legacy of ʿAllāmah as that of a mere imitator or transmitter of the doctrines of this or that authority, is simplistic in the extreme.

The most decisive influence on ʿAllāmah, as far as his jurisprudence is concerned, is that of his uncle al-Muḥaqqiq al-Ḥillī. This can be witnessed in the core structure of *Mabādiʾ*. If one draws a comparison with al-Muḥaqqiq's *Maʿārij al-uṣūl*, the latter's work on jurisprudence, one clearly sees ʿAllāmah's close emulation of al-Muḥaqqiq in the choice and emphasis of topics covered as well as in their structure and arrangement. There are, nevertheless, stark differences in this regard between the *Mabādiʾ* and al-Bayḍāwī's *Minhāj*. ʿAllāmah's *Mabādiʾ* arguably represents an effort to introduce the reader to the *Maʿārij al-uṣūl* and, similarly, his *Tahdhīb al-wuṣūl ilā ʿilm al-uṣūl* should be seen as a systemisation of the methodology of his uncle. This, in turn, was intended to facilitate his students' transition to more sophisticated works of jurisprudence by the past masters, namely *al-Dharīʿah ilā uṣūl al-sharīʿah* of al-Sayyid al-Murtaḍā and *al-ʿUddah fī uṣūl al-fiqh* of Shaykh al-Ṭāʾifah.[43] ʿAllāmah's own thought on jurisprudence culminates in his *Nihāyat al-wuṣūl ilā ʿilm al-uṣūl*, wherein the full breadth and mastery of our sage is splendidly demonstrated.

1.5 *Manuscripts and Methodology*

To the best of our knowledge there are ninety-five extant manuscripts of *Mabādiʾ al-wuṣūl ilā ʿilm al-uṣūl*. Of these we have obtained digital copies of all

---

to the critical edition of his *Minhāj al-wuṣūl ilā ʿilm al-uṣūl*, ed. Salīm Shabʿāniyah, Damascus, 1989, p. 9.

42 al-ʿAllāmah al-Ḥillī, *Mabādiʾ al-wuṣūl ilā ʿilm al-uṣūl*, ed. ʿAbd al-Ḥusayn Muḥammad ʿAlī al-Baqqāl, Najaf, 1390 AH/1970, p. 35.

43 See the editor's introduction to Ibn Idrīs al-Ḥillī, *Kitāb al-Sarāʾir al-ḥāwī li-taḥrīr al-fatāwī*, vol. 1, p. 24.

known manuscripts, which were not only copied and read in the presence of the author, and in some cases of his son, but also bear the author's signature authorising and endorsing the scribe lector to thereafter transmit the work—totalling four manuscripts in all. To these we have added an additional two manuscripts from later times. Below we have provided a list enumerating all six of these manuscripts and the symbol by which each is designated in the *apparatus criticus.*

1. *Mabādiʾ al-wuṣūl ilā ʿilm al-uṣūl*
Marʿashī Library, Qum, Iran, *fiqh, kalām, ʿarabī*, 49. 93 fols., 130 x 18 mm.
Date of Completion: 21 Shaʿbān 700 AH/1301 CE.
Symbol in app. crit.: أ

2. *Mabādiʾ al-wuṣūl ilā ʿilm al-uṣūl*
Astānah-yi Quds-i Raḍawī Library, Mashhad, Iran, *uṣūl*, 2947. 30 fols.
Date of Completion: Ramaḍān 702 AH/1303 CE.
Symbol in app. crit.: ب

3. *Mabādiʾ al-wuṣūl ilā ʿilm al-uṣūl*
Marʿashī library, Qum, Iran, *kalām, uṣūl, ʿarabī*, 4. 144 fols., 110 x 183 mm.
Date of Completion: 21 Ramaḍān 703 AH/1304 CE.
Symbol in app. crit.: ج

4 *Mabādiʾ al-wuṣūl ilā ʿilm al-uṣūl*
British Library, London, Or. 10963
Date of Completion 1 Rajab 715 AH/1315 CE.
Symbol in app. crit.: د

5. *Mabādiʾ al-wuṣūl ilā ʿilm al-uṣūl*
Kāshif al-Ghiṭāʾ Foundation, Najaf, Iraq, *uṣūl al-fiqh, ʿarabī*, 7954. 80 fols.
Date of completion 1021 AH/1612.
Symbol in app. crit.: ه

6. *Mabādiʾ al-wuṣūl ilā ʿilm al-uṣūl*
Kāshif al-Ghiṭāʾ Foundation, Najaf, Iraq, *uṣūl al-fiqh, ʿarabī*, 797. 24 fols.
Date of completion 1251 AH/1835.
Symbol in app. crit.: ط

The first of these manuscripts is deemed the *editio princeps,* and the other manuscripts have been employed as needed. An appendix has been provided containing colophons for the first and last pages for each of the foregoing manuscripts; these are designated according to the symbols in the *apparatus criticus* outlined above. Insofar as the presentation of the Arabic script is concerned, we have preserved archaic orthography in most cases. The text has been divided into paragraphs, and headings have been indented and enlarged to distinguish them from the main body of the text. References to the Qur'ān have been identified and each *ḥadīth* has been traced to the relevant sources. Persons whose names occur in the text have been identified and referenced to biographical sources. This is a dual-language critical edition, and, therefore, most of the foregoing remarks apply only to the Arabic text, which appears on the left-hand side with the corresponding English translation on the right-hand side. Although they do not appear in the Arabic text, the number of discussions in each chapter has been incorporated into the English chapter titles for purposes of clarification and for ease of navigation.

In addition to the manuscripts listed above, we have taken recourse to the Baqqāl version, which has been until now the only published edition.[44] It is most unfortunate that this edition is riddled with numerous errors in the text as well as the editor's notes. Instances of such errors, many of which have significant implications for jurisprudence, have all been pointed out in our *apparatus criticus* wherein the Baqqāl version is designated as *al-maṭbūʿah*.

Persons referenced in the *apparatus criticus* to the Arabic text have not been replicated in the notes to the English translation, but are, however, sufficiently noted in this introduction. All efforts have been made to ensure the utmost accuracy with regard to the translation of the Arabic text into English, which has entailed a careful consideration of the technical terms of jurisprudence in the source language, and appropriate terms and vocabulary for these terms have been presented in the target language. Where transliterated terms have been retained in the text, this has only been done to enable the reader to more readily and rapidly identify the concepts therein. The translation is succinct and, insofar as possible, offers a close reflection of the original rather than a discursive, pariphrastic, translation-*cum*-commentary.

2 Part Two

The following introduction presents a complete and thoroughgoing analysis of each discussion and chapter of the *Mabādi'*, with a view to drawing out the parallels and areas of intersection this text has with ʿAllāmah's most extensive contribution to Islamic jurisprudence, namely, the five-volume published *Nihāyat al-wuṣūl ilā ʿilm al-uṣūl*, (hereafter designated as *Nihāyat*). This work

44 al-ʿAllāmah al-Ḥillī, *Mabādi' al-wuṣūl ilā ʿilm al-uṣūl*, Najaf, 1390 AH/1970.

represents ʿAllāmah's magnum opus in Imamī Shīʿah jurisprudence. It is presented by the author in thirteen investigations (*maqāṣid*), with each investigation (*maqṣid*) consisting of chapters (*abwāb*) divided into sections (*fuṣūl*), and each section divided into problems (*maṭālib*), which are further divided into discussions (*abḥāth*), which are themselves sometimes divided into a station (*maqām*) and issue (*mas'alah*). There are four manuscripts of *Nihāyat al-wuṣūl ilā ʿilm al-uṣūl* extant, which were produced during the life of the author, the first of which was completed and dated 8th Ramaḍān 704 AH/1305 CE, the second and third are both from the year 705 AH/1305–6 CE, and the fourth from the year 722 AH/1322 CE.[45]

The rationale behind the following is to properly contextualise the concise and adroit discussions found in *Mabādi'* through situating them, as our translated title suggests, as the *foundation* of an enterprise in jurisprudential theory which reaches its completion in *Nihāyat*. As will be seen, this close appraisal of the two works helps to elucidate, and often to supplement, the many instances in the *Mabādi'* where our author sees fit to abridge or curtail a discussion, or else to temporarily omit from his consideration arguments and counterarguments to a position that he otherwise engages with in the full breadth of *Nihāyat*. This comparative introduction is therefore designed to abet advanced scholars of Imāmī Jurisprudence, by offering them a guide for navigating through the main writings of ʿAllāmah that intertextually maps the *Nihāyat* and *Mabādi'* onto one another.

To our knowledge this is the first such undertaking in English, making good a scholarly deficit in the study of Imāmī Shīʿī jurisprudence. However, given the subtlety and richness of the texts under examination, an exhaustive commentary would require a full monographic treatment, which shall appear shortly in our forthcoming book entitled: *The Jurisprudence of al-ʿAllāmah al-Ḥillī*—so we have, of necessity, had to limit ourselves in the ensuing to providing a cursory and descriptive overview of the discussions in each text, rather than an in-depth engagement with the intricacies of the arguments found therein.

2.1 *The Epistemology of al-ʿAllāmah al-Ḥillī*

Prior to examining the jurisprudential themes of *Mabādi'* it is first prudent to provide a broad overview of ʿAllāmah's epistemology as this is presented in *Nihāyat*, because, despite the bearing his theory of knowledge undeniably has upon the discussions of the former text, he does not see fit to outline it in any depth there. This outline is instead found within the sixth chapter (*faṣl*) of the first investigation (*maqṣid*) of *Nihāyat*, where ʿAllāmah addresses the field of

45 ʿAbd al-ʿAzīz al-Ṭabaṭabā'ī, *Maktabat al-ʿallāmah al-ḥillī*, pp. 209–10.

epistemology. Therein he explains that insofar as jurisprudence (*uṣūl al-fiqh*) constitutes a search for the evidence for rulings (*al-aḥkām*), any thoroughgoing discussion of jurisprudence must thereby require the cognisance (*maʿrifat*) of evidence (*dalīl*), and the division thereof into what conveys knowledge (*al-ʿilm*) or probability (*al-ẓann*) through theorisation (*al-naẓar*).[46] In the following six discussions, he lays out the basis of his epistemology, which is, in turn, necessary to understand his jurisprudence (*uṣūl al-fiqh*), namely his understanding of the following: knowledge, (*ʿilm*), probability (*ẓann*), conjecture (*wahm*), doubt (*shakk*), preponderance (*rujḥān*), evidence (*dalīl*), indication (*amārah*) and theorisation (*naẓar*).

ʿAllāmah agrees with al-Muḥaqqiq al-Ḥillī on the definition of knowledge (*al-ʿilm*),[47] insofar as he states that it is self-evident (*ghanī ʿan al-taʿrīf*) whilst also maintaining the position that it is immediate (*ḍarūrī*).[48] To this effect he states that knowledge entails either simple apprehension (*taṣawwur*) or judgement (*taṣdīq*), and that each one may be either 'immediate' (*ḍarūrī*) or 'acquired' (*kasbī*). An example of the former is one's immediate conception that one is in pain, for instance; where as an example of the latter is the knowledge one can acquire of another's pain. On probability (*al-ẓann*) he states that this entails the preferment of one of two sides of a matter (*tarjīḥ aḥad al-ṭarafayn*) despite the conceivability of its opposite, whilst a conjecture (*al-wahm*) is that which is outweighed by probability (*al-ẓann*), and doubt (*al-shakk*) is the negation of preponderance (*rujḥān*).[49] He further states that evidence (*al-dalīl*), according to the jurists (*fuqahāʾ*), leads to knowledge (*al-ʿilm*) through correct theorisation (*bi ṣaḥīḥ al-naẓar*).[50] Meanwhile, an indication (*al-amārah*) is said to be that which leads to probability (*al-ẓann*) through correct theorisation.[51] Finally, theorisation (*al-naẓar*) itself is said to be the arrangement of the matters of the mind (*umūr dhaniyyah*) in order to arrive at another matter, which pertains either to knowledge or to probability. [52]

2.2 Chapter One: On Languages (*al-lughāt*)

The first chapter of *Mabādiʾ al-wuṣūl ilā ʿilm al-uṣūl* can be considered an undertaking into the enterprise known as the 'philosophy of language', insofar as

46 *Nihāyat*, vol. 1, p. 75.
47 Al-Muḥaqqiq al-Ḥillī, *Maʿārij al-uṣūl*, p. 48.
48 *Nihāyat*, vol. 1, p. 75, p. 81.
49 *Nihāyat*, vol. 1, p. 82.
50 *Nihāyat*, vol. 1, p. 83.
51 *Nihāyat*, vol. 1, p. 83.
52 *Nihāyat*, vol. 1, p. 84.

in this discussion of general principles ʿAllāmah primarily considers several matters of central significance to contemporary philosophers of language, including: the nature of the relationship between meaning (or sense) and reference, that is, how the semantic properties of an utterance relate to its syntactic properties, the relationship between meaning and use, the question of whether or not connotation outstrips denotation, as well as an extended inquiry into, and theorisation upon, the proposed origins of language. The pertinence of these questions for jurisprudence can be understood when one recognises that all subsequent discussions in the *Mabādiʾ* depend on how the revealed word of the Qurʾān, as well as the recorded Prophetic and Imāmic utterances, are to be practically interpreted and understood for the purposes of jurisprudential theory—an inquiry which is as much to do with language, as it is with theology. In this chapter ʿAllāmah also provides a persuasive argument for the obligation to master Arabic, because of the dependency of the understanding of the divine law thereupon. Further discussions give close consideration to the quiddities of the Arabic language, including: the classifications of its utterances into their respective lexicographical and morphological types; the controversy surrounding the homonym, that is, those utterances which share a phonology or orthography but differ with regards to their meaning; and the crucial distinction between utterances which are veritative and those which are figurative, as well as the further subclassifications within these types of utterance. The chapter concludes with an intricate philological examination of the differences of opinion among the scholars of the Arabic language in respect to the Arabic particles, of conjunction, disjunction, delimitation, etc.

2.2.1 Discussion One: On General Principles (*aḥkām kulliyyah*)

ʿAllāmah begins the first chapter with an opening discussion on general principles wherein he states four principles.[53] The first principle concerns the epistemological debate as to whether language is bequeathed (*tawqīfiyyah*), a position he ascribes to a party (*jamāʿah*), or whether it is a product of human nomenclatures and developments (*iṣṭilāḥiyyah*), as is maintained by Abū Hāshim. In *Nihāyat* ʿAllāmah presents, altogether, five positions on who or what is taken to be the true assignor of language (*wāḍiʿ*). He ascribes the first position to ʿAbbād b. Sulaymān,[54] some others of the Muʿtazilah,[55] and the

---

53 *Nihāyat*, vol. I, pp. 150–51.

54 ʿAbbād b. Sulaymān al-Ṣaymurī, known as ʿAbbād (d. *c.* 250 AH/864 CE), was a Muʿtazilī scholar. See the critical edition of Fakhr al-Dīn al-Rāzī's (d. 606 AH/1209 CE), *al-Maḥṣūl fī ʿilm uṣūl al-fiqh*, 6 vols., ed. Ṭāha Jābir Fayyāḍ al-ʿAlawānī, Beirut, 1416 AH/1996, vol. I, p. 181.

55 Regarding this group of Sunnī rationalist-minded theologians see, *Encyclopaedia of Islam*,

practitioners of the science of letters (*aṣḥāb al-taksīr*)[56] for whom language is understood to be a natural phenomenon, which specifically means that the signification of an utterance is natural, due to its essence (*dalālat al-lafẓ ṭabīʿiyyah ay li dhātihi*). The second position, which ʿAllāmah ascribes to those whom he calls 'the verifiers' (*al-muḥaqqiqūn*)—in an epithet that could betoken his approval—is that the signification of the utterance is arrived at through the medium of assignation (*wāsiṭat al-waḍʿ*). On this position, ʿAllāmah states that there is a difference of opinion: some maintain that the assignor is God, such as Abū al-Ḥasan al-Ashʿarī,[57] Ibn Fūrak,[58] the Ẓāhiriyyah,[59] and a group of jurists (*fuqahāʾ*), with the assignation itself thereby being understood from the aspect of divine bequeathment either through revelation (*waḥy*) or through the creation of sounds (*aṣwāt*) and letters (*ḥurūf*) that are then made audible to an individual or a group of people and through the creation of *a priori* knowledge about that; whilst others, such as Abū Hāshim, his companions and a group of theologians (*mutakallimūn*), maintain that the assignation is nomenclatural (*iṣṭilāḥiyyah*). The third position, ascribed to 'others' (*ākharūn*), is that the assignation is partially nomenclatural and partially bequeathed, and, on this, the author observes that there is a difference of opinion. He quotes Abū Isḥāq[60]—citing him by his epithet of 'the teacher' (*al-ustādh*)—that 'the necessary extent by which nomenclature occurs is bequeathed and the remainder is nomenclatural'. He ascribes the opposite position to some 'others' (*ākharūn*), namely, that, although the origins of language are nomenclatural, the remainder is bequeathed. The fourth position, ascribed to the majority of

---

New Edition, Leiden, 1954–2005, vol. VII, p. 793.

56 ʿ*Ilm al-taksīr* is a branch of the esoteric science of the letters (ʿ*ilm al-jafr*). See, Muḥammad b. ʿAlī Thānvī, *Kashshāf iṣṭilāḥāt al-funūn*, Istanbul, 1899, vol. I, p. 223. However, in *Nihāyat* we find *aṣhāb al-iksīr*, which appears to be a copyist's error.

57 ʿAlī b. Isḥāq, known as, Abū al-Ḥasan al-Ashʿarī (d. 324 AH/936 CE), was the founder of the Ashʿarī theological school that bears his name, and began his career as a Muʿtazilī. His notable works include: *Maqālāt al-islāmiyyīn* and *al-Ibānah ʿan uṣūl al-diyānah*. See, Ziriklī, *al-Aʿlām*, vol. V, p. 69.

58 Muḥammad b. al-Ḥasan b. Fūrak, Abū Bakr (d. 406 AH/1015 CE), was a prominent Sunnī Ashʿarī theologian and Shāfiʿī jurist. See, Ziriklī, *al-Aʿlām*, vol. VI, p. 313.

59 Regarding this group of jurists, founded by Dāwūd b. ʿAlī b. Khalaf al-Iṣfahānī (d. 270 AH/884 CE) see, Ignaz Goldziher, *The Zahiris: Their doctrine and their History*, trans. Wolfgang Behn, Leiden, 1971.

60 Ibrāhīm b. Muḥammad b. Mihrān, known as Abū Isḥāq al-Asfarāyīnī (d. 418 AH/1027 CE), see Ziriklī, *al-Aʿlām*, vol. I, p. 59.

'the verifiers', is to suspend judgement on this matter, which he points out as the chosen stance of al-Qāḍī Abū Bakr[61] and al-Ghazālī.[62]

All the positions stated above are then analysed in detail by our author. He outright rejects the first of these as he states that all are agreed upon the invalidity of ʿAbbād's opinion. In respect to the remaining positions, and the dichotomy between the bequeathed and nomenclatural, our author provides an acute analysis of the arguments for and against whilst raising objections and counter-objections to both discussions, and it is only at the end of this particular section in *Nihāyat*—unlike in *Mabādiʾ* and *Tahdhīb* wherein he does not see fit to clearly state his own position—that his own view on the subject becomes apparent, when he states that 'since the weakness of both discussions has become clear, the most favoured opinion is the suspension of judgment whilst each of the two of them are possible even though bequeathment (*al-tawqīf*) is far stronger'.[63]

The second principle refers to the extent of linguistic utterances (*alfāẓ*), the rationale for which is given in *Nihāyat* as follows: although meanings are endless, words must at some point come to an end (*mutanāhiyah*), and so this will necessitate one of two possible outcomes; either that some meanings will be devoid of an utterance, which is the objective of ʿAllāmah's argument, or else utterances will be assigned to endless meanings, which is impossible (*muḥāl*) because the assignation of an utterance to endless meanings would necessitate their intellection and the intellection of what is endless is impossible.[64]

The third principle set forth by our author concerns the obligation for the jurist to learn the Arabic language because the understanding of the divine law (*sharʿ*) is dependent thereupon; as he explains in *Nihāyat*, legal matters necessarily make reference to the Qurʾān and the *Sunnah*, both of which are in Arabic. This in turn makes it obligatory to enter into a discussion about syntax (*al-naḥw*), morphology, and the language, since both sources are set in the language of the Arabs. This obligation is then further expounded by ʿAllāmah under the rubric that 'whatever is necessary in order to complete the obligation is obligatory' (*mā lā yatimmu al-wājib illā bi hi fa huwa wājib*).

---

61 Muḥammad b. Ṭayyib al-Bāqillānī known as Qāḍī Abū Bakr (d. 403 AH/1013 CE), was a prominent Sunnī Ashʿarī theologian. See Ziriklī, *al-Aʿlām*, vol. VII, p. 46.

62 Muḥammad b. Muḥammad b. Muḥammad al-Ghazālī al-Ṭūsī, Abū Ḥāmid (d. 505 AH/1111 CE), a very famous Shāfiʿī jurist, Ashʿarī theologian, and Ṣūfī, whose most well known work is *Iḥyāʾ ʿulūm al-dīn*, a Ṣūfī treatise explaining the five pillars of Islam. His most famous book in jurisprudence, however, is *al-Mustaṣfā*. See Ziriklī, *al-Aʿlām*, vol. VII, p. 247.

63 *Nihāyat*, vol. I, p. 158.

64 *Nihāyat*, vol. I, p. 162.

With regard to the Arabic language ʿAllāmah upholds the argument of his predecessors and calls for the same stringent procedure of examination as is applied to the examination of those who transmit the divine law (*ruwāt al-sharʿ*).[65]

The fourth principle is on what constitutes speech (*kalām*). Whilst in *Mabādiʾ* our author presents the definition of speech put forth by the Muʿtazilah, in *Nihāyat* he attributes the same definition to the masters of jurisprudence (*uṣūliyyūn*) in the discussion, On the Quiddity of Language; going on to dissect and analyse it word by word, whilst pointing out that this definition is the same as that put forward in the nomenclature of the authorities of syntax (*iṣṭilāḥ al-nuḥāt*) for what they call 'the meaningful sentence' (*al-jumlah al-mufīdah*).[66]

2.2.2 Discussion Two: On the Classification of the Utterances (*taqsīm al-alfāẓ*)

The second discussion pertains to the classification of utterances, and on this matter ʿAllāmah follows the standard procedure in jurisprudence, which is to examine an utterance from a fivefold approach, in order to classify it.

The first approach is with regard to its form (*ṣīghah*); if it relates to a tense then it is a verb (*fiʿl*), if it is independent in its signification (*dalālah*) then it is a noun (*ism*), and if neither of these applies then it is to be classified as a particle (*ḥarf*). The second approach is to classify an utterance as either simple (*mufrad*) or compound (*murakkab*). The third approach is to classify the utterance and its meaning as being either singular or numerous. The former is classified into being either a proper noun (*ʿalam*), an ellipsed noun (*muḍmar*), a univocal (*mutawāṭiʾ*) or an equivocal (*mushakkak*) utterance, and the latter are to be taken as each distinct from the other (*mutabāyinah*). However, if only the utterance is numerous then it is a synonym (*mutarādifah*) and if the meanings are many then it is classified as an improvised meaning (*murtajal*), and finally if it is used in a meaning that is unsuitable to its original assignation or else if it is used in a meaning that is suitable to the original assignation but the new meaning predominates over the first meaning, then it will be classified as either a linguistic, a customary, or a legal transfer (*al-manqūl al-lughawī aw al-ʿurfī aw al-sharʿī*). If the opposite is the case, namely, that the new meaning of the utterance does not predominate over the first meaning, then, insofar as its relationship to the first meaning is understood, it is to be classified as veritative (*ḥaqīqah*), and in its relationship with the new meaning it is to be classified as figurative (*majāz*).

65 *Nihāyat*, vol. I, p. 166.

66 *Nihāyat*, vol. I, pp. 145–47.

However, if the assignation is for two meanings without one of the meanings predominating or taking precedence over the other then, in such an instance, the utterance is classified as a homonym (*mushtarak*) in relation to both meanings, and in relation to one of the two meanings it is classified as an ambiguous (*mujmal*) utterance. The fourth approach concerns the meaningful utterance (*al-lafẓ al-mufīd*); if only one possible meaning is understood from an utterance it is classified as an explicit designation (*naṣṣ*), however if another meaning is equally possible then it falls within the category of what is known as the ambiguous (*mujmal*), otherwise the evident (*ẓāhir*) meaning becomes preferable (*rājiḥ*) to the interpreted meaning (*mu'awwal*) which is thereby outweighed (*marjūḥ*). The homonym—in-between an explicit designation and an evident utterance—is to be classified as a clear utterance (*muḥkam*), and that which is in-between an ambiguous and interpreted utterance is to be classified as an unclear utterance (*mutashābihah*). The fifth approach deals with those nouns that are classified as either concrete (*ism al-ʿayn*) or paronymous (*al-mushtaqq*), the former referring to that which signifies an essence of a thing (*al-dhāt*) and the latter being that which does not. It is noteworthy that what the author stipulates as a must (*lā budda*) regarding paronymy (*ishtiqāq*) in *Mabādi'*, is actually drawn, albeit partially, from the definition regarding its quiddity (*māhiyyah*) put forth elsewhere by al-Maydānī.[67] This definition is given in full by ʿAllāmah in his detailed discussion in *Nihāyat* on this issue, along with four principles (*arkān*) relating to the paronymic: firstly, that it is a name (*ism*) assigned (*mawḍūʿ*) to a meaning; secondly, that there is another utterance which is related (*nisbah*) to that original meaning; thirdly, that both nouns share the original letters; and fourthly, that the change (*taghyīr*) that takes place occurs only with regards to the letter or vowel (*ḥarakah*); he then gives his rational arguments that the sub-divisions (*aqsām*) of the last principle are not nine, as enumerated by Fakhr al-Dīn al-Rāzī,[68] but fifteen.[69]

2.2.3 Discussion Three: On the Homonym (*al-mushtarak*)

The next two discussions, of the homonym, and the veritative and figurative, respectively, follow naturally on from the classifications given above. The first

67 Aḥmad b. Muḥammad b. Aḥmad, Abū al-Faḍl, known as al-Maydānī (d. 518 AH/1124 CE) was a man of letters from Nishapur. See Ziriklī, *al-Aʿlām*, vol. I p. 208.

68 *Nihāyat*, vol. I, pp. 218–19. Muḥammad b. ʿUmar b. al-Ḥasan, Abū ʿAbd Allāh, known as Fakhr al-Dīn al-Rāzī (d. 606 AH/1210 CE), was an extremely prolific Sunnī Ashʿarī theologian and Shāfiʿī jurist who is perhaps best known for his commentary on the Qur'ān and his work on jurisprudence, *al-Maḥṣūl fī ʿilm uṣūl al-fiqh*. See Ziriklī, *al-Aʿlām*, vol. VII, p. 203.

69 *Nihāyat*, vol. I, pp. 187–202.

of these outlines the arguments for and against the homonym, such as the claim that it is not allowed (*imtināʿ*), which our author rejects on the basis of its philosophical possibility (*imkānihi fī al-ḥikmah*) and the existence of the homonym within language. However, when ʿAllāmah states that, '...accepted, the homonym is contrary to the principle (*al-aṣl*)'—he does not explicitly state the principle, nor does he offer clarification on this matter at any other point in the text. It is therefore worth dwelling on this elision. The principle that he alludes to in the above instance is that which is known within the works of jurisprudence as the 'lack of homonymity' (*ʿadam al-ishtirāk*), a principle that is mainly adopted by the *opponents* of the usage of the homonym. This principle is ordinarily invoked when a homonym equivocates between homonymity and the lack thereof, and in such an instance the opponents argue on the basis of one of five arguments—as detailed by Fakhr al-Dīn al-Rāzī along with several counterarguments—that homonymity is a source of unsoundness (*mafāsid*) and, even if such unsoundness does not demand the barring of such an assignation, then the least that is demanded in such a case is that the homonym is to be considered outweighed (*iqtiḍāʾ al-marjūḥiyyah*) and that an overwhelming probability (*aghlab ʿalā al-ẓann*) would constitute the lack of homonymity.

ʿAllāmah and the other proponents of homonymity supply counterarguments to each of the five arguments against the homonym. However, whilst he briefly alludes to two of these in *Mabādiʾ*, our author gives the matter much greater scrutiny in *Nihāyat*.[70] The proponents' arguments can be best summed up in the words of al-Muḥaqqiq al-Ḥillī:

> The principle of the lack of homonymity, if it were not for that no understanding would be realised except nigh the knowledge of the lack thereof, and that is void (*bāṭil*) because it necessitates the voidness of logical inference through explicit designations (*al-nuṣūṣ*) due to the possibility that utterances thereof are assigned to another meaning.[71]

ʿAllāmah goes on to state that knowledge of homonymity arises through the explicit designation thereof by the folk of the language (*ahl al-lughah*), a group to whom he takes recourse on a number of occasions in the *Mabādiʾ*. In each such instance, it could be argued that this broad designation refers to the grammarians, lexicographers, or philologists of the Arabic language. Unlike al-Muḥaqqiq al-Ḥillī, who, whilst attending more to possibility (*imkān*) than to linguistics (*al-lughah*), maintains that an utterance could be used in both of its meanings irrespective of whether it is veritative in both senses or figurative

---

70 *Nihāyat*, vol. 1, pp. 229–32.

71 *Maʿārij al-uṣūl*, p. 53.

or in either of the two, our author states that it could be used in both senses through the signs of the veritative (*ʿalāmāt al-ḥaqīqah*). However, his favoured opinion is that it is not possible to use the homonym in both of its senses except in a figurative manner, since it is not assigned for numerous meanings *qua* numerous meanings.

The issue of possibility is itself dealt with at length in *Nihāyat* wherein ʿAllāmah mentions al-Shāfiʿī,[72] Qāḍī Abū Bakr, al-Jubbāʾī,[73] Qāḍī ʿAbd al-Jabbār,[74] and al-Sayyid al-Murtaḍā as the proponents for allowing a single homonym in two senses only if it is possible, otherwise, as is the case with the imperative form (*ṣīghat ifʿal*), it should be used for a command (*al-amr bi al-shayʾ*) or a warning (*al-tahdīd ʿalayhi*). In the case of its usage without a context (*qārīnah*) that would incline its sense to one of the meanings, and he says that al-Shāfiʿī, al-Sayyid al-Murtaḍā, and ʿAbd al-Jabbār affirm that it must be predicated upon both senses together; contrary to the views of Abū Hāshim, Abū ʿAbd Allāh, Abū al-Ḥusayn al-Baṣrī,[75] al-Karkhī,[76] and Fakhr al-Dīn al-Rāzī.

2.2.4 Discussion Four: On the Veritative (*al-ḥaqīqah*) and the Figurative (*al-majāz*)

The fourth discussion brings our author to examine the utterances which should be classified as either veritative or figurative. It is noteworthy here that ʿAllāmah is at pains to explain the etymology and grammatical basis of both of these terms, like the masters of jurisprudence (*uṣūliyyūn*) who preceded him—such as al-Rāzī. In *Nihāyat* he explains that what is usually referred to as the veritative (*ḥaqīqah*) is to be found on the grammatical scale (*wazn*) of *faʿīlah* and is derived from the noun *al-ḥaqq*, and similarly that the figurative (*majāz*) is on the grammatical scale of *mafʿil* and is derived from the noun *al-jawāz*.

72 Muḥammad b. Idrīs b. al-ʿAbbās, Abū ʿAbd Allāh, known as al-Shāfiʿī (d. 204 AH/820 CE), the founder of the *madhhab* bearing his name. See, Ziriklī, *al-Aʿlām*, vol. VI, pp. 249–50.

73 Muḥammad b. ʿAbd al-Wahhāb b. Salām al-Jubbāʾī, Abū ʿAlī (d. 303 AH/916 CE) prominent Muʿtazilī scholar. See, Ziriklī, *al-Aʿlām*, vol. VII, p. 136.

74 ʿAbd al-Jabbār b. Aḥmad b. ʿAbd al-Jabbār al-Hamadhānī al-Asadābādī, Abū al-Ḥusayn known as Qāḍī al-Quḍāt or Qāḍī ʿAbd al-Jabbār (d. 415 AH/1025 CE), was a leader of the Muʿtazilah in his age and the author of an extensive theological work known as *Kitāb al-Mughnī min abwāb al-ʿadal wa al-tawḥīd*. See, Ziriklī, *al-Aʿlām*, vol. IV, p. 47.

75 Muḥammad b. ʿAlī al-Ṭayyib known as, Abū al-Ḥusayn al-Baṣrī (d. 436 AH/1044 CE), was a prominent Muʿtazilī scholar of jurisprudence who lived and died in Baghdad and authored an extremely influential work on jurisprudence entitled: *al-Muʿtamad fī uṣūl al-fiqh*. See, Ziriklī, *al-Aʿlām*, vol. VII, p. 161.

76 ʿUbayd Allāh b. al-Ḥusayn, Abū al-Ḥasan known as al-Karkhī, (d. 340 AH/952 CE), a Ḥanafī jurist. See Ziriklī, *al-Aʿlām*, vol. IV, p. 347.

These discussions grant us an insight into how ʿAllāmah, his predecessors, and his fellow masters of jurisprudence, understand these terms linguistically.[77]

The definitions of the veritative and figurative proffered in *Mabādiʾ* are succinct, for the former is stated to be the use of an utterance for the meaning it has been assigned, and the latter as the use of an utterance in another meaning from its original assignation due to a connection between the new and original assigned meaning. It is in *Nihāyat*, however, that ʿAllāmah expands upon the nature of the veritative and figurative each being opposed to the other (*mutaqābalān*), and thus explains how the definition (*ḥadd*) of one of them can serve as a guide to the definition of the other and, moreover, how the definition of one can be extracted from that of the other. He further notes that people have put forward different definitions for both terms. To illustrate this point he outlines the definition given by Abū ʿAlī al-Jubbāʾī and Abū Hāshim, which he says is also chosen by Abū al-Ḥusayn al-Baṣrī: that the veritative is an utterance which regulates the meaning thereof without any addition (*ziyādah*), subtraction (*nuqṣān*) or transference (*naql*). Now, according to ʿAllāmah, this should inform us about the definition for the figurative, which is extracted from it, and is the following: the figurative is an utterance which does not regulate the meaning thereof either due to an addition (*ziyādah*), subtraction (*nuqṣān*) or transference (*naql*).[78]

Our author then proceeds to briefly allude to the three classifications of the veritative; into either linguistic (*lughwiyyah*), customary (*ʿurfiyyah*), or legal (*sharʿiyyah*) utterances. He upholds the view that certain utterances are, undoubtedly, assigned within the language to certain meanings and used therein, an assignation which is termed linguistically veritative, or they are transferred to a second meaning and predominantly used therein and thus become customary veritative, either on the basis of a general (*al-ʿāmm*) or a specific (*al-khāṣṣ*) custom. He deals exhaustively with the third classification in *Nihāyat*, since it is obviously of paramount importance to the discussion on jurisprudence. Succinctly put, these are those utterances, which are used in meanings assigned to them within the nomenclature of divine law (*sharʿ*), regardless of whether the meaning and utterance are known or unknown to the folk of the language. The legally veritative utterance can be viewed through further sub-classifications based upon those which pertain to actions (*al-afʿāl*) and those which pertain to agents (*al-fāʿilīn*), and to differentiate the latter from the former sub-classification the legally veritative utterance is also referred to as religious (*dīniyyah*). Both classifications of legally veritative utterances are brought together through legal custom (*al-ʿurf al-sharʿī*). The

77 *Nihāyat*, vol. 1, pp. 235–6.

78 *Nihāyat*, vol. 1, pp. 235–6.

legal veritative is said by ʿAllāmah in *Mabādiʾ* to be 'truly' linguistically figurative, or, as he phrases it in *Nihāyat*, 'at best' so.[79]

This matter leads our author on to a consideration of the issue of transfer (*al-naql*) from one sense to another—in this case that of the veritative to the figurative—and, as seen above in the discussion of the homonym, he states that transfer (*al-naql*) is 'contrary to the principle' without providing any explanation of this principle.[80] Al-Muḥaqqiq al-Ḥillī explains that the principle, in *this* instance, refers to the lack of transference (*al-aṣl ʿadam al-naql*).[81] However, the two reasons that ʿAllāmah provides in *Mabādiʾ* are, as a matter of fact, the first of *three* reasons given by al-Rāzī on this matter, which are also stated in similar terms by al-Muḥaqqiq al-Ḥillī.[82] Similarly, in *Mabādiʾ*, our author states that the figurative is 'contrary to the principle', without providing any details of the principle; it is only in *Nihāyat* that this omission is made clearer, when he explains the reason behind the contrariness to the principle of transference in the following terms:

> The advantage of assignation is to make known (*ʾilām*) to the other, that which is concealed within oneself (*al-ḍamīr*) through an utterance assigned to a meaning, and, therefore, the principle is the veritative, as through it is realised the benefit of the assignation, and if it were not for the principle then either the figurative or neither of them would be the principle.

These possibilities are considered null on the basis of various arguments that he then goes on to outline in detail.[83] ʿAllāmah, contrary to the position of the Ẓāhiriyyah, maintains that the figurative has been used in the first and second source of Islamic law either by way of addition (*ziyādah*), subtraction (*nuqṣān*) or transfer (*naql*). He corrects al-Āmidī [84] on this matter, whom he considers to be mistaken about the Imāmiyyah stance on this issue.[85]

In *Mabādiʾ* our author provides only two methods on the basis of which to obtain knowledge of whether an utterance is either veritative or figurative: the first is that the folk of the language explicitly designate an utterance to be

79 *Nihāyat*, vol. I, pp. 243–61.

80 *Nihāyat*, vol. I, p. 261.

81 *Maʿārij al-uṣūl*, p. 52.

82 *Al-Maḥṣūl fī ʿilm al-uṣūl*, vol. I, p. 314; and *Maʿārij al-uṣūl*, p. 52.

83 *Nihāyat*, vol. I, pp. 282–84.

84 ʿAlī b. Muḥammad b. Sālim al-Taghlibī, Abū al-Ḥasan, known as Sayf al-Dīn al-Āmidī (d. 631 AH/1233 CE), a prominent Shāfiʿī jurist who authored the highly influential work *al-Iḥkām fī uṣūl al-aḥkām*. See Ziriklī, *al-Aʿlām*, vol. V, p. 153.

85 *Nihāyat*, vol. I, p. 226, and *al-Iḥkām fī uṣūl al-aḥkām*, vol. I, p. 63.

either veritative or figurative (*naṣṣ ahl al-lughah*) and the second of which is that the meaning presents itself to the mind upon the hearing of an utterance (*tabādur*). However, in another example of how abridged ʿAllāmah's remarks are in the *Mabādiʾ*, he discusses a further ten such methods in *Nihāyat*.[86]

2.2.5 Discussion Five: On the Contradiction of the States of Utterances (*aḥwāl al-alfāẓ*)

This is discussed and contextualised by ʿAllāmah in the seventh chapter bearing the same title in the investigation (*maqṣid*) into languages (*al-lughāt*) in *Nihāyat*, wherein he explains that those who use such utterances have extended their usage—even the assignor himself—and, in so doing, they have not confined an utterance to a single meaning nor have they obligated the confirmation thereof within its assignment, but, rather, they have permitted it to move away from the assignment and its omission (*ḥadhf*) in its entirety, despite the remaining of that which signifies it by necessity (*iltazāman*).

He further notes that such an extension of an utterance's usage by its users leads to the following: the possible unity of an utterance despite its multiple meanings, such as with the homonym (*al-mushtarak*); the transference of an utterance from its assignment without the disregarding of the assignment entirely, such as with the figurative (*al-majāz*), or else with the disregarding of the assignment entirely, such as with the transferred (*manqūl*), or else disregarding some of the instances in which it has been set forth, such as the specifier (*al-mukhaṣṣiṣ*); and the omission (*ḥadhf*) of an utterance despite its replacement by that which indicates it, such as with the ellipsis (*al-iḍmār*). ʿAllāmah observes that such things are not opposed to one another, but rather it is possible to bring them together in a single utterance or else to bring together a number of them, and it is also possible for there to be a sufficing (*al-iktifāʾ*) of one of them over another, and ʿAllāmah deems such a sufficement to be necessary if it is possible. He also regards it as obligatory to theorise on the appropriacy of the sufficed (*al-muktafā bihi*). He states that when there is a confusion in understanding (*ikhtilāl al-fahm*), appropriacy can only be realised by these five matters: homonymy (*ishtirāk*), either customary (*al-ʿurfī*) or legal (*al-sharʿī*), transference (*al-naql*), the figurative (*al-majāz*), ellipsis (*al-iḍmār*), or specification (*al-takhṣīṣ*). It is to these matters that he gives his consideration in *Mabādiʾ*.

With the foregoing in mind ʿAllāmah then presents the following discussions: On Whether Homonymy is More Appropriate When Transference and Homonymy Contradict One Another (*idhā taʿāraḍa al-naql wa al-ishtirāk fa al-ishtirāk awlā*); On the Figurative's Appropriacy Over the Homonymic

86 *Nihāyat*, vol. 1, pp. 292–98.

(*fī anna al-majāz awlā min al-ishtirāk*); On the Contradiction Between the Homonym and Other Utterances (*fī al-taʿāruḍ bayn al-ishtirāk wa al-bāqīn*), wherein the appropriacy of ellipsis (*al-iḍmār*) and specification (*al-takhṣīṣ*) over homonymy is addressed; and finally, On the Other Contradictions (*fī bāqī al-muʿāraḍāt*), wherein he addresses the appropriacy of the figurative, ellipsis, and specification over transference, the equality of the figurative and ellipsis, the appropriacy of specification over the figurative and ellipsis, the appropriacy of homonymy over abrogation, and the appropiacy of specification and the univocal over homonymy.[87]

2.2.6 Discussion Six: A Well-Needed Commentary on Particles (*ḥurūf*)

This is addressed by ʿAllāmah in the section entitled: A Commentary On the Particles Which the Jurists Discuss (*fī tafsīr ḥurūf yabḥathu ʿanhā al-fuqahāʾ*) in *Nihāyat*, which he divides into three further discussions devoted to different particles.[88]

The first of these is on the *wāw*, wherein ʿAllāmah explains that the people have differed regarding the *wāw* of conjunction (*al-ʿāṭifah*), with the majority upholding the view that it denotes absolute union (*al-jamʿ al-muṭlaq*) without denoting sequence (*tartīb*). In support of this he quotes Abū ʿAlī al-Fārisī[89] to the effect that the linguists (*al-lughawiyūn*), the authorities on syntax (*al-naḥwiyūn*), and the grammarians from the schools of Basra and Kufa, are in agreement that the *wāw* denotes absolute union (*al-jamʿ al-muṭlaq*) and not sequence (*tartīb*). He also notes that Sībawayh[90] mentions that it denotes union, and not sequence, on seventeen different occasions in his work. Furthermore, ʿAllāmah notes that it has been reported from al-Farrāʾ[91] that it denotes sequence in those instances wherein it could not possibly denote union, such as in the statement: 'bow then prostrate' (*irkaʿī wa usjudī*). In addition to the above, ʿAllāmah observes that others are of the opinion that it denotes sequence in absolute terms.[92]

The second discussion is on the particle *fāʾ*, wherein ʿAllāmah notes that: the *fāʾ* demands possible succession (*al-taʿqīb al-mumkin*); that the authori-

---

87 *Nihāyat*, vol. I, pp. 299–312.

88 *Nihāyāt*, vol. I, pp. 313–29.

89 Al-Ḥasan b. Aḥmad b. ʿAbd al-Ghaffār, known as Abū ʿAlī al-Fārisī (d. 377 AH/987 CE), a prominent grammarian. See Ziriklī, *al-Aʿlām*, vol. II, pp. 193–4.

90 ʿAmr b. ʿUthmān b. Qanbar, known as Sībawayh (d. 180 AH/796 CE), the most famous grammarian of the Arabic language and author of the celebrated *al-Kitāb*. See Ziriklī, *al-Aʿlām*, vol. V, p. 252.

91 Yaḥyā b. Ziyād b. ʿAbd Allāh, Abu Zakariyyā, known as al-Farrāʾ (d. 207 AH/832 CE) the leading grammarian of Kufa. See Ziriklī, *al-Aʿlām*, vol. IX, p. 178.

92 *Nihāyāt*, vol. I, pp. 313–21.

ties of syntax (*al-naḥwiyūn*) have reached a consensus upon its conveying the meaning of sequence (*tartīb*) without delay; and that this is the meaning of succession (*taʿqīb*). He comments on the delimitation of the above definition to the possible (*al-mumkin*), to include the example of: 'I entered Baghdad and then Basra' (*dakhaltu baghdād fa al-baṣrah*). Furthermore, he notes that there is a consensus among the folk of the language (*ahl al-lughah*) upon its conveying the meaning of succession (*al-taʿqīb*), which is to be taken as a legal proof (*ḥujjah*).[93]

In the third of these discussions ʿAllāmah addresses the five remaining particles, namely: *fī, min, ilā, bāʾ*, and *innamā*—and it is worth observing that, of these, the particle *ilā* is not addressed in *Mabādiʾ*. He states that *fī* is used to indicate time or place (*ẓarfiyyah*), and it can be tangible (*taḥqīqan*), as in the example: 'Zayd is in the house' (*zayd fī al-dār*)—which is veritative (*ḥaqīqī*) due to the fact that the noun of place and time (*ẓarf*) cannot exceed the place or time denoted (*maẓrūf*) and is figurative (*majāzī*) in such examples where it could so exceed. Also, he notes that it could be natural (*tabīʿī*) as in the example 'the cat in her fleeing' (*al-hirr fī ihābihā*) or accidental (*ʿaraḍī*), as in the example 'man in a shirt' (*al-insān fī al-qamīṣ*); or intangible (*taqdīr*) such as its usage in Qurʾānic Verse 20:72 '...on the trunk...' (*fī judhūʿ*). Our author then provides examples for the usages of the particle *min*, noting that the utterance *min* is used for: denoting the commencement of the limit from a place (*ibtidāʾ al-ghāyah min al-makān*) as in the example 'I travelled from Kufa' (*sirtu min al-kūfah*); for denoting division into parts (*al-tabʿīḍ*) as in the example 'a ring of silver' (*khātim min fiḍḍah*); denoting explanation (*al-tabyīn*) as in the example of the Qurʾānic Verse 22:30 '...of idols' (*min al-awthān*); and, finally, for denoting addition (*zāʾidah*) only after negation, as in the example 'no one came to me' (*mā jāʾnī min aḥad*). Furthermore, he states that *ilā* is used for denoting the termination of the limit (*intihāʾ al-ghāyah*), and the particle *bāʾ* denotes connection (*ilṣāq*) and seeking aid (*istiʿānah*), and that *innamā* denotes limitation (*ḥaṣr*)—which he supports by citing the view of Abū ʿAlī al-Fārisī whose opinion he regards as a proof on syntax, poetic examples from al-Aʿshā[94] and al-Farazdaq,[95] and other grammatical arguments.[96]

93 *Nihāyat*, vol. I, pp. 321–4.

94 Maymūn b. Qays b. Jandal, known as al-Aʿshā (d. 75 AH/696 CE), was among the preeminent poets of the pre-Islamic period and one of his odes is included among the so-called *Suspended Odes* (*al-Muʿallaqāt*). See Ziriklī, *al-Aʿlām*, vol. VIII, pp. 300–301.

95 Hammām b. Ghālib b. Ṣaʿṣaʿah al-Tamīmī, Abū Firās, known as al-Farazdaq (d. 110 AH/728 CE) famous poet from Basra known for his poetry in praise of the *Ahl al-Bayt*. See, Ziriklī, *al-Aʿlām*, vol. IX, pp. 96–7.

96 *Nihāyat*, vol. I, pp. 324–9.

2.3 *Chapter Two: On Rulings* (*al-aḥkām*)

The chapter On Rulings, corresponds to the foregoing chapter On Languages, insofar as this chapter's discussion of the issues surrounding the moral status of an action also constitutes a prerequisite to any thoroughgoing theorisation of its legal status. The discussions in this chapter thereby proceed to consider: the ethical evaluation and analyses of an action, the correspondent rulings that will therefore be applied to it, the conditions according to which the ruling for an action can be qualified by its manner of performance, and other related matters, with a view to articulating how these in turn inform the status of an action's ruling. In relation to this our sage also outlines, and offers his own contributions to, the prominent debate between the Ashāʿirah[97] and Muʿtazilah as to whether the status of an action can be known only through divine revelation or, rather, whether it can also be understood by means of the faculties given to the human intellect. Further discussion is given to the obligation, incumbent on all believers, of giving thanks to the Benefactor. Finally, our author concludes this chapter with a brief gloss on the initial nature of all things prior to the revelation of the divine law, which leads him to discuss the difference between necessary and non-necessary actions and his particular stance on the 'principle of indifferency' (*aṣl al-ibāḥah*).

2.3.1 Discussion One: On Action (*al-fiʿl*)

The discussion of meaning *per se* then moves on to a brief chapter addressing the ethical valuation of actions. This covers the various moral designations which actions may bear, and how these in turn relate to the performance of actions and the status of the legal rulings that concern them.

The chapter on rulings (*al-aḥkām*), as given in *Mabādiʾ* and its six discussions, is also brought forward in *Nihāyat* and examined prior to the discussion, On Language. These issues actually pertain to those matters that are considered as prerequisites (*muqaddimāt*) for the deliberation and understanding of jurisprudence.

An action is evaluated here according to the criterion of the praiseworthiness (*madḥ*) or blameworthiness (*dhamm*) of its performer, a matter that has, of course, been extensively discussed in jurisprudence. The author qualifies an action into its five well known jurisprudential classifications through the above criterion, from which he infers that an action is either of such a quality that its actor is worthy of blame, in which case such an action is considered ugly (*qubḥ*), or is not worthy of blame, in which case, such an action is considered beautiful (*ḥusn*). The same criterion is rigorously applied to each of the five classifications in *Nihāyat,* which are as follows: if the performer is

97 This term denotes those who subscribe to the Ashʿarī school of theology.

blameworthy for his act then the action is considered forbidden (*ḥarām*); if he is blameworthy for abstaining from an action and therefore he deserves punishment (*ʿiqāb*), or is praiseworthy for performing an action, then it is considered obligatory (*wājib*); if he does not deserve blame for abstaining from it, but it is preferable (*rājiḥ*) to perform it rather than abstain from it, then it is considered as an esteemed (*mustaḥabb*), approved (*mandūb*) or a supererogatory (*nafl*) conduct, a voluntary act of obedience (*taṭawwuʿ*), or a recommended form of conduct (*sunnah*); if he is not blameworthy for abstaining from it, but it is better to abstain from the action, then it is considered as a disdained action (*makrūh*); and if he is neither deserving of rebuke nor of praise for performing or abstaining from the action, then it is considered as an indifferent action (*mubāḥ*).[98]

2.3.2 Discussion Two: On the Ruling (*al-ḥukm*)

In *Nihāyat* the discussion on the ruling (*ḥukm*) is included after the discussions on soundness (*ṣiḥḥah*), voidness (*buṭlān*), and accomplishment (*ijzāʾ*) of an action. ʿAllāmah states in this text that a ruling on a matter is either about its soundness or about its voidness, and that both these judgements are accidental applications to possible actions that may occur in both of these manners. Thus, the ruling of soundness may be applied to the acts of worship (*ʿibādāt*) and to social interactions (*muʿāmalāt*). On its application to the former, he notes, in *Nihāyat*, a difference of opinion among the jurists (*fuqahāʾ*) and theologians (*mutakallimūn*), for the latter of whom the judgement of soundness on a matter is taken to be whatever agrees with the divine law irrespective of whether its compensatory performance is obligatory or not, whilst for the former the soundness of a judgement is what annuls a compensatory performance. ʿAllāmah explains that this disagreement between the jurists and the theologians comes to the fore on the issue of the prayer of the one who, on the basis of probability, considers himself to be in a state of ritual purity. According to the theologians, this ruling is to be considered sound because it is in accordance with the command (*al-amr*) and its compensatory performance is thereby obligated through a new command. The jurists consider such a ruling unsound because it does not annul the compensatory performance, which according to ʿAllāmah is not good (*laysa bi jayyid*) because of the following objections: the compensatory performance is neither commanded nor evident in the command itself (*fī nafs al-amr*), because there are on the one hand rituals that require no compensatory performance, such as the prayer of ʿĪd, and on the other hand rituals that do require a compensatory performance, despite their soundness, such as the prayer whose prerequisite of purification has not

98 *Nihāyat*, vol. 1, pp. 91–101.

been fulfilled (*fāqid al-muṭahhir*). These objections are, according to our author, compelling enough to render the position of the jurists problematic.

With regards to the application of a judgement of unsoundness to acts of worship, this is given to be the opposite of the definitions from the theologians and jurists outlined above, namely, that which does not agree with the divine law or which does not annul the compensatory performance, and *vice versa* for social interactions (*muʿāmalāt*). The author considers the unsound (*fāsid*) to be synonymous with what is termed as void (*bāṭil*), on the basis of what is well known (*al-mashhūr*), which is a contrary position to that of the Ḥanafiyyah,[99] for whom the judgement of the unsound (*fāsid*) is a middle position between that which is judged as sound or void.[100]

2.3.3 Discussion Three: On the Acts of Worship (*al-ʿibādāt*)

The issue of accomplishment (*ijzāʾ*) is discussed in the same section on the soundness and voidness of a ruling in *Nihāyat*, where he further adds to its explanation by stating that an action can be qualified by accomplishment if it's possible that its occurrence is in accordance with two manners, the first of which is that its ruling is a result thereof and the second is that its ruling is not a result thereof, such as prayer (*ṣalāt*) and other acts of worship. However, if an action occurs only in accordance with the first of these two manners, such as the knowledge of God, the Exalted (*maʿrifat Allāh*), then it cannot be properly qualified by the term accomplishment (*ijzāʾ*) as such, likewise with the returning of an item (*wadīʿah*) placed in one's trust to its rightful owner, which cannot be qualified by such terms as accomplished (*mujz*) or unaccomplished (*ghayr mujz*).[101]

Performance (*al-adāʾ*), repetition (*al-iʿādah*), and compensatory performance (*al-qaḍāʾ*) are grouped together in *Nihāyat*, wherein ʿAllāmah adds that repetition and compensatory performance can be united in a single action if no consideration is given to the time at which the action was undertaken. Moreover, repetition and performance can be united in a single action if no consideration is to be given to the undertaking of performance as foremost.[102]

2.3.4 Discussion Four: On the Beautiful (*al-ḥusn*) and the Ugly (*al-qubḥ*)

The fourth discussion in this chapter introduces the long-standing debate between the Ashāʿirah and the Muʿtazilah on the epistemology of ethics: viz.,

99 This term denotes the followers of the Ḥanafī school of law.
100 *Nihāyat*, vol. 1, pp. 107–8.
101 *Nihāyat*, vol. 1, p. 108.
102 *Nihāyat*, vol. 1, pp. 109–10.

how the status of an action can be known, whether through divine revelation or through the faculties of the human intellect. This subject is elsewhere discussed in detail in ʿAllāmah's works on theology.[103] In the *Mabādiʾ*, however, he enumerates three methods for arriving at what is beautiful or ugly, the first two of which are intellective (*ʿaqlī*), namely through the *a priori* (*ḍarūrī*) and theorisation (*naẓarī*),[104] and the third of which is the revealed method (*samʿī*), which he explains in *Nihāyat* as the intellect taking recourse to revealed sources because it can not independently realise this knowledge alone. In *Nihāyat* the chapter on rulings and the discussion on the matter of the beautiful (*ḥusn*) and the ugly (*qubḥ*) is brought forward and discussed prior to the discussion on language in those matters that are considered as prerequisites (*muqaddimāt*) for the discussion and understanding of jurisprudence. For ʿAllāmah says on this matter:

> This issue is the great battle (*al-maʿrakah al-ʿaẓīmah*) between the Ashāʿirah and the Muʿtazilah, and most of the precepts (*qawāʾid*) of the Muʿtazilah, indeed most Islamic precepts (*al-qawāʾid al-islāmiyyah*), are founded thereupon. On this matter reasonable people (*al-ʿuqalāʾ*) have become mightily muddled. The stance of all the Muʿtazilah on this issue is that both are judgements of the intellect (*al-ḥukmān al-ʿaqliyān*).[105]

With regard to the stance of the Ashāʿirah, he goes on to state that:

> The Ashāʿirah maintain that the beautiful and the ugly are subject to revealed sources (*samʿī*). The intellect only considers something beautiful through the command of God, the Exalted, and only considers something ugly through His prohibition thereof. And so, if He prohibited the beautiful it would be ugly and *vice versa*.[106]

ʿAllāmah is in concord with the Muʿtazilah on this matter. He presents fourteen arguments in this regard, that are expounded in *Nihāyat*, on the basis of which he states that this is the rightful (*al-ḥaqq*) position to adopt on this issue.[107]

---

103 For example, see, al-ʿAllāmah al-Ḥillī, *Kashf al-murād fī sharḥ tajrīd al-iʿtiqād*, Qum, 1416 AH/1995, pp. 302–305.

104 Which in *Nihāyat* he terms *istidlāl*.

105 *Nihāyāt*, vol. I, p. 118.

106 *Nihāyat*, vol. I, p. 118.

107 *Nihāyat*, vol. I, pp. 119–24.

2.3.5 Discussion Five: On Thanking the Benefactor (*shukr al-munʿim*)

The discussion on the obligation of giving thanks to the Benefactor is a theological matter, which ʿAllāmah upholds like the Muʿtazilah. In *Nihāyat* he adds three further reasons to the brief gloss on this topic in *Mabādiʾ*, which are as follows: the dispelling of fear is itself an obligation, which can only be achieved by giving thanks, therefore thanks giving becomes obligatory; when we have incompatible ways, if one of these ways leads to security and the other results in fear, then the way which leads to security is obligated, and thus, in this context, thanks giving is the way which leads to security; and, finally, if thanking the Benefactor were *not* obligatory on the basis of intellection, then knowledge (*maʿrifah*) would not be obligated, as for ʿAllāmah there is no difference between the two, because the demand for the obligation of knowledge (*maʿrifah*) is at the same time an obligation for thanks giving. ʿAllāmah then extensively analyses the arguments presented by the Ashāʿirah on this matter, along with his counterarguments, which are beyond the scope of this introduction.[108]

2.3.6 Discussion Six: On Things (*al-ashyāʾ*)

Whilst the treatment of 'things' in the *Mabādiʾ* is very condensed, *Nihāyat* elaborates in detail on the ruling on the initial nature of all things (*ashyāʾ*) prior to the revelation of divine law. In *Mabādiʾ* this is said to be indifferent (*mubāḥ*) because they are beneficial and free from any indication of unsoundness (*amārat al-mafsadah*). However in *Nihāyat* he contextualises these concepts, giving specific examples, as well as presenting the views of a number of schools of law and theology, including the differences within the Baghdādī and Baṣarī Muʿtazilah themselves, and the opinions held by scholars, which he quotes by name, some of whom maintain unique positions amidst their own schools. This is then followed by ʿAllāmah's endorsement of one of these opinions and his justifications thereof.

The discussion of things (*ashyāʾ*) in *Nihāyat* is premised on human actions, which are seen to be either necessary or non-necessary (*ḍarūrī*). The former are those actions, which it is impossible to avoid, such as breathing. Non-necessary actions are those actions, which it is possible to avoid, and the example he employs to illustrate this point is of consuming fruits and their like. This discussion actually revolves around the non-necessary actions that the intellect (*ʿaql*) cannot comprehend *a priori* as either ugly or beautiful. The Muʿtazilah of Basra, alongside some Ḥanafī and Shāfiʿī jurists, uphold the principle of indifferency (*al-ibāḥah*) with respect to things prior to the revelation of the divine law, whereas the Muʿtazilah of Baghdad, a sect from

108 *Nihāyat*, vol. 1, pp. 134–9.

among the Imāmiyyah, Abū ʿAlī b. Abī Hurayrah of the Shāfiʿiyyah,[109] are of the opinion that they were prohibited (*al-ḥaẓr*). Furthermore Abū al-Ḥasan al-Ashʿarī and Abū Bakr al-Ṣayrafī,[110] as well as a group from among the jurists, are of the opinion that judgement should be suspended in regards to these non-necessary actions, a verdict they explain on either of the following basis: firstly, there is no ruling for them—ʿAllāmah does not see this as pertaining to judgement (*al-waqf*), but as a sure exclusion of a ruling (*al-ḥukm*)—or, secondly, we are simply not aware of the ruling regarding such things. ʿAllāmah adopts the first basis, insofar as he implies that if there is no ruling for non-necessary actions then they must be neither obligatory (*wājib*) nor forbidden (*ḥarām*) and therefore neither commanded nor prohibited, and thus they are to be considered indifferent (*mūbaḥ*). ʿAllāmah subsequently presents five reasons for the justification of their permissibility. The five reasons presented in *Nihāyat* in one way or another all return to the same reason stipulated in *Mabādiʾ*.[111]

2.4 *Chapter Three: On the Commands (al-awāmir) and Prohibitions (al-nawāhī)*

An understanding of the command, along with its counterpart, the prohibition, is, of course, essential for an understanding of the law, delivered as it is through both divine commands and the commands of the Envoy of God. This chapter begins with a linguistic inquiry into which utterances constitute a command; viz. a discussion of the differences of opinion regarding the quiddity of speech and the imperative form of the verb. ʿAllāmah then offers an intensely detailed mapping and typology of the different kinds of obligation which utterances can produce, and brings to the fore the specificities of different commands and their various modalities. As is often the case in this work, ʿAllāmah occasionally departs from a step-by-step explanation to address specific questions which he deems pertinent, usually due to their having been areas of particular consternation among the different schools of thought. This chapter also briefly surveys similar matters, as they apply to prohibitions.

2.4.1 Discussion One: On the Command (*al-amr*)

On the subject of commands and prohibitions ʿAllāmah includes a preliminary (*al-muqaddimāt*) section in *Nihāyat* in which the first discussion concerns the

---

109 Al-Ḥasan b. al-Ḥusayn al-Baghdādī, Abū ʿAlī, known as Ibn Abī Hurayrah (d. 345 AH/956 CE), leader of the Shāfiʿiyyah in Iraq of his day. See Ziriklī, *al-Aʿlām*, vol. II, p. 202.

110 Muḥammad b. ʿAbd Allāh, Abū Bakr, known as al-Ṣayrafī (d. 330 AH/942 CE). See Ziriklī, *al-Aʿlām*, vol. VII, p. 96.

111 *Nihāyat*, vol. I, pp. 139–40.

quiddity of speech (*fī māhiyyat al-kalām*). The command (*al-amr*) is regarded here as a kind of speech (*naw' min al-kalām*), which in turn necessitates the discussion of its quiddity, and he further notes that even though this discussion is the outcome of the 'art of jurisprudence' it is the theologians who have most vocally deliberated and demonstrated the issues pertaining to it. He notes the difference of opinion on the quiddity of speech between the Mu'tazilah and the ancients, and the Ashā'irah, for the former of whom it consists of letters and sounds (*al-ḥurūf wa al-aṣwāt*) and is neither a distinguished genus in its essence nor a different reality from these expressions (*'ibarāt*) and the sounds (*al-aṣwāt*) that signify their meaning, whilst for the Ashā'irah speech is a meaning which is established in itself (*qā'im fī al-nafs*) and a true genus apart from the letters, sounds and expressions (*al-'ibarāt*), writing (*al-raqūm*), and forms of inscription (*al-katabah*), which signify it.[112] The second discussion considers whether the command is veritative in a specified statement (*al-qawl al-makhṣūṣ*), an opinion to which 'Allāmah grants his accord, adding that it is figurative in other cases.[113] The third discussion focusses on the definition of the command (*fī ḥadd al-amr*), which is the same as that given in the discussion under consideration in *Mabādi'*.[114]

2.4.2 Discussion Two: On the Imperative Form of the Verb (*ṣīghat if'al*) being for obligation

The second discussion in *Mabādi'*, on the imperative form of the verb (*ṣīghat if'al*), is addressed by 'Allāmah in the first discussion On the Reasons for its Usage (*fī wujūh ista'mālihā*) under the chapter dedicated to a discussion On the Form of the Command (*al-baḥth 'an al-ṣīghah*) in *Nihāyat*.[115] Therein, he clarifies the contention of the scholars of jurisprudence: that the imperative form of the verb (*ṣīghat if'al*) is employed to denote fifteen possible aspects of meaning. He notes a consensus (*ijmā'*) that not all of these usages are veritative since some of them can only be understood within a context, and in this instance he is probably alluding to linguistic consensus. However, there is a controversy (*al-nizā'*) regarding the commonality between five of these fifteen possible meanings, namely: obligation (*al-wujūb*), approvedness (*al-nudb*), indifferency (*al-ibāḥah*), refrainment (*al-tanzīh*), and forbiddance (*al-taḥrīm*). The controversy is as follows: that it is common for all the above five, or that it is common between obligation, approvedness, and indifferency, or that it is veritative at least for the meaning of indifferency, or as some have said it is for

112 *Nihāyat*, vol. I, pp. 357–8.

113 *Nihāyat*, vol. I, pp. 358–67.

114 *Nihāyat*, vol. I, pp. 367–72.

115 *Nihāyat*, vol. I, p. 373.

approvedness and obligation, whilst according to others the latter is the case only with the addition of a context, and according to others still it is for obligation and can only be employed in other meanings through the context. A few discussions later in *Nihāyat* ʿAllāmah discusses Whether or not the Command Demands Obligation (*fī ann al-amr hal yaqtaḍī al-wujūb am lā*) and his argument on this point is supported, in both works, by the same *ḥadīth* regarding the tooth-twig (*miswāk*).[116]

2.4.3 Discussion Three: On the Command (*al-amr*) Not Demanding Repetition (*al-takrār*)

The issue of a command not demanding a repetition is raised On a Command Lacking a Context (*al-amr al-mujarrad ʿan al-qarāʾin*) about which ʿAllāmah notes, in *Nihāyat,* that Abū Isḥāq al-al-Asfarāyīnī, alongside some other jurists and theologians, maintains that such a command demands repeated engagement, if at all possible, for the duration of a believer's lifetime. Others, however, including ʿAllāmah himself, al-Sayyid al-Murtaḍā, Abū al-Ḥasan al-Baṣrī and Fakhr al-Dīn al-Rāzī, uphold the position that such a command—referred to in *Mabādiʾ* as the 'absolute command' (*al-amr al-muṭlaq*)—demands neither a one-off nor a repeat engagement, insofar as it can be understood.[117]

2.4.4 Discussion Four: On the Command Demanding Neither Expedition (*al-fawr*) nor Postponement (*al-tarākhī*)

Allāmah explains the differences of opinion in relation to this matter in the third section of the fourth investigation in *Nihāyat* in the fifth discussion entitled: The Command Does not Demand Expedition (*fī anna al-amr lā yaqtaḍī al-fawr*), where he states that a group of the Ḥanafiyyah, a group of the Ḥanābilah, and whoever else obligates a repeated engagement (*al-takrār*), maintain that the command demanding neither expedition nor postponement obligates expedition (*al-fawr*); whilst the Jubbāʾiyān, Abu al-Ḥusayn al-Baṣrī, Qāḍī Abū Bakr, and a group from the Shāfiʿiyyah[118] and Ashāʿirah uphold the position of postponement (*al-tarākhī*). Furthermore, others, such as al-Sayyid al-Murtaḍā, maintain a suspension of judgement (*al-waqf*) on this matter. ʿAllāmah resolves that this kind of command signifies a demand that is common between expedition and postponement (*al-ṭalab al-mustarak bayn al-fawr wa al-tarākhī*), a verdict that he presents in *Mabādiʾ* as the 'common extent' (*al-qadr al-mushtarak*).[119]

---

116 *Nihāyat,* vol. 1, p. 414.

117 *Nihāyat,* vol. 1, pp. 435–43.

118 This term denotes those who subscribe to the Shāfiʿī school of law.

119 *Nihāyat,* vol. 1, pp. 451–2.

2.4.5 Discussion Five: On the Conditioned Command (*al-amr al-mashrūṭ*) being Non-Existent When the Condition (*al-sharṭ*) is Non-Existent

This matter is addressed in *Nihāyat* under a similar title, as part of a broader examination of the difference of opinion regarding commands that depend upon their being conditioned by the Arabic particle *in*, which is only addressed in *Mabādi'* in the example he furnishes of a master saying to his slave: 'If you enter the market then buy meat' (*in dakhalta al-sūqa fa ishtari al-laḥma*). 'Allāmah presents his reasoning and arguments—all of which are succinctly encapsulated in the short paragraph in *Mabādi'*—where he confirms that the correct opinion is that, if the condition does not exist then neither does the command. He further observes that this is the matter which so perplexed Ya'lā b. Umayyah,[120] and led him to question the shortening of prayer in times of security.[121]

2.4.6 Discussion Six: On the Command that is Delimited by an Attribute (*al-amr al-muqayyad bi al-ṣifah*) not Becoming Non-Existent With the Non-Existence of the Attribute

A similar discussion of this matter is also found in *Nihāyat* under a section entitled: The Command Delimited by an Attribute (*fī al-amr al-muqayyad bi al-ṣifah*), yet prior to this discussion a separate discussion is undertaken into The Command Delimited by a Name (*fī al-amr al-muqayyad bi al-ism*) in contrast with *Mabādi'* wherein the discussion of the name (*al-ism*) is limited to the discussion dealing with the delimitation of a command by an attribute (*al-ṣifah*). The debate in *Nihāyat* is structured around the question of whether or not the ruling (*al-ḥukm*) delimited by an attribute signifies the exclusion of that which is other than it. 'Allāmah analyses the various stances taken on this question, including by those who maintain that such an exclusion does occur, such as al-Shāfi'ī, Mālik,[122] Aḥmad b. Ḥanbal,[123] Abū al-Ḥasan al-Ash'arī, a group of

---

120 Ya'lā b. Umayyah b. Abī 'Ubaydah, was a companion of the Prophet who died alongside the forces of Imām 'Alī during the battle of Ṣiffīn in 37 AH/658 CE. See Ziriklī, *al-A'lām*, vol. IX, p. 269.

121 *Nihāyat*, vol. I, pp. 461–5.

122 Mālik b. Anas (d. 179 AH/795 CE), founder of the *madhhab* that bears his name. He was the compiler of a work known as *al-Muwaṭṭā'* for which there are roughly twelve versions. See Ziriklī, *al-A'lām*, vol. VI, p. 128.

123 Aḥmad b. Muḥammad b. Ḥanbal al-Shaybānī al-Wā'ilī, Abū 'Abd Allāh, known simply as Ibn Ḥanbal or Aḥmad Ibn Ḥanbal (d. 241 AH/855 CE), was the founder of the Ḥanbalī *madhhab* which bears his name, and is chronologically the last of the four Sunnī *madhāhib*. He was imprisoned for eighteen months by the Abbasid ruler al-Mu'taṣim for upholding the doctrine of the 'uncreated Qur'ān' (*qidam al-qur'ān*) and released

jurists and theologians, Abū ʿUbayd,[124] and a group of philologists. There are also those who uphold that it does not so occur, such as Abū Ḥanīfah[125] and his acolytes, Qāḍī Abū Bakr, al-Qaffāl,[126] and a great number of the Muʿtazilah. Our author then moves on to consider the opinion of Abū ʿAbd Allāh al-Baṣrī that it does so exclude, but only in three instances; in the address (*al-khiṭāb*) set forth for an elucidation (*al-bayān*), for instruction (*al-taʿlīm*), and thirdly in whatever is apart from an attribute included therein, such as when the ruling for two witnesses signifies the exclusion of one witness because it comes under two witnesses. ʿAllāmah asserts that the strongest opinion on this matter is that the ruling delimited by an attribute does not signify the exclusion of anything contrary to it unless the attribute itself is the cause (*ʿillah*).[127]

2.4.7 Discussion Seven: On the Chosen Obligation (*al-wājib al-mukhayyar*)

In respect to this matter our author sees fit to analyse the particularities that arise regarding any command that relates to a number of obligations by way of choice. In *Nihāyat* this issue is discussed under the chapter: On the Classifications of the Command (*al-aqsām al-amr*). The primary concern of this discussion, in both works, is to resolve the question of whether one of the obligations is the determined obligatory action according to God, or whether in fact they are all obligatory, and the charged agent must determine one out of the many by way of choice (*al-takhyīr*). This discussion gives rise to the following concepts, and subsequent implications, of choice (*takhyīr*): determination (*taʿyīn*), obligation (*wujūb*), performance (*fiʿl*), and abstainment (*tark*).[128]

---

from prison in 220 AH/835 CE, whereafter his influence increased significantly. His most important contribution is the extensive *ḥadīth* collection known as *al-Musnad*, which is organised according to the companion narrating the *ḥadīth* in question. See Ziriklī, *al-Aʿlām*, vol. I, pp. 192–3.

124 Al-Qāsim b. Sallām al-Harawī, known as Abū ʿUbayd (d. 224 AH/838 CE), was an accomplished scholar who authored works in the fields of *ḥadīth*, Arabic literature, and Islamic law, from Herat (in present day Afghanistan). He travelled to Baghdad and settled in Tarsus, visited Egypt, and finally died in Makkah. See Ziriklī, *al-Aʿlām*, vol. VI, p. 10.

125 Al-Nuʿmān b. Thābit al-Tamīmī Bālwalāʾ al-Kūfī, known as Abū Ḥanīfah or Imām al-Ḥanafiyyah (d. 150 AH/767 CE), a prominent jurist and founder of the *madhhab* that bears his name, see Ziriklī, *al-Aʿlām*, vol. IX, pp. 4–5.

126 Muḥammad b. Aḥmad b. al-Ḥusayn b. ʿUmar, Abū Bakr, known as al-Shāshī al-Qaffāl al-Fāriqī or al-Qaffāl (d. 507 AH/1114 CE), was the leader of the Shāfiʿī *madhhab* in Iraq in his day, and taught in the Niẓāmiyyah Madrasah of Baghdad. See Ziriklī, *al-Aʿlām*, vol. VI, p. 210.

127 *Nihāyat*, vol. I, pp. 470–471.

128 *Nihāyat*, vol. I, pp. 488–501.

2.4.8 Discussion Eight: On the Obligation that is to be Performed within a Broad Period of Time (*al-wājib al-muwassaʿ*)

This is discussed under a discussion of the same title in *Nihāyat* in the section, On the Classifications of the Command, wherein ʿAllāmah clarifies that in respect to time, the action should be viewed according to a threefold classification: first that the time is shorter than needed to perform the action, which would be an injunction of what is not feasible; second, that the time is adequate for the time it takes to perform the action, such as the day and the fast; and thirdly that the time is more than it takes to perform it. He says that there is no controversy regarding the first or second classifications, however some people have differed in respect to the permissibility of the third. The proponents of this, along with their differing stances, are given as Muḥammad b. Shujāʿ al-Thaljī,[129] the Shāfiʿiyyah, and the Jubbāʾiyān and their followers, al-Sayyid al-Murtaḍā, Abū al-Ḥusayn al-Baṣrī and some of the Ḥanafiyyah, whilst their opponents, along with their arguments, are given as being the Ashāʿirah and a group of the Ḥanafiyyah.[130]

2.4.9 Discussion Nine: On the Obligation On All Sufficed by the Performance of Some (*al-wājib ʿalā al-kifāyah*)

The discussion of this in *Nihāyat*, follows along the same lines as that presented in *Mabādiʾ*, as, in both works, the emphasis is placed on the objective (*gharaḍ*) of the Lawgiver either being attached to the realisation of the action by everyone who is charged, in particular, or the realisation thereof in an absolute manner. The former is obligatory upon individuals (*al-aʿyān*), and the command includes them by way of plurality (*jamʿ*). The latter is the obligation on all sufficed by the performance of some (*wājib ʿalā al-kifāyah*), and the command does not include them by way of plurality.[131]

2.4.10 Discussion Ten: On the Obligation (*wujūb*) upon Which the Absolute Obligation (*al-wājib al-muṭlaq*) Depends

ʿAllāmah discusses this in the fifth section of *Nihāyat*, in relation to the rulings of obligation (*fī ahkām al-wujūb*). However in *Nihāyat* the two classes of the obligation are given as being the conditioned (*mashrūṭ*)— which he refers to as 'the delimited' (*muqayyad*) in *Mabādiʾ*—and the absolute (*muṭlaq*). With regard to the latter the author notes the difference of opinion between the

129 Muḥammad b. Shujāʿ, Abū ʿAbd Allāh known as Ibn al-Thaljī (d. 266 AH/880 CE), was a prominent Ḥanafī jurist of Baghdad who leaned toward the Muʿtazilah in theology. See Ziriklī, *al-Aʿlām*, vol. VII, p. 28.

130 *Nihāyat*, vol. I, pp. 503–5.

131 *Nihāyat*, vol. I, p. 501.

Wāqifiyyah[132] and al-Sayyid al-Murtaḍā, on the one hand, and the Muʿtazilah and Ashāʿirah on the other. The former uphold the doctrine of the obligation thereof if the preliminary (*muqaddimah*) is a reason (*sabab*) for the commanded (*al-maʾmūr bihi*), and if it is a condition with regard to the occurrence then it is not regarded as a reason and therefore is not obligatory. The latter are of the opinion that the obligation upon which depends the existence of that which is commanded is subject to two conditions, namely the ability to perform it and that the command is set forth in absolute terms, regardless of whether it is a reason or not. ʿAllāmah subscribes to the latter position, because, he states, if it were not obligatory it would necessitate one of two matters: either the injunction of what is not feasible or the exclusion of the absolute obligation from obligation itself.[133]

2.4.11 Discussion Eleven: On the Command of a Thing (*al-amr bi al-shayʾ*) Necessitating the Prohibition (*al-nahy*) of its Opposite (*ḍiddihi*)

This section corresponds to the discussion of the same topic in *Nihāyat* which approaches this subject from two angles, firstly with regard to an utterance (*lafẓ*) and secondly with regard to its meaning (*maʿnā*). Our author thereby expands on what he presents in *Mabādiʾ*, namely that with regards to the obligation abstainment is by no means to be permitted (*manʿ*). The muted reference he makes in *Mabādiʾ* to 'the one who has acquired no knowledge' is shown here to refer to the chosen opinion among the Ashāʿirah and that of Qāḍī Abū Bakr Muḥammad b. Ṭayyib al-Bāqillānī, who maintain that 'a command of a thing is the very prohibition of its opposite' (*al-amr bi al-shayʾ nahy ʿan ḍiddihi bi ʿaynihi*).[134]

2.4.12 Discussion Twelve: When the Obligation is Abrogated (*nusikha*) the Permissibility (*al-jawāz*) Remains

This brief section is supplemented in *Nihāyat* by an intricate consideration of the differing opinions, and counterarguments to, al-Ghazālī, who is of the opinion that the abrogation of an obligation does not necessitate the permissibility to remain, and also the contrary view of Fakhr al-Dīn al-Rāzī, who upholds that the permissibility would remain in such an instance. ʿAllāmah's argument centres here on how the issue of permissibility (*al-jawāz*) is to be

132 After the martydom of the Imām Mūsā al-Kāẓim, the majority of the Shīʿah followed his son Imām ʿAlī al-Riḍā as the eighth Imām. Those who stopped with the seventh Imām and considered him to be the last of the imāms became known as the Wāqifiyyah.

133 *Nihāyat*, vol. 1, pp. 518–9.

134 *Nihāyat*, vol. 1, pp. 527–8.

understood: either as permission (*idhan*) for an action, or as an equiponderant choice for the action to be performed or not.[135]

2.4.13 Discussion Thirteen: On the Impossibility of an Injunction (*taklīf*) of the Impossible (*al-muḥāl*)

This issue is extensively discussed in *Nihāyat* under a section entitled: On What is Commanded (*fī al-maʾmūr bihi*), wherein ʿAllāmah presents the agreement of all the Muʿtazilah that such an injunction is impossible, and the differing opinions on its occurrence among the Ashāʿirah despite their agreement that such an injunction is possible.[136]

2.4.14 Discussion Fourteen: An Injunction (*al-taklīf*) on Ritual (*al-furūʿ*) is not Dependent upon Faith (*al-īmān*)

The fourteenth discussion in *Mabādiʾ* is elsewhere addressed in *Nihāyat* under a discussion on the realisation of a legal condition (*ḥuṣūl al-sharṭ al-sharʿī*) not being conditioned by an injunction (*al-taklīf*), which is the general position of the Muʿtazilah and the Ashāʿirah—except for Abū Ḥanīfah and Abū Ḥāmid al-Isfrāʾīnī who claim that disbelievers are not addressed regarding the ritual acts of worship. Another exception is the opinion of those who maintain that disbelievers are charged only insofar as the prohibitions (*nawāhī*) are concerned but not with respect to commands (*awāmir*). ʿAllāmah maintains that this dispute has no bearing insofar as the judgements of the world (*aḥkām al-dunyā*) are concerned, because the disbelief of a disbeliever (*kufr al-kāfir*) constitutes prevention for approaching Islamic ritual prayer (*al-ṣalāt*) and, after embracing Islam, the compensatory performance (*qaḍāʾ*) of prayers lapsed whilst in the state of disbelief is annulled. However, he states, this discussion has a bearing on the judgements of the hereafter (*aḥkām al-ākhirah*) insofar as the disbeliever, as he shall be chastised for disbelief, shall also be chastised for his disobedience and for abstaining from the ritual prayers—and this is the meaning, ʿAllāmah states, of our doctrine that they are commanded regarding the ritual acts of worship.[137]

2.4.15 Discussion Fifteen: On the Command (*al-amr*) Demanding Accomplishment (*al-ijzāʾ*)

The discussion of this matter in *Nihāyat* is predicated upon the notion that an accomplished action is that which is performed in a sufficient manner annulling any further devotion to it. On this, ʿAllāmah notes the difference of opin-

135 *Nihāyat*, vol. I, pp. 535–7.

136 *Nihāyat*, vol. I, p. 545.

137 *Nihāyat* vol. I, pp. 570–78.

ion between Qāḍī al-Quḍāt, Abū Hāshim and his acolytes, Qāḍī ʿAbd al-Jabbār, and al-Sayyid al-Murtaḍā, before presenting his own reasoning for the command demanding accomplishment in six points whilst noting four possible objections along with his counterarguments to each of these four points.[138]

2.4.16 Discussion Sixteen: On Whether the Impairment (*ikhlāl*) [of an act of worship] Demands the Obligation of [its] Compensatory Performance (*al-qaḍāʾ*)

In *Nihāyat* ʿAllāmah acknowledges two opinions regarding this issue, the first of which is that the command delimited by time demands the obligation (*wujūb*) of compensatory performance within the same command, as is the opinion of certain jurists, and the Hanābilah, and the second of which is that the obligation of compensatory performance requires a new command, which is the opinion of the author and those whom he calls 'the verifiers' among the Muʿtazilah and the Ashāʿirah. ʿAllāmah presents eight reasons, altogether, for his adopted position on this matter, each of which is governed by the two underlying reasons stated in *Mabādiʾ*, namely: that the command which is delimited by time only signifies that time and nothing else; and, that, although legal commands (*al-awāmir al-sharʿiyyah*) are in some instances followed by a compensatory performance, in other instances they are not. He also presents the eleven arguments of his opponents on this problem along with his counterarguments, concluding that impairment itself does not demand the obligation of compensatory performance.[139]

2.4.17 Discussion Seventeen: The Command (*al-amr*) to Command Something (*al-amr bi al-shayʾ*) does not Constitute a Command for that thing

The seventeenth discussion in *Mabādiʾ* is a concise summary in which ʿAllāmah demonstrates the concept that the command to command something does not constitute a command for that thing through reference to a prophetic statement commanding parents to command their children to perform the ritual prayer, of which he remarks that this does not constitute a command for children to pray at the age of seven, but is merely a command to their parents. Yet, despite this brevity, a further two linguistic arguments in support of this topic are presented in *Nihāyat*.[140]

138 *Nihāyat*, vol. 1, p. 578.

139 *Nihāyat*, vol. 1, pp. 582–9.

140 *Nihāyat*, vol. 1, pp. 589–91.

2.4.18 Discussion Eighteen: The Non-Existent (*al-maʿdūm*) is not Commanded

The same discussion is found in *Nihāyat* under a heading entitled: On the Impossibility of Commanding the Non-Existent (*fī istiḥālat amr al-maʿdūm*). ʿAllāmah here contests the adopted position of the Ashāʿirah on this matter on the basis of the intellect (*al-ʿaql*), and declares his astonishment that they could permit the commanding of the unmindful (*ghāfil*), the one who is asleep (*nāʾim*), the child (*ṣabī*), the mentally impaired (*majnūn*), or the intoxicated (*al-sukrān*).[141]

2.4.19 Discussion Nineteen: On the Obligation for the Intention (*qaṣd*) of Obedience (*al-ṭāʿah*)

The discussion in *Nihāyat* entitled: On the Qualifications of the Charged Agent (*fī sharāʾiṭ al-mukallaf*), provides the full context for further discussion concerning the obligation for the one who is commanded to have an intention of obedience. In *Nihāyat* ʿAllāmah enumerates five qualifications which the charged agent must fulfil for the law to be binding upon him, namely; legal maturity (*al-bulūgh*), intellect (*al-ʿaql*), absence of unmindfulness (*ʿadam al-ghaflah*), choice (*al-ikhtiyār*), and finally the aspect of intention (*jihat al-qaṣd*), which, he concludes, is obedience (*al-ṭāʿah*)—a conclusion which he supports through revelation and prophetic statements.[142]

2.4.20 Discussion Twenty: On the Timing of the Attachment (*taʿalluq*) of the Command (*al-amr*)

This is addressed by ʿAllāmah in *Nihāyat* under the discussion entitled: On the Time the Command is Confronted (*fī waqt tawajjuh al-amr*). His consideration of this issue, in both works, involves the details of when, precisely, the commanded becomes commanded in action. In *Nihāyat* ʿAllāmah elaborates on the two stances regarding this matter; namely those of the Muʿtazilah and al-Juwaynī,[143] who maintain that it is commanded prior to the occurrence of the action and not in the state of its occurrence, and the stance of the Ashāʿirah, who maintain that it is commanded in the state of action and not beforehand. ʿAllāmah subsequently verifies the argument of the Muʿtazilah, on the grounds that, if the commanded were not to become commanded in action, except in

141 *Nihāyat*, vol. I, p. 594.

142 *Nihāyat*, vol. I, pp. 597–604.

143 ʿAbd al-Malik b. ʿAbd Allāh b. Yūsuf b. Muḥammad al-Juwaynī, Abū al-Muʿālī, Rukn al-Dīn, known as Imām al-Ḥaramayn (d. 478 AH/1085 CE), was the most prominent Shāfiʿī jurist of his time as well as a noted expert in jurisprudence. His most famous student, who effectively inherited his mantle, was al-Ghazālī. See Ziriklī, *al-Aʿlām*, vol. IV, p. 306.

the state of the existence thereof, then that would necessitate an injunction of what is not feasible.[144]

2.4.21 Discussion Twenty-One: On Prohibition (*al-nahy*)

As part of his discussion of the prohibition in *Nihāyat,* ʿAllāmah includes nine distinct discussions, which are along similar lines to those he outlines in the discussion of the command (*al-amr*). They are: On the Veritability Thereof (*fī ḥaqīqatihi*); On What is Sought in the Prohibition (*fī anna al-maṭlūb fī al-nahy mādhā*); On the Prohibition Demanding Repetition (*fī anna al-nahy qad yuqtaḍī al-takrār*); On the Impossibility of Union of the Command and the Prohibition (*fī imtināʿ ijtimāʿ al-amr wa al-nahy*); On the Contradiction between the Forbiddance of the Attribute and the Obligation of the Original (*fī al-taḍādd bayn taḥrīm al-waṣf wa wujūb al-aṣl*); On Whether the Prohibition Signifies Unsoundness (*fī anna al-nahy hal yadullu ʿalā al-fasād*); On Other Topics from Among this Category Regarding Which There is Disagreement (*fī mawāḍiʿ min hādhā al-bāb waqaʿa fīhā al-khilāf*); On Whether or not the Prohibition Signifies Soundness (*fī anna al-nahy hal yadullu ʿalā al-ṣiḥḥat am lā*); and On Choice in Regards to the Prohibition (*fī al-takhyīr fī al-nahy*).[145]

2.4.22 Discussion Twenty-Two: On Whether Prohibition (*al-nahy*) Demands Unsoundness (*al-fasād*)

The twenty-second, and final, discussion in this chapter of *Mabādiʾ* corresponds to the sixth discussion in *Nihāyat*, in the chapter Regarding the Prohibition (*al-nahy*), which is further subdivided into two sections dealing with the question of the relationship between prohibition and unsoundness (*al-fasād*), firstly in regard to the acts of worship (*fī al-ʿibādāt*) and secondly in regard to social interactions (*fī al-muʿāmalāt*).[146] The conclusion of this discussion in *Mabādiʾ* is that the prohibition also does not indicate soundness, however, in *Nihāyat* ʿAllāmah devotes a separate discussion to this.[147]

2.5 *Chapter Four: On Generality* (al-ʿumūm) *and Specificity* (al-khuṣūṣ)

The fourth chapter addresses the composition of the general and the specific, outlining the various forms by which they are made manifest, and its greater part is spent in examining the process by which such specification occurs in relation to these forms. This examination takes place at once on an abstract, semantic level, considering how elements of language may act as specifiers,

144 *Nihāyat*, vol. I, p. 604.
145 *Nihāyat*, vol. II, pp. 67–105.
146 *Nihāyat*, vol. II, pp. 84–94.
147 *Nihāyāt*, vol. II, pp. 101–4.

and also at the level of scriptural hermeneutics, mapping how different proof-texts can affect each other in this regard. ʿAllāmah also considers a number of cases in which the generality or specificity of a given linguistic element, or text, has been misinterpreted by other groups, and the practical repurcussions borne out of this.

2.5.1 Discussion One: On the General (*al-ʿāmm*) and the Specific (*al-khāṣṣ*)

The discussion On the General (*al-ʿāmm*) and the Specific (*al-khāṣṣ*) in *Mabādiʾ* is addressed in *Nihāyat* in four independent chapters (*abwāb*) wherein the issues that pertain to generality (*al-ʿumūm*) and specificity (*al-khuṣūṣ*) are presented. The four chapters are: On Generality (*fī al-ʿumūm*) which consists of two sections; On Specificity (*fī al-khuṣūṣ*) which consists of seven discussions; On the Demand for Specification (*fī al-muqtaḍā li al-takhṣīṣ*) consisting of four sections; and On the Absolute and the Delimited (*fī al-muṭlaq wa al-muqayyad*) which consists of three discussions.[148] In the chapter On Generality (*fī al-ʿumūm*) ʿAllāmah includes two sections, On the Utterances Thereof (*fī alfāẓihi*), and On What is Added to the General whilst it is not Thereof (*fīmā luḥiqa bi al-ʿāmm wa laysa minhu*). He begins the first section with a discussion on the definition of generality, wherein he presents his analysis of the various linguistic expressions of the general, as he also does in *Mabādiʾ*.[149] The discussion on the specific (*al-khāṣṣ*) is addressed independently in two chapters in *Nihāyat*: the first of which, On Specificity (*khuṣūṣ*), deals with the issues of its definition and so forth, and the second is On the Demand for Specification (*fī al-muqtaḍāʾ li al-takhṣīṣ*).[150]

2.5.2 Discussion Two: On What is Added to Generality (*al-ʿumūm*) Though it is not Thereof

This is discussed in the second section, On Generality, in *Nihāyat,* wherein a further seven matters are also addressed, namely: The Transitive Verb (*al-fiʿl al-mutaʿaddī ilā mafʿūl); The Omission of the Separation (*tark al-istifṣāl*); The Conjunction to the General (*al-ʿatf ʿalā al-ʿāmm*); The Verbal Address (*al-khiṭāb al-shafāhi*); The Narration of the Reporter (*riwāyat al-rāwī*); The Implicit (*al-mafhūm*); and The Addition of the Plural to the Plural (*al-jamʿ al-muḍāf ilā al-jamʿ*).[151]

148 *Nihāyat,* vol. II, pp. 109–389.

149 *Nihāyat,* vol. II, pp. 109–201.

150 *Nihāyat,* vol. II, pp. 203–373.

151 *Nihāyāt* vol. II, pp. 164–201.

2.5.3 Discussion Three: On Specification (*al-takhṣīṣ*)

The issue of establishing specification on an evidential basis, either through a connected, or else through a separate, piece of evidence, is discussed by the author in detail in this chapter in discussions five, six, and seven of *Mabādiʾ*. In *Nihāyāt* ʿAllāmah presents the view of the Muʿtazilah that the difference between specification (*takhṣīṣ*) and abrogation (*al-naskh*) rests upon the consideration as to whether or not a postponement of time has occurred. He also enumerates the seven arguments put forward by those who do not consider specification to be a genus of abrogation, as well as the conditions that differentiate specification from exception (*istithnāʾ*).[152]

2.5.4 Discussion Four: On the Adherence to the General which is Specified (*al-ʿāmm al-makhṣūṣ*)

This discussion is contextualised by ʿAllāmah in *Nihāyat,*[153] wherein he presents an additional discussion regarding whether or not the general, which is specified, is figurative or not. He subsequently considers The Permissibility of the Adherence to the General, Which is Specified (*fī jawāz al-tamassuk bi al-ʿāmm al-makhṣūṣ*). ʿAllāmah remarks here upon the difference of opinion concerning this issue, namely that ʿĪsā b. Abān[154] and Abū Thawr[155] prohibit adherence to the general which is specified, in regard to that which is contrary to the specified object, whilst others permit the adherence to it in any case. Furthermore, al-Karkhī, al-Balkhī[156], Abū ʿAbd Allāh,[157] as well as Qāḍī al-Quḍāt permit such an adherence in some cases but not others, and yet they differ regarding the particularities of such a case.[158]

2.5.5 Discussion Five: On Exception (*al-istithnāʾ*)

ʿAllāmah considers the matter of exception in *Nihāyat* in the third chapter entitled: On the Demand for Specification (*fī al-muqtaḍī li al-takhṣīṣ*), in the fifth

152 *Nihāyat*, vol. II, pp. 207–208.

153 *Nihāyat*, vol. II, p. 216.

154 ʿĪsā b. Abān b. Ṣadaqah, Abū Mūsā (d. 221 AH/836 CE), known as ʿĪsā b. Abān; a prominent Ḥanafī judge and jurist. See Ziriklī, *al-Aʿlām*, vol. V, p. 283.

155 Ibrāhīm b. Khālid b. Abī al-Yamān al-Kalbī, known as Abū Thawr (d. 240 AH/854 CE), a prominent Shāfiʿī jurist who studied under the founder of the *madhhab*. See Ziriklī, *al-Aʿlām*, vol. I, pp. 30–31.

156 ʿAbd Allāh b. Aḥmad b. Maḥmūd al-Kaʿbī al-Balkhī al-Khurāsānī, Abū al-Qāsim (d. 319 AH/931 CE), a leading figure among the Muʿtazilah who is variously known as: al-Kaʿbī, al-Balkhī, or Abū al-Qāsim al-Balkhī. See Ziriklī, *al-Aʿlām*, vol. IV, p. 189.

157 Al-Ḥusayn b. ʿAlī b. Ibrāhīm, known variously as: Abū ʿAbd Allāh, Abū ʿAbd Allāh al-Baṣrī, or al-Juʿal al-Kāghadī (d. 369 AH/980 CE), a leading figure among the Muʿtazilah.

158 *Nihāyat*, vol. II, pp. 223–4.

investigation. The first section of this chapter, entitled: Regarding the Connected Pieces of Evidence (*fī al-adillah al-muttaṣilah*), is in turn sub-divided into two further problems; the first dedicated to exception (*al-istithnā'*) comprised of the following distinct discussions: On the Veritability of the Exception (*fī ḥaqīqat al-istithnā'*), On the Conditions for the Exception (*fī shurūṭihi*), and On the Rulings Thereof (*fī aḥkāmihi*).[159]

2.5.6 Discussion Six: On the Condition (*al-sharṭ*), the Attribute (*al-ṣifah*), and the Limit (*al-ghāyah*)

These matters are discussed in *Nihāyat* in the second problem in the first section mentioned above, Regarding the Connected Pieces of Evidence (*fī al-adillah al-muttaṣilah*). 'Allāmah presents the discussion on the condition in two distinct discussions; the first Regarding the Definition of the Condition (*ḥadd al-sharṭ*) and the second On the Rulings Thereof (*aḥkāmihi*). He dedicates the third discussion to Delimitation by Limit (*fī al-taqyīd bi al-ghāyah*), and the fourth discussion to Delimitation by an Attribute (*fī al-taqyīd bi al-waṣf*).[160]

2.5.7 Discussion Seven: On the Specification (*al-takhṣīṣ*) by Separate Pieces of Evidence (*al-adillah al-munfaṣilah*)

'Allāmah presents this discussion in *Nihāyat* within the third chapter dedicated to The Demand for Specification (*fī al-muqtaḍī lil takhṣīṣ*), wherein he includes the second section, On the Separate Pieces of Evidence (*fī al-adillah al-munfaṣilah*).[161] In *Nihāyat* he states that the specification of the general is either accomplished through intellection (*'aql*), sense perception (*ḥiss*), or revelation (*sam'*)—the latter comprising seven types, each of which form a separate discussion.[162]

2.5.8 Discussion Eight: On What is Considered a Specifier (*mukhaṣṣiṣ*) Though it is not

This matter is examined by 'Allāmah in *Nihāyat*, under the fourth section of the third chapter, across fifteen discussions.[163] To the seven matters presented in *Mabādi'* he here adds a further eight matters, namely: the Specification of the Generalities of the Qur'ān and the *Sunnah* by Analogical Reasoning (*fī takhṣīṣ 'umūm al-kitāb wa al-sunnah bi al-qiyās*); the Specification of the General by the Implicit (*fī takhṣīṣ al-'āmm bi al-mafhūm*); Regarding the Inclusion of the

---

159 *Nihāyat*, vol. II, pp. 233–60.
160 *Nihāyat*, vol. II, pp. 274–80.
161 *Nihāyat*, vol. II, pp. 281–303.
162 *Nihāyat*, vol. II, pp. 281–303.
163 *Nihāyat*, vol. II, p. 317.

Slave and the Disbeliever (*fī dakhūl al-ʿabd wa al-kāfir*); That Specification is Not Demanded by Mere Rebuke or Mere Intent (*fī anna qaṣd al-madḥ wa al-dhamm ghayr muqtaḍin li al-takhṣīṣ*); On Whether or not the Reference of a Pronoun Demands Specification (*fī anna rajūʿ al-ḍamīr ilā al-baʿḍ hal yuqtaḍā al-takhṣīṣ am lā*); On the Specific Ruling Connected to the Cause (*fī ḥukm al-khāṣṣ al-muqtarin bi al-ʿillah*); On the Address of the Prophet Demanding his Own Specification (*fī anna khiṭābahu yaqtaḍī takhṣīṣahu bihi*); and On Whether or not the Qurʾānic Verse 9:103 is for Generality (*fī anna qawlihi taʿālā 'khudh min amwālihim sadaqatan hal huwa li al-ʿumūm am lā'*).[164]

2.5.9 Discussion Nine: On the Predication of the Absolute (*al-muṭlaq*) to the Delimited (*al-muqayyad*)

Nihāyat addresses the predication of the absolute to the delimited, in the fourth chapter of the fifth investigation across three discussions, namely: On the Quiddity of These Two (*fī māhiyyatihimā*); The Ruling of Integration Between the Both of These (*fī ḥukm al-jamʿ baynahumā*); and the Integration of the Absolute and the Delimited (*fī al-jamʿ bayn al-muṭlaq wa al-muqayyad*).[165]

2.6 *Chapter Five: On the Ambiguous (al-mujmal) and the Elucidated (al-mubayyan)*

In this chapter ʿAllāmah examines the circumstances in which a given utterance or action may, or may not, fully convey the intentions of a speaker or agent. He proceeds to explain the different ways such ambiguity can arise, as well as elucidating how, and to what extent, an ambiguous expression on the part of the divine Lawgiver is logically possible. In a similar fashion to the previous chapter, the discussion of these issues is accompanied by a selection of examples illustrating their erroneous application by various parties.

2.6.1 Discussion One: On Some of the Definitions (*al-taʿārīf*)

These preliminary definitions are presented in an extensive manner by ʿAllāmah in *Nihāyat* across two discussions; On the Quiddity of the Ambiguous (*fī al-māhiyyah*), and, On the Classifications of the Ambiguous (*fī aqsām al-mujmal*), in the latter of which he explains that legal evidence (*al-dalīl al-sharʿī*) is either based on a source (*aṣl*) or else derived from it, and how, as a consequence of this, the former can either be in an utterance (*lafẓ*) or an action (*fiʿl*). As for the utterance, he states that it is either ambiguous (*mujmal*) or it is not.[166]

164 *Nihāyat*, vol. II, pp. 318–73.
165 *Nihāyat*, vol. II, pp. 378–89.
166 *Nihāyat*, vol. II, pp. 391–7.

2.6.2 Discussion Two: On the Setting Forth of the Ambiguous (*al-mujmal*)

This is addressed by ʿAllāmah in the sixth investigation in *Nihāyat* in a brief analysis contained in a discussion regarding the possibility of the setting forth of the ambiguous in the word of God, the Exalted, and in the word of His Prophet. He notes the agreement of 'the verifiers' (*muḥaqqiqūn*) on the possibility of this, due to the fact that the ambiguous has occurred in verses of the Qur'ān and prophetic statements (*hādīth*), and that such occurrence provides the evidence for permissibility (*al-wuqūʿ dalīl al-jawāz*).[167]

2.6.3 Discussion Three: On Things Which are Considered to be Ambiguous (*mujmalah*) Whilst they are Not as Such

ʿAllāmah enumerates five points in relation to this, each of which is addressed in *Nihāyat* as a distinct and independent discussion. In addition to these five discussions he also includes an additional discussion on six other matters, which are considered to be ambiguous (*fī bāqī umūr ẓunna annahā mujmalah*). These are namely: if an utterance is set forth by the Lawgiver and it is possible to predicate it upon something that conveys two meanings as well as one; if it is possible to predicate the utterance upon a new legal ruling and upon an linguistic assignment, or establish it upon a ruling that is either based upon a source (*aṣl*) or the intellect (*ʿaql*); if an utterance is set forth and the folk of the language assign it to one meaning and the Lawgiver assigns it to another; the Qur'ānic Verses 23:5, 23:6, and 9:34; the utterance of the plural which is devoid of *alif* and *lām*; and, finally, the Prophetic statement 'in a *riqqah* there is quarter of a tenth'.[168]

2.6.4 Discussion Four: On the Deferment (*ta'khīr*) of the Elucidation

In *Nihāyat* the deferment of the elucidation is examined in the context of a broader discussion On the Timing of the Elucidation (*fī waqt al bayān*), which is in itself an extended version of the argument presented in the *Mabādi'* regarding the impermissibility of the deferment of the elucidation. This discussion also contains an analysis of the opinions of various scholars, such as a group of the Ashāʿirah and Ḥanafiyyah who uphold the permissibility of the deferment of the elucidation in all aspects, whilst some of the Ashāʿirah, such as Abū Isḥāq al-Marwazī[169] and Abū Bakr al-Ṣayrafī, and some of the

167 *Nihāyat*, vol. II, p. 402.

168 *Nihāyat*, vol. II, pp. 403–26. *Riqqah* is a term used for a denomination of silver coin that was common in the era of the Prophet.

169 Ibrāhīm b. Aḥmad al-Marwazī, known as Abū Isḥāq (d. 340 AH/951 CE) leader of the Shāfiʿiyyah in Iraq after Ibn Surayj (d. 306 AH/918 CE). See Ziriklī, *al-Aʿlām*, vol. I, p. 22–3.

Ḥanafiyyah and Ẓāhiriyyah, are said to uphold the impermissibility of the deferment of the elucidation. Contrastingly, al-Sayyid al-Murtaḍā, al-Karkhī, and a group from among the jurists, permitted the deferment of the elucidation of the ambiguous in particular. Others still, permitted the deferment of the elucidation for the command but not for the narration, and the two Jubbāʾīs and Qāḍī ʿAbd al-Jabbār permitted it for abrogation but not in any other instance. Abū al-Ḥusayn al-Baṣrī permitted such a deferment for that which does not have an evident meaning (*ẓāhir*), such as the ambiguous (*mujmal*), but as for that which does have an evident meaning and is used contrarily to its evident meaning he permits the deferment of the particular elucidation without permitting the ambiguous elucidation. It is this last view that ʿAllāmah himself endorses by stating 'that is right' (*huwa al-ḥaqq*).[170]

2.6.5 Discussion Five: On the Possibility of the Charged Agent (*al-mukallaf*) Hearing the General without Hearing what Specifies it

This possibility is discussed in its entirety and also contextualised in *Nihāyat*.[171] ʿAllāmah explains that the general (*al-ʿāmm*) may be specified by revealed evidence (*samʿī*) just as it may be specified by intellective evidence (*ʿaqlī*), because the intellective may be either *a priori* (*ḍarūriyan*) or theoretical (*naẓariyan*), and thus some sort of effort and logical inference (*istidlāl*) are required in order for its realisation. With this in mind, the question arises as to whether or not it is possible for the Wise (*al-ḥakīm*) to compel the charged agent (*al-mukallaf*) to hear the general without causing him to hear the revealed specifier (*al-mukhaṣṣiṣ al-samʿī*). ʿAllāmah notes here that Abū al-Hudhayl al-ʿAllāf[172] and Abū ʿAlī al-Jubbāʾī maintain that this would not be the case, and they only permit it with regard to His causing someone to hear the general which is specified on the basis of intellective evidence, irrespective of whether the one who hears knows what it is that intellectively signifies the specification thereof; whereas, Abū Isḥāq al-Naẓẓām,[173] Abū Hāshim, and Abū al-Ḥusayn al-Baṣrī permit such a case—the position that ʿAllāmah himself also adopts on this matter. In addition to the single reason alluded to in the *Mabādiʾ* he presents four further reasons to support his position alongside the

170 *Nihāyat*, vol. II, pp. 440–76.

171 *Nihāyat*, vol. II, p. 479

172 Muḥammad b. al-Hudhayl b. ʿAbd Allāh, known as Abū al-Hudhayl al-ʿAllāf (d. 235 AH/850 CE), leader of the Muʿtazilah in his day, see Ziriklī, *al-Aʿlām*, vol. VII, p. 355.

173 Ibrāhīm b. Sayyār b. Hāniʾ al-Baṣrī, known as Abū Isḥāq al-Naẓẓām, or simply as al-Naẓẓām, (d. 231 AH/845 CE), a Muʿtazilī theologian known for his unconventional views even among the Muʿtazilah. See Ziriklī, *al-Aʿlām*, vol. I, p. 36.

six counterarguments presented by those who oppose this position, each of which he refutes in detail.[174]

2.7 *Chapter Six: On Actions (al-afʿāl)*

This chapter concerns the actions of the Prophet and the Imāms, and their status as far as the charged agent is concerned. It begins with the paramount matter of the infallibility of the Prophet and the Imāms, which the Imāmiyyah take to be absolute, in contradistinction to other Islamic sects. This leads logically on to ʿAllāmah's discussion of the implications borne out by the actions of the Prophet, with a view to his infallibility; and to an examination of particular matters of dispute in regard to these.

2.7.1 Discussion One: On the Infallibility (*ʿiṣmah*) of the Prophets

With respect to the prophet's infallibility prior to the commencement of their mission (*al-biʿthah*) and thereafter, ʿAllāmah clearly states in *Nihāyat* that the Imāmiyyah, in their entirety, uphold the doctrine that they are necessarily infallible (*ʿiṣmah*) as regards all minor and major sins whether intentional or unintentional, or with regards to interpretation (*taʾwīl*). This is because, he explains, if anything as such should occur by them it would annul their standing among individuals (*al-nufūs*) and abate their rank, which would, in turn: obligate their wrongdoing, result in their becoming disparaged, cause others to flee from following them, and prevent any acquiescence with their command and prohibitions. Such a sequence of occurrences would, evidently, negate the objective of the prophetic mission and oppose the demands of wisdom. He further observes how all other sects oppose this doctrine of the Imāmiyyah.[175]

2.7.2 Discussion Two: On the Obligation of Following (*al-taʾassī*) the Prophet (peace be upon him)

This discussion and its inter-related concepts can be found throughout three different discussions under the seventh investigation On Actions (*fī al-afʿāl*) in *Nihāyat*. The *Mabādiʾ* amalgamates these same three discussions, albeit briefly, into one terse discussion on the obligation of following the Prophet. *Nihāyat* begins with a discussion On the Meaning of Following, Agreement, and Disagreement (*fī maʿnā al-taʾassī wa al-muwāfaqah wa al-mukhālafah*). This provides an introduction to what it means to follow the Prophet, as well as what constitutes such a following. ʿAllāmah claims that because consensus and explicit textual designation (*naṣṣ*) signify the obligation of following the Prophet, the knowledge (*maʿrifah*) of what it means to follow, agree, and

---

174 *Nihāyat*, vol. II, pp. 479–84.

175 *Nihāyat*, vol. II, p. 525.

disagree is therefore obligatory. Thus, one may follow the Prophet in regards to his action or to his abstaining from something. As for the action (*al-fiʿl*), this is to be enacted in the same form (*ṣūrah*), manner (*ʿalā al-wajh*), and according to the same reason (*ajal*), that he performed it. As far as abstaining (*al-tark*) is concerned it should be similar (*mithl*); undertaken in the same manner and for the self-same reason on behalf of which he abstained from something. ʿAllāmah illustrates this point through an example: if he prayed, and we fasted, that would not constitute following (*taʾassī*). Insofar as the manner (*wajh*) of following is concerned, the objective (*gharaḍ*) of following and the intention of the follower should be united with the intention of the Prophet, either of obligation (*wujūb*) or of approvedness (*nudb*). For example, if the Prophet undertook an action as obligatory and the follower undertook the same action as something merely *approved* then such a case would not constitute an example of true following (*taʾassī*).[176]

The third discussion on this topic, in *Nihāyat,* concerns whether or not the action of the Prophet, peace be upon him, signifies a ruling with regard to us (*fī anna fiʿalahu hal yadullu ʿalā ḥukm fī haqqinā am lā*). ʿAllāmah presents the actions of the Prophet as threefold, namely: those actions that are natural (*afʿāl al-jibilliyyah*) such as standing, sitting, eating and drinking, and so forth, which he says there is no dispute on the permissibility thereof for his followers; those actions which are particular for him and actions according to consensus (*ijmāʿ*), some of which are not obligatory for his followers, such as the night prayers (*al-witr wa al-tahajjud bi al-layl*), nor are they indifferent for his followers, such as entering Makkah without the garbs of pilgrimage (*iḥrām*) or having more than four wives; and, finally, those actions which he clearly set forth as an elucidation for his followers, such as saying: 'pray as you have seen me pray and adopt from me your rites of pilgrimage' or through circumstantial context (*bi-qarāʾin al-aḥwāl*), both of which ʿAllāmah claims constitute evidence (*dalīl*) according to consensus (*ijmāʿ*).[177]

Above and beyond the three types of action outlined above, are those actions which are to be considered from the perspective of whether or not they were undertaken with the intention of gaining greater proximity to God (*qaṣd al-qurbah*). Those that were undertaken with such an intention are deemed to be obligatory for the Prophet and his followers; as is the opinion of

---

176 *Nihāyat*, vol. II, p. 528.

177 *Nihāyat*, vol. II, p. 533.

Ibn Surayj,[178] Abū Saʿīd al-Iṣṭakhrī,[179] Ibn Abī Hurayrah, Abū ʿAlī b. Khayrān,[180] the Ḥanābilah,[181] a group from among the Muʿtazilah, and al-Sayyid al-Murtaḍā—who reported it from Mālik. They are otherwise regarded as approved (*al-nudb*) actions, as in the opinion of al-Juwaynī, which he takes from al-Shāfiʿī, and others who uphold the principle of indifferency with respect to such actions, as is also reported from Mālik. However, al-Ṣayrafī, most of the Muʿtazilah, and al-Sayyid al-Murtaḍā suspend judgement on this matter. As for those actions wherein there is no intention of gaining divine proximity, the controversy is as above, except that more are inclined to the suspension of judgement or of indifferency, than to its being obligatory or approved. ʿAllāmah states that, according to him, the correct opinion is that wherever the intention of gaining divine proximity is to be found then that is to be taken for the common extent between obligation and indifferency, which is an absolute preferment with regard to the Prophet and his followers, and in other cases where such an intention is not evident then that is to be taken for the common extent between the above two and permissibility, which thereby removes sin from the action.[182]

It is the fourth discussion in *Nihāyat* that most directly addresses the obligation of following the Prophet (*fī wujūb al-taʾassī*), and ʿAllāmah contextualises this discussion by indicating the differences of opinion regarding this topic. The multitude of the jurists, and the Muʿtazilah, are said to maintain that following the Prophet is obligatory; if we know the manner in which he performed an action, then we are to perform it according to such a manner in order to be followers, a process of reasoning similar to that which ʿAllāmah presents in the second paragraph of this section in *Mabādiʾ*.[183] He subsequently analyses the reasoning of those who maintain the view that the Prophet is only to be followed in matters of worship, a position that he refutes on the grounds that, as it is obligatory to follow the Prophet, this means performing an action in the exact manner as he performed it—when this can be known. The same Qurʾānic verses as those presented in *Mabādiʾ* are given in this section as the justification for ʿAllāmah's argument. This is then followed

178 Aḥmad b. ʿUmar b. Surayj, Abū al-ʿAbbās, known as Ibn Surayj (d. 306 AH/918 CE), a well-known Shāfiʿī jurist of his era, see Ziriklī, *al-Aʿlām*, vol. I, pp. 178–79.

179 Al-Ḥasan b. Aḥmad b. Yazīd al-Iṣṭakhrī, known as Abū Saʿīd al-Iṣṭakhrī (d. 328 AH/940 CE), a Shāfiʿī jurist. See Ziriklī, *al-Aʿlām*, vol. II, p. 192.

180 Al-Ḥusayn b. Sāliḥ b. Khayrān al-Baghdādī, Abū ʿAlī, known as Abū ʿAlī b. Khayrān (d. 320 AH/932 CE), one of the leaders of the Shāfiʿī *madhhab*. See al-Rāzī, *al-Maḥṣūl fī ʿilm uṣūl al-fiqh*, vol. III, p. 229.

181 This term denotes the followers of the Ḥanbalī school of law.

182 *Nihāyat*, vol. II, pp. 533–5.

183 *Nihāyat*, vol. II, p. 552.

by the fifth and sixth discussions entitled: The Manner of the Knowledge of Following the Prophet (*fī jihat al-ʿilm bi al-taʾassī*) and The Method of Knowing His, peace be upon him, Actions (*fī tarīq maʿrifat afʿālihi*), the latter of which addresses the issue of how to determine whether the Prophet acted according to obligation (*wujūb*), approvedness (*nudb*), or indifferency (*ibāḥah*), and the methodology for ascertaining the aforementioned.[184]

2.7.3 Discussion Three: On the Preferment between the Statement (*al-qawl*) and the Action (*al-fiʿl*)

ʿAllāmah approaches this issue, in *Nihāyat*, from the angle of contradiction (*taʿāruḍ*) instead of preferment (*tarjīḥ*). His discussion is divided into three classifications, which each correspond to the main points presented in *Mabādiʾ*. These involve the resolution of the putative differences between the statements and actions of the Prophet. When determining which of these to take recourse to, a pivotal factor is shown to be the knowledge of which preceded the other, the statement or the action—and thus the three classifications are as follows: firstly, that the statement precedes the action, secondly, that the action precedes the statement, and thirdly, that the date is unknown and it is therefore not known which of the two preceded the other.[185]

2.7.4 Discussion Four: On the Prophet's Following (*taʿabbud*) Prior Revealed Laws

This is examined in *Nihāyat* across three discussions: On Whether the Prophet, Prior to the Commencement of his Prophetic Mission, Followed Prior Revealed Laws or not (*fī annahu hal kāna mutaʿabbidan qabl al-nubuwwah bi sharʿi man qablahu am lā*); On the Permissibility of the Prophet's Following the Similar Laws of Any Prophet who Preceded Him (*fī jawāz taʿabbud nabī bi mithil sharīʿah nabī taqaddamahu*); and On the State of the Prophet After Prophethood (*fī ḥālihi baʿd al-nubuwwah*). In the first of these discussions ʿAllāmah brings to light the difference of opinion between those, such as Abū al-Ḥusayn al-Baṣrī and some others, who uphold that prior to the commencement of his Prophetic mission, he did not follow the law of the prophets who preceded him, whereas others are absolutely certain that he did follow the preceding revealed laws. This latter group, however, dispute whether it was the law of Noah, Abraham, Moses, Jesus, or his own self-legislated commands. As for the remaining masters of jurisprudence, such as al-Sayyid al-Murtaḍā, Qāḍī ʿAbd al-Jabbār, al-Ghazālī and others, they suspended judgement regarding this issue and allowed for the possibility of both matters, a position which ʿAllāmah

184 *Nihāyat*, vol. II, pp. 556–68.
185 *Nihāyat*, vol. II, pp. 569–77.

recognises as the strongest opinion, yet his position on this matter receives its clearest statement in *Mabādiʾ*.

In addition to the two reasons proffered by those who maintain that the Prophet did not follow any prior laws, ʿAllāmah includes two further reasons, which those who maintained that he did not follow, based their argument upon: firstly, that the mission (*daʿwah*) of the preceding prophets was general and therefore included him, due to the absence of any abrogation prior to his Prophetic mission; and secondly, that prior to the commencement of his mission he prayed, performed the *Ḥajj*, the *ʿUmrah*, the *Ṭawāf* of the Kaʿbah and venerated it, ritually slaughtered meat himself and consumed it, journeyed on animals, and abstained from consuming the meat of animals that were not slaughtered according to the correct rite—and all the above was not done on the basis of mere reason.[186]

2.8 *Chapter Seven: On Abrogation (al-naskh)*

The question of abrogation, a concept of paramount significance for, almost all, Islamic jurisprudential systems, is not unlike the question of the general and the specific inasmuch as it concerns the relationship between different scriptural injunctions. In the case of abrogation, however, one scriptural text is superseded by another, later, one. Unsurprisingly this requires careful definition and regulation. The concept also demands the negotiation of some complex theological semantics; indicating, as it does, a change in the revealed law of God, and so a debate thereby arises as to when exactly this may be said to occur, as well as regarding the status of the abrogated law.

2.8.1 Discussion One: On the Definition (*taʿrīf*) Thereof

The definition of abrogation is addressed within *Nihāyat* across a number of discussions of investigation eight under the section On its Veritability (*fī ḥaqīqatihi*), namely: The Quiddity Thereof (*fī māhiyyatihi*), The Definition Thereof (*fī ḥaddihi*), Whether Abrogation is an Abolition or an Elucidation (*fī anna al-naskh rafʿun aw bayān*), The Difference Between Abrogation and Appearance (*fī al-farq bayn al-naskh wa al-badāʾ*), and The Difference Between Specification and Abrogation (*fī al-farq bayn al-takhṣīṣ wa al-naskh*). In the discussion of its quiddity ʿAllāmah explains that insofar as jurisprudence (*uṣūl al-fiqh*) is an investigation into the methods of law (*fiqh*), which largely refer to the Qurʾān and the *Sunnah*, then abrogation will lead to these two and by the consideration thereof exclude the abrogated (*al-mansūkh*) from being an appropriate method for logical inference (*istidlāl*) and the abrogator (*al-nāsikh*) will also be determined.

186 *Nihāyat*, vol. IV, pp. 407–20.

He further states that it is obligatory for the master of legal methodology (*al-uṣūlī*) to have knowledge of the following: abrogation, the conditions and soundness thereof, the abrogator, the abrogated, the difference between abrogation and the concept of appearance (*badā'*), what is added to it, what is excluded from it, and what is included therein whilst not constituting it, and, finally, the method to ascertain whether something is an abrogator or the abrogated. He then proceeds to state that, linguistically, the noun abrogation (*naskh*) is assigned to elimination (*izālah*), to removal (*naql*), and to modification (*taḥwīl*).[187]

2.8.2 Discussion Two: On the Possibility (*jawāz*) Thereof

ʿAllāmah addresses the possibility of abrogation across three distinct discussions in a section of the same title in *Nihāyat*. The first of these discussions considers the conditions for abrogation (*sharāʾiṭ al-naskh*), the second is on the possibility of abrogation (*jawāz al-naskh*), and the third concentrates on the possibility of abrogation in the Qur'ān (*jawāz al-naskh fī al-qur'ān*). It is in the second discussion that ʿAllāmah provides the context for the debate surrounding the possibility of abrogation, wherein he notes that Muslims are agreed on the possibility of abrogation on the basis of intellect, and that this is by and large also the opinion of the masters of revealed laws (*arbāb al-sharāʾiʿ*) except for some of the Jews. It would seem that ʿAllāmah is alluding to the Jewish sects known as the Sadducees and the Karaites, both of whom reject the abrogation of Mosaic law, whereas the Rabbanites, partisans of rabbinical authority, uphold a doctrine of abrogation of laws.[188] Furthermore, ʿAllāmah says that the Muslims have all agreed on the occurrence of abrogation in revelation, except for the reports of Abū Muslim b. Baḥr Al-Iṣfahānī,[189] and again some of the Jews, who rejected it in regard to revealed matters and only deemed it possible in regard to matters of intellection, and others among the masters of revealed laws, who consider it to be possible in revealed matters as well as on the basis of intellection. ʿAllāmah, of course, considers abrogation to be both possible and permissible because he argues that the actions of God, the Exalted, are either caused (*muʿallalatan*) for such objectives as welfare and wisdom, or they are not, and thus the possibility of abrogation is evident.

---

187 *Nihāyat*, vol. II, pp. 579–99.

188 Mielziher, Moses, 'Abrogation of Laws', *The Jewish Encyclopedia*, New York, 1901–1906, 12 vols., vol. I, pp. 131–33.

189 Muḥammad b. Baḥr al-Iṣfahānī known as Abū Muslim al-Iṣfahānī (d. 322 AH/934 CE), an erudite Muʿtazilī scholar who also happened to be governor of Isfahan, see Ziriklī, *al-Aʿlām*, vol. VI p. 273.

'Allāmah then goes on to present his counterarguments to the group of the Jews who reject the concept of abrogation with regard to revealed matters. He notes a number of instances from the Torah, which he presents as evidence for the occurrence of abrogation therein. He also engages with the arguments put forward by Abū Muslim in the third discussion on the possibility of abrogation in the Qur'ān, and he maintains that Muslims are in agreement about the possibility of abrogation taking place with regard to certain Qur'ānic rulings. In addition to the five instances alluded to in *Mabādi'* he also adds the Qur'ānic Verse 2:106 which he cites to demonstrate this issue along with Abū Muslim's objection, and his own counterarguments to these objections.[190]

2.8.3 Discussion Three: On the Abrogation (*naskh*) of a Thing Prior to the Expiration of its Time of Performance

This is discussed in *Nihāyat* under the first discussion of section three on the Abrogated, entitled Abrogation Prior to the Action (*fī naskh qabl al-fi'l*), wherein 'Allāmah explains that the discussion pertaining to this issue comprises two aspects: firstly, the abrogation of something after the expiration of its time of performance, which there is no dispute as to the possibility thereof, and secondly, the abrogation of something prior to the arrival (*ḥuḍūr*) of the time for its performance and its expiration, upon which there has arisen a difference of opinion. He states that the Mu'tazilah, along with some of the companions of Abū Ḥanīfah and Abū Bakr al-Ṣayrafī of the Shāfi'iyyah, do not allow for this, whilst the Ashā'irah and the majority of the Shāfi'iyyah maintain that it is possible. The different stances on this issue are a point of thorough analysis for 'Allāmah, and one which he exhaustively discusses.[191]

2.8.4 Discussion Four: On What it is Possible to Abrogate (*naskh*)

'Allāmah's discussion of what it is possible to abrogate can be found within various discussions of the third and fourth sections on abrogation in *Nihāyat*. The former of which concerns the abrogated (*fī al-mansūkh*) and the latter the abrogator (*fī al-nāsikh*). In the first of these 'Allāmah discusses: The Possibility of Abrogation by That Which is of Greater Importance (*fī jawāz al-naskh ilā al-athqal*), The Possible Abrogation of the Recitation of a Verse Without the Abrogation of its Ruling and *vice versa* (*fī jawāz naskh al-tilāwah dūna al-ḥukm wa bi al-'aks*), The Abrogation of a Narration (*fī naskh al-khabar*), The Possible Abrogation of a Command Delimited by Perpetuity (*fī jawāz naskh al-amr al-muqayyad bi al-ta'bīd*), and The Impossibility of Abrogating Consensus (*fī*

190 *Nihāyat*, vol. II, pp. 600–621.

191 *Nihāyat*, vol. III, pp. 23–43.

istiḥālat naskh al-ijmāʿ). In the last of these, the following matters are addressed: The Abrogation of the Qur'ān by its Like and by the Continuous Tradition (*al-sunnah al-mutawātirah*); The Abrogation of the Continuous Tradition by its Like and by the Qur'ān; and the abrogation of the Solitary Narration (*khabar al-wāḥid*), and his arguments for why consensus does not abrogate.[192]

2.8.5 Discussion Five: Addition to (*ziyādah*) and Omission of (*nuqṣān*) Acts of Worship

This is addressed within *Nihāyat* in two distinct discussions which centre on the following questions; on whether addition to the text (*al-naṣṣ*) constitutes abrogation or not, and whether or not omission constitutes abrogation.

With respect to the former of these ʿAllāmah states that an addition can either be connected with that to which it is added to or to a separate matter. As for the connected, it can be effective upon that which it is added to, by taking into consideration the fact of its wisdom in the divine law, such that if it occurs independently (*mustaqill*) without that which it is added to, then it would not be considered. An example he gives to illustrate this is of the addition of two inclinings (*rakʿatayn*) to the two inclinings; as it has been transmitted that although the duty of ritual prayer (*farḍ al-ṣalāt*) prescribes two inclinings, this is to be increased whilst present in one's house (*al-ḥaḍar*). The connected can also be non-effective, such as with the addition of twenty lashes to the legal punishment (*ḥadd*) for the false accuser (*qādhif*), the addition of banishment (*taghrīb*) to the legal punishment for the adulterer (*zānī*), and the addition of lapidation to the legal punishment for the married man (*muḥṣin*). As for the separate matters, such as the addition of a sixth prayer (*ṣalāt*), a second month of fasting, or charitable pursuits (*ṣadaqah*) other than the alms (*zakāh*), all the scholars (*ʿulamā'*) are in agreement upon the fact that the separate matter is not an abrogator (*nāsikh*), because it does not abolish a legal ruling (*ḥukman sharʿiyyan*). ʿAllāmah points out that the people of Iraq considered that the addition of a sixth prayer to the five prayers constituted an abrogation due to His word, the Exalted: 'Be you watchful over the prayers, and the midmost prayer (*al-ṣalāt al-wusṭā*)'[193] as any such addition to the prayers would thereby render 'the midmost' as other than the midmost.

In the latter discussion, on whether or not omission constitutes abrogation, ʿAllāmah also observes the total agreement of the people on the following two matters: the fact that an omission from an act of worship constitutes an abrogation insofar as it annuls, and the fact that when the soundness of an

192 *Nihāyat*, vol. III, pp. 43–91.

193 Q. 2:238.

act of worship does not depend upon an abrogation, then its abrogation does not constitute an abrogation for that act of worship. However, he discusses in detail a dispute regarding those abrogations upon which the soundness of an act of worship rests and whether or not these constitute an abrogation for such an act of worship. Our author notes a variety of disputing views on this issue: Abū al-Ḥusayn al-Baṣrī and Abū al-Ḥasan al-Karkhī maintain that it does not constitute an abrogation of an act of worship; a group of theologians are said to uphold the opinion that it constitutes an absolute abrogation for the act of worship, a view that al-Ghazālī also inclines towards; Qāḍī ʿAbd al-Jabbār obligates the abrogation of an act of worship through the abrogation of a part thereof and not an abrogation of a condition thereof; and al-Sayyid al-Murtaḍā is of the opinion that if whatsoever remains from an act of worship after an omission occurs were to be performed then there would be no ruling for it in the law and it would not take the place of the performance prior to the omission. This would thereby constitute an abrogation, such as the omission of an inclining in prayer, otherwise if it were not as such it would not constitute an abrogation, such as the omission of twenty lashes from a legal punishment.[194]

2.9 *Chapter Eight: On Consensus* (*al-ijmāʿ*)

ʿAllāmah justifies the legal force of consensus to function as a proof on the grounds of a long-standing Imāmī argument to the following effect: since it is known that the hidden Imām, though he may be in occultation, is present among the community, if the community arrives at a consensus then that consensus must contain the view of the Imām, and, *ipso facto*, it must be taken to carry within it the infallible legal force of his words. From this argument ʿAllāmah then goes on to discuss the question of whether a consensus can be challenged once it has been formed, and he also considers whether a point which was once under dispute may later be agreed upon and so become a consensus. The most elaborate discussion of all, however, centres upon the question as to whose opinion is to be taken into account in the formation of a consensus.

2.9.1 Discussion One: On the Consensus (*ijmāʿ*) of the *Ummah* of Muḥammad

This matter is addressed in *Nihāyat* across a number of discussions in the ninth investigation dedicated to consensus. These include the four discussions of the first section therein: On the Quiddity Thereof (*fī māhiyyatihi*); On the Verification Thereof (*fī taḥaqquqihi*); On Consensus Being a Legal Proof (*fī anna*

194 *Nihāyat*, vol. III, pp. 101–121.

al-ijmāʿ ḥujjah); and On the Proofs Put Forth by the Masses For it Being a Legal Proof (*fī ḥujjaj al-jumhūr ʿalā kawnihi ḥujjah*).

In the first of these discussions ʿAllāmah considers the term itself and its dual-assigned meanings in the language, signifying both resolution (*al-ʿazm*) and agreement (*al-ittifāq*). As for its nomenclatural understanding, our author notes that this is a matter of contention among scholars. He presents four distinct definitions for consideration in this discussion, two of which are attributed to al-Naẓẓām and al-Ghazālī, whilst the other two are alluded to without mention of their authors. The first of these unnamed definitions is in fact from al-Rāzī and the second comes from al-Āmidī. ʿAllāmah's own position on the nomenclatural understanding of consensus can be gleaned from the qualifications he introduces to these author's definitions.[195]

In the second discussion on the verification of consensus (*ijmāʿ*) our author maintains that this is a well-known matter because of the possibility that all skilled practitioners of juristic reasoning (*mujtahid*) should be informed about the evidence of a ruling and the agreement of opinions concerning it, and that therefore consensus (*ijmāʿ*) is verified. In this discussion he also examines the arguments for and against this position.[196]

In the third discussion, on consensus being a legal proof (*ḥujjah*), ʿAllāmah upholds that the veracity of consensus as a legal proof is a well known matter (*mashūr*) nigh the majority of people. Of course, he notes the denial of al-Naẓẓām and the Khawārij on this issue. Our author states that:

> The Imāmiyyah maintain that it is correct because the consensus, by which we mean the agreement (*ittifāq*) of the *ummah,* the believers (*al-muʾminūn*), and the scholars (*al-ʿulamāʾ*), is to be considered in whatever therein, and in all these categories it is a must that the statement (*qawl*) of the infallible Imām is included therein, because he is the lord of the believers, the lord of the *ummah,* and the lord of the scholars. Accordingly, the name (*ism*) is inclusive of him, and it cannot be established without him, and whatever the infallible states is, indeed, a legal proof (*ḥujjah*), correct (*ṣawāb*), and true (*ḥaqq*), not due to the consideration of consensus but rather due to the consideration that it includes the statement of the infallible. Even if it stood alone his view would constitute a legal proof, and we only maintain that the view of the group (*jamāʿah*), with which his view is in agreement, is a legal proof, because of his view. Others maintain that He, the Exalted, knows that this entire *ummah* can

195 *Nihāyat*, vol. III, pp. 125–27.

196 *Nihāyat*, vol. III, pp. 128–31.

> not agree upon an error—even though error is possible for everyone individually—and that, therefore, consensus is effective (*ta'thīr*).

Our author then proceeds to present the arguments of the Imāmiyyah for the legal validity of consensus, on the premise that consensus constitutes a legal proof because the era of injunction (*zamān al-taklīf*) cannot be devoid of an infallible Imām. It is worth observing here that he establishes this argument on the precept of grace (*qāʿidat al-luṭf*), as first outlined by Shaykh al-Ṭā'ifah in his discussion on consensus (*ijmāʿ*).[197]

In the fourth discussion ʿAllāmah presents the pieces of scriptural evidence solicited by those whom he refers to in *Mabādi'* as 'our opponents' (*al-mukhālif*), and in *Nihāyat* as 'the masses' (*al-jumhūr*). Moreover, in addition to the verses presented in *Mabādi'*, he brings forward other pieces of scriptural evidence in this particular discussion, such as the Qur'ānic verses 4:59 and 3:103 as well as considering the other intellective arguments that are employed by the proponents for the veracity of consensus as a legal proof from among 'the masses'.[198]

2.9.2 Discussion Two: On Introducing (*iḥdāth*) a Third Opinion (*qawl thālith*)

This is presented in *Nihāyat* as being merely the first of eight distinct discussions, which constitute the second section of the investigation into consensus, entitled On that which is Excluded from Consensus Whilst it Pertains to it (*fīmā ukhrija min al-ijmāʿ wa huwa minhu*). Herein ʿAllāmah explains that if a legal issue is comprised of a total assignment in absolute terms (*mawḍūʿ kullī ʿalā al-iṭlāq*) then the ruling therein is either by total affirmation, total negation, or affirmation of a part and negation of the remainder. He further explains that when the people of an era differ with respect to two opinions from among the aforementioned three likelihoods; then, in such a case it is possible for those who come after to uphold a third opinion. For instance, some of them may maintain total affirmation whilst others maintain total negation, or some may maintain a divided opinion (*iqtisām*), or some of them maintain total negation whilst others maintain a divided opinion. ʿAllāmah states that the masses (*jumhūr*) and the Imāmiyyah do not allow the introduction of a third opinion, however, the Ẓāhiriyyah and some of the Ḥanafiyyah do allow for it. He alludes to what has been suggested by al-Āmidī,[199] without mentioning him by name, and corrects his allegation that the Shīʿah allow such a stance on this

197 *Nihāyat*, vol. III, pp. 131–44.

198 *Nihāyat*, vol. III, pp. 144–92.

199 *Al-Iḥkām fī uṣūl al-aḥkām*, vol. I, p. 384.

matter. ʿAllāmah asserts that al-Āmidī is mistaken, because the legal proof of the Shīʿah on this matter is evident, and he further argues that if the *ummah* disagree on two opinions then only one of them can be true and this will be whichever of the two includes the opinion of the infallible, rendering the second opinion void and thus the third more appropriate for invalidity.[200]

In his discussion of this topic in *Mabādiʾ*, ʿAllāmah briefly touches upon the issue of differentiating between two legal issues, however he gives this a far greater scope in a distinct discussion in *Nihāyat* entitled: The Lack of Differentiation Between Two Legal Issues (*fī ʿadam al-faṣl bayn al-masʾalatayn*). This discussion is undertaken as an effort to resolve the question of whether, in those instances where the *ummah* has not differentiated between two legal issues, it is permissible for those who come after them to differentiate between these hitherto undifferentiated issues. Our author then verifies that, in cases where the *ummah* stipulated the lack of differentiation between these issues, then differentiation is not allowed, irrespective of whether they had ruled the lack thereof in all things or in some rulings. Furthermore, he categorises this matter thus: first, the *ummah* rules with one ruling for both issues deciding upon either permissibility (*taḥlīl*) or forbiddenness (*ḥurmah*); second, that some rule regarding them with forbiddenness (*taḥrīm*) whilst others rule permissibility (*taḥlīl*); or third, that their ruling regarding these has not been reported to us. In such instances (*ṣuwar*) if evidence signifies on a ruling regarding one of the two then it would do likewise for the other; and if they did not stipulate the undifferentiability of the issues, but there are none among them who actually differentiated between the two issues, then if the unity of the method of the ruling is known it will take the place of the designation (*naṣṣ*) for the undifferentiability thereof. This point is explained through reference to the same examples presented in *Mabādiʾ* on the issue of inheritance pertaining to the paternal and maternal aunts. However, our author states that if the unity of the method of the ruling is unknown, then the truth is that it is permissible to differentiate for those who come after, by basing the action on a sound source which does not contradict or oppose the agreed upon ruling or its cause.[201]

2.9.3 Discussion Three: On That by Which Consensus (*al-ijmāʿ*) is and is not Established

This discussion comprises a number of premises, which correspond to the discussions in *Nihāyat* that are included by ʿAllāmah in the second and third sections on consensus. ʿAllāmah dedicates the former of these to That Which

200 *Nihāyat*, vol. III, pp. 193–4.

201 *Nihāyat*, vol. III, pp. 193–200.

is Excluded from Consensus Whilst Pertaining to it (*fīmā ukhrija min al-ijmāʿ wa huwa minhu*), and the latter to That Which is Included in Consensus Whilst not Pertaining to it (*fīmā udkhila fī al-ijmāʿ wa laysa minhu*). Within the former he includes the following discussions: On the Permissibility of Consensus after Disagreement (*fī jawāz al-ijmāʿ baʿd al-khilāf*); On the Permissibility of the Agreement of the People of the Second Era (*fī jawāz ittifāq ahl al-ʿaṣr al-thānī*); On Whether or not the End of an Era Constitutes a Condition (*fī anna inqirāḍ al-ʿaṣr hal huwa sharṭ am lā*); On the Legal Proof of Consensus as Reported by a Solitary Narration (*fī anna al-ijmāʿ al-manqūl bi khabar al-wāḥid ḥujjah*); On the Consensus of the Descendants of the Prophet Constituting a Legal Proof (*fī anna ijmāʿ al-ʿiṭrah ḥujjah*); and On the Establishment of Consensus Despite the Opposition of Those Mistaken in the Principles of Religion from Among the Muslims (*fī inʿiqād al-ijmāʿ maʿa mukhālafat al-mukhṭiʾīn fī al-uṣūl min al-muslimīn*). In the latter he includes discussions on the following: On Consensus by Silence (*fī al-ijmāʿ al-sukūtī*); On the Opinion of a Companion When no Opposition to Him is Known, (*fī qawl al-ṣaḥābī idhā lam yuʿraf lahu mukhālif*); On the Logical Inference of an Era's People Through the Evidence or Their Reliance upon Interpretation (*fī istidlāl ahl al-ʿaṣr bi dalīl aw maṣīruhum ilā taʾwīl*); On the Consensus of the People of Madīnah not Constituting a Legal Proof (*fī anna ijmāʿ al-madīnah laysa ḥujjah*); On the Consensus of the Four Caliphs, (*fī ijmāʿ al-khulafāʾ al-arbaʿah*); On the Consensus of the Companions Despite the Opposition of a Follower from the Subsequent Generation (*fī ijmāʿ al-ṣaḥābah maʿa mukhālafat man adrakahum min al-tābiʿīn*); and On the Consensus of the Majority not Constituting a Legal Proof (*fī anna ijmāʿ al-akthar laysa bi ḥujjah*).[202]

2.9.4 Discussion Four: On the Conditions (*sharṭ*) for Consensus

This discussion considers the matter of whose opinion should be taken into consideration with regard to law, legal issues, and legal rulings (*fiqh wa al-masāʾil wa al-aḥkām*), an issue which is also extensively addressed by ʿAllāmah across the scope of the following four sections in *Nihāyat*: On the Means to Know if Consensus has Taken Place (*fī madrak al-ijmāʿ*); On Those who Form the Consensus (*fī al-mujmaʿīn*); On The Ruling Confirmed by Consensus (*fī al-ḥukm al-thābit bi al-ijmāʿ*); and On the Ruling of Consensus (*fī ḥukm al-ijmāʿ*).[203]

---

202 *Nihāyat*, vol. III, pp. 193–247.

203 *Nihāyat*, vol. III, pp. 248–80.

2.10 *Chapter Nine: On Narrations (al-akhbār)*

The potential authority of narrations has been a prevailing debate in Shīʿah Imāmiyyah scholarship. In this chapter ʿAllāmah makes two key assertions in connection to this; firstly, that the continuous narration (*khabar al-mutawātir*) avails certain knowledge, and secondly, that the solitary narration (*khabar al-wāḥid*) avails probable knowledge which can, and should, be used in the derivation of legal rulings. This is accompanied by a wider discussion on what constitutes each of these two classifications, as well as the general criteria for determining whether or not a narration is to be accepted as true or rejected as false.

2.10.1 Discussion One: On the Definition (*taʿrīf*) of a Narration (*al-khabar*) and its Classifications

The definition of a narration (*khabar*) and its classifications is considered in the tenth investigation of *Nihāyat* in the extensive section On the Quiddity of the Narration (*fī māhiyyatihi*), which is in turn comprised of six distinct discussions.

In the first discussion, regarding the term 'narration' (*lafẓ al-khabar*), ʿAllāmah states that it applies to a specified statement (*al-qawl al-mukhṣūṣ*) and to other matters such as indications (*ishārāt*) and pieces of evidence (*dalāʾil*). He further notes that the term 'narration' is veritative with regard to the specified statement in accordance with consensus, and figurative in other instances, because the former meaning, rather than the latter, immediately occurs to the mind (*tabādur*) upon the utterance of the statement 'inform so and so of such and such, and so and so is the informer (*mukhbir*)'. Furthermore, he maintains the position that in most cases the term is only employed in its veritative sense and not in its figurative. He notes that the Ashāʿirah are of the opinion that the term 'narration' (*al-khabar*) is common between the specified statement and the meaning which arises of itself (*al-maʿnā al-qāʾim bi al-nafs*), whilst according to others it is figurative in the latter and veritative in the former because that is the meaning that suggests itself to the understanding and not the latter. He also notes that according to the Muʿtazilah it is veritative in the statement (*al-qawl*) and neither veritatively nor figuratively employed in the meaning which arises of itself, because this is non-existent according to them.

In the second discussion, On Whether or not the Term 'Narration' Can be Defined (*fī annahu hal yaḥuddu am lā*), ʿAllāmah notes that some people uphold the view that it cannot be defined because it is known *a priori* (*ḍarūrī*), whilst others are of the opinion that it can be defined and that this is known through acquisition (*al-iktisāb*).

The third discussion concerns The Definition of a Narration (*fī ḥaddihi*), wherein ʿAllāmah notes the disputing stances of those who are of the opinion that a narration can be defined. He adds that the two Jubbāʾīs, Abū ʿAbd Allāh al-Baṣrī, al-Qāḍī ʿAbd al-Jabbār, and others from among the Muʿtazilah, uphold the view that the narration is that speech (*al-kalām*) which could be inclusive of truth or falsity.

The fourth and fifth discussions are not addressed in *Mabādiʾ*. In the former of these ʿAllāmah briefly touches upon the issue, as stated by al-Sayyid al-Murtaḍā and Abū al-Ḥusayn, that intent and form are a must regarding narrations. He also notes the variant stances of the Ashāʿirah and the two Jubbāʾīs on this matter. In the latter discussion he succinctly notes what a narration signifies (*madlūl al-khbar*).

It is in the sixth discussion, On the Classifications Thereof (*fī aqsāmihi*), that ʿAllāmah discusses the threefold types of the narration (*al-khabar*). These are as follows: first into true (*al-ṣidq*) or false (*al-kidhb*); second into continuous (*al-tawātur*) or solitary (*al-āḥād*); and third into what is known to be true, what is known to be false, or that about which neither of these two matters can be known.[204]

2.10.2 Discussion Two: On Continuance (*al-tawātur*) Conveying Knowledge (*al-ʿilm*)

This matter is addressed in the first and second discussions of the second section On the Continuous Narration (*fī al-mutawātir*), of ʿAllāmah's investigation of the narration. In the discussion, On the Continuous Narration Conveying Knowledge (*fī annahu yufīd al-ʿilm*), our author introduces the term continuance (*al-tawātur*), in its linguistic sense, as denoting the sequence of one coming after another with an interval between the two. To support this he presents the Qurʾānic Verse 23:44: 'Then we sent our envoys one after another', which he explains as referring to the sequence of an envoy after another envoy with an interval between them. He then presents the nomenclatural understanding (*al-iṣṭilāḥ*) as meaning:

> The successive coming forth of narrations to the ear (*ʿalā al-samʿ*), narration after narration, however, with the condition that the abundance of narrations leads to the realisation of knowledge through their word.

He notes the definition of continuance (*al-tawātur*) as it is given by the Ashāʿirah: '…of a group, which reaches a great number in such a manner that knowledge (*al-ʿilm*) is realised by their word'. Our author states that this is

204 *Nihāyat*, vol. III, pp. 283–98.

mistaken, as 'continuance is not of a group' (*al-tawātur laysa huwa al-jamā'ah*). 'Allāmah continues to argue that:

> We maintain that the majority of the people have upheld the opinion that continuance conveys knowledge, regardless of whether it is a narration of affairs present in our time, such as the narrations about large cities, or of passed affairs, such as the existence of the prophets and kings of the past.

He notes the denial of this notion by the Sumaniyyah[205] and Barāhimah[206] who instead maintain that it only conveys probability (*al-ẓann*), as well as those among them who uphold that it would only convey knowledge about present matters and not historical ones.

In the second discussion 'Allāmah affirms that the majority of reasonable people (*al-'uqalā'*) are of the view that the knowledge conveyed by the continuous narration is *a priori* (*ḍarūrī*). However, Abū al-Ḥusayn al-Baṣrī, Abū al-Qāsim, al-Balkhī of the Mu'tazilah, and al-Juwaynī, al-Ghazālī, and al-Daqqāq of the Ashā'irah are of the opinion that it is acquisitional (*kasabī*), and that al-Sayyid al-Murtaḍā suspended judgement regarding this matter. In his third discussion he presents and analyses the arguments of those who claim that it is acquired (*fī iḥtijāj man idda'ā al-iktisāb*).[207]

2.10.3 Discussion Three: On the Conditions for the Continuous Narration (*al-mutawātir*)

These conditions are addressed in *Nihāyat* in the fourth discussion of the section, On the Continuous Narration (*fī al-mutawātir*), which is then further divided into two problems; the first, On the Correct Conditions (*fī al-sharā'iṭ al-ṣaḥīḥah*), containing a further elaboration upon what he states in the first three statements in *Mabādi'*—where it becomes clear that 'Allāmah draws upon the view of al-Sayyid al-Murtaḍā with respect to the position it should not be preceded by uncertainty (*shubhah*). The second problem is, On Those Matters, Which are Considered to be Conditions (*fī umūr ẓunna annahā shurūṭ*) which he notes as sevenfold. For 'Allāmah, all these seven putative conditions are mistaken: the first is about the number (*al-'adad*), which is the only one of these matters to be noted in *Mabādi'*; the second is that some conditioned

205 The Sumaniyyah were a group from India who rejected the knowledge presented through narrations. See Ibn Manẓūr, *Lisān al-'arab*, 6 vols., Beirut, n.d., vol. III, p. 2105.

206 The Barāhimah were a group who upheld the doctrine that it is not permissible for God to send forth His Envoys. See Ibn Manẓūr, *Lisān al-'arab*, vol. I, p. 271.

207 *Nihāyat*, vol. III, pp. 299–318.

that the people of continuance are not contained within a city or restricted in number; third, that the Jews conditioned that they are not of one religion; the fourth that some conditioned that they are neither of one genealogy nor of one city; fifth, that Ibn al-Rāwandī[208] conditioned the presence of an infallible among them so that they can not agree upon a lie; sixth, that some have conditioned Islam and justness; and the seventh being that the Jews conditioned that it includes the narration of base people and so forth.[209]

2.10.4 Discussion Four: On the Classifications which Signify the Truth (*ṣidq*) of a Narration (*al-khabar*)

These classifications are addressed in the third section entitled: On the Remaining Narrations Known to be True (*fī bāqī al-akhbār al-maʿlūmat al-ṣidq*) within the investigation On the Narration (*fi al-khabar*) in *Nihāyat*. The discussions within this section are: On the Narration from Him, the Exalted, (*fī khabarihi taʿālā*); On the Narration from the Envoy (*fī khabar al-rasūl*); On the Narration which is Supported by Contextual Evidence (*fī khabar al-muḥataff bi al-qarāʾin*); On the Remaining True Narrations (*fī baqāyā al-ikhbārāt al-ṣādiqah*), and a fifth discussion, Regarding That Which is Considered to be of This Chapter (*fīmā ẓunna annahu min hādhā al-bāb*). In the discussions regarding the narration from God and the Prophet, ʿAllāmah presents arguments for their truth, and in the third discussion he presents the difference of opinions regarding whether knowledge is realised from the narration whose truth is not known when it is nonetheless supported by external contextual evidence, wherein he notes that, as al-Naẓẓām, al-Ghazālī and al-Juwaynī have maintained, it does so—whilst the others have rejected this. Subsequently, in the fourth discussion, ʿAllāmah enumerates six types of true narrations, and it is here that he includes the narration from the Imām and the narration from the *ummah* as together constituting the third type. He states that:

> The narration of the entire *ummah* is true; as far as we are concerned it is because of the inclusion of the infallible and, as far as the masses (*jumhūr*) are concerned, it is due to the evidences which signify upon the truth of consensus (*al-ijmāʿ*).[210]

---

208 Aḥmad b. Yaḥyā b. Isḥāq, Abū al-Ḥusayn al-Rāwandī, known as Ibn al-Rāwandī. He was a prominent sceptic in an age of faith. Our sources are not clear about the exact year of his death, but it is known that he flourished in the third century of the Hijrah, which corresponds to the ninth/tenth century of the Common Era. See ʿAbd al-Raḥmān Badawī, *Min tārīkh al-ilḥād fī al-islām*, Beirut 1980, pp. 68, 146–54.

209 *Nihāyat*, vol. III, pp. 319–26.

210 *Nihāyat*, vol. III, pp. 338–40.

Nihāyat also has a fourth section On the Narration That is Assured of its Falseness (*fī al-khabar al-maqtūʿ bi kidhbihi*).[211] This fourth section contains the following discussions: On the Narration that Opposes What is Known (*fī al-khabar al-mukhālif li al-maʿlūm*); On the Abundant Claims for Reporting a Narration (*fī mā yutawaffaru al-dawāʿī ʿalā naqlihi*); On the Presence of a Lie in the Narrations (*fī wujūd al-kiḍb fī al-akhbār*); and, Regarding the Rulings of the Companions (*fī aḥkām al-ṣaḥābah*).[212]

2.10.5 Discussion Five: On the Solitary Narration (*khabar al-wāḥid*)

The solitary narration is extensively discussed by ʿAllāmah in *Nihāyat* under the fifth section of the same title. The points presented in *Mabādiʾ* with respect to the solitary narration are generally encompassed within the following four discussions: On the Definition Thereof (*fī ḥaddihi*), wherein ʿAllāmah notes the argument presented by al-Āmidi on the position of some of the Ashāʿirah that the solitary narration does not convey probability (*al-ẓann*). This is then followed by another three discussions: On the Solitary Narration not Conveying Knowledge (*fī anna khabar al-wāḥid lā yufīd al-ʿilm*); On the Permissibility to Follow the Solitary Narration on the Basis of the Intellect (*fī jawāz al-taʿabbud ʿaqlan bi khabar al-wāḥid*); and finally, On the Occurrence of Following it (*fī wuqūʿ al-taʿabbud bihi*).[213]

2.10.6 Discussion Six: On the Qualifications (*sharāʾiṭ*) for a Transmitter of a Narration

These qualifications are outlined by ʿAllāmah in *Nihāyat* under the sixth section entitled: On the Qualifications of the Transmitter of a Narration (*fī sharāʾiṭ al-rāwī*). In the first discussion, which is On the Issue of Being of Age (*al-bulūgh*), he presents a further qualification of his position that it is obligatory to act in accordance with the solitary narration:

> It should be known that not every narration is accepted; only those which bring together the qualifications that refer to the transmitter and to others. There are five matters that refer to the transmitter that are regulated by one thing, viz.; that he is preferable insofar as there is a conviction about his veracity over the conviction about his falsity.[214]

211 *Nihāyat*, vol. III, p. 345.

212 *Nihāyat*, vol. III, p. 345–69.

213 *Nihāyat*, vol. III, pp. 370–413.

214 *Nihāyat*, vol. III, p. 414.

He then lists the five qualifications that a transmitter must fulfil in order for his narration to be accepted (*maqbūl*), namely: sanity (*al-ʿaql*); being of age (*al-bulūgh*); being Muslim (*al-islām*); justness (*al-ʿadālah*); and exactitude (*al-ḍabṭ*). The remainder of the first discussion is On the Discerning Child (*al-ṣabī al-mumayyiz*), the second is On [the Qualification of] Islam (*fī al-islām*), the third is On [the Issue of] Justness (*al-ʿadālah*), the fourth is On the Transmission of a Person Whose State is not Known (*fī riwāyat al-majhūl*), the fifth is On the Method to Ascertain Justness (*fī ṭarīq maʿrifat al-ʿadālah*), the sixth, On Rulings on Invalidation and the Attestation of Integrity (*fī aḥkām al-tazkiyah wa al-jarḥ*) which is also discussed in the ninth discussion of this chapter in *Mabādiʾ*, the seventh is On Exactitude (*fī al-ḍabṭ*), and, finally, discussion eight focuses On Matters That Justify the Transmission (*fī musawwighāt al-riwāyah*).[215]

2.10.7 Discussion Seven: On that which is Considered a Condition (*sharṭ*) Whilst it is not

This matter is addressed by ʿAllāmah in *Nihāyat*'s seventh section under the same name in the investigation on narrations. This chapter consists of thirteen detailed discussions, which are as follows: On Number (*al-ʿadad*), which is the opening issue addressed in this same discussion in *Mabādiʾ*; On the Absence of Denial of the Original Transmitter (*fī ʿadam takdhīb al-aṣl*); On the Legal Competence of the Transmitter, The Reasonability of his Transmission, and the Knowledge of his Lineage not Being a Condition (*fī annahu lā yushtaraṭ fiqh al-rāwī wa lā yuʿqal riwāyatuhu wa lā maʿrifat nasabihi*)—a matter which is only briefly examined in the second issue presented in this discussion in *Mabādiʾ*; On the Ruling Regarding the Narration along with what Opposes it (*fī ḥukm al-khabar maʿa al-muʿāriḍ*); On the Narration Contradicted by Analogical Reasoning (*fī al-khabar al-muʿāriḍ bi al-qiyās*), in respect to which ʿAllāmah notes that most scholars and a group from among some others have absolutely banned action on the basis of analogical reasoning; On the Narration which Contradicts the Action of the Prophet and the Action of the Majority (*fī al-khabar al-muʿāriḍ li fiʿlihi wa li ʿamal al-akthar*); The Lack of the Obligation of its Critical Examination on the Basis of the Qurʾān (*fī ʿadam wujūb arḍihi ʿalā al-kitāb*); On the Opposition of the Action of the Transmitter to the Narration (*fī muʿāraḍah ʿamal al-rāwī li al-khabar*); On the Relation of the Text to the Known and to Other General Matters (*fī nisbat al-matan ilā al-maʿlūm wa ghayrihi mimmā taʿummu al-balwā bihi*): Regarding the Narration Which does not Include the Name of its Original Transmitter (*fī al-mursal*); On the Reporting of a Tradition by Meaning (*fī naql al-ḥadīth bi al-maʿnā*), which is concisely

215 *Nihāyat*, vol. III, pp. 414–36.

alluded to by ʿAllāmah as the fourth point in this discussion in *Mabādiʾ*; On the Modality of the Utterances of the Transmitter (*fī kayfiyyat alfāẓ al-rāwī*): and finally, Regarding an Isolated Addition [to the narration] by a Transmitter (*fī infirād al-rāwī bi al-ziyādah*).[216]

2.10.8 Discussion Eight: On Rejected Narrations (*al-akhbār al-mardūdah*)
ʿAllāmah briefly states in *Mabādiʾ* that a narration would not be accepted in the following cases: firstly, when a solitary narration demands knowledge (*ʿilm*) and no decisive piece of evidence is to be found that signifies such knowledge; secondly, when the narration does not include the name of its original transmitter (*al-mursal*); and thirdly, when the transmitter of the source is absolutely certain as to the falsity of the transmission of a second person then, in such a case, the transmission of the second person is not accepted.

The first of the above points is covered in *Nihāyat* in the fifth section on narrations, entitled: On the Solitary Narration, wherein under the discussion On Following the Solitary Narration on the Basis of the Intellect (*fī jawāz al-taʿabbud ʿaqlan bi khabar al-wāḥid*), ʿAllāmah notes that the majority are of the opinion that it is permissible to do so if such a narration has been reported by a just person—contrary to the position of al-Jubbāʾī on this matter, as well as that of a certain group of theologians.[217]

The second of the above points, regarding the narration which does not include the name of its original transmitter (*fī al-mursal*), is addressed in a discussion of the same title in the seventh section on narrations, entitled: On What is Considered to be a Condition Whilst it is not (*fī mā ẓūnna annahu sharṭ wa laysa kadhālika*). It is in this discussion that ʿAllāmah remarks on the difference of opinion regarding such a narration and its forms. He considers the statement of a just person who did not meet the Envoy and says that 'the Envoy of God said such and such' as well as the statement of one who did not meet Ibn ʿAbbās and says that 'Ibn ʿAbbās said such and such'. Our author notes that Abū Ḥanīfah, Mālik, Aḥmad, and the masses (*jumhūr*) of the Muʿtazilah such as Abū Hāshim and his followers, accept such a narration as one of the two well-known transmissions. Furthermore, he states that this opinion is also found among the ancients (*qudamāʾ*) of the Imāmiyyah, specifically Muḥammad b. Khālid. He also notes the stance of al-Shāfiʿī who upholds the opinion that such a narration is not to be accepted unless it fulfils one of six conditions. Furthermore, he observes that ʿĪsā b. Abān maintains that only the narrations that do not include the names of their original transmitters (*al-marāsīl*) from the companions (*al-ṣaḥābah*), the followers

---

216 *Nihāyat*, vol. III, pp. 437–97.
217 *Nihāyat*, vol. III, pp. 375–81.

of the companions (*al-tābiʿīn*), and the follower of the followers of the companions (*tābiʿ al-tābiʿīn*), and from one who is an authority on reports, are to be absolutely accepted. Our author also notes that as far as Qāḍī Abū Bakr and a further group of jurists are concerned, they agreed with the stance of al-Shāfiʿī on this issue. Among the many reasons that ʿAllāmah enumerates in defence of his stipulation that such narrations should be rejected, is the first reason listed in *Nihāyat* and also stated in this discussion in *Mabādiʾ*, namely that the justness of the original transmitter is unknown and therefore his transmission cannot be accepted.[218]

The third of the points outlined above is addressed in *Nihāyat*, albeit from the perspective of viewing the issue within the second discussion of section seven: On the Absence of the Denial of the Original Transmitter (*fī ʿadam takdhīb al-aṣl*). ʿAllāmah notes here that the majority Ḥanafiyyah position on the matter is that, if the transmitter of the source (*rāwī al-aṣl*) does not accept the tradition (*al-ḥadīth*) then that constitutes a rebuke (*qadḥ*) of the transmission of the second person, irrespective of whether he is absolutely certain of falsehood (*takdhīb*) or says, for example, that 'I do not know and it is a transmission of Aḥmad'.[219]

2.10.9 Discussion Nine: On Invalidation (*al-jarḥ*) and Validation (*al-taʿdīl*)

The four brief points detailed in *Mabādiʾ* on invalidation (*al-jarḥ*) and validation (*al-taʿdīl*) are further embellished in the sixth section of *Nihāyat* in the investigation of narrations entitled: On the Qualifications For the Transmitter (*fī sharāʾiṭ al-rāwī*), under the sixth discussion, entitled: On the Rulings of Attestation of Integrity and Invalidation (*fī aḥkām al-tazkiyah wa al-jarḥ*). Herein our author notes that there are four rulings on this matter: firstly, that the people have differed regarding whether it is obligatory to mention the reason for invalidation (*al-jarḥ*) and validation (*al-taʿdīl*); secondly, that the majority have upheld the opinion that number (*ʿadad*) is not a condition for scrutinising the attester of integrity (*al-muzakkī*) or the invalidator (*al-jāriḥ*) with regard to the transmission (*al-riwāyah*), but is, instead, a condition in the matter of testimony regarding both; thirdly, that if an invalidation and validation contradict one another but do not deny each other, by the fact that the validator applies the attestation of integrity and the invalidator mentions a reason for invalidation that is not known to the invalidator, then in such an instance the statement (*qawl*) of the invalidator takes precedence; and fourthly, that abstaining from

218 *Nihāyat*, vol. III, pp. 459–70.

219 *Nihāyat*, vol. III, pp. 440–41.

passing a judgement on the basis of testimony does not constitute invalidation or rebuke (*qadḥ*) with regard to the transmission.[220]

2.11 *Chapter Ten: On Analogical Reasoning* (*al-qiyās*)

The debate about analogical reasoning (*qiyās*) is a long-standing and significant one in Islamic jurisprudence, in general, and Imāmī jurisprudence in particular. In many of the earlier Imāmī sources, analogical reasoning (*qiyās*) stands alongside personal opinion (*raʾy*), disputation (*ikhtilāf*) and other such notions as emblems of the misguided, arbitrary, and opinion-based thought practiced by those who lacked the guidance of the infallible Imām, and as such these notions were thoroughly denounced, taken as evidence for the epistemological failings of other schools of thought who lacked the Imām's guidance. In later periods this dispute increasingly developed into a discussion of terminology, and so it is here in *Mabādiʾ*. ʿAllāmah agrees with his teacher al-Muḥaqqiq al-Ḥillī that a known ruling for a given situation may be applied to another situation where the ruling is unknown if the cause for the known ruling is given in scripture, and it is known that the same cause is in effect in the situation for which the ruling is unknown.[221] However, while al-Muḥaqqiq al-Ḥillī names such an operation 'analogical reasoning', ʿAllāmah declares that this is not the case, contending rather that analogical reasoning is the term for the impermissible types of analogy practised by other schools in cases where the cause of a ruling is not sufficiently clear. He thus maintains his teacher's sanction of a kind of analogy when all the necessary components are supplied in scripture (*al-qiyās al-manṣūṣ ʿalā ʿillatihi*), thereby minimising the fallible, human component of a ruling. However, by declaring that the foregoing is not technically analogical reasoning he allows himself to cite the many available traditions (*ḥadīth*) condemning analogical reasoning in support of his position.

2.11.1 Discussion One: On the Definition (*taʿrīf*) of Analogical Reasoning (*al-qiyās*)

The issue of analogical reasoning is discussed at great length in *Nihāyat*. ʿAllāmah initiates the investigation of analogical reasoning with a section comprised of the following three discussions: On the Quiddity of Analogical Reasoning (*fī al-māhiyyah*); On the Foundations Thereof (*fī arkānihi*); and On its Classifications (*fī taqsīm al-qiyās*). In the first of these discussions, ʿAllāmah contextualises the concept under consideration, by examining the linguistic meaning of the term 'analogical reasoning' (*qiyās*), apart from its legal context. ʿAllāmah defines it as a measure (*al-taqdīr*), adducing the following examples

220 *Nihāyat*, vol. III, p. 430–33.

221 *Maʿārij al-uṣūl*, pp. 182–94.

in support: 'I measured the ground with a cane and the garment with the arm' (*qistu al-arḍ bi al-qaṣabah wa al-thawb bi al-dhirāʿ*). He then proceeds to discuss the two meanings upheld by the jurists regarding analogical reasoning. The first of these is analogical reasoning by way of co-exclusion (*qiyās al-ʿaks*) which is an expression about the realisation of the opposite (*naqīḍ*) of the known ruling in another case due to their separation with regards to the cause of the ruling, and the second is analogical reasoning by way of co-extension (*qiyās al-ṭard*), for which various definitions have been put forth, including those of Abū Hāshim, Qāḍī ʿAbd al-Jabbār Abū al-Ḥusayn al-Baṣrī, and Qāḍī Abū Bakr. ʿAllāmah notes these definitions along with his criticisms, recommendations, and remarks, the basic definition noted is: the reaching of the truth (*iṣābat al-ḥaqq*).

With this context firmly established he then presents a further explanation of the matter in the second discussion, by detailing how analogical reasoning involves: 'the extension of a ruling from a principle case to a secondary case through a cause that unites them both' (*al-qiyās huwa taʿdiyat al-ḥukm min al-aṣl ilā al-farʿ bi ʿillah muttaḥidah fī himā*), to which he adds that the quiddity of analogical reasoning cannot be established except by these four matters:

> Because the relationship between two things is that of equality—not from every aspect but rather regarding the legal ruling (*al-ḥukm al-sharʿī*), and that too not figuratively, but because of an appropriate uniting matter for the causation.

Our author then presents the four necessary foundations, as they are given in *Mabādiʾ*, namely:

a. the principle case (*al-aṣl*)
b. the secondary case (*al-farʿ*)
c. the cause (*al-ʿillah*)
d. the ruling (*al-ḥukm*).

ʿAllāmah employs the practical example of wine to demonstrate how these four fundamental components interact with one another in such a case.

In the third discussion ʿAllāmah presents six distinct aspects of the classifications of analogical reasoning. These are: its classification with relation to knowledge (*al-ʿilm*) and probability (*al-ẓann*), through which analogical reasoning can be either definite (*qaṭʿī*) or probable (*ẓannī*); its classification in relation to the ruling, which of these takes precedence in the secondary case, and the lack thereof (*awlawiyyat al-ḥukm fī al-farʿ wa ʿadamihā*); that analogical reasoning is either obvious (*jalī*) or not obvious (*khafī*); analogical reasoning can be either be effective (*muʾaththir*) or appropriate (*mulāʾim*); that an instance of analogical reasoning can be classified either through the cause (*qiyās al-ʿillah*), through its signification (*qiyās dalālah*), or through its original meaning (*maʿnā al-aṣl*); and that if analogical reasoning occurs by way of the confirmation of the derived cause, wherein there is a suitability (*munāsabah*), then it will be called analogical reasoning by way of the imagination (*qiyās al-ikhālah*), and if there is a resemblance (*al-shabah*) involved it will be called analogical reasoning by way of resemblance (*qiyās al-shabah*), and if there is probing and division (*sabr wa al-taqsīm*) it will be called analogical reasoning by way of probing (*qiyās al-sabr*), and if there is co-extension and co-exclusion (*al-ṭard wa al-ʿaks*) it will be called analogical reasoning by way of co-extension (*qiyās al-ṭard*). It is this final classification that constitutes the object of ʿAllāmah's attention in the fifth discussion of the tenth chapter of *Mabādiʾ*.[222]

2.11.2 Discussion Two: On Analogical Reasoning not being a Legal Proof (*ḥujjah*)

This discussion corresponds to the fuller argument presented in *Nihāyat* across a number of discussions which, altogether, comprise the second section entitled: On Whether to Reckon on the Basis of Analogical Reasoning or not (*fī annahu hal yuʿtaddu bi al-qiyās am lā*). The discussion On Analogical Reasoning not being a Legal Proof, as it is given in *Mabādiʾ*, is thus compartmentalised across the discussions within this section, some of which include: On its Intellective Permissibility (*fī jawāzihi ʿaqlan*), and On the Prohibition of Following Analogical Reasoning (*fī al-manʿ min al-taʿabbud bi al-qiyās*). In the former discussion ʿAllāmah notes that there is a difference of opinion on this matter among various groups. He observes that the majority of the companions and their followers, some of the Imāmiyyah, including al-Sayyid al-Murtaḍā and others, al-Shāfiʿī, Abū Ḥanīfah, Mālik, Aḥmad, and the majority of the jurists and theologians, permitted it on the basis of the intellect. On the other hand, he mentions that some of the Shīʿah, al-Naẓẓām, a group from the Muʿtazilah of Baghdad such as Yaḥyā al-Iskāfī,[223] Jaʿfar b. Mubashshir,[224] and Jaʿfar b.

---

222 *Nihāyat*, vol. III, pp. 501–17.

223 Yaḥyā al-Iskāfī (d. 240 AH/854 CE) was a Muʿtazilī scholar of Baghdad. See the critical edition of Ṭāhā Jābir Fayyāḍ al-ʿAlwānī of Fakhr al-Dīn al-Rāzī's (d. 606 AH/1209 CE), *al-Maḥṣūl fī ʿilm uṣūl al-fiqh*, vol. VI, p. 73.

224 Jaʿfar b. Mubashshir b. Aḥmad al-Thaqafī (d. 234 AH/848 CE), an early Muʿtazilī authority who lived in Baghdad, see Ziriklī, *al-Aʿlām*, vol. II, p. 121.

Ḥarb,[225] consider it absurd to set forth the following of analogical reasoning, although ʿAllāmah notes that the individuals mentioned above differ with regards to the source from whence it is taken, as he explains that some of them are of the opinion that the prohibition of this matter is specific to Islamic law (*sharʿ*) whilst others are of the opinion that the prohibition of following analogical reasoning applies to all laws (*sharāʾiʿ*). Furthermore al-Qaffāl of the Shāfiʿiyyah, and Abū al-Ḥusayn al-Baṣrī, maintain the position that intellection obligates the setting forth of following analogical reasoning. Our author asserts that ultimately, although it is allowed intellectively, it is prohibited according to revealed sources.[226]

In the latter discussion ʿAllāmah explains that those who uphold the opinion that it is permissible to follow analogical reasoning on the basis of the intellect, have disagreed on this matter, with some maintaining that following analogical reasoning has occurred whilst others uphold the contrary. The former agree as to the signification of revelation (*al-samʿ*) on this point, and yet they differ on three points. The first of these points concerns whether the intellect (*ʿaql*) signifies such accordance; this is affirmed by Abū al-Ḥusayn al-Baṣrī and al-Qaffāl of the Ashāʿirah, whilst the rest of the Ashāʿirah and Muʿtazilah reject this. The second point of contention concerns the signification of revelation (*dalālat al-samʿ*); Abū al-Ḥusayn is of the opinion that this is probable (*ẓanniyyah*) whilst the others maintain that it is definite (*qaṭʿiyyah*). The third point is that al-Nahrawānī[227] and al-Qāshānī[228] assert that action on the basis of analogical reasoning can take two forms: firstly, the cause can designate it by a clear utterance (*ṣarīḥ al-lafẓ*); and secondly, there is the forbiddance of hitting one's parents which is arrived at on the basis of analogical reasoning by way of the forbiddance of expressing anger and displeasure (*qiyās taḥrīm al-ḍarb ʿalā taḥrīm al-taʾfīf*).

225 Jaʿfar b. Ḥarb al-Hamadhānī (d. 236 AH/850 CE), a leading Muʿtazilī scholar from Baghdad who studied under Abū al-Hudhayl al-ʿAllāf (d. 235 AH/850 CE). See Ziriklī, *al-Aʿlām*, vol. II, pp. 116–17.

226 *Nihāyat*, vol. III, pp. 518–9.

227 Al-Muʿāfī b. Zakariyyā b. Yaḥyā al-Jarīrī al-Nahrawānī, Abū al-Faraj Ibn Ṭarār, known as al-Nahrawānī or Ibn Ṭarār (d. 390 AH/1000 CE), was a jurist and man of letters from Nahrawān, Iraq. He was a follower of the Jarīrī *madhhab* founded by the famous jurist, exegete, and historian Muḥammad b. Jarīr al-Ṭabarī (d. 310 AH/922 CE). See Ziriklī, *al-Aʿlām*, vol. VIII, p. 169.

228 Muḥammad b. Isḥāq al-Qāshānī, known as al-Qāshānī (n.d.), was a follower of Dāwūd b. ʿAlī b. Khalaf al-Iṣfahānī (d. 270 AH/884 CE) who was the founder of the Ẓāhirī *madhhab*. He left this school and later became a prominent Shāfiʿī jurist and composed a treatise defending analogical reasoning against the objections of his former teacher. See Fakhr al-Dīn al-Rāzī, *al-Maḥṣūl fī ʿilm uṣūl al-fiqh*, vol. V, p. 22.

Among those who uphold the view that following of analogical reasoning has not occurred, there are some who maintain that whatever signifies the occurrence of following analogical reasoning is not found through revelation (*al-samʿ*), thereby obligating the prohibition of acting in accordance with it. ʿAllāmah states that: 'there are also those from among them who are not content with this, but they adhere to the revealed evidences (*al-adillah al-samʿiyyah*) regarding its exclusion (*nafyihi*)'. According to ʿAllāmah this is the right position on this matter (*wa huwa al-ḥaqq*). Our author then proceeds to present fifteen arguments in support of this objection to analogical reasoning, comprising Qur'ānic verses, prophetic narrations, statements from the *Ahl al-Bayt*, their doctrines, their consensus (*ijmāʿ*), and the sayings of the companions. For example, in the tenth argument, he states:

> For we know through necessity that the doctrine (*madhhab*) of al-Bāqir, al-Ṣādiq, al-Kāẓim, peace be upon them, their forefathers, and their sons, is the rejection of analogical reasoning (*al-qiyās*), they denounced it, and prohibited action on its basis, just as we know of the reported doctrines (*al-madhāhib al-manqūlah*) of al-Shāfiʿī, Abū Ḥanīfah and others. As has already been stated, the consensus of the descendants of the Prophet is a legal proof (*ijmāʿ al-ʿitrah ḥujjah*).[229]

2.11.3 Discussion Three: On the Connection of the Unspoken (*al-maskūt*) to the Spoken (*al-manṭūq*)

To demonstrate how this concept does not constitute a form of analogical reasoning ʿAllāmah examines an actual case, the forbiddance of striking ones parents, which is implied by the obvious ruling on the forbiddance of expressing anger or displeasure. Two corresponding discussions are found in *Nihāyat*'s second section in the eleventh investigation into analogical reasoning, which centres the discussion around the above case as demonstrated by the headings: On the Extension of the Forbiddance of the Expression of Anger and Displeasure to Other Types of Inflicting Harm (*fī taʿdiyyat al-taḥrīm min al-taʾfīf ilā bāqī anwāʿ al-adhā*), and On the Harmony Between the Ruling of the Principle and Secondary Case (*fī al-tanāsub bayn ḥukm al-aṣl wa al-farʿ*). In the former of these discussions, ʿAllāmah explains the difference of opinion among the people regarding the connection that obtains between the forbiddance of striking (*taḥrīm al-ḍarb*) and the forbiddance of expressing anger and displeasure (*taḥrīm al-taʾfīf*). Here he remarks that some have said that it is a form of analogical reasoning that is to be termed 'obvious' (*jalī*), whilst others have said that it is not a form of analogical reasoning but a customary transfer

229 *Nihāyat*, vol. III, pp. 538–49.

from its linguistic assignment to the prohibition of all manners of inflicting harm. In the latter discussion On the Harmony between the Ruling of the Principle and Secondary Cases (*fī al-tanāsub bayn ḥukm al-aṣl wa al-farʿ*) ʿAllāmah states that if the confirmability (*thubūt*) of the ruling in the principle case is certain (*yaqīnan*) then it would be impossible for the ruling in the secondary case to be the stronger (*aqwā minhū*). He explains this on the epistemological basis that there is no level above that of certainty (*yaqīn*).[230]

2.11.4 Discussion Four: On the Ruling (*al-ḥukm*) in Which the Cause is Explicitly Designated (*al-manṣūṣ ʿalā ʿillatihi*)

ʿAllāmah addresses this in the second section on analogical reasoning under the discussion: On Analogical Reasoning in Which the Cause is Explicitly Designated (*fī al-qiyās al-manṣūṣ ʿalā ʿillatihi*). Here he notes the difference of opinion among the people with regards to whether the explicit designation of the cause of a ruling is the following of analogical reasoning thereof or whether it is a must to follow something additional instead. ʿAllāmah notes the various arguments on this matter presented by Abū al-Ḥusayn, Abū Isḥāq al-Naẓẓām, the jurists, the Ẓāhiriyyah, Abū Hāshim, and Abū ʿAbd Allāh al-Baṣrī. ʿAllāmah himself adopts the position of al-Naẓẓām on this matter, which is that the explicit designation of a cause for a ruling is sufficient to follow analogical reasoning. He goes on to present four arguments in defence of his position, the summary of which is presented in *Mabādiʾ*. However, the last issue in this section in *Mabādiʾ* is independently addressed in much greater detail in *Nihāyat* in the second discussion entitled: On the Explicit Designation of the Cause (*fī al-naṣṣ ʿalā al-ʿillah*) of the third section entitled: On the Methods of Causational Inference (*fī ṭuruq al-taʿlīl*). Here, ʿAllāmah explains that sometimes the explicit designation of the cause (*al-naṣṣ ʿalā al-ʿillah*) is either definite (*qaṭʿī*) and that is evident with regard to efficacy (*ṣarīḥ fī al-muʾaththiriyyah*) as stated either in the Qurʾān or the *Sunnah*; or it is evident and indefinite (*ẓāhir ghayr qaṭʿī*) as in statements wherein a particle of causation (*ḥurūf al-taʿlīl*) is brought forth, such as: *lām, kay, min, in* and *bāʾ*.[231]

2.11.5 Discussion Five: On the Derived Cause (*al-ʿillah al-mustanbiṭah*)

This discussion corresponds to ʿAllāmah's third section in *Nihāyat*, in the investigation of analogical reasoning, entitled: The Methods of Causational Inference (*fī ṭuruq al-taʿlīl*), in which all of the six methods mentioned in *Mabādiʾ* are extensively addressed in independent discussions, viz.: suitability (*munāsabah*), the effective (*muʾaththir*), resemblance (*al-shabah*), rotation

230 *Nihāyat*, vol. III, pp. 609–12.

231 *Nihāyat*, vol. III, pp. 603–608; pp. 622–40.

(*al-dawrān*), the method of probing (*al-sabr*) and division (*al-taqsīm*), and co-extension (*al-ṭard*). However, prior to the discussion of these methods, our author presents a discussion on the possibility of causational inference (*fī imkānihi*) wherein he states that the main object of analogical reasoning (*ḥāṣil al-qiyās*) refers to two fundamental principles (*aṣlayn*); the ruling in the principle case giving the cause as such and such and the confirmability of that same quality in the secondary case, with the former being, of course, the most significant of the two. Our author then presents the four arguments of those who reject analogical reasoning on this matter: what is meant by the cause (*al-ʿillah*) is either the effective (*al-muʾaththir*) regarding the ruling, or else it is that which calls upon the divine law for the confirmation thereof, or what defines it, or a fourth meaning. He then states that the first three classifications are void and likewise is the case for the fourth classification because of the lack of the conveyance of the conception thereof. This is followed by an extensive argument in support of his position.[232]

2.12 *Chapter Eleven: On Preferment* (*al-tarjīḥ*)

This chapter covers the phenomenon of apparent contradictions in scriptural evidence, and the intellectual procedures which relate to this. It begins by asking how the occurrence of two irreconcilable pieces of evidence, which are of equal strength, are considered in the divine law. The latter part of the chapter discusses the various means by which one piece of evidence may be demonstrated to be reconcilable with, or to take precedence over, another. As such, it is largely an elaboration on material that is elsewhere covered in previous chapters, dealing with recurrent questions such as abrogation, specification, and so forth. Where the chapter opens new ground is in its opening sections, which discuss correct practice in the consideration of two pieces of evidence whose contradiction seems insoluble. Here one discovers the reason that ʿAllāmah, unlike al-Muḥaqqiq al-Ḥillī in *Maʿārij al-uṣūl*, allocates an entire chapter to this question, and one also gains an insight into why this penultimate chapter is situated where it is in the structure of the *Mabādiʾ*: viz. that such issues as preferment can only be properly considered once the foregoing groundwork given in the previous chapter has been established. ʿAllāmah argues against the position of those who advocate choice (*takhyīr*) or suspension of judgement (*tawaqquf*) in a situation when two equal pieces of evidence present themselves. Instead, he advocates the obligation of preferment, thereby rendering the discussion that follows as a veritable manual on how this may be achieved—even in the most apparently intractable of cases.

232 *Nihāyat*, vol. III, pp. 614–40; *Nihāyat*, vol. IV, pp. 91–157.

2.12.1 Discussion One: On the Contradiction of Two Pieces of Evidence (*al-dalīlayn*)

The matters succinctly stated herein are addressed by ʿAllāmah in *Nihāyat* in the opening discussion of the section, On Two Equal Pieces of Evidence (*taʿādul*). The issue is related to the apparent contradiction of two equal pieces of evidence; if they are both definite (*qaṭʿī*) then the issue does not arise as it pertains instead to those equal pieces of evidence that are probable (*ẓanniyān*), and if they contradict one another the question arises as to which course of action is to be taken. In such a case the option of choice (*takhyīr*) is presented as a course of action for anyone insofar as his or her action is concerned.[233]

2.12.2 Discussion Two: On the Course of Action When Two Equal Pieces of Evidence Present Themselves (*al-taʿādul*)

ʿAllāmah states that in the resolution of such a case, preferment (*tarjīḥ*) is obligatory; it is therefore essential to understand what he means by 'preferment'. Such an explanation is to be found in the discussion On the Quiddity Thereof (*fī māhiyyatihi*), wherein he explains that:

> Preferment (*al-tarjīḥ*) is the strengthening of one of two methods over the other in order to know the strongest (*al-aqwā*) so that action can then be carried out on its basis and the weakest one abandoned.[234]

ʿAllāmah addresses the other matters briefly stated in this discussion in the discussion in *Nihāyat*: On Preferment Through Abundant Pieces of Evidence (*fī al-tarjīḥ bi kathrat al-adillah*), wherein he notes that preferment is realised with regard to pieces of evidence through their abundance, a view which he explains by affirming that when one of two possible rulings is signified by several pieces of evidence then it will be more appropriate than the ruling that is inferred from fewer pieces of evidence. He notes that this is also maintained by al-Shāfiʿī, contrary to those who uphold the opinion that preferment is not realised by an abundance of evidence, as for example with the preferment of one of two narrations due to the abundance of transmitters (*ruwāt*). Our author presents two reasons in support of this argument: firstly, that probability following from indication (*al-amārah*) is stronger if there are abundant indications and is weaker if there are fewer indications and it is obligatory to act according to the strongest of the two probabilities;[235] and, secondly, that violation of the evidence (*mukhālafat al-dalīl*) is contrary to the principle (*aṣl*). Our

233 *Nihāyat*, vol. v, pp. 275–82.

234 *Nihāyat*, vol. v, p. 285.

235 *Nihāyat*, vol. v, pp. 290–1.

author explains that if, on the one side, there are numerous pieces of evidence and, on the other, a single piece of evidence, then the violation of the former is to be more severely cautioned than the latter. He also explains that although one should exercise caution in respect to both sides, one side is specified with an additional caution. If, he states, it were not for preferment then there would be a perpetration of something which is severely cautioned, which, according to ʿAllāmah, would be unthinkable (*wa huwa muḥāl*).[236]

The last matter examined in this discussion in *Mabādiʾ* is addressed by ʿAllāmah in *Nihāyat* in a discussion entitled: The Uniting of Contradictory Pieces of Evidence (*fī al-jamʿ bayn al-adillah al-mutaʿāriḍah*). Here our author writes that when two pieces of evidence contradict one another it is not possible to act in accordance with each of the two from every aspect, otherwise there would be no contradiction, but rather it is a must that either one of them is voided from every aspect or some aspects, or else they are both of them voided from every aspect or some aspects. However, if it is possible to act in accordance with both pieces of evidence when they are considered from one aspect but not from the other then that would be more appropriate than acting in accordance with one of the two and rendering the other void in its entirety, because the signification of the utterance for a partial understanding follows the signification thereof for the whole understanding, and that is the original signification. So if an action were in accordance with each of the two from one particular aspect but not from another, then action according to the signification that follows would have to be abandoned, and if an action were in accordance with one of the two and not the other then action according to the original signification would have to be abandoned. Our author upholds the view that the former option is the most appropriate course to adopt and states that: ' action according to each of the two from one aspect, and not from the other, is more appropriate than action according to one of the two from every aspect, and not from the other'.[237]

2.12.3 Discussion Three: On the Ruling of Contradictory Pieces of Evidence (*al-adillah al-mutaʿāriḍah*)

This corresponds to the discussion in *Nihāyat* entitled, On the Classification of Contradictory Pieces of Evidence (*fī taqsīm al-adillah al-mutaʿāriḍah*), wherein ʿAllāmah explains that when two pieces of evidence contradict each other they can either both be: general (*ʿāmm*) in absolute terms; or specific (*khāṣṣ*); or one of them can be general whilst the other is specific; or both of them can be more general (*aʿamm*) than another in regard to some aspect;

236 *Nihāyat*, vol. v, p. 292.

237 *Nihāyat*, vol. v, pp. 295–6.

or more specific (*akhaṣṣ*) in regard to another aspect. Thus, the classifications for contradictory pieces of evidence are fourfold, and it is according to these four assessments (*taqādīr*) that they can either be: known (*maʿlūmayn*), probable (*maẓnūnayn*), or differentiated (*bi al-tafrīq*). Furthermore, according to all assessments (*taqādīr*) they are subdivided into either the earlier (*al-mutaqaddim*) or the later one (*al-muta'akhkhir*). The first category is that both are general, the second is that both are specific, the third that both of them are general and specific in consideration of the Qur'ānic Verse 4:23 with verse 4:24, and the fourth is that one of the two is general whilst the other is specific.[238]

2.12.4 Discussion Four: On the Preferment of the Narrations (*tarjīḥ al-akhbār*)

Our examination of this particular discussion in *Mabādi'* has brought to light that it can be classified into five broad topics of concern, all of which are addressed by ʿAllāmah as independent discussions in *Nihāyat*.

The first of these topics is entitled: On the Preferment Realised by Virtue of the Transmitter (*fī al-tarājīḥ al-ḥāṣilah bi sabab al-rāwī*), wherein ʿAllāmah notes that the preferment of one of two narrations over the other, with regard to the transmitter, can either occur due to the abundance of transmitters or on the basis of their states (*aḥwālihim*). He then proceeds to enumerate the two reasons for the occurrence of such a preferment, on the basis of abundance (*kathrah*). The first reason he gives is that:

> The transmitters of one of the two are more numerous than the transmitters of the other, and therefore it is most preferable (*arjaḥ*), contrary to the position on this matter adopted by al-Karkhī, because the probability realised through this one is greater than the other one. This is because the likelihood (*al-iḥtimāl*) of a mistake (*ghalaṭ*) or lie (*kidhb*) occurring among a greater number is less than the likelihood of its occurrence among a fewer number, since the narration (*khabar*) of every one conveys probability and collective probability is stronger than individual probability.

The second reason proffered by ʿAllāmah is:

> That one of the two narration's chain of transmission is superior and therefore it is more preferable than the other, because whenever the transmitters are fewer then the likelihood of a mistake or a lie is lesser, and whenever that is lesser then the likelihood of soundness (*al-siḥḥah*)

238 *Nihāyat*, vol. v, pp. 296–300.

> is more evident (*aẓhar*), and in such an instance action is obligatory according to it. The superiority of the chain of transmission is more preferable according to this aspect; otherwise it is outweighed (*marjūḥ*) due to the consideration of its rarity.

ʿAllāmah then goes on to qualify these remarks by adding that:

> The likelihood of an error or lie from a fewer number is only less if the personages of the transmitters are either the same for both narrations or are equal in their attributes. However, if they are numerous and their attributes are many, then the likelihood of an error or a mistake is greater than otherwise.

Preferment occurs on the basis of the state (*aḥwāl*) of a transmitter either by virtue of: knowledge (*ʿilm*), God-fearingness (*warʿ*), acumen (*dhakāʾ*), fame (*shuhrah*), the time of the transmission (*zamān al-riwāyah*), or the modality of the transmission (*kayfiyyat al-riwāyah*). ʿAllāmah then presents detailed reasons for each of the above-mentioned states, the specificities of which lie beyond the scope of this introduction.[239]

The second of the broad topics addressed in *Nihāyat* is: On Preferment Relying On the State Wherein the Narration Was Set Forth (*fī al-tarjīḥ al-mustanid ilā ḥāl wurūd al-khabar*), wherein ʿAllāmah discusses, altogether, eight issues such as the role of location in evaluating Makkī versus Madanī narrations.[240]

The third topic addressed in *Nihāyat* is: On That Which Refers to the Utterance (*fī mā yarjiʿu ilā al-lafẓ*) wherein ʿAllāmah discusses thirty-four issues, such as the eloquence of the narration, the precedence of the veritative over the figurative, and so forth.[241]

The fourth topic addressed is: On Preferment Reverting to the Ruling (*fī al-tarājīḥ al-ʿāʾidah ilā al-ḥukm*) wherein ʿAllāmah's discussion encompasses five aspects of this matter along with its various ramifications, such as the preferability of the narration that excludes legal punishment over the one that confirms it.[242]

The fifth, and final, of the topics addressed in *Nihāyat* is found across the following two discussions: On Preferment Through External Matters (*fī al-tarājīḥ bi al-umūr al-khārijiyyah*); and, On the Remaining Preferment of

---

239 *Nihāyat*, vol. v, pp. 301–10.

240 *Nihāyat*, vol. v, pp. 310–12.

241 *Nihāyat*, vol. v, pp. 312–18.

242 *Nihāyat*, vol. v, pp. 318–30.

the Narrations (*fī baqāyā tarājīḥ al-akhbār*). In these discussions 'Allāmah approaches the issue of the narration which some of the scholars have based their action upon; an issue that is also mentioned in *Mabādi'* but is here considered from a different perspective.[243]

2.13 *Chapter Twelve: On Juristic Reasoning (al-ijtihād) and its Dependents*

The final chapter examines how the endeavour to infer the divine law, which all hitherto preceding sections sought to introduce, becomes an applied reality for the Muslim community through the mediation of the skilled practitioners of juristic reasoning (*al-mujtahidūn*). It is in this chapter that one first encounters 'Allāmah's adoption of a new definition of juristic reasoning (*ijtihād*) for Imāmī jurisprudence. He then goes on to define, in much greater depth, the numerous strict qualifications which are necessary for its valid undertaking. This leads to a discussion outlining the controversy on the 'doctrine of resemblance', and whether or not problems pertaining to juristic reasoning are determined by a ruling from God. 'Allāmah proceeds to outline the intricacies of the system of juristic reasoning and its related issues. The chapter concludes with a brief examination of the pragmatics of implementing the doctrine of the 'presumption of continuity', specifically in relation to a ruling that has been arrived at beforehand.

2.13.1 Discussion One: On Juristic Reasoning (*al-ijtihād*)

'Allāmah's chapter On Juristic Reasoning (*ijtihād*) in *Mabādi'* is to be found in his final investigation, in *Nihāyat*. The section is divided into four problems, the first of which is: On the Quiddity of Juristic Reasoning (*fī māhiyyatihi*), wherein 'Allāmah explains that, linguistically, the term *ijtihād* is an expression used to denote the utmost exertion of one's ability (*istifrāgh al-wus'*) to accomplish something that entails an inconvenience (*al-kulfah*) and hardship (*al-mashaqqah*). For example it is said: exert your utmost ability in carrying the load (*ijtahid fī ḥaml al-thaqīl*), to wit, he exerted his utmost ability regarding that (*ay istafragha wus'ahu fīhi*); and it is not said: exert your utmost ability in carrying the date pit (*ijtahid fī ḥaml al-nawāt*). As far as the customary understanding held by the jurists (*'urf al-fuqahā'*) is concerned, 'Allāmah explains that *ijtihād* means: the exertion of one's utmost ability in search for the probability (*al-ẓann*) of something from the divine legal rulings insofar as this excludes any blame for falling short (*istifrāgh al-wus' fī ṭalab al-ẓann bi shay' min al-aḥkām al-shar'iyyah bi hayth yantafī al-lawm 'anhu bi sabab al-taqṣīr*). 'Allāmah notes that the phrase 'exertion of one's utmost ability' (*istifrāgh al-wus'*) serves as a

243 *Nihāyat*, vol. v, pp. 331–6.

genus for the linguistic and nomenclatural meanings, and its jurisprudential meaning is thereafter distinguished from its linguistic meaning.

The customary understanding of the jurists, stated above, is then qualified by ʿAllāmah, who attests that the statement 'in search of probability' excludes definite rulings (*al-aḥkām al-qaṭʿiyyah*), and that which is 'of something from the legal rulings' excludes matters pertaining to intellection (*al-umūr al-ʿaqliyyah*), and, insofar as the statement 'excludes any blame for falling short', it thereby excludes the juristic reasoning of one who falls short (*al-muqaṣṣir*), accompanied by the possibility that more could have been added thereupon because that is not nomenclaturally counted as an instance of reliable juristic reasoning. ʿAllāmah notes that this method is only applied to problems (*masāʾil*) that pertain to the domain of ritual (*furūʿ*), and hence these problems are called 'the problems of juristic reasoning' (*masāʾil al-ijtihād*) and the one who investigates them (*al-nāẓir fīhā*) is the 'skilled practitioner of juristic reasoning' (*mujtahid*) and that this is not the state of affairs with regard to matters pertaining to the domain of faith (*al-uṣūl*)—a point that he revisits in *Mabādiʾ* in the fifth discussion of this chapter. On the basis of the above points ʿAllāmah concludes that juristic reasoning involves the relation and connection between two matters (*nisbah wa iḍāfah bayn amrayn*), one of which is the skilled practitioner of juristic reasoning (*al-mujtahid*) who is the investigator (*al-nāẓir*) qualified with the attribute of juristic reasoning, and the other of which is the object of juristic reasoning (*al-mujtahad fīhi*), which are those problems that pertain to the domain of ritual (*al-masāʾil al-farʿiyyah*).[244]

Insofar as juristic reasoning and the Prophet are concerned, this issue is extensively addressed by ʿAllāmah in an independent discussion in *Nihāyat* entitled: On the Prophet not Following Juristic Reasoning (*fī ann al-nabī lam yakun mutaʿabbidan bi al-ijtihād*). Here our author writes that the doctrine of the Imāmiyyah and the two Jubbāʾīs is that the Prophet did not follow juristic reasoning on anything. However, al-Shāfiʿī and Abū Yūsuf are of the opinion that it was possible and allowed for him to do so (*al-jawāz*), some are of the opinion that he followed juristic reasoning on matters related to battles (*al-ḥurūb*) but not on judgements related to religion (*aḥkām al-dīn*), and others suspended judgement on this matter. ʿAllāmah enumerates fourteen arguments comprising the doctrine of the Imāmiyyah; these also include the five presented in this discussion in *Mabādiʾ* but with further elaborations. Furthermore, ʿAllāmah discusses the objections of opponents such as Qāḍī al-Quḍāt and Abū al-Ḥusayn to these arguments, one by one,

244 *Nihāyat*, vol. v, pp. 167–8.

and then presents his refutations of them.[245] In addition to the above discussion, ʿAllāmah also considers further matters relating to the Prophet and juristic reasoning in the following discussions: On the Impossibility of Him Committing an Error (*fī ʿadam jawāz al-khaṭaʾ ʿalayhi*), and, On Juristic Reasoning in His Time (*fī al-ijtihād fī zamānihi*).[246]

As our author writes in *Mabādiʾ*, according to the Imāmiyyah the practice of juristic reasoning is not possible as far as the Twelve Imāms are concerned, due to their infallibility (*ʿiṣmah*) and because the source of their knowledge is prophetic instruction (*taʿlīm al-rasūl*) and divine inspiration (*ilhām min allāh taʿālā*). However, for ʿAllāmah, insofar as the scholars (*al-ʿulamāʾ*) are concerned, juristic reasoning is to be permitted with regard to the derivation of rulings through the generalities of the Qurʾān, the *Sunnah*, and through the preferment of contradictory pieces of evidence.

In the last sentence of this discussion in *Mabādiʾ* our author briefly alludes to the view that the 'principle of juristic approbation' (*al-istiḥsān*) is neither appropriate nor allowed for the derivation of rulings. This matter is taken up in full in *Nihāyat* in the third section entitled: Juristic Approbation (*al-istiḥsān*), presented in the twelfth investigation entitled: On Logical Inference (*fī al-istidlāl*)—wherein ʿAllāmah discusses juristic approbation in two discussions, namely: On the Quiddity Thereof (*fī māhiyyatihi*); and, On That it is not a Legal Proof (*fī annahu laysa bi ḥujjah*). In the former of these he examines the etymology of the term and presents the definitions supplied by the followers of Abū Ḥanīfah. In the latter he discusses the difference of opinion on this matter among the people. Our author writes that the Ḥanafiyyah and Aḥmad b. Ḥanbal uphold the view that it is a legal proof (*ḥujjah*), whilst the Imāmiyyah, al-Shāfiʿī and the remaining masses have rejected it. He notes the famous statement of al-Shāfiʿī: 'whosoever arrives at a ruling on the basis of juristic approbation has made up the divine law (*man istaḥsana faqad sharraʿa*)'.[247]

2.13.2 Discussion Two: On the Qualifications of the Skilled Practitioner of Juristic Reasoning (*al-mujtahid*)

This corresponds to the first discussion in *Nihāyat* similarly entitled: On His Qualifications (*fī sharāʾiṭihi*) found in the second problem: On the Skilled Practitioner of Juristic Reasoning (*fī al-mujtahid*) in the section on juristic reasoning. ʿAllāmah notes here that, insofar as it is possible for them to infer (*istidlāl*) rulings (*aḥkām*) through legal evidence, the skilled practitioner of ju-

245 *Nihāyat*, vol. v, pp. 172–82.

246 *Nihāyat*, vol. v, pp. 186–91.

247 *Nihāyat*, vol, iv, pp. 395–401.

ristic reasoning is legally charged (*mukallaf*) to do so and that this responsibility is the one thing that regulates the qualifications. Our author then explains that this ability is conditioned by three matters: firstly, the skilled practitioner's cognisance of the demands of the utterance and its meaning, without which he would avail nothing from it, and his cognisance of the language, and the customary (*al-ʿurfī*) and legal (*al-sharʿī*) assignments (*al-waḍʿ*), so that it is possible for him to report about it; secondly, that he knows about the state of the addressed (*ḥāl al-mukhāṭab*), the meaning of the utterance, and what its evident meaning demands in isolation or in a context, if one is to be found—a condition for which ʿAllāmah presents several arguments along with an objection raised by the Ashāʿirah; and thirdly, that the skilled practitioner knows if the utterance is either isolated or connected to a context if accompanied by one.[248]

Insofar as the context (*al-qarīnah*) is concerned ʿAllāmah says that it is either intellective (*ʿaqliyyah*) or revealed (*samʿiyyah*). He presents a further eight matters, the knowledge of which, he says, is a must for any skilled practitioner of juristic reasoning, which are: the Qurʾān; the *Sunnah*; consensus (*ijmāʿ*); intellect (*ʿaql*); the conditions of the definition (*al-ḥadd*) and logical demonstration; the Arabic language, its syntax (*al-naḥw*) and morphology (*al-taṣrīf*); the abrogator (*al-nāsikh*) and the abrogated (*al-mansūkh*); and the status of the transmitters and subjects that are connected with this science (*maʿrifat al-rijāl*).[249]

In *Mabādiʾ*, the reader will notice that ʿAllāmah does not mention the intellect (*al-ʿaql*) but refers instead to the 'principle of exemption' (*al-barāʾah al-aṣliyyah*), which is the intellective principle that he lists whilst discussing the intellect (*al-ʿaql*) in *Nihāyat*. He states that:

> Insofar as the intellect (*al-ʿaql*) is concerned it is to have knowledge concerning the principle of exemption (*al-barāʾah al-aṣliyyah*) because we are legally charged to adhere to it except when there is established evidence that says otherwise, such as the explicit designation of a text (*naṣṣ*) or consensus (*ijmāʿ*) and other matters.[250]

ʿAllāmah briefly alludes to the notion that juristic reasoning is achievable in a single science or even in a single legal problem for an individual. This issue is taken up in *Nihāyat* in the fifth discussion entitled: On Partial Juristic Reasoning (*fī tajazzuʾ al-ijtihād*). In outlining one of the arguments presented therein

248 *Nihāyat*, vol. v, pp. 168–72.

249 *Nihāyat*, vol. v, pp. 168–70.

250 *Nihāyat*, vol. v, p. 171.

by the proponents of this matter, our author notes that: 'According to consensus Mālik was a jurist, despite the fact that he was questioned about forty legal problems and to thirty-six of which he responded by saying: 'I do not know!' (*lā adrī*).[251]

The final issue, very briefly touched upon in this discussion in *Mabādī'*, is the focus of the third problem, in the section On Juristic Reasoning (*fī al-ijtihād*) in *Nihāyat*, entitled: Wherein Juristic Reasoning Applies (*mā fīhi al-ijtihād*). Our author notes that its application encompasses every legal ruling (*ḥukm sharʿī*) for which there is no definite evidence (*dalīl qaṭʿī*). He qualifies this by stating that the term 'legal' (*sharʿī*) excludes problems that pertain to intellection (*al-ʿaqlī*) and theology; and that the phrase 'for which there is no definite evidence' excludes all matters for which there is definite evidence, such as the obligation of the five daily ritual prayers and the giving of alms and all other evident issues (*al-masā'il al-ẓāhirah*) upon which the *ummah* agrees. Furthermore, our author notes the opinion of Abū al-Ḥusayn that a problem pertaining to juristic reasoning (*al-mas'alah al-ijtihādiyyah*) is that which the skilled practitioners of juristic reasoning differ upon with respect to legal rulings (*al-aḥkām al-sharʿiyyah*). He argues that the objection al-Rāzī raises to the above necessitates a circular argument, and concludes that:

> There is no circular argument regarding the conditioning of the possibility of legal disputes (*al-ikhtilāf al-sharʿī*) to a problem that pertains to juristic reasoning and the definition of 'pertaining to juristic reasoning' (*taʿrīf al-ijtihādiyyah*) on that upon which the difference between the scholars has occurred.[252]

2.13.3 Discussion Three: On the Correctness (*taṣwīb*) of the Skilled Practitioner of Juristic Reasoning

This particular discussion parallels 'Allāmah's discussion in *Nihāyat*: On Whether or not the Skilled Practitioner of Juristic Reasoning is Correct in the Domain of Ritual in Absolute Terms (*fī anna al-mujtahid fī al-furūʿ mutlaqan hal huwa muṣīb am lā*). Herein our author notes that there is a difference of opinion among people on whether or not every skilled practitioner of juristic reasoning in legal rulings is correct. 'Allāmah states that this gives rise to the question of whether or not the problem that pertains to juristic reasoning is determined by a ruling from God, the Exalted, prior to the practice of juristic reasoning. Those who maintain that He does not have a determined ruling are

251 *Nihāyat*, vol. v, p. 191.
252 *Nihāyat*, vol. v, p. 192.

those who judge that every skilled practitioner of juristic reasoning is correct. He reports that this is the doctrine of Abū al-Ḥasan al-Ashʿarī and Qāḍī Abū Bakr of the Ashāʿirah, and also the view of Abū al-Hudhayl al-ʿAllāf, Abū ʿAlī and Abū Hāshim and their followers, from the Muʿtazilah. Our author then states that the above mentioned have variant positions on this issue; there are those who say, in respect to an incident for which there is no ruling to be found, that if it were to be found that would be the ruling God would judge by. This opinion is also known as the 'doctrine of resemblance' (*qawl bi al-ashbah*) and it is upheld by many of those who consider the skilled practitioner to be correct (*al-muṣawwibūn*). However, there are some who do not subscribe to this stance. ʿAllāmah then proceeds to discuss the various positions that branch out from these two positions, which he summarises in the following terms:

> The strongest opinion regarding these issues is that God, the Exalted, has a determined ruling (*ḥukm muʿayyan*) with regard to every incident (*fī kull wāqiʿah*), for which there is an evident evidence (*dalīl ẓāhir*) which is not definite (*lā qāṭiʿ*), and that, [furthermore], the one who is incorrect therein is excused.[253]

2.13.4 Discussion Four: On the Changing (*taghyīr*) of Juristic Reasoning
ʿAllāmah addresses this matter in the second section entitled: Compliance With the Conclusions of the Skilled Practitioner of Juristic Reasoning (*al-taqlīd*), which is to be found in the final investigation of *Nihāyat* in a discussion entitled: On the Repetition of Juristic Reasoning (*fī takarrur al-ijtihād*). It is here that our author raises the complex question as to whether or not, when a skilled practitioner of juristic reasoning arrives at a ruling through his juristic reasoning, and makes an edict based upon it, and he is questioned a second time about that selfsame problem, it is obligatory for him to practice juristic reasoning anew. By way of resolving this problem, our author details three possible responses: firstly, that it would be obligatory to repeat the process of juristic reasoning because of the likelihood (*iḥtimāl*) that the skilled practitioner's juristic reasoning would have undergone a change, and that he would thereby come to know what had not dawned upon him initially; secondly, that it is not obligatory because he would have performed the obligation and would thereby be freed from the charge of the injunction to practice juristic reasoning, because the command does not demand repetition and the principle in this case is that he is unaware of that which did not dawn upon him initially; and thirdly, that if the skilled practitioner of juristic reasoning can recollect the method of the initial process of juristic reasoning, he is thus a *skilled* practitioner of

253 *Nihāyat*, vol. v, pp. 198–200.

juristic reasoning, and it is thereby permissible for him to make an edict, so it would be as if he had practiced juristic reasoning in the here and now (*al-ḥāl*). However, if he can not so recollect the process of juristic reasoning then it is necessary for him to embark on it anew, because he comes under the ruling of one who has not practiced juristic reasoning.[254]

2.13.5 Discussion Five: On the Permissibility of Compliance with the Conclusions of the Skilled Practitioner of Juristic Reasoning (*taqlīd*)

This discussion is contextualised by ʿAllāmah in *Nihāyat* under the third problem entitled: On the Seeker of an Edict, The Conditions for Seeking an Edict, and its Place (*fī al-mustaftī wa sharāʾiṭ al-istiftāʾ wa maḥallihi*), which is situated in the section: On Compliance with the Conclusions of the Skilled Practitioner of Juristic Reasoning (*taqlīd*). This problem is composed of a number of discussions, and in the discussion: On the Layperson (*fī al-ʿāmmī*), ʿAllāmah writes that:

> The verifiers (*muḥaqqiqūn*) are in agreement that it is permissible for the layperson (*al-ʿāmmī*) to comply with the conclusions of the skilled practitioners of juristic reasoning (*taqlīd*) regarding the laws (*al-sharʿ*) that pertain to the domain of ritual (*al-furūʿ*), [and] likewise is the case for the one who is not a skilled practitioner of juristic reasoning even though such an individual is learned in one of the sciences that is taken into account with regard to juristic reasoning. Rather, it is obligatory for such a person to comply with the conclusions of the skilled practitioner's juristic reasoning, and to adopt the view of the one who makes edicts (*muftī*).

ʿAllāmah presents four reasons for his position on this matter; he also notes possible objections, along with his counterarguments to these objections. Our author also notes here that some from among the Muʿtazilah of Baghdad are of the opinion that compliance with the conclusions of the skilled practitioner of juristic reasoning is not permissible, unless the skilled practitioner elucidates to the layperson the soundness of his juristic reasoning with the evidence thereof. However, Abū ʿAlī al-Jubbāʾī is of the opinion that it is permissible regarding legal problems which pertain to juristic reasoning (*masāʾil al-ijtihād*) but not with respect to other matters such as the five acts of ritual worship (*al-ʿibādāt al-khams*).[255]

254 *Nihāyat*, vol. v, p. 247.

255 *Nihāyat*, vol. v, pp. 250–57.

2.13.6 Discussion Six: On the Conditions for Seeking an Edict (*al-istiftā'*)

This matter is addressed by 'Allāmah in a discussion of the same name, within the third problem, On Compliance With the Conclusions of the Skilled Practitioner of Juristic Reasoning (*taqlīd*). Herein 'Allāmah notes that there is a consensus that it is only permissible to seek an edict from one who possesses the two qualities of juristic reasoning and God-fearingness (*al-war'*). Our author considers these qualities to be obligatory for the one who makes edicts (*al-muftī*). Also, he asserts that it is not obligatory for the one who seeks an edict to do his utmost to obtain knowledge of the God-fearingness of the skilled practitioner of juristic reasoning. The sufficient extent, he attests, is to base this matter upon that which is evident (*al-ẓāhir*), which is that he sees him holding an office of ediction, which is witnessed among mankind.

Furthermore, our author states that there is a consensus that it is not permissible to comply with the conclusions of one about whom there is any probability that he is neither knowledgeable (*'ālim*) nor religious (*mutadayyin*). In the case where there are numerous skilled practitioners of juristic reasoning, he then maintains that it is obligatory upon the one seeking an edict to act according to their ruling if all are in agreement about that particular ruling. However, if they differ with regards to a particular ruling then it is obligatory upon the one seeking an edict to do his utmost to gain knowledge of the most learned scholar (*a'lam*) and the most God-fearing (*awra'*) among them, because this method will strengthen his probability which will then take the same place as that of the probability of the skilled practitioner of juristic reasoning. 'Allāmah notes that this is the opinion of a group from among the masters of jurisprudence (*al-uṣūliyyūn*), the jurists (*al-fuqahā'*), Aḥmad b. Ḥanbal, Ibn Surayj of the Shāfi'iyyah, and al-Qaffāl. In support of the above point, our author presents the following Qur'ānic verse as evidence: '...He who guides to the truth or he who guides not unless he is guided? What then ails you, how you judge?'[256] Others, such as Qāḍī Abū Bakr, are said by our author to be of the opinion that it is not obligatory upon the one seeking an edict to do his utmost, but he can instead choose to refer to whomsoever he wishes from among them.[257]

2.13.7 Discussion Seven: On the Ediction (*iftā'*) of One Who is not a Skilled Practitioner of Juristic Reasoning

The seventh discussion in chapter twelve of *Mabādi'* corresponds to 'Allāmah's discussion in *Nihāyat* entitled: On the Ediction by Means of an Account (*fī al-iftā' 'an al-ḥikāyah*), wherein he notes the differing opinions regarding the

256 Q. 10:35.
257 *Nihāyat*, vol. v, pp. 263–4.

one who is not qualified for juristic reasoning; and whether it is permissible to make an edict in accordance with the doctrines of other skilled practitioners of juristic reasoning insofar as this constitutes relating from another. ʿAllāmah presents the three variant positions on this matter. The first of these is that of Abū al-Ḥusayn al-Baṣrī and a group from the masters of legal methodology, who prohibit the above. Their justification for this is that such a person can only be questioned about his opinion and not about another's and, furthermore, if it were permissible to make an edict through the method of relating it from another's doctrine then it would also be permissible for the layperson. They argue that because the latter is void, on the basis of consensus, likewise is true for the former. The second position he discusses belongs to those who uphold permissibility in this regard, as in the case where it is confirmed that the view of the one who is not a skilled practitioner of juristic reasoning is founded on the basis of a report (*naql*) from one whose opinion is reliable. The third position is that of those who have discussed this matter in relation to two aspects. Firstly, if the one who makes edicts is a skilled practitioner of juristic reasoning in a doctrine—insofar as he is qualified to know the sources of the absolute skilled practitioner of juristic reasoning, possesses the ability to understand the ramifications of the precepts and views of his leader (*imām*), is adept at drawing matters together and differentiation (*al-jamʿ wa al-farq*), and is also adept at theorisation and argumentation (*al-naẓar wa al-munāẓarah*), then he can make an edict and is distinguished from a layperson because there is an established consensus by the people of every era with respect to the acceptance of such a type of edict. Secondly, if he is relating from the deceased then it is not permissible to adopt his view because the deceased has no view and because consensus can be established, despite his opposition, after his death but not whilst he is alive, and this signifies that his opinion is no longer pertinent.[258]

2.13.8 Discussion Eight: On the One Who has not Attained the Degree of Juristic Reasoning (*al-ijtihād*)

This matter is examined in *Nihāyat* in the discussion: On the Non-Layperson (*fī ghayr al-ʿāmmī*) within the third problem on the compliance with the conclusions of the skilled practitioner of juristic reasoning (*taqlīd*). Here, ʿAllāmah explains that if an incident takes place for someone who is a mere layperson (*ʿāmmī*), it is obligatory upon him to seek an edict. However, if he is a scholar (*ʿālim*), then he has either attained the degree of juristic reasoning or has not, and in the latter case, on the basis of the strongest opinion (*ʿalā al-aqwā*), it is permissible for him to seek an edict. In the former case, our

258 *Nihāyat*, vol. v, pp. 248–50.

author notes that either he has practiced juristic reasoning or he has not—and if he has practiced it, and reached an overwhelming probability regarding a ruling, then in such a case it is not permissible for him to comply with the conclusions of someone who opposes him in his opinion and to base his action upon the probability of another, according to consensus. However, if he has not practiced juristic reasoning then it is also impermissible for him to comply with the conclusions of another skilled practitioner of juristic reasoning—as is the doctrine of the majority of the Ashāʿirah. ʿAllāmah notes that according to Aḥmad b. Ḥanbal, Isḥāq b. Rāhwayh,[259] and Sufyān al-Thawrī,[260] it is permissible for a scholar (*ʿālim*) to comply with the conclusions of another scholar (*ʿālim*) in absolute terms. Furthermore, he notes that there are two transmissions about this matter from Abū Ḥanīfah. In addition to the above, he also notes that there are others who have provided further details on this matter from various aspects, such as: al-Shāfiʿī, who upholds that it is permissible for one who came after the companions (*ṣaḥābah*) to comply with the conclusions of the companions but not for others; Muḥammad b. al-Ḥasan al-Shaybānī,[261] who is of the opinion that it is permissible for a scholar (*ʿālim*) to comply with the conclusions of the most learned scholar (*aʿlam*); some of the Iraqi's, who maintain that compliance with the conclusions of the skilled practitioner of juristic reasoning is permissible in the matter which is specific to him, and not in that which he pronounces an edict upon; and Ibn Surayj, who maintains that it is permissible to comply with the conclusions of the skilled practitioner of juristic reasoning in the matter which is specific to him when he fears that time would lapse if he engaged with juristic reasoning.[262]

2.13.9 Discussion Nine: On the Presumption of Continuity (*al-istiṣḥāb*)

This issue is addressed by ʿAllāmah in the twelfth investigation in *Nihāyat,* entitled: Logical Inference (*istidlāl*), under the second section, On the Presumption of Continuity (*fī al-istiṣḥāb*). In this section our sage presents the following discussions, which remove the matter from the context of juristic reasoning

259 Isḥāq b. Ibrāhīm b. Makhlad al-Ḥanẓalī al-Tamīmī al-Marwazī, Abū Yaʿqūb, known as Ibn Rāhwayh (d. 238 AH/853 CE), was a very accomplished scholar of *ḥadīth* from Khurāsān who taught many well-known Sunnī *ḥadīth* scholars including al-Bukhārī (d. 256 AH/870 CE), Muslim (d. 261 AH/874 CE), al-Tirmidhī (d. 279 AH/892 CE), al-Nasāʾī (d. 303 AH/915 CE), and Aḥmad b. Ḥanbal (d. 241 AH/855 CE). See Ziriklī, *al-Aʿlām*, vol. I, p. 284.

260 Sufyān b. Saʿīd b. Masrūq, Abū ʿAbd Allāh, known as Sufyān al-Thawrī (d. 161 AH/778 CE) was a well known jurist, who founded a now extinct *madhhab.* See Ziriklī, *al-Aʿlām*, vol. III, p. 158.

261 Muḥammad b. al-Ḥasan al-Shaybānī (d. 189 AH/804 CE), an extremely prominent Ḥanafī jurist who was a direct disciple of Abū Ḥanīfah. See Ziriklī, *al-Aʿlām*, vol. VI, p. 309.

262 *Nihāyat*, vol. V, pp. 258–63.

within which it is found in *Mabādi'*: On Whether it is a Legal Proof or not (*fī annahu hal huwa ḥujjah am lā*); On the Ruling on the Presumption of Continuity of Consensus on Points of Disagreement (*fī ḥukm istiṣḥāb al-ijmāʿ fī maḥall al-khilāf*); and, On Whether or not There is Evidence for the Negation (*fī anna al-nāfī hal ʿalayhi dalīl am lā*). In the first of these discussions, he notes that the majority of the Ḥanafiyyah, and a group of theologians such as Abū al-Ḥusayn al-Baṣrī, al-Sayyid al-Murtaḍā, and some others, uphold the view that it is not a legal proof. From the same group are those who permit preferment (*al-tarjīḥ*) on the basis thereof and nothing else. Furthermore our author notes that a group of the Shāfiʿiyyah such as al-Muzanī,[263] al-Ṣayrafī, al-Ghazālī, and others, uphold the view that it is a legal proof. In the third discussion, On Whether or not There is Evidence for the Negation (*al-nāfī*), a matter briefly covered in *Mabādi'*, he notes that some are of the opinion that there is no evidence thereupon, whilst others, such as al-Sayyid al-Murtaḍā, Abū al-Ḥusayn al-Baṣrī, and al-Ghazālī, maintain that it is a must that there is evidence for it, a view which our author certifies as the truth (*al-ḥaqq*).[264]

*

Our examination of the *Mabādi'*, has brought to the fore a number of characteristic features of ʿAllāmah's contribution to the development of Imāmī legal theory and the distinctive stance he takes upon certain jurisprudential matters. These can be summarised in the following manner,[265] ʿAllāmah upholds: the principle of indifferency (*al-ibāḥah*) regarding the state of all things prior to the revelation of divine law (*al-sharʿ*); that some utterances are legally veritative (*al-ḥaqīqah al-sharʿiyyah*); that the command (*al-amr*) neither signifies a one-off (*al-marrah*) nor a repeat performance (*al-takrār*); that with respect to social interactions the prohibition (*al-nahy*) does not demand the unsoundness (*al-fasād*) of the thing which is prohibited; that the utterances of generality (*alfāẓ al-ʿumūm*) are assigned for the arrival at a general meaning (*al-maʿnā al-ʿāmm*); that it is permissible to act in accordance (*taʿabbud*) with the solitary

263 Ismāʿīl b. Yaḥyā b. Ismāʿīl, Abū Ibrāhīm, known as al-Muzanī (d. 264 AH/878 CE), a prominent Egyptian jurist who was a disciple of al-Shāfiʿī (d. 204 AH/820 CE). See Ziriklī, *al-Aʿlām*, vol. I, p. 327.

264 Here ʿAllāmah is alluding to the concept of *iṣtiṣḥāb al-ʿadam al-aṣlī*, which is presumption of the original absence. For further details see: al-Rāzī, Fakhr al-Dīn Muḥammad b. ʿUmar, *al-Maḥṣūl ilā ʿilm al-uṣūl*, vol. VI, pp. 121–2, and *Nihāyat*, vol. IV, pp. 363–94.

265 See part five (*al-faṣl al-khāmis*) of the Introduction to: al-ʿAllāmah al-Ḥillī, *Mabādi al-wuṣūl ilā ʿilm al-uṣūl*, edited by Sayyid Amjad H. Shah Naqavi, London, 2016.

narration on the basis of intellection (*ʿaql*) and the divine law (*sharʿ*); and that the term juristic reasoning (*al-ijtihād*) ought to be understood according to the new nomenclature (*iṣṭilāḥ*) first employed by his uncle al-Muḥaqqiq al-Ḥillī: as an utmost scientific endeavour undertaken in order to infer a legal ruling (*al-ḥukm al-sharʿī*) from the evidence.

The preceding summary is, of course, only a mere selection of ʿAllāmah's most significant points; we have aimed to contextualise all of these foregoing points, insofar as possible, into their correct place within the development of Imāmī Shīʿī jurisprudence in our forthcoming title, *The History of Imāmī Shīʿī Uṣūl al-Fiqh Without Any Gaps*. A comprehensive analysis of ʿAllāmah's contribution to the subject of jurisprudence (*uṣūl al-fiqh*), shall be presented in full in our forthcoming monograph *The Jurisprudence of al-ʿAllāmah al-Ḥillī*.

بنده شیرخدا
Sayyid Amjad H. Shah Naqavi
Bloomsbury, London
ʿĪd al-Ghadīr 1437 AH / 20th September 2016

Mabādiʿ al-Wuṣūl Ilā ʿIlm al-Uṣūl

مبادئ الوصول إلى علم الأصول

The Foundations of Jurisprudence

An Introduction to Imāmī Shīʿī Legal Theory

 | DOI 10.1163/9789004311770_003

[خطبة]

بِسم الله الرّحمٰن الرّحيم، وبه نستعين ربّ يسّر[1] 75b

الحمدُ للهِ المتفرّدِ بالأزليّة والدّوام، المتوحّدِ بالجلالِ والإكرام، المتفضّلِ بسوابغِ الإنعام، المتقدّسِ عن مشابَهَةِ الأعراضِ والأجسَام. وصلّىٰ الله علىٰ سيّدِ الأنام محمّد المصطفىٰ وآله[2] الأماجدِ الكرام. صَلوٰةً تتعاقب عليهم تعاقُب اللّيالي والأيّام.[3]

أمّا بعد،

فهٰذا كتاب مبادىء الوصول إلىٰ علم الأصول قد اشتَمَلَ من عِلمِ[4] أصُولِ الفِقه علىٰ مَا لابُدَّ منه واحتَوىٰ عَلىٰ مَا لا نستغني[5] عنه. نرجو بوضعه التّقرُّبَ إلىٰ الله تعالىٰ وهو حسبنا ونعمَ الوكيل. ورتّبته علىٰ فصول.

---

1 في "ج": (ربّ سهل ويسّر). و في "د": (وبه ثقتي). والعبارة: (وبه نستعين ربّ يسّر) لا توجد في "ب" و"ه" و"ط". 2 في الهامش الأيمن مِن "أ" وكل من "ب" و"ج" و"د" و"ه" و"ط": (عترتِهِ). 3 لا توجد العبارة (صَلوٰةً تتعاقب عليهم تعاقُب اللّيالي والأيام) في "ب" و"ج". 4 لم ترد (عِلمِ) في "أ" ووردت في "ج" و"د" و"ه" و"ط" ولعله الصّواب كما أثبتناه. 5 في "د" و"ه" و"ط": يستغني.

Prologue

In the name of God, the Oft-Compassionate, the Ever-Merciful, by Him we seek besteading, my Lord make it easy.

Praise is for God, the one who is alone in eternity and perpetuity, the one who is unique in majesty and munificence, the one who is alone in excellence in bestowing ample blessings, and the one who is far removed from the likeness of accidents and bodies. May the blessings of God be upon the lord of Mankind, Muḥammad, the Chosen, and upon his most glorious and illustrious descendants. A blessing that follows them as night follows day.

Now then,

This book, *Mabādiʾ al-wuṣūl ilā ʿilm al-uṣūl,* encompasses those matters which are necessary for the knowledge of jurisprudence (*ʿilm uṣūl al-fiqh*), and includes what is indispensable. By putting it forth we hope for closeness to God the High, He is sufficient for us, and He is the most excellent Guardian. I have arranged it in [the] chapters [which follow].

الفَصْلُ[1] الأَوَّل

فِي اللُّغَات، وفيه مباحث

الأوّل: في أحكام كلية

ذهب جماعة إلىٰ أنّ اللّغات توقيفية. لقوله[2] تعالىٰ: ﴿وَعَلَّمَ ءَادَمَ ٱلۡأَسۡمَآءَ كُلَّهَا﴾ [سُورة البقرة:٣١]، وقوله تعالىٰ: ﴿وَٱخۡتِلَٰفُ أَلۡسِنَتِكُمۡ﴾ [سُورة الرّوم:٢٢]، والمراد به اللّغات. وقال أبو هاشم[3]: إنّها إصطلاحية لقوله تعالىٰ: ﴿وَمَآ أَرۡسَلۡنَا مِن رَّسُولٍ إِلَّا بِلِسَانِ قَوۡمِهِۦ﴾ [سُورة إبرَاهِيم:٤].

ولا يجب أن يكون لكلّ معنىً لفظ، وإلّا لزَمَ عدَم تناهي الألفاظ، بَل الوَاجب وَضعُ اللّفظ لما تكثر الحَاجَةُ إلىٰ التّعبير عَنه.

وَالعِلم باللّغة وَاجب لِوجوب مَعرفَة الشّرع المتوقّف عليهَا.

والكلام عند المعتزلة هوالمنتظم منَ الحرُوف المَسمُوعَةِ المتميّزةِ المتواضعِ عليها، إذا صدر[4] عَن قادِر وَاحد. ويطلق[5] علىٰ الجملة المفيدة.

---

1 لا توجد (الفَصْلُ) في "أ" و"ب" و"ج" و"د" و"ه" وموجودة في "ط". 2 في "ه": كقوله.

3 عبد السلام بن محمد بن عبد الوهاب الجبّائي، من أبناء أبان مولىٰ عثمان: عالم بالكلام، من كبار المعتزلة. له آراء انفرد بها. وتبعته فرقة سميت "البهشمية" نسبة إلىٰ كنيته "أبي هاشم" وله مصنفات في الإعتزال كما لأبيه من قبله. ولد في بغداد سنة ٢٤٧ ه/٨٦١م، وفيها توفي سنة ٣٢١ ه/٩٣٣م. لاحظ الأعلام، خير الدين زركلي، ١٢ مجلدات، بيروت: ١٣٨٩ه / ١٩٦٩م، ج٤ /ص١٣٠-١٣١. 4 في "ب" و"ج" و"د" و"ه" و"ط": صدرت؛ ولعله مصحّف.

5 في "أ": تطلق. وفي "ج" و"ه" و"ط": يطلق؛ ولعلّه الصواب. وفي "د": وقد يطلق.

CHAPTER ONE

On Languages (*al-lughāt*)–Consisting of Six Discussions

1 Discussion One: On General Principles (*aḥkām kulliyyah*)

A party is of the opinion that languages are bequeathed (*tawqīfiyyah*), due to His word, the Exalted, 'And He taught Adam all the names'[1] and due to His word, the Exalted, 'And the differences of your tongues',[2] by which the intended meaning is 'languages'. Abū Hāshim upheld the opinion that languages are nomenclatural (*iṣṭilāḥiyyah*), due to His word, the Exalted, 'And we sent no envoy save with the tongue of his people'.[3]

It is not obligatory that there should be for every meaning an utterance (*lafẓ*); otherwise, it would necessitate the lack of an ending of the utterances. Rather, the obligation is to assign (*waḍʿ*) an utterance for that which is much in need of expression.

The knowledge of the [Arabic] language is obligatory because of the obligation to know the divine law (*sharʿ*), which is dependent thereupon.

According to the Muʿtazilah, speech (*kalām*) is that which is arranged from distinguished audible letters upon which there is agreement, if it is issued from an able individual. This [definition also] applies to the meaningful sentence (*al-jumlah al-mufīdah*).

---

1 Q. 2:31.

2 Q. 30:22.

3 Q. 14:4.

البَحْث الثاني: فِي تقسيم الألفاظِ[6]

وهو من[7] وجوه. أحدُها، أنّ اللّفظ[8] إن دَلّ علىٰ الزّمانِ المعيّن بصيغته فهوَ الفِعل، وإلّا فهوَ الإسمُ إن استقل بالدّلالةِ، وإلّا فهو الحرْف.

الثّاني، اللّفظ[9] إمّا مفرد وإمّا[10] مركّب، فالأوّل ما لا يدلّ جزؤه علىٰ جزء معناه[11] حين هو جزؤه والثاني | ما يدُل. 76a

الثّالث، اللّفظ وَ المعنىٰ إن اتحدا فإن منع نفس[12] تصوّر المعنىٰ من الشّركة[13] فهوَ العَلمُ أو[14] المضْمَرُ،[15] وإلّا فهو المتَواطئ إن تساوت أفراده فيه[16] والمشكك إن اختلفت[17]. وإن تكثرا فهي الألفاظ المتبَاينة. وإن تكثّر اللّفظ[18] خاصّة فهيَ المتَرادفة. وإن تكثّر المعنىٰ خاصّة، فإن كان قد وُضع أوّلا لمعنىً ثمّ استُعمل في الثّاني فهو المرْتَجل إن نقل لا لمنَاسبَة.[19] وإن نقل لمنَاسبة فهوَ المنقول اللّغَويّ[20] أو العرفيّ أو الشرعيّ إن غَلبَ المنقول إليه. وإلّا فَهو حقيقة بالنسبَة إلىٰ الأوّل، ومجاز بالنسبة إلىٰ الثّاني.

---

6 في "ه": اللّفظ. 7 في "ه": علىٰ. 8 في "ه": الأوّل اللّفظ. 9 في "ط": والثاني ان اللفظ. 10 في "د" و"ه": أو. 11 توجد في "ه": كزيد هو حسن. 12 لا توجد كلمة (نفس) في "ب" و"ج" و"د". 13 في الهامش الأيسر مِن "أ": فإن منع نفس تصوره من وقوع الشركة فيه الخ كذا في النسخة التي قرئت علىٰ الشيخ فخر الدين رحمه الله. 14 وردت واو العطف في كلّ من "ب" و"ج" و"د" و"ه" و"ط" وكذٰلك في النسخة المطبوعة وهو تصحيف والصحيح: (أو) كما وردت في "أ" فأثبتناه. 15 لا توجد العبارة (فإن منع نفي تصور المعنىٰ من وقوع الشّركة فهوَ العلم أو المضمر) في "ط". 16 لا توجد كلمة (فيه) في "ج". 17 في "ه": اختلف. 18 في "ه": الألفاظ. 19 لا توجد العبارة (وإن تكثّر اللّفظ خاصّة فهيَ المتَرادفة. وإن تكثّر المعنىٰ خاصّة فإن كان قد وضع أوّلا لمعنىً ثمّ استعمل في الثّاني فهو المرْتَجل إن نقل لا لمناسبَة) في "ط". 20 في "ه": الاصطلاحية.

2 Discussion Two: On the Classification of Utterances (*taqsīm al-alfāẓ*)

This classification is of [a number of] aspects.

The first of them, if the utterance by its form (*ṣīghah*) signifies a particular tense[4] then it is a verb (*fiʿl*), otherwise, if it is independent in its signification (*al-dalālah*), it is a noun (*ism*), and if not it is a particle (*ḥarf*).

The second, the utterance is either simple (*mufrad*) or compound (*murakkab*). The simple is the utterance whose part does not signify a part of its meaning when it is a part thereof. The complex (*murakkab*)[5] is the utterance whose part does signify a part of its meaning when it is a part thereof.

The third, if the utterance and the meaning are united and if its conceptualisation precludes the meaning from being shared, then it is a proper noun (*ʿalam*) or an implicit pronoun (*muḍmar*), otherwise it is univocal (*mutawāṭiʾ*) if all its members are similar, and equivocal (*mushakkak*) if they differ. If the utterance and meaning are numerous, then each is distinct from the other (*mutabāyinah*). If the utterance, in particular, is numerous then it is a synonym (*mutarādifah*). If the meaning, in particular, is numerous, then if it was initially assigned (*wuḍiʿa*) to one meaning and subsequently employed in another, it is an improvised meaning (*murtajal*) that is moved to an entirely new meaning that has no suitability (*munāsabah*). However, if it is moved to a new meaning due to its suitability—if the second meaning predominates over the first meaning in its usage—then it is a transfer by language (*al-manqūl al-lughawī*), a transfer by custom (*al-manqūl al-ʿurfī*), or a transfer by divine law (*al-manqūl al-sharʿī*). If the second meaning does not predominate, then its usage is veritative (*ḥaqīqah*) in relation to its first meaning, and figurative (*majāz*) in relation to the second meaning.

---

4 The Arabic word here is *al-zamān*, which simply means 'time'; 'tense' is employed in the first sense given by the *Oxford English Dictionary* (hereafter referred to as the OED), which is 'time'.

5 It is also known as *qawl*.

وإِنْ وضع لهما معًا[21] فهو المشترك بالنّسبة إليهما معًا والمجمل بالنّسبة[22] إلىٰ كل واحد منهما.

الرابع، اللَّفظ المفيد. إن لم يحتمل غير مَا فُهِمَ عَنه، فهوَ النَّص. وإن احتمَل فإن تساويا فالمجمل، وإلّا فالرّاجح ظاهر والمرجوح مؤوّل. والمشترك بين النصّ والظّاهر هوَ المحكَم، وبين المجمل والمؤوّل هوَ المتشابه.

الخامس، الإسم إن دلّ علىٰ الذّات فهو اسمُ العين. وإلّا فهو المشتقّ. ولابدّ في الإشتقاق من اتحاد بين اللّفظين، وتناسب في المعنىٰ والتركيب. ولا يشترَط بقاء المعنىٰ في صِدقه.

البحْث الثالث: في المشترِك

ذهب قوم إلىٰ امتناعه،[23] وهو خطأ، لا مكانه في الحكمة. وَ وجوده في اللّغة. نعم، هو علىٰ[24] خلاف الأصل، وإلّا لما حصل التّفاهُم حَالة التّخاطب من دون القرينة، ولما استفيد من السّمعيات شيء أصلاً. ويُعلم الإشتراك بنصّ أهل اللّغة، وبعلامات الحقيقة في كلا المعنيين. والأقرب أنّه لا يجوز استعمالُ اللفظ المشترك[25] في كلا معنييه،[26] إلّا علىٰ سَبيل المجاز، لأنه غير موضوع للمجموع[27]، من حيث هو[28] مجموع.

---

21 لا توجد في "ط": معًا. 22 في الهامش الأيسر مِن "أ": بالنسبة، صح، كذا وجد في النسخة التي قرئ علىٰ الشيخ فخر الدين. 23 في "د": امتناع المشترك. 24 لا توجد في "ط": علىٰ. 25 في الهامش الأيسر مِن "أ": كذا في النسخة التي قرئ علىٰ الشيخ فخر الدين رحمه الله. 26 في "ه": في المعنيين. و في "ط": كلا المعنيين. 27 في "ط": المجمع.
28 في "ط": أنه.

If it were assigned (*wuḍiʿa*) to both meanings together (*maʿan*), then it is a homonym (*mushtarak*) in relation to both of the meanings together, and ambiguous (*mujmal*) in relation to any one of its meanings.

The fourth, the utterance that conveys meaning (*al-lafẓ al-mufīd*): if the likelihood is to only understand one meaning from it, then it is an explicit designation (*al-naṣṣ*). If another meaning is likely and both are equal, then it is ambiguous (*al-mujmal*). Otherwise, the evident (*ẓāhir*) meaning is preferable (*rājiḥ*) and the interpreted (*al-muʾawwal*) meaning is outweighed (*al-marjūḥ*). The homonym between the explicit designation (*al-naṣṣ*) and the evident (*al-ẓāhir*) is a clear utterance (*al-muḥkam*), and between the ambiguous (*al-mujmal*) and interpreted (*al-muʾawwal*) is an unclear (*al-mutashābihah*) utterance.

The fifth, if the noun (*al-ism*) signifies the essence (*al-dhāt*) then it is a concrete noun (*ism al-ʿayn*). Otherwise, it is a paronymic noun (*ism al-mushtaqq*). It is a must regarding paronymy (*al-ishtiqāq*) that there is unity between the two utterances and harmony in their meaning and construction. The permanence of the meaning is not a condition regarding the truth thereof.

3 Discussion Three: On the Homonym (*al-mushtarak*)

Some people are of the opinion that homonyms are not allowed (*imtināʿ*), and this is an erroneous opinion, due to their philosophical possibility (*al-ḥikmah*) and the existence in language thereof. Accepted, the homonym is contrary to the principle (*aṣl*); otherwise no understanding would be achieved in discourse without the context (*qarīnah*), and nothing would have been conveyed at all by way of meaning from audible matters (*samʿiyyāt*).[6] The homonym is known through the explicit designation (*naṣṣ*) of the folk of the language and through the signs of the veritative (*ḥaqīqah*) in both of the meanings (*al-maʿnayayn*). The most favoured opinion is that the use of a homonym in both of its meanings is not permissible except in a figurative (*majāz*) manner, because it is not assigned (*mawḍūʿ*) for numerous meanings *qua* numerous meanings.

6 ʿAllāmah is alluding here, in particular, to revealed matters such as the Qurʾān and *ḥadīth*.

76b

البحث الرابع: في الحقيقة والمجاز

الحقيقة[29] : استعمال اللّفظ فيما وضع له، في الإصطلاح الّذي وقع به التّخاطب.

والمجاز : استعماله في غير ما وضع له، في أصل تلك المواضعة، للعلاقة.

والحقيقة: لغويّة، وعرفية، وشرعيّة. والحقّ أنّ الشرعيّة مجاز لغويّ، وإلّا لخرج القرآن عن كونه عربيّاً.

واعلم أنّ النّقل علىٰ خلاف الأصل، وإلّا لما حصَل التّفاهم حالة التّخاطب، قبل البحث عن التّعيين. ولتوقّفهِ علىٰ الوَضع الأوّل وَنسخهِ والوضع الثّاني، فيكون مَرجوحًا بالنّسبَة إلىٰ ما يتوقّف علىٰ الأوّل خاصّة.

وكذٰلك المجاز، علىٰ خلافِ الأصلِ، فيجب الحمل علىٰ الحقيقة، ما لم يدلّ دليل علىٰ عدم إرادتها. لأنّ الواضع إنّما وضع اللّفظ، ليكتَفي به في الدّلالة عَلىٰ ما وضعه له. وانّما يتمّ ذٰلك بإرادة المَعنىٰ الموضوع له اللّفظ، عند التجرّد عَن المعارض. ولأنَّ المجاز لوساوىٰ الحقيقة، لما حَصل التفاهمُ عند المخاطبة[30]، كما قلناه أوّلاً.

واعلم أنَّ المجاز واقع في القرآن والسنّة. و[31] قد يكون بالزيادة والنقصان، وبالنقل. [32]

ويعلم كون اللّفظ حقيقة ومجازًا بالنص من أهلِ اللّغةِ وَمبادرة المعنىٰ إلىٰ الذّهن في الحقيقَة، واستغنائه عن القرينةِ فيها[33] وبضدّ ذٰلك في المجَاز، وبتعلّقه بما يستَحيل تعلّقه عليه.

---

29 في "ه": فالحقيقة. 30 في "ه": حالة التخاطب. 31 توجد في "ه": هو.

32 توجد في "ط": وبالإستعارة. 33 لا توجد في "ج": فيها.

4 Discussion Four: On the Veritative (*al-ḥaqīqah*) and the Figurative (*al-majāz*)

The veritative is the usage of the utterance [in the meaning] for which it has been assigned (*wuḍiʿa*), according to the nomenclature within which discourse occurs.

The figurative is the usage of the utterance in [a meaning] other than that for which it was originally assigned (*muwāḍiʿah*) due to a connection [between the two meanings].

The veritative is linguistic, customary, or legal. The truth is that the legal veritative is linguistically figurative; otherwise, the Qurʾān would depart from being Arabic.

Let it be known that transference (*naql*) [of meaning] is contrary to the principle (*aṣl*), otherwise no understanding would be achieved in discourse prior to the discussion on determination [of a meaning], and because transference is dependant upon the initial assignment, the abrogation thereof, and the second assignment. Therefore, it is outweighed (*marjūḥ*) in relation to that which is dependent upon the initial [assignment], in particular.

Likewise, the figurative (*majāz*) is contrary to the principle (*al-aṣl*); therefore, it is necessary to predicate[7] it upon its veritative meaning, so long as there is no evidence signifying the absence of the intent (*irādah*) thereof, because the assigner only assigned the utterance to be enough to signify to what he assigned it. This can only be accomplished by intending the assigned meaning of the utterance (*mawḍūʿ*), whilst being free from any obliquity, and because if the figurative were equal to the veritative, no understanding would be achieved through discourse, as we have formerly stated.

Let it be known that the figurative occurs in the Qurʾān and the *Sunnah*, it may occur through addition (*ziyādah*) and subtraction (*nuqṣān*), or through transference (*naql*).

An utterance is known to be veritative or figurative through the explicit designation (*naṣṣ*) of the folk of the language. Regarding the veritative (*ḥaqīqah*), [it is known] by the immediacy of the meaning that suggests itself to the mind, and its needlessness of context. The opposite is the case for the figurative and by its connection to what is impossible to connect it to.

---

7 The word 'predicate' is given as a translation for *ḥaml*, according to third sense given in the OED—which is to affirm a statement or the like *on* some given grounds; hence 'to found a proposition, or argument, and so forth, *on* some basis or data'.

وقَد يكثر استعمال المجاز وتقلّ الحقيقة، فتصير الحقيقة مجازًا عرفيًا، والمجاز حقيقة عرفية، فيحمل علىٰ[34] أحدهما بالقرينة.

البحْث الخامس: في تعارض أحوال الألفاظ

النقل أولىٰ من الإشتراك، لاتّحاد المعنىٰ في النّقل دائمًا، فيحصل الفهم بخلاف المشترك.

والمجاز أولىٰ من الإشتراك، لأنّ اللّفظ إن تجرّد عَن القَرينةِ، حُمل عَلىٰ الحقيقة | والاّ فَعلىٰ المجاز. 77a

والإضمار أولىٰ مِنَ الإشتراك، لأنّ صحّته مشروطة بالعلم بتعيينه، بخلاف المشترك.

والتخصيص أولىٰ من الإشتراك، لأنه خير من المجاز.

والمجاز أولىٰ من النّقلِ، لافتقار النّقلِ إلىٰ الإتفاق[35] عليه بين أهل اللّغة.

والإضمار أولىٰ منه، لما تقدّم.

والتّخصيص أولىٰ من النّقل، لأنّه خير من المجاز. والمجاز أولىٰ من الإضمار لكثرته.[36]

والتخصيص أولىٰ من المجاز، لاستعمال[37] اللّفظ مع التخصيص في بعض موارده، ومن الإضمار لأنّه أدون من المجاز.

---

34 لا توجد في "ط": علىٰ. 35 في "د": لاتفاقه. 36 لا توجد العبارة (والتخصيص أولىٰ من النقل، لأنّه خير من المجاز. والمجاز أولىٰ من الإضمار لكثرته) في "ط". 37 في "ط": لأنه.

Sometimes the usage of the figurative is frequent and the usage of the veritative is infrequent. Consequently the veritative becomes customarily figurative and the figurative becomes customarily veritative and so it will be predicated on one of the two according to the context.

5 Discussion Five: On the Contradiction of the States of the Utterances (*aḥwāl al-alfāẓ*)

Transference (*naql*) is more appropriate than (*awlā*) homonymy (*ishtirāk*), because the meaning is always united in transference, thus understanding is achieved, contrary to the homonym.

The figurative is more appropriate than the homonymic; because, if the utterance were free from the context then it would be predicated upon the veritative, otherwise upon the figurative.

Ellipsis (*iḍmār*) is more appropriate than homonymy because its soundness is conditioned by the knowledge of its determination, contrary to the homonym.

Specification (*takhṣīṣ*) is more appropriate than homonymy because it is better than the figurative.

The figurative is more appropriate than transference (*naql*) because transference is in need of agreement thereupon among the folk of the language.[8]

Ellipsis (*iḍmār*) is more appropriate than transference for the reason presented earlier.

Specification (*takhṣīṣ*) is more appropriate than transference because it is better than the figurative.

The figurative (*majāz*) is more appropriate than ellipsis due to its numerosity.

Specification (*takhṣīṣ*) is more appropriate than the figurative (*majāz*) due to the use of the utterance with specification in some of its places, and it is more appropriate than ellipsis since it is less appropriate (*adwan*) than the figurative.

8 The literal translation of the Arabic is given here and through out the translation, namely 'the folk of the language (*ahl al-lughah*)', however, in each instance of usage 'Allāmah could be referring to the grammarians, lexicographers, or philologists of Arabic language.

البحْث السادس[38]: في تفسير حروف يحتاج إليها

"الواو" للجَمع المُطلق[39]. لعدم التناقض في مثل: "رَأَيْتُ زَيدًا وَعمرًا قَبلَه"، وللتكرار[40] لو قيل بعده. ولسؤال الصّحابة عن البداءة بالصّفا و[41] المروة[42]. ولأنّ أهل اللّغة قالوا إنّها كواوِ الجَمع. وقيل للتّرتيب للحاجة إلىٰ التّعبير عنه، وهو معارض بمطلق الجمع[43]، مع أولويّة[44] ما[45] قلناه.

و[46]"الفاء" للتّعقيب، علىٰ حسب ما يمكن.

و"في" للظرفيّة، تحقيقًا أو تقديرًا.

و"من" لابتداء الغاية، وللتّبعيض، والتّبيين، وصلة.

و"الباء" قيل للتّبعيض، فيما يتعدّى بنفسه.

و"إنّما" للحَصر بالنّقلِ.

---

38 لا توجد في "ط": البحْث السادس. 39 في "ب" و"ج" و"د": مطلقًا. 40 في "أ" و"د" و"ه" و"ط": التكرار. وفي "ج": للتكرار، ولعلّه الصّواب. 41 في "أ" و"ه": الصّفا أو. وفي "ج" و"د" و"ط": الصّفا و. ولعلّه الصّواب. 42 المحصول في علم أصول الفقه، فخر الدّين محمّد بن عمر بن الحسين الرّازي، ٦ مجلدات، بيروت: ١٤١٢ه / ١٩٩٢م، ج ١ / ص ٣٦٥-٣٦٦. 43 في "ه": الجمع بمطلق. 44 في الهامش الأيسر مِن "أ": ووجه الأولوية ان الجمع اعم من الترتيب فكونه حقيقة في الأعم أولىٰ من الأخص لأن الأعم اكبر وجودا. 45 لا توجد في "ط": ما. 46 لا توجد في "ط": و.

6 Discussion Six: A Well-Needed Commentary on Particles (*ḥurūf*)

The particle *wāw* denotes absolute union: due to the lack of contradiction in the following example: 'I saw Zayd and 'Amr before him (*qablahu*)'—denoting repetition (*takrār*) if it is said '[I saw Zayd and 'Amr] after him' (*ba'dahu*)—and due to the question of the companions about starting at Ṣafā and Marwah,[9] because the folk of the language have said that it is like the *wāw* denoting union. It is said that it is used for denoting sequence (*tartīb*) for the need of the expression thereof; this is oblique (*mu'āriḍ*) for absolute union, despite the appropriateness of what we have stated.

The particle *fā'* is used for succession (*ta'qīb*) whenever possible.

The particle *fī* is used to indicate time or place, whether tangible or intangible.

The particle *min* is used for denoting the commencement of the limit (*ibtidā' al-ghāyah*), division into parts (*tab'īḍ*), explanation (*tabyīn*), and conjointment (*ṣilah*).

It is said that the particle *bā'*, when used with transitive verbs, is for indicating division into parts.

The particle *innamā*, is used for limitation in accordance with that which has been reported.

---

9 These are two hills located near the Ka'bah. A part of the ritual of the *Ḥajj* and the *'Umrah* is the undertaking of a ritual walk (*sa'y*) between these hills; the question of the companions is related to the beginning of this ritual walk.

الفَصْلُ الثّاني[1]

فِي الأَحْكَام، وفيـه مبـاحث

الأوّل[2]: [في الفعـل]

الفعل إِمّا أن يكون علىٰ صفة، لأجلها يستحق فاعِله الذمّ، وهو القَبيحُ. أو لاَ، وهوَ الحسن. وَ القبيح حرام، ويقال محظور.[3] وَالحسن إما أن يذم تاركه شرعًا، وهو الواجب، ويسمّىٰ أيضًا[4] الفرض، أو لا يذمّ.[5] فإن كان فعله راجحًا في الشرع فهو المستحبّ، والمندوب والنفل[6] وَ التطوّع وَ السنّة. وإن كان مرجوحًا فهو المكروه. وإِن تساويا فمباح وحلال وطِلقٌ. فالأحكام هٰذه الخمسَة لا[7] غير.

الثاني: [في الحكم]

الحكم قد يكون صحيحًا، وهو في العبادات، ما وافق الشّريعة، وفي المعاملات،[8] ما يترتّب عليه أثره. وقد يكون فاسدًا وهو ما يقابلها. ويطلق عليه الباطل. 77b

الثالث: [في العبادات]

الإجزاء في العبادات ما أسقط الأمر. والأداء ما فُعل في وقته. والإعادة ما فُعل ثانيًا، لوُقوعِ خللٍ في الأوّل. والقضاء هو فعل الفائِت في غير وقته المحدود.[9]

---

1 لا توجد في "ط": الفَصْلُ الثّاني. 2 لا توجد في "ط": الأوّل. 3 في "ط": له
المحظور. 4 لا توجد في "ط": أيضا. 5 توجد في "ط": تاركه. 6 لا توجد في
"ط": النفل. 7 في "ط": اما. 8 في "د": العقود. 9 لا توجد في "ط": المحدود.

CHAPTER TWO

On Rulings (*al-aḥkām*)–Consisting of Six Discussions

1 Discussion One: On Action (*al-fiʿl*)

An action is either of such a quality that its actor becomes deserving of rebuke, and that is ugly (*al-qabīḥ*), or it is not, in which case that is beautiful (*al-ḥasan*). The ugly is forbidden (*ḥarām*) and it is also called the prohibited (*maḥẓūr*). [With regards to] the good (*ḥasan*): either the abstainer from it is blameworthy in law in which case it is obligatory (*wājib*), also known as duty (*farḍ*), or they are not blameworthy; if its performance is preferable in the law then it is esteemed (*mustaḥabb*), approved (*mandūb*), supererogatory (*nafl*), a voluntary act of obedience (*taṭawwuʿ*), or a recommended conduct (*sunnah*). If it is outweighed (*marjūḥ*) then it is disdained (*makrūh*). If both are equal then it is indifferent (*mubāḥ*), permitted (*ḥalāl*), or allowed (*ṭilq*). Thus, the rulings for actions are these five and no other.

2 Discussion Two: On the Ruling (*al-ḥukm*)

The ruling (*ḥukm*) may be sound (*ṣaḥīḥ*) and that in the acts of worship is what agrees with the divine law (*sharīʿah*), and, in social interactions (*muʿāmalāt*), whatever results from its effect; or it may be unsound (*fāsid*) and that is what opposes it [the above] and the term void (*bāṭil*) applies thereupon.[1]

3 Discussion Three: On the Acts of Worship (*al-ʿibādāt*)

Accomplishment (*ijzāʾ*), in the acts of worship, is that which makes the command annulled; performance (*adāʾ*) is a term given to an act carried out in its time; repetition (*iʿādah*) is an act performed for a second time due to a fault having occurred in the first performance; and compensatory performance (*qaḍāʾ*) is to perform a missed act of worship outside its fixed time.

1 Void, as a translation for *bāṭil*, is used in the seventh sense given by the OED, namely: having no legal force, not binding in law, being legally null, invalid, or ineffectual.

الرابع: [في الحسن والقبح]

الحكم بالحسن والقُبح قد يكون ضروريًا، كحسن الصّدق النّافع، وقبح الكذب الضّار، ونظريًا كحسن الصّدق الضّار، وقبح الكذب النّافع، وسمعيًا كحسن صوم شهر[10] رَمضان، وقبح صوم العيدِ.

لأنّا نعلم بالضّرورَة حسن الصّدق وقبح الكذب معَ تساويهما في المنافع. وللفرق[11] بين الصّادق والكاذب في مدّعي النبوّة. وللوثوق بوعده تعالىٰ[12] ووعيده. ومَن جعل ذٰلك شرعيًا أبطل هٰذه الأحكام ولزم[13] بطلان الشريعة.

الخامس: [في شكر المنعم]

شكر المنعم واجب عقلاً والضرورة قاضية به.

السّادس: [في الأشياء]

الأشياء قبل ورود الشّرع علىٰ الإباحة، لأنها نافعة خالية عن أمارة[14] المفسدة، ولا ضرر علىٰ المالكِ في تناولها فكانت مباحةً.

10 لا توجد في "ج" و"د" و"ط": شهر. 11 في "أ": الفرق. ولعلّه مصحّف. وفي "ج" و"د" و"ه" و"ط": للفرق. ولعلّه الصّواب. 12 لا توجد في "ط": تعالىٰ. 13 في "د": لزمه.
14 في "د" و"ط": امارات.

4 Discussion Four: On the Beautiful (*al-ḥusn*) and the Ugly (*al-qubḥ*)

The ruling of the beautiful and the ugly may be *a priori* (*ḍarūriyyan*), as in the case of the beauty of the beneficial truth, or the ugliness of the detrimental lie, or it may be theoretical (*naẓarī*), such as the beauty of the detrimental truth and the ugliness of the beneficial lie, or it may be subject to revealed sources (*samʿī*),[2] like the beauty of fasting in Ramaḍān and the ugliness of fasting on the day of ʿĪd.

We know *a priori* (*ḍarūrah*) the beauty of the truth and the ugliness of the lie, despite the equality of both in benefit. This is so we may distinguish between true and false claimants to prophecy, and so that we may be convinced of God's promise and His threat. Whosoever makes that to be [a matter] of the divine law renders these rulings void and necessitates the voidness of the divine law (*sharīʿah*).

5 Discussion Five: On Thanking the Benefactor (*shukr al-munʿim*)

Thanking the Benefactor (*munʿim*) is obligatory according to the intellect (*ʿaql*), and necessity decrees that.

6 Discussion Six: On Things (*al-ashyāʾ*)

All things are [a matter of] indifferency prior to the appearance of a revealed law, for all things are beneficial and free from the indication of unsoundness (*amārat al-mafsadah*). There is no harm for the owner [of an object] in consuming them,[3] for they are indifferent (*mubāḥ*) [for him].

2 Transmitted and narrated—revealed either through the Qurʾān or the *Sunnah*.

3 Here the pronoun refers to things (*ashyāʾ*).

الفَصْلُ الثّالِث[1]

فِي الأَوَامِرْ والنّواهِي، وفيه مباحث

الأوّل[2]: [في الامر]

الأمر هو اللّفظ الدّال علىٰ طلب الفعل علىٰ جهة الإستعلاء. وهو حقيقة في القول، مجاز في الفعل، وإلّا لزم الإشتراك. والطلب هو إرادة المأمور به.

والأمر إسم للصيغة الدالة علىٰ الترجيح لا لنفس الترجيح لأنهم قالوا الأمر من الضرب: "إضرب".

ودلالة الصيغة علىٰ الطلب، لا يتوقّف علىٰ الإرادة، لأنّها مَوضوعة له كغيرها من الألفاظِ، خلافًا للجُبائيين.[3]

1 لا توجد في "ط": الفَصْلُ الثّالِث. 2 لا توجد في "ط": الأوّل. 3 المراد بالجبائين أبي علي وابنه أبي هاشم، وهما: محمد بن عبد الوهّاب بن سلام الجبائي أبو علي: من رؤوس المعتزلة. وإليه نسبت الطائفة "الجبائية". له مقالات وآراء انفرد بها فى المذهب. نسبته إلىٰ جبىٰ (من قرىٰ البصرة) اشتهر في البصرة، ودفن بجبىٰ. له "تفسير" حافل مطول، ردّ عليه الأشعري؛ وابنه أبو هاشم عبد السّلام مرت ترجمته.

CHAPTER THREE

On the Commands (*al-awāmir*) and Prohibitions (*al-nawāhī*)–Consisting of Twenty-Two Discussions

1 Discussion One: On the Command (*al-amr*)

The command (*al-amr*) is an utterance that signifies a demand for an action by direction of superiority. It is veritative in utterance and figurative with regard to the action; otherwise, it would necessitate homonymy (*al-ishtirāk*).

The demand (*al-ṭalab*) is a desire (*al-irādah*) for what has been commanded.

The command (*al-amr*) is a name for the form (*al-ṣīghah*), which signifies preferment (*tarjīḥ*),[1] not a name for preferment itself, for they[2] have said that the command (*al-amr*) for striking (*ḍarb*) is: 'strike' (*iḍrib*).

The signification of the form for demand is not dependent upon the intent (*al-irādah*), because the meaning of demand is assigned to the form, as is the case with other utterances (*al-alfāẓ*), contrary to the view of the two Jubbāʾīs.

1 In other words, it signifies preferment for the action.

2 This alludes to the grammarians and scholars of legal theory.

البحْث الثاني[4]: في أن صيغة افعل للوجوب

ذهب الأكْثر إلىٰ أنّ صيغَة إفعَل[5] للوجوب. | لقوله تعالىٰ: ﴿مَا مَنَعَكَ أَلَّا تَسْجُدَ إِذْ 78a
أَمَرْتُكَ﴾ [سُورة الأعْرَاف:١٢] ولولا أنه للوجوب لما ذمّه. وكذا قوله تعالىٰ: ﴿وَإِذَا قِيلَ لَهُمُ ٱرْكَعُواْ لَا يَرْكَعُونَ﴾ [سُورة المرْسَلات:٤٨]. ولقوله عليه السلام: "لولا أن أشقّ علىٰ أُمّتي لأمرتهم بالسّواك"[6] مع ثبوت النّدبيّة. ولأنّ تارك المأمور[7] عاصٍ والعاصي يستحقّ العِقاب لقوله تعالىٰ: ﴿وَمَن يَعْصِ ٱللَّهَ وَرَسُولَهُ﴾ [سُورة الجِنّ:٢٣].

وقال آخرون: إنّه للقدر المشترك بين الوجوب والنّدب لأنّه قد استعمل فيهما والمجاز والإشتراك علىٰ خلاف الأصل وهو جيّد. إذا عرفت هٰذا فالأمر الوارد بعد الحَظر[8] كالأمر المبتدأ عند المحققين.

البحْث الثالث[9]: في أنّ الأمر لا يقتضي التّكرار

الحقّ أن الأمر[10] المطلق لا يقتضي الوحدة ولا التكرار خلافًا لقوم فيهما. لأنّ الصيغة وردت فيهما، والمجاز والإشتراك علىٰ خلاف الأصل، فوجب جعله حقيقة في القدر المشترك وهو مطلق طلب الماهية. ولقبوله التقييد بكل واحد منهما.

ولأنه لو دلّ علىٰ التكرار فإمّا[11] دائمًا فهو[12] باطل بالإجماع، أو بحسب وقت معين، وهو باطل[13] لإنتفاء دلالة اللّفظ عليه أو غير معين وهو تكليف ما لا يطاق.

4 لا توجد في "ط": البحْث الثاني. 5 في "ط": الأمر. 6 الكافي، أبو جعفر محمد بن يعقوب بن إسحاق الكليني، ٨مجلدات، طهران: ١٣٨٨هـ، ج ٣ / ص٢٢. 7 توجد في "هـ" و"ط": به. 8 لا توجد في "ط": بعد الحَظر. 9 لا توجد في "ط": البحْث الثالث.
10 لا توجد في "ط": الأمر. 11 توجد في "ط": أن يكون. 12 في "د" و"هـ" و"ط": وهو.
13 في "ج" و"د" و"هـ" و"ط": (باطل بالإجماع) ولعلّه الصّواب.

2 Discussion Two: On the Imperative Form of the Verb (*ṣīghat ifʿal*) being for Obligation

The majority are of the opinion that the imperative form of the verb is for obligation (*al-wujūb*), due to His word, the Exalted, 'what prevented you from prostrating when I commanded you',[3] and if it were not for obligation God would not have rebuked Iblīs. Similarly, His word, the Exalted, 'And when it is said to them bow down they do not bow down',[4] and due to his word, peace be upon him, 'Had I not thought it burdensome upon my *ummah* I would have commanded them to use the tooth–twig' (*al-siwāk*) despite the confirmability (*thubūt*) of its approval (*al-nudbiyyah*). Furthermore, the abstainer of what is commanded is disobedient and the disobedient deserve punishment, due to His word, the Exalted, 'whoever disobeys God and His Envoy…'[5]

Others are of the opinion that the imperative form of the verb is the common extent (*al-qadr al-mushtarak*) between obligation (*al-wujūb*) and that of approvedness (*al-nudb*) because it has been used regarding both of these cases; and that the figurative and the homonymic (*al-ishtirāk*) are contrary to the principle (*al-aṣl*), which is a good opinion. When this is understood, then, according to the verifiers (*muḥaqqiqīn*), the command which is set forth after a prohibition (*al-ḥaẓr*) is like the original command.

3 Discussion Three: On the Command (*al-amr*) Not Demanding Repetition (*al-takrār*)

The truth is that the absolute command (*al-muṭlaq*) neither demands a one-off (*al-waḥdah*) nor a repeat engagement, contrary to the view of some people regarding both of these cases, because the form has been set forth for both of them—and the figurative or homonymic use is contrary to the principle (*al-aṣl*). Therefore it is obligatory to render it veritative to a common extent and that is the absolute demand that seeks the quiddity of something—and because of the form's receptivity to delimitation (*taqyīd*) by either one of these meanings.

Furthermore, if it were to signify repetition, then this must either be perpetual, which is void due to consensus, or in accordance with a determined time (*waqt muʿayyan*), which is also void because of the lack of signification of the utterance thereupon, or in accordance with a determined time, which would be an injunction of what is not feasible (*taklīf mā lā yuṭāq*).[6]

---

3 Q. 7:12.

4 Q. 77:48.

5 Q. 72:23.

6 The word feasible is used in the first sense given in the OED, namely, 'capable of being done'

البحْث الرابع[14]: في أن الأمر لا يقتضي الفور ولا التراخي

الحقّ أن الأمر المطلق لا يقتضي الفور ولا التراخي خلافًا لقوم فيهما. لأن الأمر ورد بالمعنيين، فيكون حقيقة في القدر المشترك دفعًا للمجاز والإشتراك. ولأنه قابل للتقييد بهما.

إحتجوا بقوله تعالىٰ: ﴿مَا مَنَعَكَ أَلَّا تَسْجُدَ إِذْ أَمَرْتُكَ﴾ [سُورة الأَعْرَاف: ١٢]. ولأنّ التأخير إن كان دائمًا، انتفى الوُجوب. وإن كان إلىٰ وقت معيّن وجب وجود ما يدلّ
78b عليه في اللّفظ. وإن كان إلىٰ غير معيّن، لزم | تكليف ما لا يطاق.

والجواب عن الأوّل أنّه حكاية حال، فلعلّ أمره كان مقرونًا بما يدلّ علىٰ الفور، ولأن إبليسَ ترك السّجود لا بعزم الفِعل، فاستحقّ الذمّ لا مِن حيث التّأخير.

و[15] عن الثّاني أنّه منقوض بقوله: أوجبت عليك[16] الفعل، في أيّ وقتٍ شئت[17]. ثم التّحقيق أن التّأخير يجوز إلىٰ وقت معيّنٍ، وهو حصول ظنّ الموتِ بعد وقت الفِعل بلا فصل.

---

14 لا توجد في "ط": البحْث الرابع. 15 توجد في "ط": الجواب. 16 في "ط": عليكم.
17 في "ط": شئتم.

4 Discussion Four: On the Command Demanding Neither Expedition (*al-fawr*) Nor Postponement (*al-tarākhī*)

The truth is that, contrary to some people, the absolute command (*al-amr al-muṭlaq*) demands neither expedition nor postponement for the command has been set forth in both meanings, therefore it is veritative to the common extent (*al-qadr al-mushtarak*), rejecting figurativeness and homonymy, and it is receptive to delimitation by either of the two.

They have argued on the basis of His word, the Exalted: 'What prevented you from prostrating when I commanded you?'[7] Contending that, if the deferment (*al-ta'khīr*) was perpetual, then the obligation (*al-wujūb*) would cease to exist, and if it were until a determined time then it would be obligatory for there to exist within the utterance that which signifies it, and if it were until a non-determined time then it would necessitate an injunction of what is not feasible.

The answer to the first argument is that it is an account of a state and perhaps the command thereof was linked with what signifies expedition; because Iblīs abstained from the prostration without the resolve for the action and so he became deserving of rebuke, and not because of the deferment.

The statement: 'I have made the action obligatory upon you in whatever time you wish to do so' disproves the second argument. Furthermore, the fact is that the deferment is permissible until a determined time, and that is the realisation of the probability of death following the time of the action without intermission.

7 Q. 7:12.

البحْث الخامس: في أنّ الأمر المشروط يعدم[18] عند عدم الشرط

لأنّ قضيّة الشّرط ذٰلك ولعَدم الإستلزام وجودًا. فلولا[19] التّلازم[20] عدمًا لكان كلّ شيء شرطًا لغيره ولأنّه مفهوم منه. ولهٰذا سأل يَعْلى بن أميّة[21] عَن سبب القصر مع الأمن ولا يلزم تكرر الأمر المعلق[22] عليه، ولا علىٰ الصفة بتكريرهما. لعدم التكرّر في قول السّيد لعبده: "إِنْ دَخَلْتَ السُّوقَ فَاشْتَرِ اللَّحْمَ" ولأنّ مطلق التّعليق أعمّ منه مع قيد التّكرار[23] ولا دلالة للعامّ علىٰ الخاصّ.

البحْث السادس: في أن الأمر المقيّد بالصفة لا يعدم بعدمها

لأنّه لو دلّ تقييد الحكم بالوصفِ علىٰ نفيه عمّا عَداه، لدَلّ التّخصيص بالإسم، علىٰ نفيه عما عداه، والتّالي باطل إتّفاقًا فكذا المقدَّم. بيان الشّرطية أنّ المقتضي للنّفي هناك إنّما هو ثبوت غرض في التّخصيص، وانتفاء الأغراض سوىٰ النّفي، وهٰذا ثابت في الإسم.

ولأنّ التّقييد[24] قَد وُجِد[25] من دون التخصيص، كما في قوله تعالىٰ: ﴿وَلَا تَقۡتُلُوٓاْ أَوۡلَٰدَكُمۡ خَشۡيَةَ إِمۡلَٰقٍ﴾ [سُورة الإِسْرَاء:٣١]، ﴿وَمَن قَتَلَهُۥ مِنكُم مُّتَعَمِّدٗا فَجَزَآءٞ مِّثۡلُ مَا قَتَلَ مِنَ ٱلنَّعَمِ﴾ [سُورة المَائِدَة:٩٥].

---

18 في الهامش الأيسر مِن "ب"، و في الهامش الأيمن مِن "ج"، و في "د" و "ه": عدم. 19 في "ط": ولولا. 20 في "ه": الاستلزام. 21 يعلىٰ بن أمية بن أبي عبيدة (واسمه عبيد، ويقال زيد) ابن همام التميمي الحنظلي. وهو صحابي، من الولاة. ومن الأغنياء الأسخياء من سكان مكة، كان حليفًا لقريش. وأسلم بعد الفتح. وشهد الطائف وحنينًا وتبوك مع النبي (ص). لاحظ الأعلام للزركلي: ج ٩ / ص٢٦٩. 22 في "ط": المتعلق. 23 توجد في "ه": والوحده. 24 توجد في "د": بالصفة. 25 في الهامش الأيمن مِن "أ": قد وجد.

5 Discussion Five: On the Conditioned Command (*al-amr al-mashrūṭ*) being Non-Existent When the Condition (*al-sharṭ*) is Non-Existent

This is due to the matter of the condition being as such, and there being nothing which necessitates [the command's] existence [if the condition is non-existent]. For if there were no correlation in terms of lack [of fulfilment between the condition and the conditioned command], then everything would be a condition for everything else; and also because [the conditioned command] is implied by the [existence of the condition]. It was due to this that Yaʿlā b. Umayyah enquired about the reason for the shortening of the prayer (*al-qaṣr*) in times of security. Furthermore, it is not necessary to repeat the command that is dependent upon a condition or attribute (*al-ṣifah*) with the repetition of either of the two (*takrīr*), because there is no repetition in the master's statement to his slave, 'If you enter the market then buy meat'. This is because the absoluteness of the dependence upon a condition (*al-taʿlīq*) is more general than it, despite the delimitation (*qayd*) of the repetition (*al-takrār*), and there is no signification for the general (*al-ʿāmm*) over the specific (*al-khāṣṣ*).

6 Discussion Six: On the Command that is Delimited by an Attribute (*al-amr al-muqayyad bi al-ṣifah*) not Becoming Non-Existent With the Non-Existence of the Attribute

This is because: first, if a ruling delimited by an attribute (*waṣf*) signifies that it[8] excludes anything that is contrary to it, then specification [of something] by name signifies that anything contrary to it is excluded. The latter is void on the basis of agreement, thus, such is the case regarding the former.[9]

Elucidation of the nature of conditionality: the demand for the exclusion (*al-nafī*), here, is only confirmable (*thubūt*) by the objective regarding specification (*al-takhṣīṣ*) and the lack of objectives (*al-aghrāḍ*) is equivalent to exclusion (*al-nafī*), and this is confirmed (*thābit*) in [the case of] the name (*al-ism*).

Second, delimitation has been found without specification, as in His word, the Exalted, 'And slay not your children for fear of poverty',[10] and 'Whosoever of you slays it wilfully, there shall be recompense—the like of what he has slain, in flocks'.[11]

8 This pronoun refers to the attribute.

9 The author now begins to explain the connection between the latter and the former: i.e., restriction by a noun's being similar to the cases where there is restriction by an attribute.

10 Q. 17:31.

11 Q. 5:95.

البحْث السابع: في الواجب المخير

الأمر بالأشياء علىٰ سبيل التخيير، يقتضي وصف كل واحد منها بالوجوب. وعلىٰ معنىٰ أنّ المكلّف لا يحلّ له الإخلالُ بالجميع، ولا يجب عليه الإتيان|بالجميع. وأيّها 79a
فَعَلَ كان واجبًا بالأصالة، والتّعيين موكول[26] إلىٰ اختياره. وَإِنْ فَعَلَ الجميع استحقّ الثّواب علىٰ فِعْلِ أمور، كلّ واحد منها واجب مخيّر. وأمّا مَا يُقال، من أنّ الواجب منها واحد، غير معيّن عندنا، وهو معيّن عند الله فهو باطل. لأن التعيين يقتضي إيجاب ذٰلك المعيّن، وعدم جواز تركه وقد وقع الإتفاق علىٰ التخيير، ومعناه جواز ترك كل واحد بشرط الإتيان بالآخر. وذٰلك تناقض.

البحْث الثامن: في الواجب الموسع

اعلم أنه لا يجوز أن يكون وقت العبادة يقصر عن فعلها إلّا أن يكون المقصود منه[27] القضاء، ويجوز أن يساويه إجماعًا. [28] والحقّ أنّه[29] يجوز أن يكون الوقت يفضل منه، وهوَ الواجب الموسع، وهو ثابت لقوله تعالىٰ: ﴿أَقِمِ ٱلصَّلَوٰةَ لِدُلُوكِ ٱلشَّمْسِ إِلَىٰ غَسَقِ ٱلَّيْلِ﴾ [سُورة الإِسْرَاء:٧٨].

وتخصيص آخر الوقت[30] بالوجوب أو أوّله – كما ذهب إليهما من لا تحقيق له[31] – ترجيح من غير مرجّح. واعلم أنّ هٰذا الواجب في الحقيقة، يرجع إلىٰ الواجب المخير، فكأن الشارع قال له: "ٱفْعَلْ إِمّا فِي أَوّلِ ٱلْوَقْتِ أَوْ وَسَطِهِ أَوْ آخِرِهِ". وإذا لم يبقَ من الوقت إلّا قدر فعله، تعيّن عليه لا محالة وحرم تركه.

---

26 في "ه": موكولا. 27 في الهامش الأيسر من "أ": منه. وفي "ط": غرضه. 28 لا توجد في "ط": ويجوز أن يساويه اجماعًا. 29 لا توجد في "ط": والحق أنه. 30 توجد في "د": ما هو. 31 لا توجد في "ط": له.

7 Discussion Seven: On the Chosen Obligation (*al-wājib al-mukhayyar*)

A command regarding matters by way of choice (*al-takhyīr*) demands the description of each one of them as obligatory. This means that the charged agent (*mukallaf*) is not permitted to go beyond all the choices, nor is the performance of all obligatory upon him, and, of them, whatever he performs is deemed obligatory in principle (*wājib bi al-aṣālah*), and the determination (*taʿyīn*) [of one of the choices] is entrusted to his choosing (*ikhtiyār*). If the charged agent (*mukallaf*) performs all of the choices he would be worthy of the reward for the performance of matters, each one of which is a chosen obligation (*wājib mukhayyar*). However, the doctrine that the obligation from them is one, [which is] not determined (*muʿayyan*) nigh us, whilst it is determined nigh God, is void. This is because determination (*taʿyīn*) demands the obligation (*ījāb*) of that which is determined (*muʿayyan*), and the lack of permissibility of abstaining (*tark*) from it. Agreement has occurred regarding choice (*takhyīr*), and the meaning thereof is the permissibility to abstain from each one with the condition of the performance of the other, and that is a contradiction.

8 Discussion Eight: On the Obligation that is to be Performed within a Broad Period of Time (*al-wājib al-muwassaʿ*)

Let it be known that it is not permissible for the time of the act of worship to be less than it takes to perform it, except where the intention thereof is compensatory performance (*al-qaḍāʾ*). According to consensus (*ijmāʿ*) it is permissible that the time be equal to it. The fact is that, it is permissible that the time exceeds it and that is the obligation that is to be performed within a broad period of time (*al-wājib al-muwassaʿ*), and this is confirmed (*thābit*) due to His word, the Exalted, 'Perform the prayer at the sinking of the sun until the darkening of the night'.[12]

The specification of the last portion of the time with obligation or the foremost of it—as is the opinion on these two matters of those who possess no verification—constitutes a preferment without a preferrer (*tarjīḥ min ghayr murajjiḥ*). Let it be known that this obligation, in reality, refers to the chosen obligation. Thus, it is as if the Lawgiver said to him, 'perform, either at the onset of the time, or its midmost, or its end', when only the time for the performance thereof remains then without doubt it is determined (*taʿayyana*) upon him and the abstaining thereof is forbidden.

12 Q. 17:78.

واعلم أن السّيد المرتضىٰ[32] اوجب العزم لينفصل من المندوب. وعلىٰ الوجه الذي لخّصناه -من أنّه راجع إلىٰ الواجب المخيّر- إنفصل[33] عن المندوب، ولا حاجة إلىٰ العزم.

البحْث التاسع: في الواجب علىٰ الكفاية

إذا تعلّق غرض الشّارع بتحصيل الفعل من الجماعة لا علىٰ سَبيل الجمع، كان واجبًا علىٰ كلّ واحد، ويسقط عنه[34] بفعل غيره.

فإن ظنّ جماعةٌ فِعْلَ غيرهم له، سَقَطَ عنهم وإلّا فلا. ولو ظنّ كل طائفة[35] قيام

79b غيرهم | به، يسقط عن الجميع.

32 توجد في "ه": رحمه الله. علي بن الحسين بن موسى بن محمد بن موسى بن ابراهيم بن الامام موسى الكاظم (ع) السيد الشريف المرتضى علم الهدى أبو القاسم أخو الشريف الرضي الأكبر منه فإنه ولد ٣٥٥ ه وولد الرضي ٣٥٩ ه، وتوفي المرتضى في الثمانين من عمره في ٤٣٦ ه، ويقال له الثمانيني. كان عماد الشيعة ونقيب الطالبيين ببغداد وأمير الحاج والمظالم بعد أخيه الرضي، وهو منصب والدهما. وكان يدرُّ على تلاميذه، فعلى أبي جعفر الطوسي، يدرّ كل شهر اثني عشر ديناراً، وعلى القاضي ابن البرّاج ثمانية دنانير، وعمدة مشايخه المفيد. ومع ذلك فقد روى هو عن بعض مشايخ المفيد أيضاً، منهم أبو عبد الله محمد بن عمران المرزباني البغدادي المتوفى ٣٧٨ ه، فإنه يروي عنه كثيراً، منها "حديث خطبة الزهراء (ع)"، رواه عنه في "الشافي"، وذكرت ديوانه مفصلاً في "الذريعة ٩: ٧٣٥ - ٧٣٦". وفصّل فهرس مؤلفاته في "أدب المرتضى". لاحظ طبقات أعلام الشيعة، النابس في القرن الخامس، الشيخ آغا بزرگ الطهراني، بيروت: ١٣٩١ ه/ ١٩٧١ م، ص ١٢٠ - ١٢١. 33 في "ج": منفصل. وفي "د" و"ه" و"ط": انفصل. 34 لا توجد في "ط": عنه. 35 "ب": منهما.

Let it be known that al-Sayyid al-Murtaḍā makes the resolve obligatory for it to be separated from what is approved (*al-mandūb*). However, on account of what we have briefly explained, it refers to a chosen obligation, [thus] it is separated from the approved (*al-mandūb*) and there is no need for the resolve.

9 Discussion Nine: On the Obligation on All Sufficed by the Performance by Some (*al-wājib ʿalā al-kifāyah*)

When the objective of the Lawgiver depends upon the realisation of the action by the congregation, not collectively, then it is an obligation upon every individual, which is annulled for all by its performance by any one [or more] of them.

If the congregation deems it probable that others have performed it, then it is annulled for them, otherwise not, and if each group deems it probable that the other has risen to it, then it is annulled for all.

البحْث العاشر: في وجوب ما يتوقّف عليه الواجب المطلق

الواجب قسمان، مطلق كالصلاة، ومقيد كالزكاة. فالثّاني لا يستلزم[36] وجوب ما يتوقّف عليه من القيد. والأوّل يستلزم وجوب ما لا يتم إلاّ به، إذا كان مقدورًا لأنّ الأمر ورد مطلقًا، فلو لم تجب المقدمة لكان الفعل واجبًا، حال عدمها وهو تكليف ما لا يطاق.

البحْث الحادي عشر: في أنّ الأمر بالشّيء يستلزم النّهي عن ضدّه

قد بيّنا أنّ الأمر يستلزم الوجوب، ولا بدّ في الوجوب[37] من المنع من الترك. فالأمر[38] يستلزم النهي عن الترك، وليس هو نفسه، كما ذهب إليه من لا[39] تحصيل[40] له.

البحْث الثاني عشر: في أنه إذا نُسِخَ الوجوب بقي الجواز

والدّليل عليه أنّ الوجوب ماهية مركبة، من الإذن في الفعل والمنع من الترك. ورفع المركب لا يستلزم رفع جزئيْه معًا، بل أحدهما لا بعينه. وإنما قلنا ببقاء الجواز، لوجود اللّفظ الدّال عليه وهوَ الأمر.

---

36 توجد في "ط": وجوبه. 37 في "ط": الواجب. 38 توجد في "ط": بالشيء.
39 لا توجد في "ط": لا. 40 في "ب": تحقيق.

10 Discussion Ten: On the Obligation (*wujūb*) upon Which the Absolute Obligation (*al-wājib al-muṭlaq*) Depends

The obligation (*al-wājib*) is of two classes: absolute (*muṭlaq*), such as the ritual prayer (*ṣalāh*), and delimited (*muqayyad*), such as the prescribed alms (*zakāh*). The latter does not necessitate the obligation of what depends upon it of the delimitation (*al-qayd*), whilst the former necessitates the obligation of what is not completed save by it, if it were decreed. This is because the command (*amr*) is set forth in absolute terms (*muṭlaqan*), and if the prerequisite (*al-muqaddimah*) were not obligatory then the action would be obligatory whilst it were lacking—and that is an injunction of what is not feasible.

11 Discussion Eleven: On the Command of a Thing (*al-amr bi al-shay'*) Necessitating the Prohibition (*al-nahy*) of its Opposite (*ḍiddihi*)

We have elucidated that a command necessitates obligation (*al-wujūb*), and regarding the obligation it is a must that abstainment not be permitted (*al-manʿ*). Therefore, the command necessitates the prohibition (*al-nahy*) of the abstainment, and not the prohibition itself, as is the opinion, about it, of one who has acquired no knowledge.

12 Discussion Twelve: When the Obligation is Abrogated (*nusikha*) the Permissibility (*al-jawāz*) Remains

The argument (*al-dalīl*) for this is that obligation (*al-wujūb*) is a compound quiddity (*māhiyyah murakkabah*) of the permission (*al-idhn*) for the action and of the prohibition (*al-manʿ*) of the abstainment. The removal of the compound (*al-murakkab*) does not necessitate the removal of both of its parts together, rather [it removes only] one of the two, not the totality thereof. We only uphold the opinion on the remaining of permissibility because of the existence of the utterance that signifies thereupon, and that is the command.

البحث الثالث عشر: في امتناع التكليف بالمحال

تكليف ما لا يطاق قبيح بالضّرورة، والله تعالىٰ لا يفعل القبيح[41] لحكمته، فاستحال منه وقوع التكليف بالمحال. ونزاع الأشعرية في ذٰلك باطل، وقد بيّناه في كتبنا الكلامية. ومن هٰذا الباب تكليف[42] المكره، إن بَلَغَ الإكراه إلىٰ حدّ الإلجاء[43] وإلّا كان جائزًا.

البحث الرابع عشر: في أن التّكليف بالفروع لا يتوقف علىٰ الإيمان

ذهبت الحنفيّة إلىٰ أنَّ الكفّار غير مخاطبين بفروع العبادات. وهو[44] خطأ لقيام المقتضي، وهو الأمر مع إنتفاء المانع إذا المانع عندهم هو الكفر لا غير وهو لا يصلح للمانعيّة. لأن الكافر يتمكن من الإيمان حتّى يتمكّن من الإتيان بالفروع. ولأنه تعالىٰ 80a
يعاقبهم علىٰ ذٰلك لقوله تعالىٰ: ﴿مَا سَلَكَكُمْ فِي سَقَرَ ۝ قَالُوا لَمْ نَكُ مِنَ الْمُصَلِّينَ﴾ [سُورة المدَّثِّر: ٤٢،٤٣].

احتجوا بأنّه[45] حالَ الكفر لا يصحّ منه وبعده يسقط عنه.

والجواب أنّ المراد بالوجوب هنا مؤاخذتهم علىٰ تركها في الآخرة مع استمرار كفرهم.

---

41 توجد في "ج" و"ه" و"ط": القبيح. 42 في "د": التكليف. 43 توجد في "ط": به.
44 في "د": هٰذا. 45 في "د" و"ط": بأنّ.

13 Discussion Thirteen: On the Impossibility of an Injunction (*taklīf*) of the Impossible (*al-muḥāl*)

An injunction (*taklīf*) of what is not feasible is ugly through necessity (*qabīḥ bi al-ḍarūrah*) and God, the Exalted, does not do anything [ugly] due to His wisdom. Therefore, the occurrence of an injunction (*taklīf*) of the impossible (*al-muḥāl*) from Him is impossible. The controversy of the Ashʿarīs concerning this matter is void, as we have elucidated in our books on theology.[13] The injunction of the compelled, falls within this category, if the compulsion reaches the extent of denying any choice,[14] otherwise it is permissible.

14 Discussion Fourteen: An Injunction (*al-taklīf*) on Ritual (*al-furūʿ*) is not Dependant upon Faith (*al-īmān*)

The Hanafiyyah are of the opinion that the disbelievers are not addressed regarding the ritual acts of worship. That is incorrect, due to the arising of the demand, which is the command (*al-amr*), with the absence of a preventer (*al-māniʿ*), since, according to them, the preventer is none other than disbelief (*al-kufr*). This, however, is not appropriate for prevention, because a disbeliever is capable of faith, he is even capable of the performance of the ritual, and because He, the Exalted, shall chastise them regarding that, due to His word, the Exalted, 'What thrusted you into *Saqar*?[15] They shall say, "We were not of those who prayed..."'[16]

The Ḥanafīs have argued that in the state of disbelief (*al-kufr*) [such acts] are not correct and after the state of disbelief,[17] those acts are annulled for him.

The answer is that the meaning of obligation (*al-wujūb*) here[18] is that they are held to account in the Hereafter for abstaining from them as well as for their continuous disbelief.

---

13 See 'Allāmah al-Ḥillī, *Nahj al-ḥaqq wa kashf al-ṣidq*, Beirut, 1982, pp. 99–100. For the Ashʿarī position, see Fakhr al-Dīn al-Rāzī, *al-Maṭālib al-ʿāliyyah fī al-ʿilm al-ilāhiyyah*, Beirut, 1407 AH/1987, vol. III, pp. 305–15.

14 In other words if compulsion reaches a level at which choice is denied, then it would be considered ugly through necessity.

15 *Saqar* is one of the Qur'ānic terms for the Hellfire.

16 Q. 74:42–43.

17 'After the state of disbelief refers' to when the disbeliever accepts the faith, then all the former injunctions are annulled for him. In other words their compensatory performance is annulled.

18 That the rituals (*furūʿ*) are necessary for the non-believers.

البحْث الخامس عشر: في أن الأمر يقتضي الاجزاء

الحقُّ ذٰلك.

والمراد بالإجزاء خروجه عن عهدة التّكليف، بفعل المأمور به علىٰ وجهه. لأنّه لولا ذٰلك لكان الأمر إمّا أن يتناول عين ما فَعَلَ فيلزم تحصيل الحاصِل أوغَيْره، فلا يكون المأتي به تمام ما أمر به والتقدير خلافه.

وذهب أبو هاشم إلىٰ أنّه لا يقتضيه لأنّ الحجّ الفاسِدَ مأمور به ولا يجزئ. والجواب عنه أنه مجزٍ[46] بالنسبة إلىٰ الأمر الوارد به[47]. وغير مجزٍ[48] بالنّسبة إلىٰ الأمر الأوّل.

البحْث السادس عشر: في أنّ الإخلال هل يقتضي وجوب القضاء[49]

الحقّ إن الأمر إذا كان مقيّدًا بوقت ولم يفعل فيه، لا يقتضي وجوب القضاء، وإنّما يجب القضاء بأمر جديد. لأنّ الأمر الأوّل لا يتناول ما عدا وقته فلا يدلّ عليه، ولأنّ أوامر الشّرع تارة يُستعقب[50] القضاء وتارة لا يستعقبه[51]. فدلّ[52] علىٰ أن مجرّد الأمر الأوّل غير كافٍ في القضاء.

46 في "ب" و"ج" و"د" و"ه": مجزى. 47 توجد في "ط": ثانيا. 48 كذا في "أ" و"د" و"ط"، وفي "ب" و"ج": مجزٍء، وفي "ه": مجزى. 49 توجد في "د": ام لا. 50 في "د" و"ه": تستعقب. 51 في "د" و"ه": تستعقبه. 52 لا توجد في "ط": ولأنّ أوامر الشرع: تارة يُستعقب القضاء، وتارة لا يستعقبه. فدل.

15 Discussion Fifteen: On the Command (*al-amr*) Demanding Accomplishment (*al-ijzāʾ*)

That is the truth.

The meaning of accomplishment (*al-ijzāʾ*) is to be free from the charge of the injunction (*ʿuhdat al-taklīf*) by performing what is commanded as prescribed. If this were not the case then the command would either include the essence of what was performed, in which case it would be the realisation of the realised (*taḥṣīl al-ḥāṣil*), or other than it, in which case the performed would not be all of what was commanded; this is contrary to the assumption.

Abū Hāshim is of the opinion that the command (*al-amr*) does not demand accomplishment (*al-ijzāʾ*) because a defective *ḥajj* is commanded and yet it is not accomplished. The answer to his view is that it is accomplished in relation to the command that is set forth regarding it and it is not accomplished in relation to the first command.

16 Discussion Sixteen: On Whether the Impairment (*ikhlāl*) [of an act of worship] Demands the Obligation of [its] Compensatory Performance (*al-qaḍāʾ*)

The truth is that if a command is delimited by time and is not performed therein, then it does not demand the obligation (*wujūb*) of a compensatory performance (*al-qaḍāʾ*) and the compensatory performance only becomes obligatory through a new command. This is because the first command does not include its time and therefore it does not signify thereupon. Furthermore, because sometimes the compensatory performance (*al-qaḍāʾ*) follows the commands of the law and at other times it does not. Thus signifying that the sole first command is not sufficient regarding the compensatory performance (*al-qaḍāʾ*).

البحْث السابع عشر: الأمر بالأمر بالشيء ليسَ أمرًا بذٰلك الشيء

لأنّ قوله عليه السلام: "مروهم بالصّلاة وهم أبناء سبع"[53] لا يقتضي الوجوب. والأمر بالماهية الكليّة، ليسَ أمرًا بشيء من جزئيّاتها لأنّ الكليّ مغاير للجزئيّ وغير مستلزم له.

البحْث الثامن عشر[54]: في أنّ المعدوم غير مأمور

الأشاعرة خالفت سائر العقلاء في ذٰلك. والدّليلُ عليه أنّ الأمر من غير مأمور عبث. وهو قبيح والله تعالىٰ لا يفعل القبيح. والنبيّ | عليه السلام غير آمر لنا[55] حقيقةً، بل هو 80b
مخبر عن الله تعالىٰ بأنّه[56] يأمر كلّ واحد بما جاء به حال وجوده.

وكذٰلك الغافل غير مأمور، لأنّ تكليف مَنْ لا يَعلم الخطاب -حَال التكليف-، تكليف بما لا يطاق. ولقوله عليه السلام: "رُفِعَ القَلمُ عَن ثَلاث..."[57] الحديث.[58]

البحْث التاسع عشر: [في وجوب قصد الطاعة]

يجب علىٰ المأمور قصد الطّاعة لقوله تعالىٰ: ﴿وَمَآ أُمِرُوٓاْ إِلَّا لِيَعۡبُدُواْ ٱللَّهَ مُخۡلِصِينَ لَهُ ٱلدِّينَ﴾ [سُورة البَيِّنَة:٥]. ولقوله[59] عليه السلام: "إنّما الأَعْمَالُ بِالنّيات...".[60] وهٰذا حكم واجب في كل عبادة، سوىٰ شيئين: النّظر المعرِّف للوجوب، وإرادة الطّاعة.

---

53 الكافي ج ٣/ص ٤٠٩. 54 لا توجد في "ط": (لا يقتضي الوجوب... البحْث الثامن عشر). 55 توجد في "د": الآن. 56 في "أ" و"د" و"ط": أنه. وفي "ج" و"هـ": بأنّه. ولعلّه الصّواب. 57 كتاب الخصال، الشيخ الصدوق أبي جعفر محمد بن علي بن الحسين بن بابويه القمي، طهران: ١٣٨٩هـ / ١٣٤٨ش، ص ١٧٥. 58 لا توجد في "ط": الحديث. 59 في "د": قوله. 60 تهذيب الأحكام، شيخ الطّائفة أبي جعفر محمد بن الحسن الطّوسي، ١٠ مجلدات، طهران: ١٣٩٠هـ، ج ١/ ص٨٣.

17 Discussion Seventeen: The Command (*al-amr*) to Command Something (*al-amr bi al-shay'*) does not Constitute a Command for that thing

For the saying of the Prophet, peace be upon him, 'Command them to pray when they are seven years old' does not demand obligation (*al-wujūb*).

Furthermore, the command for the whole quiddity (*al-māhiyyah al-kulliyyah*) is not a command for some of its parts. This is because the whole (*al-kullī*) is different from the part (*juz'ī*) and does not necessitate it.

18 Discussion Eighteen: The Non-Existent (*al-ma'dūm*) is not Commanded

The Ash'ārīs have opposed all other reasonable people (*'uqalā'*) in this matter.[19]

The argument for this is that the commanding of the one who is not charged (*ghayr ma'mūr*) is useless and that is ugly and God, the Exalted, does nothing ugly. The Prophet, peace be upon him, in the true sense is not the one who commands us; rather, he announces on behalf of God, the Exalted, of what God commands everyone in the state of their existence according to what he has brought forth.

Likewise, the one who is unmindful (*al-ghāfil*) is not charged (*ghayr ma'mūr*), since the injunction of the one who does not know the address (*al-khiṭāb*)—the state of the injunction—would constitute an injunction of what is not feasible (*taklīf bimā lā yuṭāq*). And due to his saying, peace be upon him, 'The law does not apply to the following three…'

19 Discussion Nineteen: On the Obligation for the Intention (*qaṣd*) of Obedience (*al-ṭā'ah*)

It is obligatory for the one who is commanded to have an intention of obedience (*ṭā'ah*) due to His word, the Exalted: 'They were commanded not save to worship God sincerely'[20] and due to his saying, peace be upon him, 'Verily, deeds are through intentions'. This is an obligatory ruling in every act of worship except in two cases: the perception that informs of the obligation, and the will to obey.

---

19 Ash'arī theology is based on a firm subordinating of the laws of causality to God's will. Thus, according to them, if he willed it, God could command the non-existent.

20 Q. 98:5.

البحْث العشرون: [في وقت تعلق الامر]

المأمور[61] يصير مأمورًا قبل الفعل، لأنّ القدرة شرط الأمر وهي إنّما تحقّق قبل الفعل، لأنّ الفعل حال وجوده واجب فلا قدرة عليه، فلا يتعلق به أمر.

وعند الأشاعرة أنّه مأمور حال[62] الفِعل، لأنّها[63] حالة[64] القدرة[65] وقد بيّنا فساده في علم الكلام.

البحْث الحادي والعشرون: في النهي

الخلاف في أنّ النّهي يقتضي التّحريم، كالخلاف في أنّ الأمرَ يقتضي الوجوب.

والحقّ أنه يقتضيه. لقوله تعالىٰ: ﴿وَمَا نَهَىٰكُمْ عَنْهُ فَٱنتَهُوا۟﴾ [سُورة الحَشْر:٧]، ووجوب الإنتهاء يستدعي[66] تحريم المنهيّ عنه، وفي اقتضائه التكرار كما قلنا في الأمر.

وهل يجوز أن يكون الشّيء الواحد مأمورًا به منهيًّا عنه. كالصلاة في الدّار المغصوبَة.

الوجه عدم الجواز، لأنّ كونه مأمورًا به يستلزم نفي الحرج، وكونه منهيًّا عنه يستلزم ثبوت الحرج.

والجمع بينهما محال، فإن شغل الحيّز جزء من ماهية الصّلاة وهو منهيّ عنه. والأمر بالصلاة أمر بأجزائها. فيلزم الأمر بذٰلك الشّغل والنّهي عنه،[67] وهو محال.[68]

---

61 في "ط": ان المأمور. 62 في "ط": حالة. 63 في "ج" و"ه": لأنّه. 64 في الهامش الأيسر مِن "أ": حالة الفعل. 65 في الهامش الأيمن مِن "د": صح، الفعل.
66 في "ه": يقتضي. 67 وهناك تصحيح بنفس خط المتن بالهامش الأيمن من "أ": (النهي عنه)، وبالمتن (المنهي عنه) والصّواب ما أثبتناه. 68 لا توجد في "أ" و"د" و"ط": وهو محال. وفي "ج": وهو محال. ولعلّه الصّواب.

20 Discussion Twenty: On the Timing of the Attachment (*taʿalluq*) of the Command (*al-amr*)

The commanded (*al-maʾmūr*) becomes commanded before the action (*fiʿl*), for ability (*al-qudrah*) is a condition for the command, and that is only realisable prior to the action (*al-fiʿl*); this is because the action, in the state of its existence, is obligatory and the inability to act would mean that no command is attached to it.

However, according to the Ashʿarīs, it is commanded in the state of action because that is the state of ability. We have elsewhere elucidated upon the unsoundness (*fasād*) of this in theology (*ʿilm al-kalām*).[21]

21 Discussion Twenty-One: On Prohibition (*al-nahy*)

The difference of opinion regarding the prohibition (*nahy*) demanding forbiddance (*al-taḥrīm*) is the same as the difference of opinion regarding the command (*al-amr*) demanding obligation (*al-wujūb*).

The truth is that prohibition demands forbiddance, due to His word, the Exalted, 'and refrain from what he prohibits'.[22] The obligation of refrainment calls for the forbiddance of that which is prohibited. Regarding prohibition demanding repetition (*al-takrār*), it is just as we stated regarding the command.

Is it permissible for something to be both commanded and prohibited, such as prayer in a usurped house?

The guiding principle is the lack of permissibility, because its being commanded necessitates the exclusion of sin (*nafī al-ḥaraj*) and its being prohibited necessitates the confirmability of sin (*thubūt al-ḥaraj*).

The drawing together of the two is impossible, for the occupancy of the seized (*shaghl al-ḥayyiz*) is a part of the quiddity of prayer and that is prohibited. The command for the prayer is a command of the parts thereof thus necessitating the command of that occupancy and the prohibition thereof, and that is impossible.

---

21 See al-ʿAllāmah al-Ḥillī, *Nahj al-ḥaqq wa kashf al-ṣidq*, p. 385. For the Ashʿarī position see Fakhr al-Dīn al-Rāzī, *al-Maḥṣūl fī ʿilm al-uṣūl*, 6 vols., ed. Ṭāha Jābir Fayyāḍ al-ʿAlawānī, Beirut, 1416 AH/1996, vol. II, pp. 271–4.

22 Q. 59:7.

البحْث الثّاني والعشرون: في أنّ النّهي هل[69] يقتضي الفساد

الحقّ أنّه يقتضي الفساد[70] في العبادات لا في المعاملات. أمّا الأوّل، فلأنّه[71] لم يأت
81a بالمأمور به فيبقى في عهدة التّكليف. وأمّا| الثّاني، فلإمكان النّهي عن البيع مع وقوع
الملك به كما في وقت النّداء. ولا ينتقض بالعبادات لأنّ الفساد هناك معناه عدم
الإجزاء. وهنا معناه عدم ترتّب حكمه عليه ومع اختلاف التفسير لا يتمّ النّقض.

واعلم أن النّهي كما لا يدلّ علىٰ الفَساد في التصرّفات[72] فإنّه[73] لا يدل علىٰ الصحة.

---

69 لا يوجد (هل) في "أ" و"ه"، وأمّا في "ج" و"د" و"ط"، فإنّه موجود. ولعلّ الصّواب ما أثبتناه.

70 لا يوجد في "ط": الحق أنه يقتضي الفساد. 71 في "ط": فانه. 72 في "ه": المعاملات.

73 في "ه" و"ط": كذا.

22 Discussion Twenty-Two: On Whether Prohibition (*al-nahy*) Demands Unsoundness (*al-fasād*)

The truth is that it demands unsoundness in the acts of worship (*ʿibādāt*) and not in social interactions (*muʿāmalāt*). As for the former, because he has not performed what he is charged [with] (*al-maʾmūr bihi*) he therefore remains within the charge of the injunction (*ʿuhdat al-taklīf*). As for the latter, due to the possibility of the prohibition of the trafficking (*al-bayʿ*) although the commodity in question may be possessed, as is the case at the time of the call to prayer.[23] It would not be an infringement regarding the acts of worship, since unsoundness (*al-fasād*), there[24] means the lack of accomplishment (*al-ijzāʾ*), and here[25] it means the non-assignment of the ruling of unsoundness upon it. Whilst there exist differences regarding interpretation of this point, infringement is not complete.

Let it be known that just as the prohibition (*al-nahy*) does not signify unsoundness regarding modes of conduct (*al-taṣarrufāt*), similarly it does signify soundness (*al-ṣiḥḥah*).

---

23 The time to the call of prayer is a reference to the *adhān* for the Friday congregational prayer, see Q. 62:9.

24 There (*hunāka*) refers to the acts of worship.

25 Here (*hunā*) refers to matters of social interactions.

الفَصْلُ الرّابِع

فِي العُمُوم وَالخصوص، وفيه مباحث

الأوّل: [في العام والخاص]

العامّ، هو اللّفظ المستغرق لجميع ما يصلح له بحسبِ وضعٍ واحدٍ. والمطلق، هو اللّفظ الدّال علىٰ الحقيقة، من حيث هي هي من غير أنْ يكون فيه دلالة، علىٰ شيءٍ من القيود.

وصيغ العموم: "كلٌّ" و"جميع"[1] و"أيّ" و"ما" و"متىٰ" و"مَنْ" و"أين" في المُجازات والإستفهام. والنّكرة في سياق النّفي والجمع المعرَّف باللّام الجنسيّة والمضاف.

لأنَّ قولنا: "جاءَني كلُّ رَجلٍ" يناقض قولنا: "ما جاءَني كلُّ رَجلٍ".

والثّاني، ما[2] يفيد العموم، فوجبَ كونُ[3] الأوّل مفيداً للعموم. لأنَّ السّلبَ الجزئيَّ إنّما يناقضه الإيجاب الكليّ. وكذا في الـ"جميع".

وأمّا ألفاظ المجازات والإستفهام، فلأنّها لو لم تُفِد العموم لكانت إمّا مفيدة للخصوص، وهو باطل لحسن الجواب[4] بذكر كلِّ[5] العقلاء. وإما للعموم والخصوص معًا، وهو باطل وإلّا لما حَسُنَ الجواب إلّا بعد الإستفهام عن جميع الإحتمالات الممكنة. أو لا لواحدٍ منها وهو باطلٌ بالإجماع. وأيضًا فإنّه يصحُّ استثناءُ أيِ عددٍ كان منها.

والإستثناء إخراج ما لولاه لدَخَلَ، وهو دليلُ عامٍّ في جميع ما ادعينا عمومه.

---

1 توجد في "د" و"ه" و"ط": وجميع. 2 في "د": لا. وفي "ه" و"ط": لم. 3 في "ط": ان يكون. 4 في "ط": والا لما حسن الجواب. 5 في الهامش الأيسر مِن"أ": كلِّ.

CHAPTER FOUR

On Generality (*al-ʿumūm*) and Specificity (*al-khuṣūṣ*)–Consisting of Nine Discussions

1 Discussion One: On the General (*al-ʿāmm*) and the Specific (*al-khāṣṣ*)

The general (*al-ʿāmm*) is an utterance that engages wholly all that is appropriate for it in accordance with a single assignation (*waḍʿ*).

The absolute (*al-muṭlaq*) is an utterance signifying the veritative insofar as it is itself, without there being within it signification of any of the delimitations.

The forms of generality (*al-ʿumūm*) are: 'every' (*kull*), 'whole' (*jamīʿ*), 'any' (*ayy*), 'whatever' (*mā*), 'whenever' (*matā*), 'whoever' (*man*), 'wherever' (*ayna*), in conditional and interrogative sentences, the indefinite noun after negation (*al-nafī*), and the defined plural, either by *lām* denoting genus or by its being a genitive (*muḍāf*).

This is because our statement 'every man came to me' (*jāʾanī kullu rajulin*) contradicts our statement 'every man did not come to me' (*mā jāʾanī kullu rajulin*).

In the second statement, the particle *mā* of negation conveys the meaning of generality (*al-ʿumūm*). Therefore, it is obligatory that the first statement conveys the meaning of generality, because a partial negation is only contradicted by a total affirmation. This is the case in all such instances.

As for the conditional and interrogative utterances, if they did not convey the meaning of generality they would either convey the meaning of specificity (*al-khuṣūṣ*), which is void due to the properness of the response by all reasonable people (*al-ʿuqalāʾ*) at its mention; or it would convey the meaning of the generality and the specificity together and this is void, otherwise it would not be proper to answer except after enquiring about all possible probabilities; or it would not convey the meaning of any one of the two, and that is void according to consensus (*ijmāʿ*). Also, it is correct to make an exception (*istithnāʾ*) of any number, however many they may be.

Exception (*istithnāʾ*) means the exclusion of whatever would have been included, were it not for the exception. This is a general argument (*dalīl*) regarding everything whose generality we have claimed.

وأمّا النّكرة المنفيّة، فإنّها[6] نقيض المثبتة، وهي غير عامةٍ في الإثبات فتعمّ[7] في النّفي.

وأمّا الجمع المعرَّف، فإنه يؤكّد بما يفيد العموم، والتأكيد تقوية ما يُفيده الموكَّد[8]. وأمّا المضاف فللإستثناء.

البحْث الثاني: في ما أُلحق بالعموم وليس منه

وهوستّة. الأوّل، الواحد المعرّف بلام الجنس لا يفيد العموم، لعدم إفادته في مثل: "لَبِسْتُ الثّوبَ وشَرِبْتُ المَاءَ"، ولإمتناع تأكيده ووصفه بما يفيده. 81b

الثاني، الجمع المنكر لا يفيد العموم، لأنّه يوصف بالأقلّ نحو: "جَاءَنِي رِجَال ثَلَاثة وأَرْبَعَة وخَمْسَة" والمفهوم[9] قابل للتّقسيم إلىٰ هٰذه المراتب ومورد التّقسيم مغاير لأقسامه وغير مستلزم لها.

إذا عرفتَ هٰذا فنقول، أقلُّ[10] الجمعِ ثلاثة، وقيل إثنان. لنا أنَّ أهلَ اللّغة فرّقوا بين الصّيغتين وبين ضميريهما ولعدم قبولِه الوصف بالإثنين.

الثالث، قوله تعالىٰ: ﴿لَا يَسۡتَوِيٓ أَصۡحَٰبُ ٱلنَّارِ وَأَصۡحَٰبُ ٱلۡجَنَّةِ﴾ [سُورة الحَشْر: ٢٠]، لا يقتضي نفي الإستواء في جميع الأمور، لأنَّ نفي الإستواء أعمُّ من نفيهِ من كلِّ وجهٍ ومن نفيه[11] من وجهٍ[12] دون وجهٍ، ولا دلالة للعامّ علىٰ الخاصّ.

---

6 لا توجد في "ط": فانها. 7 "ب": فيعمّ. 8 لا توجد في "ط": وأما الجمع المعرَّف: فإنه يؤكّد بما يفيد العموم، والتأكيد تقوية ما يُفيده الموكَّد. 9 توجد في "ط": منه. 10 في الهامش الأيمن مِن "أ": أقلُّ. 11 لا توجد في "ه": من نفيه. 12 لا توجد في "ط": ومن نفيه من وجه.

As far as the indefinite negative [noun] (*al-nakirah al-manfiyyah*) is concerned, it is the opposite of the affirmative (*al-muthbitah*), and it is not general in the affirmation (*al-ithbāt*) but it is general in the negative.

As for the definite plural (*al-jamʿ al-muʿarraf*), it is corroborated by that which conveys the meaning of generality, and corroboration (*al-taʾkīd*) strengthens what the corroborated conveys.

As for that which is defined by the genitive (*muḍāf*), it is general by virtue of exception (*istithnāʾ*).[1]

2 Discussion Two: On What is Added to Generality (*al-ʿumūm*) Though it is not Thereof

And these are six: Firstly, the definite singular (*al-wāḥid al-muʿarraf*) with *lām* denoting the genus that does not convey the meaning of generality, because of the lack of its conveyed meaning in the example, 'I wore the garment' (*labistu al-thawb*) or 'I drank the water' (*sharibtu al-māʾ*), and due to the impossibility of its corroboration and its description by what conveys the meaning of generality.

Secondly, the indefinite plural (*al-jamʿ al-munakkar*) does not convey the meaning of generality because it can be described with the smallest of numbers, such as 'three, four, or five men came to me', and the notion thereof (*al-mafhūm*)[2] is capable of classification into these degrees. The thing that is classified is different to its classifications and does not necessitate them.

If this has been understood, then we [can] maintain the view that the least number for the plural is three; and it has been said that it is two. Our proof is that the folk of the language have differentiated between the two forms and their pronouns, and that the plural is indescribable by the number two.[3]

Thirdly, His word, the Exalted, 'Not equal are the inhabitants of the Fire and the inhabitants of Paradise'.[4] This does not demand the exclusion of equality in all matters because the exclusion of equality is more general than its exclusion from every aspect and its exclusion from one aspect rather than another, and there is no signification for the general (*al-ʿāmm*) over the specific (*al-khāṣṣ*).

---

1 See Ryding, Karin, 'Aspects of the Genitive: Taxonomy' in *al-Jumal fī al-naḥw*' in *Early Medieval Arabic: Studies on al-Khalīl ibn Aḥmad*, edited by Karin C. Ryding, Washington DC, 1998, pp. 92–142.

2 In other words, the notion of the indefinite plural (*mafhūm al-jamʿ al-munakkar*) is classifiable.

3 In Arabic, singular, dual, and plural are distinct.

4 Q. 59:20.

الرابع، خطاب الرّسول ﷺ في مثل قوله تعالىٰ: ﴿يَـٰٓأَيُّهَا ٱلنَّبِيُّ﴾[13]، لا يتناول الأمّة وقيل يتناولهم وهٰؤلاء إن زعموا أنّه مستفادٌ من هٰذا اللّفظ فهو خطأ فاحش، وإن زعموا استفادته من دليلٍ آخر فهو خروجٌ عن هٰذه المسألة.

الخامس، الصيغة المتناولة للذّكور والإناث عامة فيهما، إن لم يظهر فيه علامة كـ"مَنْ" و"أَيٌّ". للإجماع علىٰ عتقِ جميع الذكور والإناث من مماليكه، عند قوله: "مَنْ دَخَلَ دَارِي فَهُوَ حُرٌّ". وأمّا إن ظَهَرَ فيه[14] علامة – كقوله: قامَ، قاما، قاموا، قامت، قامتا، قُمْنَ – فالمؤنّث لا يتناول المذكّر إجماعًا. وفي العكسِ خلاف، الأقرب أنه كذٰلك، لأنّ الجمعَ تضعيفُ الواحد، والواحد لا يتناول المؤنث فكذا الجمع.

السّادس، حكاية الحال لا تعمّ. لأنّ قولنا: "فُلانٌ فَعَلَ" يكفي في صدقه صدور الفعل عن الفاعل مرّةً واحدةً.

البحْث الثالث: في التّخصيص

وهو إخراج بعض ما تناوله الخطاب عنه. وهو إمّا بمتّصلٍ أو منفصِلٍ. فالأوّل الإستثناء والشّرط والصّفة والغاية. والثّاني عقليّ وسمعيّ.

---

13 هٰذه العبارة وردت مطلعًا لآيات عدة منها سُورَة الأَنفَال–٨ آية ٦٤، وسُورَة التَّوبَة–٩ آية ٧٣.

14 لا توجد (فيه) في "أ". وأمّا في "ج" و"د" و"ه" و"ط" فإنّها موجودة، ولعلّ الصّواب ما أثبتناه.

Fourthly, the address to the Envoy, peace be upon him, as in the example of His word, the Exalted, 'O ye Prophet'[5] does not include the *ummah,* however it has been said that it does include the *ummah.* Those who hold this position either claim that is understood from this utterance, and that is a clear mistake, or they claim that it is understood from another argument, and that is beyond the scope of this issue.

Fifthly, the form (*al-ṣīghah*) that includes the masculine and the feminine is general with regard to both of them, if no sign (*'alāmah*) appears therein such as *man* (whoever) and *ayyu* (whichever). This argument is based on the consensus concerning the manumission (*'itq*) of every male and female from the master's possession, when he says, 'Whoever enters my house is free'. If there appears therein a sign (*'alāmah*) such as his saying, 'He stood up, those two stood up, they stood up, she stood up, those two females stood up, those females stood up…' then, according to consensus, the feminine does not include the masculine. However, in the opposite case there is a difference of opinion. The favoured opinion is that it is as such, because the plural is the multiplication of the one (*al-wāḥid*), and the one does not include the feminine, and likewise is the [case for] the plural.

Sixthly, the account of the state (*al-ḥāl*) is not a form of the general, because our statement that 'so and so did something', it is sufficient for its truth that the actor performed the action once.

3 Discussion Three: On Specification (*al-takhṣīṣ*)

Specification is the exclusion of a part of what has been included in the address and it is either connected (*muttaṣil*) or separate (*munfaṣil*). The former are the exception (*al-istithnā'*), the condition (*al-sharṭ*), the attribute (*al-ṣifah*), and the limit (*al-ghāyah*). The latter are either the intellective (*'aqlī*) or the revealed (*sam'ī*).[6]

---

5 Q. 8:65.

6 Revealed sources, that is to say the Qur'ān and the *Sunnah.*

والفرق بينه وبين النّسخ، أنّه |لا يصحُّ[15] إلّا في اللّفظ،[16] والنّسخ يصحُّ[17] فيما عُلِمَ بالدّليل 82a
إرادته. ولأنَّ نسخ الشريعة بمثلها جائز، بخلاف التّخصيص. ولأنَّ النسخ[18] يجب فيه التراخي دون التخصيص.

والحقّ إن التخصيص جنس للنسخ والإستثناء وغيرهما. ويصحُّ إطلاق العام وإرادة الخاص في الخبر والأمر، كقوله تعالىٰ: ﴿ٱللَّهُ خَٰلِقُ كُلِّ شَيْءٍ﴾ [سُورة الرَّعد:١٦]، وقوله: ﴿فَٱقْتُلُواْ ٱلْمُشْرِكِينَ﴾ [سُورة التَّوبَة:٥]. ولا بدّ في العام المخصوص من بقاء كثرة بعد التخصيص لقبح اكلت كلّ الرّمان وقد اكل واحدة.[19]

البحث الرابع: في التمسك بالعام المخصوص

الحقّ أنه مجازٌ إن خُصَّ بمنفصلٍ، عقلياً كان أو نقلياً وحقيقةٌ إن كان متّصِلاً.[20]

ويجوز التمسّك به إن لم يكن التّخصيص مجملاً وإلّا فلا. لأنّ كونه حجّةً في بعضِ موارده، لا يتوقّف علىٰ كونه حجّة في الأخرىٰ،[21] وإلّا دارَ[22] أو لزِم الترجيح من غير مرجّح فإذا خَرَجَ عن[23] كونهِ حجّةً في بعضِ الموارد، لم يزل عنه كونُهُ[24] حُجةً في الأخرين[25]. ولأنَّ أكثر العمومات مخصوصة، مع إحتجاج العلماء كافة بها.

---

15 في "د" و"ط": لا يصلح. 16 في الهامش الأيسر مِن "ب": الملفوظ. 17 في "ط": يجوز. 18 لا توجد في "ط": النسخ. 19 والعبارة (ولا بدّ في العام...اكل واحدة) بأسرها غير موجودة في النسخة المطبوعة، هذا مع أنّها وردتْ في جميع النسخ الخطيّة التي اعتمدنا عليها، فليت شعري كيف غفل عنها المحقق ومَن قرّظ عمله؟ 20 في "ط": بمتّصل. 21 في "ب": الآخرين، وفي "د" و"ه" و"ط": الاخر. 22 في "ط": لدار. 23 لا توجد في "ب" و"ط": عن. 24 في "د": لم يلزم عدم كونه. وفي "ه": لم يخرج عن كونه. 25 في "د" و"ه" و"ط": الاخر.

The difference between specification (*takhṣīṣ*) and abrogation (*naskh*) is that specification is only correct regarding the utterance, whereas abrogation is correct wherever the intention thereof is known through evidence (*dalīl*), and because abrogation of the divine law (*sharīʿah*) by its like is permissible, contrary to specification. Furthermore, postponement (*al-tarākhī*) regarding abrogation is obligatory while this is not the case regarding specification.

The truth is that specification is a genus of abrogation, and of exception, and of other than these two.

The application of the general (*al-ʿāmm*) whilst intending the specific, regarding the narration (*al-khabar*) and the command (*al-amr*), is correct, as in His word, the Exalted, 'God is the Creator of all things'[7] and His word, 'And so slay the polytheists'.[8]

It is a must regarding the specified general that the multiple abides after specification due to the unseemliness of the construction: 'I ate all of the pomegranates' whilst in fact he consumed one.

4 Discussion Four: On the Adherence to the General which is Specified (*al-ʿāmm al-makhṣūṣ*)

The truth is that it is figurative (*majāz*) if specified by a disconnected (*munfaṣil*) evidence, whether it be intellective (*ʿaqlī*) or reported, (*naqlī*), and it is veritative (*ḥaqīqah*) if it is by a connected (*muttaṣil*) evidence.[9]

It is permissible to adhere to it if the specification is not ambiguous (*mujmal*) otherwise it is not. This is because the specified general's (*al-ʿāmm al-makhṣūṣ*) being a legal proof (*ḥujjah*) in some cases, is not dependant upon its being a legal proof in others, otherwise it would lead to a circular argument or it would necessitate preferment without a preferrer. Meanwhile, if in some cases it ceases to be a legal proof (*ḥujjah*), it will not cease to be a legal proof in others. Furthermore, [it is permissible] because most generalities are specified according to the argumentations of all scholars regarding that.

---

7 Q. 13:16.

8 Q. 9:5. The author employs this example where a general term is employed for a specific case. The example of 'slay' is as such.

9 The author is here alluding to the general which is specified by a disconnected or connected piece of evidence (*al-dalīl*).

البحْث الخامس: في الإستثناء

وهو إخراج بعضِ الجملةِ منها بلفظة[26] "إلّا" أو ما يقوم مقامَهَا، ويجب اتّصالها[27] بالمستثنى منه عادةً. وهو قسمان: حقيقة، وهو الإستثناء من الجنس، ومجاز، وهو الإستثناء من غيره. وشرطه عدم الإستغراق، ويجوز أن يكون المستثنى أكثر من الباقي.

وإذا ورد عقيب الإثبات، أفاد النّفي إجماعًا. وإذا ورد عقيب النفي أفاد الإثبات، خلافًا لأبي حنيفة.

لنا[28] لو لم يكن كذٰلك لم يكن[29] قولنا: "لَا إله إلا الله" موجبًا لثبوتِ الإلهيّة[30] وبالإجماع دلَّ علىٰ تمامِ الإسلام به.[31]

وإذا تعدّد الإستثناء فإن كان بحرف عطفٍ، كان الجميع راجعًا إلىٰ المستثنىٰ منه. وإن كان بغيره فكذٰلك إن كان الثاني أكثر من الأول أو مساويًا،[32] وإلّا عاد إلىٰ الأوّل[33] | القربِه. 82b

وإذا ورد عقيبَ الجمل اختصَّ بالأخيرة. وقال الشافعي[34] يعود إلىٰ الجميع. وقال السيد المرتضىٰ بالإشتراك.

---

26 في "ب" و"د": بلفظ. 27 في "ب" و"د": اتصاله. 28 توجد في "ط": انه. 29 لا توجد في "ط": كذٰلك لم يكن. 30 في المطبوع زيادة "له تعالىٰ" من طرف المحقق. 31 لا توجد في "د": به. 32 توجد في "ط" وفي النسخة المطبوعة: له. 33 في "هـ": الاخير.

34 محمد بن إدريس بن العباس بن عثمان ابن شافع الهاشمي القرشي المطّلبي، أبو عبد الله: أحد زعماء المذاهب الأربعة عند أهل السنّة. وإليه نسبة الشافعية كافة. ولد في غزّة "بفلسطين" سنة ١٥٠ هـ/ ٧٦٧ م، وحمل منها إلىٰ مكة وهو ابن سنتين. وزار بغداد مرتين. وقصد مصر سنة ١٩٩ فتوفي بها سنة ٢٠٤ هـ/ ٨٢٠ م، وقبره معروف في القاهرة. لاحظ الأعلام للزركلي: ج ٦/ص ٢٤٩ - ٢٥٠.

5 Discussion Five: On Exception (*al-istithnā'*)

Exception (*istithnā'*) is the exclusion of a part of a clause by the utterance 'except' (*illā*) or that which takes its place. Its conjointment with the clause from which it is excluded is obligatory in the usual manner. It is of two classes: the veritative (*ḥaqīqah*), and that is the exception from the genus, and the figurative (*majāz*), which is the exception from anything other than that. The condition thereof is that it should not exclude the whole clause, however, it is permissible that the excluded be greater than the remaining clause.

According to consensus, if the exception (*istithnā'*) is set forth following an affirmation (*al-ithbāt*), it will convey the meaning of negation (*al-nafī*). If the exception (*istithnā'*) is set forth following a negation, it will convey the meaning of affirmation, contrary to the opinion of Abū Ḥanīfah.

Our argument is that if it were not thus, then our statement, 'There is no god except God', would not be a cause for affirming (*thubūt*) His divinity, the Exalted, and according to consensus, the complete profession of Islam is signified through this statement.

If exceptions (*istithnā'*) are numerous and they are by means of a conjunction (*ḥarf ʿaṭf*), then all shall refer to the clause from which they are excluded. And likewise is the case if they are by some other means, if the second part of the clause is greater than or equal to the first. Otherwise they will refer to the first clause, due to the proximity thereof.

If the exception (*istithnā'*) is set forth following many clauses, it will be specified with the last clause. Shāfiʿī is of the opinion that it will refer to all of them. Al-Sayyid al-Murtaḍā upholds the opinion of the common extent.[10]

10 Al-Sayyid al-Murtaḍā upholds both the above opinions, referring to all as ascribed to Shāfiʿī and referring to the last clause as ascribed to Abū Ḥanīfah. See Al-Sharīf al-Murtaḍā, *al-Dharīʿah ilā uṣūl al-sharīʿah*, ed. Abū al-Qāsim Gurjī, Tehran, 1363 SH/1984, vol. I, p. 248, and *Nihāyat*, vol. II, p. 260.

لنا أنَّهُ علىٰ خلافِ الأصل، فتُرِكَ العملُ به في الأخير لدفع محذور الهَذرِيَّة، وللقرب فيبقى الباقي علىٰ الأصل. ولأنَّ الإستثناء عقيب مثله، يعود إليه دون المُستثنى منه ولأنَّ الظّاهرَ عدم الإنتقال من الجملةِ قبل استيفائها.[35]

البحْث السادس: في الشرط والصفة والغاية

الشّرط ما يتوقّف عليه تأثير المؤثّر. وله صيغتان: "إن"، ويختص بالمحتمل، و"إذا"، ويدخل عليه وعلىٰ المتحقّق. وإذا تعقَّبَ الجُمل رجع إلىٰ الجميع. وقيل يختصُّ بالأخيرة. والأولىٰ تقديمه لفظًا، وإنْ جاز تأخيره.

وأمَّا الصّفة، فإنْ كانت عقيبَ جملةٍ واحدة، عادت إليها. وإن كانت عقيب أكثر، فإن تعلَّقت إحديْهما بالأخرىٰ عادت إليهما معًا، وإلا فالأقرب عودها إلىٰ الأخيرة.

وأمّا الغاية، فهي نهاية الشَّيء. وصيغتها "حتىٰ" و"إِلى". والحكم فيما بعدها مخالف لحكم ما قبلها، إن كانت منفصلة بمنفصل محسُوس، وإلّا فلا.

البحْث السابع: في التّخصيص بالأدلة المنفصلة

أمّا التخصيص بالعقل فكقوله تعالىٰ: ﴿خَٰلِقُ كُلِّ شَىۡءٖ﴾ [سُورة الرّعْد:١٦]، وقوله: ﴿وَأُوتِيَتۡ مِن كُلِّ شَىۡءٖ﴾ [سُورة النّمْل:٢٣].

35 "ب": استثنائها.

Our argument is that it is contrary to the principle (*aṣl*),[11] and so abstaining from acting in accordance with it, with regards to the last clause, is for averting the peril of prattle, and due to the proximity. Thus, the other clauses shall remain in accordance to the principle; also because the exception (*istithnāʾ*), following its like, will refer to it and not to the clause from which it is excluded. Furthermore, it is apparent that transference of the clause, prior to the completion thereof, cannot take place.

6 Discussion Six: On the Condition (*al-sharṭ*), the Attribute (*al-ṣifah*), and the Limit (*al-ghāyah*)

The condition (*al-sharṭ*) is that upon which the effect of the cause depends. It has two forms; 'if' (*in*) which is specific to something that is likely (*al-muḥtamal*), and 'when' (*idhā*), which applies both to the former[12] and to something that is assured (*al-mutaḥaqqiq*). When the condition follows the clauses it will refer to all of them, and it is said that it is specific to the last clause. It is most appropriate that it be uttered first even though it is permissible to defer its mention.

As for the attribute (*al-ṣifah*), if it follows a single clause then it will refer to it; and if it follows more than one clause, then if one of them is connected to the other, the attribute will refer to both together; otherwise the most favoured opinion is that its reference is to the latter.

As for the limit (*al-ghāyah*), it denotes the end of a thing and its forms are: 'until' (*ḥattā*) and 'to' (*ilā*). The ruling for what follows it is contrary to what is prior to it, if it is separated by a separator that is perceptible through the senses (*munfaṣil maḥsūs*), otherwise not.

7 Discussion Seven: On the Specification (*al-takhṣīṣ*) by Separate Pieces of Evidence (*al-adillah al-munfaṣilah*)

As for the specification by intellection (*al-ʿaql*) it is like His word, the Exalted, 'Creator of all things'[13] and His word, 'And she has been given of everything'.[14]

---

11 The principle in this case being 'the application of the general in accordance to its generality' (*ijrāʾ al-ʿāmm ʿalā ʿumūmmihi*). See *Mabādiʾ al-wuṣūl ilā ʿilm al-uṣūl*, ed. ʿAbd al-Ḥusayn Muḥammad ʿAlī al-Baqqāl, Najaf, 1348 SH/1969, pp. 136–7 n.5.

12 The former referring to something that is likely (*al-muḥtamal*).

13 Q. 13:16.

14 Q. 27:23.

وأمّا بالنقل فله أقسام: أحدها، تخصيص الكتاب بالكتاب[36] وهو جائز، خلافًا للظّاهريّةِ لقوله تعالىٰ: ﴿وَٱلْمُطَلَّقَٰتُ يَتَرَبَّصْنَ بِأَنفُسِهِنَّ ثَلَٰثَةَ قُرُوٓءٍ﴾ [سُورة البقَرَة:٢٢٨]، ومع قوله: ﴿وَأُوْلَٰتُ ٱلْأَحْمَالِ أَجَلُهُنَّ أَن يَضَعْنَ حَمْلَهُنَّ﴾ [سُورة الطَّلاق:٤].

الثّاني، تخصيصه بالسنّة المتواترة جائزٌ خلافًا لبعض الشّافعية، لقوله عليه السلام: "القَاتِل لَا يَرِثُ"[37]، في تخصيص قوله تعالىٰ: ﴿يُوصِيكُمُ ٱللَّهُ فِيٓ أَوْلَٰدِكُمْ﴾ [سُورة النِّسَاء:١١]، وكتخصيص آية الجلد، برجم المُحْصِن.

الثّالث، تخصيصه بالإجماع وهو جائز. للإجماع علىٰ تخصيص العبد من آية الميراث ومن آية الجلد.

83a الرّابع، تخصيصه بفعله عليه السلام[38] إن | كان حكم العامّ متناولاً له، وثَبَتَ أنَّ حكمَ غيره مثل حكمه. و[39] إن كان غيرَ متناولٍ له، كان مخصوصًا في حقِّ غيره إن ثَبُتَ أنَّ حكمَ غيره حكمه. وإلّا فلا.

الخامس، تخصيصه بخبر الواحد جائز، لأنّهما دليلان تعارضا، فَقُدِّمَ الأخصُّ جمعًا بين الدّليلين. وقد وقع كما في تخصيص: ﴿فَٱقْتُلُواْ ٱلْمُشْرِكِينَ﴾ [سُورة التَّوبَة:٥]، بقوله: "سُنّوا بهم سُنَّةَ أهلِ الكتاب"[40]. والسيّد المرتضىٰ منع من ذٰلك لأنَّ خبر الواحد ليس بحجّة عنده.

---

36 لا توجد في "ط": بالكتاب. 37 الكافي ج ٧ / ص ١٤١؛ تهذيب الأحكام ج ٩ / ص ٣٧٨.
38 توجد في "ط": جائز. 39 لا توجد في "ط": (إن كان حكم العام... غيره مثل حكمه).
40 من لا يحضره الفقيه، الشيخ الصدوق أبي جعفر محمد بن علي بن الحسين بن بابويه القمي، ٤ مجلدات، طهران: ١٣٩٠ هـ، ج ٢ / ص ٢٩.

As for the specification by revealed sources (*al-naql*), it has numerous classes: the first of them is the specification of the Book by the Book. This is permissible, contrary to the Ẓāhiriyyah, due to His word, the Exalted, 'Divorced women shall wait by themselves for three periods',[15] in addition to His word, 'And those who are with child, their term is when they bring forth their burden'.[16]

The second is the specification of the Qur'ān by the continuous tradition (*sunnah mutawātirah*), which is permissible, contrary to some of the Shāfiʿiyyah, due to the statement of the Prophet, peace be upon him, 'The murderer does not inherit', on the specification of His word, the Exalted, 'God charges you concerning [the inheritance of] your children',[17] and alike the specification of the verse on flogging[18] by the lapidation of the married man (*muḥṣin*).

The third is the specification of the Qur'ān by consensus (*al-ijmāʿ*) and that is permissible, due to the consensus of the specification of the slave from the verse on inheritance and the verse on flogging.[19]

The fourth is the specification of the Qur'ān by his action, peace be upon him, if the ruling of the general includes him, and it is confirmed that the ruling for others is like the ruling for him. If the ruling does not include him, it will be specified for the right of others, if it is confirmed that the ruling for others is the ruling for him, otherwise not.

The fifth is the specification of the Qur'ān by a solitary narration (*khabar al-wāḥid*), which is permissible, because both of them are two pieces of evidence in contradiction of each other, and so the most specific (*al-akhaṣṣ*) takes precedence in order to hold together the two pieces of evidence. This has occurred in such instances as in the specification of 'Slay the polytheists'[20] by his word, 'Treat them as you treat the People of the Book'. Al-Sayyid al-Murtaḍā denied this for the solitary narration because he did not deem the solitary narration as legal proof.[21]

---

15 Q. 2:228.

16 Q. 65:4.

17 Q. 4:11.

18 An allusion to Q. 24:2.

19 Q. 4:11–12 and 24:2.

20 Q. 9:5.

21 See al-Sharīf al-Murtaḍā, *al-Dharīʿah ilā uṣūl al-sharīʿah*, vol. II, pp. 41–79. Al-Mufīd also does not permit the specification of any general by means of the solitary narration. See al-Mufīd, *al-Tadhkirah bi-uṣūl al-fiqh*, in: *Muṣannafāt, al-Shaykh al-Mufīd,* 14 vols., Qum, 1414 AH/1993, vol. IX, p. 38.

السّادس، لا يجوز تخصيصه بالقياس. لأنَّ القياسَ عندنا باطل علىٰ ما يأتي، فكيف إذا عارض القرآن.

السابع، يجوز تخصيص السُنّة المتواترة بمثلها. لأنَّ العمل بهما وتركهما وترك الخاص، باطلٌ بالإجماع فتعيَّنَ ما قلناه.

فَائِدة

إذا ورد خبران عام وخاصّ واقترنا، كان الخاصّ مُخصِّصًا[41] للعامّ. وكذا إن ورد الخاص متأخرًا قبل حضور وقت العمل بالعام. وإن كان بعده كان نسخًا. وإن تأخر العام فعند أبي الحسين[42] يُبنى العام علىٰ الخاص لأنَّ الخاص أقوىٰ دلالة.

وعند أبي حنيفة[43] العام ناسخٌ لأنَّ مع التعارض يُعمَل بالأخير. وإن جُهِلَ التأريخ، توقَّف أبو حنيفة لتردّد الخاصّ بين كونه منسوخًا وتخصيصًا وناسخًا.

---

41 في "ط": مختصا. 42 محمد بن علي الطيب، أبو الحسن، البصري: أحد رؤوس المعتزلة. ولد في البصرة وسكن بغداد وتوفي بها سنة ٤٣٦هـ/١٠٤٤م. ومن كتبه "المعتمد فى أصول الفقه" و"تصفح الأدلة" و"غرر الأدلة" و"شرح الأصول الخمسة" كلها في الأصول، وكتاب في "الإمامة" و"شرح أسماء الطيبي". لاحظ الأعلام للزركلي: ج٧/ص ١٦١. 43 النعمان بن ثابت، التيمي بالولاء، الكوفي، أبو حنيفة: رأس الحنفية، أحد زعماء المذاهب الأربعة عند أهل السنة. قيل: أصله من أبناء فارس. ولد سنة ٨٠ هـ/ ٦٩٩ م بالكوفة ونشأ فيها. وكان يبيع الخز ويطلب العلم في صباه، ثم انقطع للتدريس والإفتاء. وأراده عمر بن هبيرة (أمير العراقيين) على القضاء، فامتنع ورعًا. وأراده المنصور العباسي بعد ذٰلك علىٰ القضاء ببغداد، فأبىٰ، فحلف عليه ليفعلن، فحلف أبو حنيفة أنه لا يفعل، فحبسه إلىٰ أن مات سنة ١٥٠ هـ/ ٧٦٧ م. لاحظ الأعلام للزركلي: ج٩/ص ٤-٥.

The sixth is that the specification of the Qur'ān by analogical reasoning (*al-qiyās*) is not permissible. This is because analogical reasoning is, in our opinion, void, according to what will follow—how then, if it contradicts the Qur'ān?

The seventh is that the specification of the continuous tradition (*al-sunnah al-mutawātirah*), is permissible by its like. This is because acting in accordance with both of them, abstaining from both of them and abstaining from the specific is void according to consensus. Therefore, what we have said is determined.

Availment

When two reports are set forth, one general (*'āmm*) and the other specific (*khāṣṣ*), and both are connected, then the specific specifies the general. The same is the case if the specific is set forth later prior to the arrival of the time of action in accordance with the general; and if it were after it, then it would be a case of abrogation (*naskh*). If the general were deferred, then, according to the opinion of Abū al-Ḥusayn, the general will be based upon the specific, because the specific is stronger in signification (*dalālah*); according to the opinion of Abū Ḥanīfah, the general is an abrogator, because, in the case of contradiction, action (*'amal*) is to be carried out in accordance with the last [report].

Abū Ḥanīfah has suspended judgement when the date [of the issuance of the narration] is unknown because the specific could be confused for being either abrogated, a specification, or an abrogator.

البحْث الثامن: فيما ظنّ أنّه مخصِّص وليس كذٰلك

وهو سبعة. الأوّل، السّبب ليس مخصِّصًا خلافًا للشافعيِّ، لوجود المقتضي للعموم وهو لفظه، وخصوص السبب لا يصلح للمنع لأنه لو صرح [44] وقال: عليك بالعام كان جائزًا. ولأنَّ الظهار واللعان وغيرهما، وردت علىٰ أسباب خاصة[45] مع عمومها.

الثاني، مذهب الرّاوي ليس بمخصّص، خلافًا لابن أبان[46] لإحتمال استناده إلىٰ ما ليس بدليل، وقد أخطأ في ظنّه.

83b الثالث، لا يجوز تخصيص العموم بذكر بعضه، لعدم التّنافي والمفهوم[47] ليس بحجّة خصوصًا مع معارضة العموم.

الرابع، العادة غير مخصّصة، إلّا أن يقع في زمانه ﷺ ويقرّرهم[48] عليها، لأنَّ فعل العبيد[49] ليس بحجة علىٰ الشّرع.

الخامس، المخاطِب لا يخرج عن عموم الخطاب، كقوله تعالىٰ: ﴿إِنَّ ٱللَّهَ بِكُلِّ شَىْءٍ عَلِيمٌ﴾ [سُورة العَنكبُوت:٦٢].

السّادس، الخطاب المتناول للرّسول ﷺ والأمّة، لا يختص بالأمّة لعموم اللّفظ.

---

44 توجد في "ط": به. 45 في "ط": اشياء. 46 عيسىٰ بن أبان بن صدقة، أبو موسىٰ: قاضٍ من كبار فقهاء الحنفية. خدم المنصور العباسي مدة. وولي القضاء بالبصرة عشرة سنين، وتوفي بها سنة ٢٢١هـ/ ٨٣٦م. له كتب، منها "إثبات القياس" و"اجتهاد الرأي" و"الجامع في الفقه، و"الحجة الصغيرة" في الحديث. لاحظ الأعلام للزركلي: ج ٥/ص٢٨٣. 47 في "ط": العموم. 48 في "ه": يقرّهم. 49 في "د" و"ه": العبد.

8 Discussion Eight: On What is Considered a Specifier (*mukhaṣṣiṣ*) though it is not

They are seven: The first is that the cause (*al-sabab*) is not a specifier, contrary to the opinion of Shāfiʿī, due to the existence of the demand for generality, and that is the utterance thereof. Specifically the cause is not appropriate for prevention, for if he were to explicitly say: 'adhere to the general!' (*ʿalayka bi al-ʿāmm*), it would be permissible, and because of divorce, by stating *tu mihi ut dorsum matris meæ* (*ẓihār*), divorce by mutual execration (*liʿān*), and so forth, each were set forth on the basis of specific causes, despite the generality thereof.

The second is that the opinion of the transmitter (*madhhab al-rāwī*) is not a specifier, contrary to the opinion of Ibn Abān, due to the likelihood (*iḥtimāl*) that he did not base it on a piece of evidence (*dalīl*) and might [thus] be mistaken in his thinking.

The third is that it is not permissible to specify the generality by mentioning a part thereof due to the lack of mutual exclusion (*al-tanāfī*), and what is implicit (*al-mafhūm*) is not a legal proof (*ḥujjah*), especially when it contradicts the generality.

The fourth is that custom (*al-ʿādah*) is not a specifier; except if it occurred during his[22] era, peace be upon him, and he approved it for them, for the action of mere men is not a legal proof (*ḥujjah*) for the divine law (*sharʿ*).

The fifth is that the one who makes the address (*mukhāṭib*) is not beyond the generality of the address, due to His word, the Exalted, 'And He is of all things Ever-Knowing'.[23]

The sixth is that the address, including both the Envoy, peace be upon him, and the *ummah*, is not specific for the *ummah* due to the generality of the utterance.

---

22 This pronoun refers to the Prophet.

23 Q. 29:62.

السّابع، عطف الخاصّ علىٰ العامّ لا يقتضي التّخصيص، خلافًا للحنفيّة، كقوله ﷺ: "لا يقتل المؤمن بكافرٍ ولا ذو عهدٍ في عهده". لأنّ العطف لا يقتضي الإشتراك من كلّ الوجوه.

البحث التاسع: في حمل المطلق علىٰ المقيد

إن كان حكم المطلق مخالفًا لحكم المقيّد، لم يُحمل المطلق عليه. وإن ماثله فإن اتّحد السبب، حُمل المطلق عليه. وإن اختلف، لم يجب الحمل إلا بدليلٍ منفصل. وقال بعض الشافعيّة: تقييد أحدهما يقتضي تقييد الآخر لفظًا وهو خطأ، لأنّه لو قال[50] الشّارع، أوجبت أيَّ رقبةٍ كانت في الظّهار، لم ينافِ التقييد بالإيمان في القتل.

---

50 لا توجد في "ط": قال.

The seventh is that the conjunction (*ʿaṭf*) of the specific to the general does not demand specification, contrary to the opinion of the Ḥanafīs, due to his saying, peace be upon him, 'A believer shall not be slain for a non-believer nor the possessor of a position whilst in his position', because the conjunction (*al-ʿaṭf*) does not demand the common extent (*ishtirāk*) in all aspects.

9 Discussion Nine: On the Predication of the Absolute (*al-muṭlaq*) to the Delimited (*al-muqayyad*)

If the ruling of the absolute (*al-muṭlaq*) is different to the ruling of the delimited (*al-muqayyad*) then the absolute will not be predicated thereupon. However, if it is similar, then, if the cause (*al-sabab*) is one, the absolute (*al-muṭlaq*) will be predicated thereupon. However, if it differs, then the predication is not obligatory save with a separate piece of evidence (*dalīl munfaṣil*). A group of Shāfiʿīs uphold the opinion that the delimitation of one of them demands the delimitation of the other in utterance. This opinion is incorrect; for, if the Lawgiver were to say, 'I obligate the freeing of any slave in the case of *ẓihār*', this would not be incompatible with the delimitation of faith in the case of murder.

الفَصْلُ الخَامِس

فِي المُجْمَل وَالمبَيَّن، وفيه مباحث

الأوّل: [في بعض التّعاريف]

البيان، هو الذي دلَّ علىٰ المراد بخطابٍ لا يستقل بنفسه في الدلالة علىٰ المراد.

والمُبَيَّن، يُطلَق علىٰ المُستغني عن البيان وعلىٰ ما ورد عليه بيانه. والمُجمل، ما أفاد شيئًا معيّنًا في نفسه واللّفظ لا يُعيّنه. والتأويل، إحتمال يعضده دليل يصير به أغلب علىٰ الظن من الذي دلَّ الظاهرُ عليه.

ثم المجمل قد يكون لفظًا، باعتبار إرادة خلاف الظّاهر منه، كالعامّ المخصوص. أولا، كالمتواطيء والمشترك. وقد يكون فعلاً، باعتبار عدم ما يدلّ علىٰ جهة وقوعه.

البحْث الثاني: [في ورود المجمل]

يجوز ورود المجمل في كلام الله تعالىٰ، وكلام الرّسول صلىٰ الله عليه وآله وسلّم
84a لإمكانه في الحكمة، ووقوعه | فيهما.

البحْث الثالث: في أشياء ليست مجملة وظن أنّها كذٰلك

فمنها، التّحليل والتحريم المضافان إلىٰ الأعيان، خلافًا للكرخي،[1] لإفادتهما المعنىٰ المطلوب من تلك الذّات.

---

1 عبيد الله بن الحسين الكرخي، أبو الحسن: فقيه، انتهت إليه رئاسة الحنفية بالعراق. مولده في الكرخ سنة ٢٦٠ هـ/ ٨٧٤ م، ووفاته ببغداد سنة ٣٤٠ هـ/ ٩٥٢ م. له "رسالة في الأصول التي عليها مدار فروع الحنفية" و"شرح الجامع الصغير" و"شرح الجامع الكبير". لاحظ الأعلام للزركلي: ج٤/ص٣٤٧.

CHAPTER FIVE

On the Ambiguous (*al-mujmal*) and the Elucidated (*al-mubayyan*)–Consisting of five Discussions

1 Discussion One: On some of the Definitions (*al-ta'ārīf*)

The Elucidation (*al-bayān*) is that which signifies the intended by the address that does not itself independently signify the intended.

The elucidated (*al-mubayyan*), applies to that which is needless of an elucidation (*al-bayān*) and for what the elucidation (*bayān*) thereof is set forth.

The ambiguous (*al-mujmal*), does not convey anything determined by itself and the utterance does not determine it.

The interpretation (*al-ta'wīl*) is a likelihood that is supported by a piece of evidence, by which it becomes more overwhelmingly probable than that which is signified by the evident meaning (*al-ẓāhir*).

Furthermore, the ambiguous (*al-mujmal*) may be an utterance, considering the desire for its difference to the evident meaning (*al-ẓāhir*) thereof, like the general that has been specified, or it may not be that, such as the univocal (*al-mutawāṭi'*), and the homonym (*al-mushtarak*), and sometimes it may be an action (*fi'l*), considering the absence of what signifies the status of its occurrence.

2 Discussion Two: On the Setting Forth of the Ambiguous (*al-mujmal*)

The setting forth of the ambiguous is permissible in the words of God, the Exalted, and the words of the Envoy, due to its philosophical possibility (*al-ḥikmah*), and due to the fact that it has occurred in their words.

3 Discussion Three: On Things Which are Considered to be Ambiguous (*mujmalah*) Whilst They are not as Such

Among these are permissibility (*al-taḥlīl*) and the forbiddance (*al-taḥrīm*) that is added to entities (*al-a'yān*), contrary to the opinion of al-Karkhī, because they both convey the desired meaning of those essences.

ومنها، قوله تعالىٰ: ﴿وَٱمۡسَحُواْ بِرُءُوسِكُمۡ﴾ [سُورة المَائِدَة:٦]، خلافًا لبعض الحنفيّة.

لأنَّ الباء إمّا للتبعيض، وإما للقدر المشترك بين الجميع والبعض، ومعهما لا إجمال.

ومنها الفعل المنفي، خلافًا لأبي عبد الله البصريّ، لأنّ الإضمار لابدّ منه، وإضمار الصحّة أولىٰ، لأنّه أقرب مجاز إلىٰ الحقيقة.

ومنها، آية السّرقة ليست مجملة في اليد ولا[2] القطع، لأنّ اليد الموضوعة للعضو من المنكب واستعماله في البعض علىٰ سبيل المجاز، وأمّا القطع فهو الإبانة.

ومنها قوله عليه السلام: "رُفِعَ عَنْ أُمّتِي الخَطَأ والنِّسْيَانُ"[3] لأنّ المراد منه رفع المؤاخذة.

البحْث الرابع: في تأخير البيان

قد وقع الإجماع علىٰ أنه لا يجوز تأخير البيان عن وقت الحاجة، وإلّا لزم تكليف ما لا يطاق.

وأمّا تأخيره عن وقت الخطاب، فقد منع أبو الحسين من تأخير البيان، فيما له ظاهر وقد استعمل في خلافه وزعم أن البيان الإجماليّ كافٍ فيه، وجوّز تأخير البيان فيما ليس له ظاهر إلىٰ وقت الحاجة. والأشاعرة جوّزوا التّأخير مطلقًا.

احتج أبو الحسين[4] بأنَّ القصد من الخطاب الإفهام، وإلّا كان عبثًا. فإن كان المراد إفهام ظاهره مع عدم إرادته، كان إغراءً بالجهل. وإن كان غير ظاهره مع عدم بيانه، لزم تكليف ما لا يطاق.

---

2 توجد في "ط": في. 3 توجد في "ط": وما استكرهوا عليه. من لا يحضره الفقيه ج ١ / ص ٣٦. 4 توجد في "ه": البصري.

Among them is His word, the Exalted, 'Anoint your heads',[1] contrary to the opinion of some of the Ḥanafīs, because the particle *bāʾ* is either for division into parts (*al-tabʿīḍ*) or for the common extent between the whole (*al-jamīʿ*) and the part (*al-baʿḍ*), and regarding these two there is no ambiguity (*ijmāl*).

Among them is the negative verb (*al-fiʿl al-manfī*), contrary to the opinion of Abū ʿAbd Allāh al-Baṣrī, because ellipsis (*iḍmār*) is a must, and the ellipsis of correctness is more appropriate, for it is the nearest figuratively to the veritative (*al-ḥaqīqah*).

Among them is the verse on theft;[2] this is not ambiguous, neither as regards 'the hand' (*al-yad*), nor regarding 'cutting' (*al-qaṭʿ*), because hand (*al-yad*) is assigned (*mawḍuʿah*) for a limb from the shoulder (*al-mankib*) and its usage, for some of it,[3] is in a figurative manner. As for cutting (*al-qaṭʿ*), it means separation (*al-ibānah*).

Among them is his saying, peace be upon him, 'Error and forgetfulness are removed from my *ummah*'. What is intended by this is the removal of being held to account.

4 Discussion Four: On the Deferment (*taʾkhīr*) of the Elucidation

Consensus has occurred (*al-ijmāʿ*) on the impermissibility of the deferment of the elucidation beyond the time of need, otherwise it would necessitate an injunction of what is not feasible.

As for the deferment of the elucidation (*bayān*) beyond the time of address (*al-khiṭāb*), Abū al-Ḥusayn considered the deferment of the elucidation regarding that which is evident and has been employed in a meaning contrary thereto, to be forbidden. He claimed that the ambiguous elucidation (*al-bayān al-ijmālī*) is sufficient therein. However, he permitted the deferment of the elucidation (*al-bayān*) regarding that which is not evident until the time of need.

The Ashʿarīs have absolutely permitted the deferment.

Abū al-Ḥusayn argued that the intention of the address (*al-khiṭāb*) is to make something understood as it would otherwise be nonsense. Thus, if the intention is to make the evident meaning thereof understood without desiring it, then that would be an incitement to ignorance and if it were the non-evident meaning thereof, without the elucidation (*bayān*) thereof, this would necessitate an injunction of what is not feasible.

---

1 Q. 5:6.

2 Q. 5:38.

3 This pronoun refers to the hand.

أحتجّت الأشاعرة بأنّ الله تعالىٰ كلّف بني إسرائيل ذبح بقرةٍ معيّنة، لقوله تعالىٰ: ﴿قَالُوا۟ ٱدْعُ لَنَا رَبَّكَ يُبَيِّن لَّنَا مَا هِىَ قَالَ إِنَّهُۥ يَقُولُ إِنَّهَا بَقَرَةٌ﴾ [سُورة البَقَرَة:٦٨]، ثمّ إنّه تعالىٰ ما بيّنها لهم حتىٰ سألوا. ولقوله تعالىٰ: ﴿فَإِذَا قَرَأْنَٰهُ فَٱتَّبِعْ قُرْءَانَهُۥ ۝ ثُمَّ إِنَّ عَلَيْنَا بَيَانَهُۥ﴾ [سُورة القِيَامَة:١٨–١٩]، وثمّ للتراخي.

83b والجواب | أنّهما دلّتا علىٰ تأخير البيان عن وقت الحاجة، وهو غير جائز إجماعًا فلابدّ من التأويل.

البحْث الخامس: [في جواز سماع المكلف العام من غير سماع ما يخصصه]

يجوز أن يسمع المكلف العام من غير أن يسمع ما يخصصه خلافًا لأبي علي ولأبي الهذيل[5]. لأنّه يجوز في المخصوص بدليل العقل،[6] وإن لم يعلم السّامع في العقل ما يدلّ عليه عندهما. فكذا هنا وقد سمعوا ﴿فَٱقْتُلُوا۟ ٱلْمُشْرِكِينَ﴾ [سُورة التَّوْبَة:٥]، ولم يسمعوا "سُنّوا بِهِمْ سُنَّةَ أَهْلِ الكِتَاب"،[7] إلّا بعد حين.

---

5 محمد بن الهذيل بن عبد الله بن مكحول العبدي، مولىٰ عبد القيس، أبو الهذيل العلّاف: من رؤوس المعتزلة. ولد في البصرة سنة ١٣٥ هـ / ٧٥٣ م، واشتهر بعلم الكلام. قال المأمون: أطل أبو الهذيل علىٰ الكلام كإطلال الغمام على الأنام. له مقالات في الإعتزال ومجالس ومناظرات. وكان حسن الجدل قوىٰ الحجّة، سريع الخاطر. كفّ بصره في آخر عمره، وتوفي بسامرّاء سنة ٢٣٥ هـ / ٨٥٠ م. له كتب كثيرة، منها كتاب سماه "ميلاس" علىٰ اسم مجوسي أسلم علىٰ يده. لاحظ الأعلام للزركلي: ج ٧ / ص ٣٥٥.

6 في "ط": فعل.

7 من لا يحضره الفقيه ج ٢ / ص ٢٩.

The Ashʿarīs argued that God, the Exalted, charged the children of Israel to slaughter a marked cow, due to His word, the Exalted, 'They said, "Pray to thy Lord for us, that He may elucidate for us what she may be"',[4] and furthermore God did not elucidate until they asked, and due to His word, the Exalted, 'So, when We recite it, follow thou its recitation. Then upon us is the elucidation thereof'.[5] The utterance 'then' (*thumma*) denotes postponement (*al-tarākhī*).

The answer is that both verses signify the deferment of the elucidation (*al-bayān*) beyond the time of need and this is not permissible, according to consensus (*ijmāʿ*). Therefore, it is a must to resort to interpretation (*al-taʾwīl*).

5 Discussion Five: On the Possibility of the Charged Agent (*al-mukallaf*) Hearing the General without Hearing what Specifies it

It is possible for the charged agent (*al-mukallaf*) to hear the general without hearing what specifies it, contrary to the opinions of Abū ʿAlī and Abū al-Hudhayl. This is because, according to them it is permissible regarding that which is specified (*al-makhṣūṣ*) by arguments based on intellection (*bi dalīl al-ʿaql*), even though the one who hears them does not intellectively understand what they signify. Likewise the case here, when they heard, 'Slay the polytheists', and did not hear, until after a period of time had passed, 'Treat them as you treat the People of the Book'.

4 Q. 2:68.
5 Q. 75:18–19.

الفَصْلُ السَّادِس

فِي الأَفْعَال، وفيه مباحث

الأوّل: [في عصمة الأنبياء]

مذهَبُنَا أنَّ[1] الأنبياء معصومون عن الكفر والبدعة خلافًا للفُضيليّة،[2] وعن الكبائر خلافًا للحشوية،[3] وعن الصّغائر عمدًا خلافًا لجماعة من المعتزلة، وخطأ في التّأويل خلافًا للجبائي،[4] وسهوًا خلافًا للباقين.

وبالجملة فالعصمة واجبة في كل زمان، وقد بيّنا ذٰلك في علم الكلام، فلا حاجة إليه هنا.

---

1 لا توجد في "ط": أنَّ. 2 هم فرقة من الخوارج، أتباع فضل بن عبد الله، ومن عقائدهم: أنّ من قال: لا اله الّا الله محمد رسول الله بلسانه ولم يعتقد ذلك بقلبه بل اعتقد الدهرية أو اليهودية أو النصرانيّة، فهو مسلم عند الله مؤمنٌ، ولا يضرّه إذا قال الحقّ بلسانه ما اعتقد بقلبه. لاحظ معجم الفرق الإسلامية، شريف يحيى الأمين، بيروت، ١٤٠٦ ه، ص ١٨٦. ولاحظ الحور العين، ابو سعيد نشوان الحميري (المتوفى سنة ٥٧٣ ه)، تحقيق كمال مصطفى، القاهرة ١٣٦٨ ه / ١٩٤٨ م، ص ١٧٧ و٢٧٣ و٢٧٤. 3 قال الحميري: سميت "الحشوية" حشوية لأنهم يحشون الأحاديث التي لا أصل لها في الأحاديث المروية عن رسول الله (ص)، أي: يدخلون فيها وليست منها. ثم قال: وجميع الحشوية يقولون بالجبر والتشبيه. لاحظ الحور العين ص ٢٠٤. 4 في المطبوعة: للجبائيين، وهو خطأ. والصحيح كما أثبتناه من جميع المخطوطات.

CHAPTER SIX

On Actions (*al-afʿāl*)–Consisting of Four Discussions

1 Discussion One: On the Infallibility (*ʿiṣmah*) of the Prophets

Our doctrine is that the prophets are infallible (*maʿṣūmūn*) in regard to disbelief (*al-kufr*) and innovation (*al-bidʿah*), contrary to the opinion of the Fuḍayliyyah; in regard to major sins (*al-kabāʾir*), contrary to the opinion of the Ḥashawiyyah; in regard to intentional minor sins (*al-ṣaghāʾir*), contrary to the opinion of a group of Muʿtazilīs; in regard to erring in interpretation (*al-taʾwīl*), contrary to the opinion of Jubbāʾī; and in regard to unintentional (*sahw*) [minor sins], contrary to the opinion of others.

In sum, infallibility (*al-ʿiṣmah*) is a necessity in every epoch; we have elucidated this in theology (*al-kalām*), and thus there is no need for it here.[1]

---

1 See al-ʿAllāmah al-Ḥillī, *Kashf al-murād fī sharḥ tajrīd al-iʿtiqād*, Qum, 1416 AH/1995 pp. 364–5.

البحْث الثاني: في وجوب التأسي بالنبيّ عليه السلام

والحق ذٰلك خلافًا لقوم، لنا قوله تعالىٰ[5]: ﴿فَٱتَّبِعُوهُ﴾ [سُورة الأَنْعَام:١٥٣]. وقوله[6]: ﴿لَّقَدْ كَانَ لَكُمْ فِي رَسُولِ ٱللَّهِ أُسْوَةٌ حَسَنَةٌ﴾ [سُورة الأَحْزَاب:٢١]. وقوله[7]: ﴿قُلْ إِن كُنتُمْ تُحِبُّونَ ٱللَّهَ فَٱتَّبِعُونِي يُحْبِبْكُمُ ٱللَّهُ﴾ [سُورة آلِ عِمْرَان:٣١].

إذا عرفت هٰذا فمعنىٰ التأسي به أنّه عليه السلام إذا فعل فعلاً علىٰ وجه الوجوب، يجب علينا أن نفعله علىٰ وجه[8] الوجوب، وإن تنفَّل به، كنّا متعبدين بالتنفّل، وإن فعله علىٰ وجه الإباحة[9] كنّا متعبدين بإعتقاد إباحته، وجاز لنا فعله. هٰذا إذا عُلِمَ وجه الفعل. أمّا إذا لم يعلم، فقال ابن سُريج[10]: "إنَّه لِلوُجُوب فِي حَقِّنَا" وقال الشَافعي للندب، وقال مالك[11] للإباحة، وأكثر المعتزلة علىٰ[12] الوقف،[13] وهو الأقرب[14]. لأنَّ عصمته تنفي القبح عنه والوجوب والنّدب زائدان. فالمشترك هو الجواز.

---

5 في "أ" اللَّفظة "تعالىٰ" غير موجودة. وفي "ج" و"د" و"ه" و"ط" اللّفظة "تعالى" موجودة.

6 لا توجد في "ج": قوله. وفي "ط": قوله تعالىٰ. 7 توجد في "ط": تعالىٰ. 8 في "ط": سبيل. 9 لا توجد في "ط": إن تنفَّل به كنّا متعبدين بالتنفّل وإن فعله علىٰ وجه الإباحة.

10 أحمد بن عمر بن سريج البغدادي، أبو العباس: فقيه الشافعية في عصره. ولد في بغداد سنة ٢٤٩هـ/٨٦٣م، وفيها توفيّ سنة ٣٠٦هـ/٩١٨م. له نحو ٤٠٠ مصنف. وكان يلقب بالباز الأشهب. ولي القضاء بشيراز. انظر الأعلام للزركلي: ج١/ص١٧٨–١٧٩.

11 مالك بن أنس بن مالك الأصبحي الحميري، أبو عبد الله: أحد زعماء المذاهب الأربعة عند أهل السنة، وإليه تنسب المالكية كافة. مولده في المدينة سنة ٩٣هـ / ٧١٢م، وفيها توفي سنة ١٧٩هـ / ٧٩٥م. وصنف "الموطأ". وله تصانيف أخرىٰ. انظر الأعلام للزركلي: ج٦/ص١٢٨.

12 لا توجد في "ب": علىٰ. 13 في "ط": التوقف. 14 توجد في "د": عندي.

2 Discussion Two: On the Obligation of Following (*al-taʾassī*) the Prophet

This is the true doctrine, contrary to the opinions of some people, and our opinion is based on His word, the Exalted, 'So follow him'[2] and, 'You have had a good example in the Envoy of God',[3] and His word, 'Say, "If you love God, follow me, and God shall love you"'.[4]

If this is understood, then the meaning of 'following him' (*al-taʾassī*) is that, if he, peace be upon him, performed an action by way of obligation, it is obligatory for us to perform it by way of obligation, and if he supererogated it then we should follow it by way of supererogation, and if he performed it in an indifferent manner then we should follow through belief in its indifferency and it would be permitted for us to perform it. This is the case when the manner of the action is known. However, if the manner of the action is not known then, according to Ibn Surayj, it will be obligatory with regard to us. Shāfiʿī is of the opinion it would be approved. Mālik is of the opinion that it would be [a matter of] indifferency and the majority of the Muʿtazilah suspended judgment on this matter. That is the favoured opinion, because his infallibility excludes unseemliness (*al-qubḥ*) from him. Obligation (*al-wujūb*) and approvedness (*al-nudb*) are additions (*zāʾidān*) and so the common [extent] is permissibility.

---

2 Q. 6:153.
3 Q. 33:21.
4 Q. 3:31.

البحْث الثالث: في الترجيح بين القول والفعل

إذا ورد خطاب متناول للأمة خاصّة ثم فَعَلَ ﷺ فِعْلاً[15] ينافيه،[16] وجب المصير إلىٰ القول.[17]

وإن كان متناولاً لنا وله وتراخى[18]| فعله، صار منسوخًا عنه وعنّا للتأسّي.[19] وإن تناوله[20] دوننا، كان منسوخًا عنه. وإن كان الفعل[21] متقدّمًا، وجب التأسّي. فإن كان القول متناولاً له خاصّة، كان مخصِّصًا له عن ذٰلك العموم. وإن تناول أمّته خاصّة، كان حكم[22] الفعل مختصًا[23] به. وإن كان عامًّا لنا وله،دلّ علىٰ سقوط حكم[24] الفعل عنه وعنّا. 85a

وإن لم يعلم تقدّم أحدهما، قُدِّم[25] القول لأنه أقوىٰ دلالة من الفعل.

البحْث الرابع: [في تعبده بشرع من قبله]

الحقّ أنه ﷺ لم يكن متعبّدًا بشرع من قبله، قبل[26] النبوّة ولا بعدها. وإلّا لاشتهر، ولافتخر به أهل تلك الملّة، ولوجب مراجعة[27] من تقدَّم، لوكان متعبدًا بعد النبوّة، ولعلّمَ مُعاذًا[28] عند سؤاله.

---

15 لا توجد في "ط": فعلاً. 16 في "ط": يتنافيه. 17 في "د" وردت العبارة:(أي إلىٰ الخطاب) بين السطرين. وأمّا النسخة المطبوعة ففيها (إلىٰ الفعل) وهو خطأ أفحش. 18 في "د": يتراخى. 19 توجد في "ط": وان تعقب الفعل القول كان الفعل مخصصا للقول في حقه لا في حق الأمة دفعا للغوّ. 20 زيادة في "ط": الخطاب. 21 لا توجد في "ه": الفعل.

22 لا توجد في "ط": حكم. 23 في "ه": مخصوصا. 24 لا توجد في "ط": حكم.

25 في "ط": تقدم. 26 توجد في "ط": لا قبل. 27 توجد في "ط": الى. 28 معاذ بن جبل عمرو بن أوس الأنصاري الخزرجي، أبو عبد الرحمٰن: كان صحابيًا. وشهد العقبة مع الأنصار السبعين. وشهد بدرًا وأحدًا والخندق والمشاهد كلها مع رسول الله (ص) وبعثه رسول الله، بعد غزوة تبوك، قاضيًا لأهل اليمن فبقي في اليمن إلى أن توفي النبي (ص). توفي بناحية الأردن سنة ١٨ هـ / ٦٣٩ م، ودفن بالقصير المعيني (بالغور). لاحظ الأعلام للزركلي: ج ٨/ص ١٦٦.

3 Discussion Three: On the Preferment between the Statement (*al-qawl*) and the Action (*al-fiʿl*)

When an address (*khiṭāb*) is set forth including the *ummah* in particular, then if he, peace be upon him, performs an action that is lacking in agreement with it, then it is obligatory to take recourse to the statement.

If the address includes him and us and he postpones its performance, it will become abrogated for him and for us, on account of the need to follow him (*al-taʾassī*), and if the address includes him and excludes us then it will be abrogated for him. If the action is prior to the address it is obligatory to follow him. If the statement were to include him in particular then it would be specific to him from that generality, and if it were to include his *ummah* in particular then the ruling for the action will be exclusively for it. If it were general for us and for him, it will signify the annulment of the ruling for the action for him and for us.

If the precedence of one of them is not known, then the statement takes precedence because it has a stronger signification than that of the action (*al-fiʿl*).

4 Discussion Four: On the Prophet's Following (*taʿabbud*) of Prior Revealed Laws

The truth is that the Prophet, peace be upon him, did not follow the law (*sharʿ*) of those who came before him, before the announcement of his prophethood (*nubuwwah*), nor after it. Otherwise, this would have become well known and the people of those creeds would have boasted about it. Furthermore, after the announcement of his mission it would have been obligatory for him to refer to those who came before him if he had followed their laws. In addition, he would have briefed Muʿādh of this issue when he asked him about it.

الفَصْلُ السَّابِع

فِي النَّسخ، وفيه مباحث

الأوّل: في تعريفه

النّسخ في اللّغة[1] النّقل والتّحويل وقيل الإبطال. وفي عرف الفقهاء رفع الحكم الثّابت بالخطاب المتقدّم بخطاب مُتراخٍ عنه، علىٰ وجه لولاه لكان ثابتًا.

واختلفوا فقال القاضي أبو بكر[2]: "النّسْخُ رفعٌ"[3]، ومعناه أنَّ خطابه تعالىٰ تعلّق بالفعل، بحيث لولا طريان النّسخ لبقي.

وقال أبو اسحاق[4]: "إنّه بيان انتهاء مدة الحكم"، بمعنىٰ أنّ الخطاب الأوّل انتهى بذاته في ذٰلك الوقت، وحصل بعده حكم آخر.

البحْث الثاني: في جوازه

أكثر المسلمين علىٰ ذٰلك. وخالف فيه أبو مسلم الأصفهاني،[5] وجماعة من اليهود.

---

1 توجد في "ط": عبارة عن. 2 محمد بن عبد الله بن محمد المعافري الإشبيلي المالكي، أبو بكر ابن العربي: قاضٍ، من حفاظ الحديث. ولد في إشبيلية سنة ٤٦٨ هـ/١٠٧٦ م، ورحل إلى المشرق، وبرع في الأدب، وصنف كتبًا في الحديث والفقه والأصول والتفسير والأدب والتاريخ. وولي قضاء إشبيلية، ومات بقرب فاس سنة ٥٤٣ هـ/١١٤٨ م، ودفن بها. لاحظ الأعلام للزركلي: ج ٧/ص ١٠٦. 3 توجد في "ط": الحكم. 4 إبراهيم بن أحمد المروزي، أبو إسحاق: فقيه انتهت إليه رئاسة الشّافعية بالعراق بعد ابن سريج. مولده بمرو الشهجان (قصبة خرسان) وأقام ببغداد أكثر أيامه وله تصانيف. وتوفي بمصر سنة ٣٤٠ هـ/٩٥١ م. لاحظ الأعلام للزركلي: ج ١/ص ٢٢-٢٣. 5 محمد بن بحر الإصفهاني، أبو مسلم: والٍ، من أهل إصفهان. معتزلي. من كبار الكتّاب. كان عالمًا بالتفسير وبغيره من صنوف العلم، وله شعر. ولي إصفهان وبلاد فارس، للمقتدر العباسي، واستمر إلىٰ أن دخل ابن بويه إصفهان سنة ٣٢١هـ، فعزل. من

CHAPTER SEVEN

On Abrogation (*al-naskh*)–Consisting of Five Discussions

1 Discussion One: On the Definition (*taʿrīf*) Thereof

Abrogation (*al-naskh*) in language (*fī al-lughah*) means removal (*al-naql*) and modification (*al-taḥwīl*). It has been said that it means annulment (*al-ibṭāl*). According to the custom of the jurists, (*al-fuqahāʾ*) it means the abolition of a ruling (*al-ḥukm*) confirmed by a previous address (*khiṭāb*) or by a subsequent address, in such a manner that if it were not for that [abolition] it would still be confirmed.

There are different opinions regarding this issue. Qāḍī Abū Bakr is of the opinion that abrogation is abolition (*rafʿ*), which means that the address of the Exalted is attached to the action and if it were not for the coming forth of the abrogation (*al-naskh*) then the ruling would have remained.

Abū Isḥāq is of the opinion that an abrogation is an elucidation denoting that the period of the ruling has ended. It means that the first address ended of itself at that time, and that after it another ruling was obtained.

2 Discussion Two: On the Possibility (*jawāz*) Thereof

The majority of Muslims are in agreement regarding this. Abū Muslim al-Iṣfahānī and a group from among the Jews have opposed its possibility.[1]

1 See Mielzner, Moses, 'Abrogation of laws', *The Jewish Encyclopedia*, 12 vols., New York: 1901–1906., vol. I, pp. 131–33.

لنا أنَّ الأحكام منوطة بالمصالح،[6] ولا امتناع في كون الوجوب مثلاً مصلحة في وقتٍ، ومفسدة في آخر. فلو كُلِّف به دائمًا، لزم التكليف بالمفسدة، فيجب رفعه في وقت كونه مفسدة وهو المطلوب. ولقوله تعالىٰ: ﴿مَا نَنسَخْ مِنْ ءَايَةٍ أَوْ نُنسِهَا نَأْتِ بِخَيْرٍ مِّنْهَآ أَوْ مِثْلِهَآ﴾ [سُورة البَقَرَة:١٠٦]. ولأنَّ النّسخ وقع في شرع اليهود، كتحريم كثير من الحيوان علىٰ لسان موسىٰ عليه السلام مع إباحته[7] الجميع عدا الدم علىٰ لسان نوح، وغير ذٰلك من الأحكام.

85b واحتجاج اليهود بقول | موسىٰ عليه السلام: "تمسّكوا بالسّبت أبدًا" ضعيف. لأنَّ التّأبيد يطلق علىٰ الزّمان الطويل. كقوله في التّوراة: "يُستخدم العبد ست سنين، ثم يُعرض عليه العتق، فإن أبى ثُقِبت أذنه، واستخدم أبدًا" وفي موضوع آخر: "يستخدم العبد خمسين سنة ثم[8] يعتق في تلك السنة". وأيضًا تواتر اليهود انقطع، لأنَّ بختنصر[9] أفناهم إلا من شذَّ.

إذا عرفت هٰذا فالنّسخ قد وقع في القرآن كما في القبلة، والإعتداد للوفاة وثبات الواحد، للعشرة ووجوب تقديم الصّدقة علىٰ المناجاة.

---

6 توجد في "ط": الخلايق. 7 في "د" و"ه" و"ط": اباحة. 8 لا توجد في "ط": ثم.
9 لا توجد في "ط": لأنَّ بختنصر. بخت نصر: -بالتشديد- ملك بابل (٦٠٥- ٥٦٢ ق.م) احتلّ فلسطين وخرب اورشليم وسبى اليهود ٥٨٦ ق.م وأحرق التوراة وقتل منهم مقتلة عظيمة. و"بخت نصر" يعني: ابن الصنم لأنّه وجد عند صنم ولم يعرف له أب فنسب إليه ويعرف بنبوخذ نصّر. لاحظ نهاية الوصول إلىٰ علم الأصول ج٣/ص٣٠٣.

Our argument is that rulings (*al-aḥkām*) are entrusted with welfare (*maṣāliḥ*). There is no impossibility of an obligation (*wujūb*) being, for example, good at a particular time and bad (*mafsadah*) at another time. Therefore, if it were charged perpetually, it would necessitate an injunction for the detrimental (*al-taklīf bi al-mafsadah*). Therefore, its abolition is obligatory when it is detrimental (*mafsadah*), and this is what is sought. Also it is due to His word, the Exalted, 'And for whatever verse We abrogate or cast into oblivion, We bring a better or the like of it'.[2] And because abrogation has occurred in the law of the Jews, such as the forbiddance (*taḥrīm*) of many animals by Moses, despite the indifferency of all animals with the exception of blood by Noah, and other such rulings.

The argument of the Jews, based upon the statement of Moses, 'Forever keep the Sabbath',[3] is weak because perpetuity (*al-ta'bīd*) applies to a lengthy time, like his saying in the Torah, 'A slave may be worked for six years then he may be given the offer of freedom and if he refuses his ears should be pierced and he shall remain a slave forever',[4] whereas he said in another place, 'The slave is to be worked for fifty years, then he should be freed in that year',[5] and also the continuity (*al-tawātur*) of the Jews was disrupted because Nebuchadnezzar annihilated them save a few.[6]

Whenas this is understood, it accounts for why abrogation (*al-naskh*) has occurred in the Qur'ān as in the case of the direction for prayer (*al-qiblah*),[7] the prescribed period for waiting for women before remarrying in case of the husband's death,[8] the endurance of one against ten,[9] and the obligation for offering alms before a private audience with the Prophet.[10]

---

2 Q. 2:106.

3 Exodus 31:16.

4 This is an abbreviated paraphrase of Exodus 21:1–6.

5 Leviticus 25:39–40.

6 *Tawātur* is a term generally used to denote information's being transmitted in a continuous manner from generation to generation in such a way that the information gives rise to certainty.

7 Q. 2:115 is seen to be abrogated by 2:144 and 2:150.

8 Q. 2:240 is seen to be abrogated by 2:234.

9 Q. 8:65 is seen to be abrogated by 8:66.

10 Q. 58:12 is seen to be abrogated by 58:13.

وقوله تعالىٰ: ﴿لَّا يَأْتِيهِ ٱلْبَـٰطِلُ مِنۢ بَيْنِ يَدَيْهِ وَلَا مِنْ خَلْفِهِۦ﴾ [سُورة فُصِّلَت:٤٢]، يريد به لم[10] يتقدمه من كتب الله تعالىٰ ما يبطله ولا يأتيه من بعده ما يبطله، لا ما توهّمه[11] أبو مسلم من نفي النسخ.

البحْث الثالث: في نسخ الشيء قبل مضيّ وقت[12] فعله[13]

ذهب[14] المعتزلة إلىٰ بطلانه. لاستحالة كون الشيء[15] حسنًا وقبيحًا في وقتٍ واحد، والأمر بالقبيح والنّهي عن الحسن. فذٰلك الفعل في ذٰلك الوقت إن كان حسنًا استحال النّهي عنه، وإن كان قبيحًا استحال الأمر به.

والأشعرية ذهبوا إلىٰ جوازه. لأنه تعالىٰ أمر إبراهيم بذبح ولده، لقوله تعالىٰ: ﴿إِنِّىٓ أَرَىٰ فِى ٱلْمَنَامِ أَنِّىٓ أَذْبَحُكَ﴾ [سُورة الصَّافَّات:١٠٢]، ثم نسخ عنه بالفدية. وهٰذا عندي أقوىٰ.

والجواب عن حجّة المعتزلة أنّ الحسن والقبح، كما يوصف الفعل بهما فكذا يلحقان الأمرَ فجاز أن يكون الشّيء حسنًا. إلّا أن الأمر به يشتمل علىٰ نوع مفسدة، فيلحقه النسخ بإعتبار لحوق القبح للأمر لا للمأمور.

البحْث الرابع: [في ما يجوز نسخه]

يجوز نسخ الشّيء إلىٰ غير بدل، كالصدقة أمام المناجاة وإلىٰ ما هو أثقل. ونسخ التّلاوة دون الحكم، وبالعكس. ونسخ الخبر مع تعدّد مقتضاه، كقوله: "أعمرت نوحًا

---

10 في "ط": لمن. 11 في "ط": توهم. 12 في "ط": وقته. 13 لا توجد في "ط": فعله.
14 في "ط": ذهبت. 15 لا توجد في "ط": الشيء.

Furthermore, His word, the Exalted, 'Falsehood comes not to it from before it nor from behind it',[11] which means that no books have come from God, the Exalted, before the Qur'ān which abolish the Qur'ān, and nothing shall come after it to abolish it; nor what Abū Muslim has imagined concerning the denial of abrogation (*al-naskh*)

3 Discussion Three: On the Abrogation (*naskh*) of a Thing Prior to the Expiration of its Time of Performance

The Muʿtazilīs uphold the view that the abrogation of a thing prior to the expiration of its time of performance is invalid due to the impossibility of a thing being both beautiful and ugly at the same time and due to the impossibility of the command for the ugly and the prohibition of the beautiful. Therefore, if action at that time is beautiful then the prohibition thereof would be impossible and if it is ugly then the command thereof would be impossible.

The Ashʿarīs uphold the opinion that it is possible because He, the Exalted, ordered Abraham to sacrifice his son due to His word, the Exalted, 'I see in the dream that I shall sacrifice thee',[12] then He abrogated it for him through the ransom. In my view, this is the stronger opinion.

The answer to the argument of the Muʿtazilīs is that just as an act could be described by both the beautiful and the ugly; likewise, they could both be attached (*ilḥāq*) to the command. Thus, it is possible that a thing could be beautiful, except that the command of it includes a type of detriment, in which case abrogation will be attached to it, through the consideration of the attachment (*luḥūq*) of the ugly to the command, not to that which is commanded.

4 Discussion Four: On What it is Possible to Abrogate (*naskh*)

It is possible: to abrogate something without a substitute, such as dispensing alms prior to the private audience with the Prophet[13] and something of greater importance still; to abrogate the recitation of a verse without the abrogation of its ruling and *vice versa*; to abrogate a narration (*al-khabar*) despite the plurality of its demands, such as His statement that He caused Noah to live for

11 Q. 41:42.

12 Q. 37:102. See also, Fakhr al-Dīn al-Rāzī, *al-Maḥṣūl fī ʿilm al-uṣūl*, vol. III, pp. 311–9.

13 Q. 57:12.

ألف سنة" ثم يقول[16]: "عمّرته ألف سنة إلّا خمسين عامًا". ونسخ الأمر المقيّد بالتأبيد لأنّه شرطه. ونسخ المتواتر من السنة بمثله وبخبر الواحد عقلاً غير | واقع[17]. ونسخ[18] 86a
خبر الواحد بمثله وبالمتواتر. ونسخ الكتاب بمثله، خلافًا للشّافعي، كالقبلة والعدّة.

ونسخ الكتاب بالسنة المتواترة، كالحبس في البيوت خلافًا له. أمّا الإجماع، فلا يَنْسَخُ، لأنّ شرط إنعقاده وفاة الرسول ﷺ ولا يُنْسَخ به لأنّ وقوعه علىٰ خلاف النّص خطأ.

البحث الخامس: [في زيادة العبادة أونقصانها]

لا خلاف في أن زيادة عبادة[19] علىٰ العبادات ليس بنسخ للعبادات، وزيادة غيرها نسخ عند أبي حنيفة، خلافًا للشافعي.

والحقّ ما قاله أبو الحسين، وهو أنّ[20] الزيادة لا شكّ أنّها تقتضي زوال أمرٍ وأقلّه عدمها. فإن كان الزايل[21] حكمًا شرعيًا، وكانت الزّيادة متراخية عنه، سُمِيّت تلك الإزالة نسخًا وإلّا فلا.

وزيادة التّغريب تزيل عدمه، وهو حكم عقلي مستند إلىٰ البراءة الأصلية، لأنّ[22] إيجاب الحدّ لا إشعار فيه، ينفي الزائد ولا إثباته.

---

16 لا توجد في "ط": "أعمرت نوحًا ألف سنة" ثم يقول. 17 لا توجد في "ط": وبخبر الواحد عقلاً غير واقع. 18 لقد وردت (نسخ) في "ج" و"د" و"ه"، ولم ترد في "أ" و"ط". ولعلّ الصّواب ما أثبتناه. 19 توجد في "ط": مستقلة. 20 لا توجد في "ط": أن. 21 في "د": حكم الزائل. 22 لا توجد في "ط": لأن.

'a thousand years' and then His saying that He caused him to live a thousand years, 'save fifty years'; to abrogate a command delimited by perpetuity because that is its condition; to abrogate the continuous tradition by its like whilst a solitary narration is not conceivable by intellection; to abrogate a solitary narration by its like and by a continuous narration; to abrogate the Qur'ān by its like—contrary to the opinion of Shāfiʿī—as in the cases of the direction of prayer and the waiting period for women (after divorce or the death of the husband); and to abrogate the Qur'ān by the continuous tradition (*al-sunnah al-mutawātirah*), such as with the matter of confinement within the house, which is contrary to the Qur'ān. However, as for consensus (*al-ijmāʿ*), it cannot abrogate because the condition for its formation is the death of the Prophet, peace be upon him, and it cannot be abrogated, for its occurrence in contradiction of the text (*al-naṣṣ*) would be a mistake.

5 Discussion Five: Addition to (*ziyādah*) and Omission of (*nuqṣān*) Acts of Worship

There is no disagreement that the addition of an act of worship to the [existing] acts of worship is not an abrogation of the acts of worship. However, according to Abū Ḥanīfah, contrary to al-Shāfiʿī, an addition to anything else[14] is a form of abrogation.

The truth is what Abū al-Ḥusayn maintained, and that is that there is no doubt that the addition demands the removal of a matter, even if what is removed is only the absence of what is added.[15]

If the removed were a legal ruling (*ḥukm sharʿī*) and the addition was postponed thereafter, then that removal would be called an abrogation; and if it is not called an abrogation, then there is no addition.

The addition of banishment (*al-taghrīb*)—[as an element of a punishment for a *ḥadd* crime]—removes the lack of it, and that is a intellective ruling (*ḥukm ʿaqlī*) based upon the principle of original exemption (*al-barā'ah al-aṣliyyah*), for the obligation of the punishment (*al-ḥadd*) contains no indication (*ishʿār*) therein of the negation of the addition or of its affirmation.

---

14 To laws other than the acts of worship, such as those which pertain to social interactions.

15 Al-Baṣrī, Abū al-Ḥusayn, Muḥammad b. ʿAlī b. al-Tayyib, *al-Muʿtamad fī uṣūl al-fiqh*, 2 vols., Damascus, 1964–5, vol. 1, pp. 384–5.

أمّا زيادة ركعة علىٰ الصّبح، فإنّها ترفع وجوب التشهد عقيب الركعتين. فكان نسخًا لهٰذا الحكم لا للرّكعتين،[23] لأنّ النسخ لا يرد علىٰ الأفعال ولا لوجوبهما، ولا[24] لأجزائهما، لأنهما كانتا مُجزِئتين والآن إنما لم تجزِ بالوجوب الثالثة، ووجوب الثالثة إنّما يرفع نفي وجوبها، ونفي وجوبها عقلي.

وأمّا نقصان جزء العبادة، فالحقّ أنه ليس نسخًا للعبادة، لأنّ المقتضي للجزئين ثابت، وخروج احدهما لا يقتضى خروج الآخر، وكذا شرطها. نعم، إنّه نسخ للجزء أو الشرط.[25]

---

23 في "ط": الى الركعتين. 24 لا توجد في "ط": ولا لوجوبهما ولا. 25 في "ه" و"ط": للجزء والشرط.

As for the addition of an inclining of prayer (*rakʿah*) to the morning prayer (*al-ṣubḥ*), that would lift the obligation for the testimony in prayer (*tashahhud*) following the two inclinings of prayer. This would be an abrogation for this ruling[16] not for the two inclinings of prayer—because abrogation is not set forth upon actions—neither for the obligation of the two inclinings nor for their accomplishment, because they have been accomplished. Now, however, the third inclining (*rakʿah*) is not accomplished by way of the obligation of the third. The obligation of the third inclining only lifts the negation of the obligation thereof and the negation of its obligation is intellective.

As for the omission (*nuqṣān*) of a part of an act of worship, the fact is that it is not an abrogation of the act of worship, because the demand of the two parts is confirmed and the exclusion of one of them does not demand the exclusion of the other, and similarly the condition thereof. In fact, it is an abrogation of the part or of the condition.

16 In other words: this ruling of the testimony.

الفَصْلُ الثّامِن

فِي الإِجْمَاع، وفيه مباحث

الأوّل: [في إجماع أمة محمد]

إجماع أمّة محمد صلى الله عليه وآله حق. أمّا علىٰ قولنا فظاهر، لأنّا نوجب المعصوم في كلِّ[1] زمان، وهو سيّد الأمّة، فالحجّة في قوله.

وأمّا المخالف فلقوله تعالىٰ: ﴿وَمَن يُشَاقِقِ ٱلرَّسُولَ مِنۢ بَعۡدِ مَا تَبَيَّنَ لَهُ ٱلۡهُدَىٰ وَيَتَّبِعۡ غَيۡرَ سَبِيلِ ٱلۡمُؤۡمِنِينَ نُوَلِّهِۦ مَا تَوَلَّىٰ﴾ [سُورة النِّساء:١١٥]. والتوعُّد علىٰ اتباعِ غير سبيل المؤمنين[2] يقتضي وجوب إتباع سبيلهم. ولقوله تعالىٰ:| ﴿وَكَذَٰلِكَ جَعَلۡنَٰكُمۡ أُمَّةٗ وَسَطٗا﴾ 86b
[سُورة البَقَرة:١٤٣]، والوسط العدل[3]. ولقوله تعالىٰ: ﴿كُنتُمۡ خَيۡرَ أُمَّةٍ أُخۡرِجَتۡ لِلنَّاسِ تَأۡمُرُونَ بِٱلۡمَعۡرُوفِ وَتَنۡهَوۡنَ عَنِ ٱلۡمُنكَرِ﴾ [سُورة آلِ عِمْرَان:١١٠]، وهو يقتضي أمرهم بكلِّ معروف، ونهيهم عن كلِّ منكر. ولقوله عليه السلام: "لا تَجْتَمِعُ أُمَّتِي عَلىٰ الضَّلَالَة"[4].

البحْث الثاني: [في إحداث قول ثالث]

لا يجوز إحداث قولٍ ثالثٍ، إن لزم منه إبطال ما أجمعوا عليه. كالجَدِّ قيل: له المال، وقيل: يقاسمه الأخ، فِحرمانُهُ باطل. وإن لم يستلزم بطلان الإجماع، جاز لعدم المانع. ولو لم تَفْصِل الأمّة بين المسألتين. فإن نصّوا علىٰ عدمه، امتنع الفصل، وكذا إن عُلِمَ إتحاد طريقة الحكم في المسألتين، كالعمّة والخالة، علّة إرثهما كونهما من ذوي

---

1 لا توجد في "ط": كل. 2 لا توجد في "ط": والتوعُّد علىٰ اتباعِ غير سبيل المؤمنين.

3 لا توجد في "ط": ولقوله تعالىٰ:﴿وَكَذَٰلِكَ جَعَلۡنَٰكُمۡ أُمَّةٗ وَسَطٗا﴾ والوسط العدل.

4 سنن الترمذي، أبي عيسىٰ محمد بن عيسىٰ بن سورة، ٥ مجلدات، بيروت: ١٩٣٧م، ج ٤/ص ٤٦٦.

CHAPTER EIGHT

On Consensus (*al-ijmāʿ*)–Consisting of Four Discussions

1 Discussion One: On the Consensus (*ijmāʿ*) of the *ummah* of Muḥammad

The consensus of the *ummah* of Muḥammad, may God bless him and his descendants, is a fact (*ḥaqq*). As far as our doctrine is concerned this is evident because we deem it necessary that there be an infallible (*maʿṣūm*) in every age and that he is the lord of the *ummah*, therefore the legal proof (*al-ḥujjah*) is within his word (*qawl*).

As far as our opponents are concerned, consensus is a fact, due to His word, the Exalted: 'And whoso makes a breach with the Envoy after the guidance has been elucidated for him, and follows a way other than the believers, him We shall turn over to what he has turned to…'[1] the threat regarding following other than the path of the believers demands the obligation to follow their path, due to His word, the Exalted, 'Thus we have appointed you a midmost (*wasaṭan*) nation',[2] and 'midmost' means just (*al-ʿadl*)His word, the Exalted, 'You are the best nation ever brought forth to men; enjoining the accepted and forbidding the rejected',[3] this demands that they enjoin all that is accepted (*al-maʿrūf*) and forbid all that is rejected (*al-munkar*), and due to his saying, peace be upon him, 'My *ummah* cannot agree upon an error'.

2 Discussion Two: On Introducing (*iḥdāth*) a Third Opinion

It is not possible to introduce a third opinion, if due to it the consensus is made void. Such as in the case of the grandfather inheriting, since it is said that he will inherit the entire sum and it is also said that the sum will be shared between him and the brother, therefore his dispossession would be void. However, if it[4] does not necessitate the consensus to be void then it would be permissible due to the absence of a preventer, even if the *ummah* does not

1 Q. 4:115.
2 Q. 2:143.
3 Q. 3:110.
4 This pronoun refers to the third opinion.

الأرحام، فَمَنْ ورَّث إحداهما ورَّث الأخرىٰ وَمَنْ منع إحداهما منع الأخرىٰ[5]. وإن لم يكن كذٰلك جاز.

البحْث الثالث: [في ما وما لا ينعقد الاجماع به]

يجوز الإتّفاق بعد الخلاف. وإذا أجمع أهل العصر الثاني، علىٰ أحد قوليَ العصر الأوّل انعقد الإجماع. ولو أجمع أهل العصر علىٰ حكم، بعد إختلافهم علىٰ قولين، إنعقد أيضًا. وانقراض العصر غير معتبر، لتناول أدلّة الإجماع مع عدم الإنقراض.

ولو قال بعض أهل العصر قولاً، وسكت الحاضرون، فالحقّ أنّه ليس[6] بإجماع، لإحتمال السّكوت غير الرضا.

ولو قال بعض الصّحابة قولاً،[7] ولم يوجد له مخالف لم يكن إجماعًا. وإجماع أهل المدينة ليس بحجّة، خلافًا لمالك، لأنّهم بعض المؤمنين.

أما إجماع العترة فإنه حجة، لقوله تعالىٰ: ﴿إِنَّمَا يُرِيدُ ٱللَّهُ لِيُذْهِبَ عَنكُمُ ٱلرِّجْسَ أَهْلَ ٱلْبَيْتِ وَيُطَهِّرَكُمْ تَطْهِيرًا﴾ [سُورة الأَحْزَاب:٣٣]. ولقوله[8] عليه السلام: "إني تارك فيكم الثقلين[9] ما إن تمسكتم بهما[10] لن تضلّوا بعدي[11] كتاب الله وعترتي أهل بيتي".[12]

---

5 العبارة (ومَنْ منع... وزيادة في) لم ترد في "أ"، ووردت في "ج" و"د" و"ه" و"ط"، ولعلّ الصّواب ما أثبتناه. 6 توجد في "ه" و"ط": ذٰلك. 7 في "ب": قول. 8 في "ط": ولقول النبي.
9 كذا في "د" و"ه" و"ط"، واللّفظة (الثقلين) لا توجد في "أ" و"ب" و"ج". 10 كذا في "ط"، وفي "أ" و"ب" و"ج" و"د" و"ه": به. 11 كذا في "ط"، وساقطة في "أ" و"ب" و"ج" و"د" و"ه": بعدي. 12 الكافي ج ١/ ص ٢٩٤. موسوعة كتاب الله و أهل البيت في حديث الثقلين، ٤ مجلدات، قم، ١٤٢٩هـ.

differentiate between the two legal issues, since if the *ummah* stipulated the lack of it, differentiation would be impossible. Similarly, if the unity of the method (*ṭarīqah*) of the ruling in the two legal issues is known, such as in the case of the paternal aunt and the maternal aunt, the reason for them being inheritors is that they are relatives through blood and, therefore, if one of them is to inherit the other is also to inherit, and if one of them is barred the other will be barred. However, if the unity of the method (*ṭarīqah*) of a particular ruling is not known then differentiating between the two issues is allowed.

3 Discussion Three: On That by which Consensus (*al-ijmāʿ*) is and is not Established

Agreement (*al-ittifāq*) is permissible after disagreement (*al-khilāf*). Whenas the people of the second era form a consensus about one of the two opinions held by the people of the first era, then a consensus will be established. If the people of a particular era form a consensus about a ruling after having differences about the two views, a consensus will be established. The end of an era is not to be taken in consideration because of the inclusiveness of the arguments of a consensus despite the lack of an ending.

If some people in an era uphold a view whilst others who are present remain silent, then, as a matter of fact, a consensus will not be established because of the likelihood that silence means non-consent.

If some of the companions upheld a view and a contrary view is not to be found, in such a case, it would not constitute a consensus.

The consensus of the folk of Madīnah is not a legal proof, contrary to the opinion of Mālik, because they constitute only some of the believers.

As for the consensus of the Family of the Prophet (*ʿitrah*), it is a legal proof (*ḥujjah*) due to the saying of the Most High, 'Verily, God desires to keep away from you abomination (*rijs*) and to purify you with a purification.[5] [Furthermore], due to the statement of the Prophet, peace be upon him, 'I am leaving among you, two weighty matters, as long as you cleave to them you will never stray, the Book of God and my offspring (*ʿitrah*), who are the People of my House'.

5 Q. 33:33.

البحْث الرابع: [في شرط الإجماع]

لا يجوز الإجماع إلّا عن دليل، وإلّا لزم الخطأ علىٰ كلّ الأمّة. وهل يُعتبر قول العوام[13] في الإجماع. الحقّ عدمه لأنّ قول العامي[14] لا لدليل،[15] فيكون خطأً.

87a فلوكان قول العالم | خطأً، لزم إجماع الأمة علىٰ الخطأ. ولا عبرة بقول الفقيه في مسائل الكلام، ولا بالمتكلم في مسائل الفقه، ولا بقول الحافظ للمسائل[16] والأحكام إذا لم يكن متمكّنًا من الإجتهاد، لأنّهم كالعوام فيما لا يتمكنون من الإجتهاد فيه.

ويُعتبر[17] الأصولي[18] في الأحكام، إذا كان متمكنًا من الإجتهاد فيها، وإن لم يكن حافظًا لها.

وإجماع غير الصّحابة[19] حجة، لتناول الأدلّة له. ولا يجوز وقوع الخطأ من أحد شطري الأمّة في مسئلة، ومن الشطر الآخر في أخرىٰ، لإستلزامه تخطئة[20] كل الأمة.

---

13 في "ط": العامي. 14 في "ط": العامين. 15 توجد في "ط": فيه. 16 في "هـ": للمذاهب. وفي "ط": بالمسائل. 17 في النسخة المطبوعة زيدت هنالك (قول) مع أنّها لم ترد قطّ في النسخ الخطيّة التي اعتمدنا عليها. 18 في "ط": الاصول. 19 لا توجد في "ط": الصحابة. 20 في النسخة المطبوعة: (بخطيئة) وهو خطأ، والصّواب ما أثبتناه.

4 Discussion Four: On The Conditions (*sharṭ*) for Consensus

Consensus is not permissible without evidence (*dalīl*); otherwise, error is imposed upon the whole *ummah*.

Is the opinion of the laymen to be considered regarding consensus? The fact is that it is not, because the opinion of the layman is not based upon evidence (*dalīl*) and therefore it will be erroneous. However, if the opinion of a scholar were mistaken, it would necessitate the consensus of the *ummah* being based upon a mistake.

There is no consideration for the jurist's (*al-faqīh*) view regarding theological issues, nor the opinion of a theologian (*al-mutakallim*) regarding issues of law (*al-fiqh*), nor the opinion of one who knows the Qur'ānic text by heart (*al-ḥāfiẓ*) regarding legal issues (*al-masā'il*) and rulings (*al-aḥkām*) if they do not have the ability to practice juristic reasoning. This is because all of them are like the laymen with regard to that in which they do not have the ability to practice juristic reasoning.

The master of legal methodology (*al-uṣūlī*) should be considered regarding legal rulings (*al-aḥkām*), if he were able to practice juristic reasoning regarding those matters, even if those matters are not committed to his memory.

The consensus of those other than the companions is a legal proof (*ḥujjah*), because the arguments (*adillah*) for consensus are inclusive thereof.

It is not permissible for a mistake to occur in one of the groups of the *ummah* regarding a legal issue and then from the remaining group, regarding another issue, since this would necessitate the error of the whole *ummah*.

الفَصْلُ التَّاسِع

فِي الأَخْبَار، وفيه مباحث

الأوّل: [في تعريف الخبر وأقسامه]

ماهيّة الخبر معلومة بالضّرورة. وإن[1] عُرِض اشتباه، مُيِّز بما يحتمل الصِّدق والكذب ولا يخلو عنهما. وهو إمّا أن يكون مقطوعًا بكونه صدقًا، أو بكونه كذبًا، أو يجوز فيه الأمران.

والأوّل سبعة: المتواتر، وما عُلم وجودُ مُخبَرِهِ إمّا بالضّرورة أو بالإستدلال، وخبر الله، وخبر رسوله، وخبر الإمام عندنا، وخبر كلّ الأمّة، والخبر المعتضد بالقرائن.

والثّاني: الخبر الذي ينافي مُخبَرُهُ وجودَ ما عُلِمَ بالضّرورة أو بالإستدلالِ.

البحْث الثّاني: في إفادة التواتر العلم

الحقّ أنّ خبر المتواتر يفيد العلم الضّروري خلافًا، للسّيد المرتضىٰ حيث وقف،[2] ولأبي الحسين حيث قال انّه نظريّ. لأنّ جزمنا بوقوع الحوادث العِظام كوجود محمّد ﷺ، وحصول البلدان[3] الكبار، لا يَقْصُر عن العلم بأن الكلّ أعظم من الجزء وغيره من الأوليّات. وهو حاصلٌ للعوام، ومن لم يمارس الإستدلال، ولا يُقبل التشكيك.

---

1 في "ب" و"د" و"ه" و"ط": فإن. 2 في "ط": توقف. 3 توجد في "ط": النائية.

CHAPTER NINE

On Narrations (*al-akhbār*)–Consisting of Nine Discussions

1 Discussion One: On the Definition (*taʿrīf*) of a Narration (*al-khabar*) and its Classifications

The quiddity (*māhiyyah*) of a narration is known through necessity (*al-ḍarūrah*), and if any ambiguity were put forth then it would be distinguished by what takes into consideration the likelihood of its truth or its falsity, since it must be one or the other. The narration is either assured (*maqṭūʿ*) in its truth or in its falsity; or both matters are possible regarding it.

The first is sevenfold: a continuous narration (*al-mutawātir*), the existence of the reported content of which is known either through necessity (*al-ḍarūrah*) or through logical inference (*al-istidlāl*); a narration from God (*khabar Allāh*); a narration from His Envoy; a narration from an Imām according to us; the narration of the entire *ummah*; and a narration which is supported by contextual evidence.

The second is the narration whose reported content contradicts the existence of that which is known through necessity (*al-ḍarūrah*) or logical inference (*al-istidlāl*).

2 Discussion Two: On Continuance (*al-tawātur*) Conveying Knowledge (*al-ʿilm*)

The truth is that the continuous narration (*al-mutawātir*) conveys necessary knowledge (*al-ʿilm al-ḍarūrī*), contrary to the opinion of al-Sayyid al-Murtāḍā, insofar as he suspended judgement on this matter[1] and the opinion of Abū al-Ḥusayn, insofar as he upholds the view that it is theoretical (*naẓarī*),[2] because our absolute certainty of the occurrence of great events, such as the existence of Muḥammad, peace be upon him, and the existence of large cities, does not fall short of knowledge that the whole is greater than the part, and other such axioms. This is realisable for the laity and for those who do not practice the art of logical inference (*al-istidlāl*), and it is not receptive to doubt (*al-tashkīk*).

---

1 See al-Sharīf al-Murtaḍā, *al-Dharīʿah ilā uṣūl al-sharīʿah*, vol. II, p. 485.

2 Abū al-Ḥusayn al-Baṣrī, *al-Muʿtamad fī uṣūl al-fiqh*, vol. II, pp. 80–82, 86–92.

البحْث الثّالث: في شرائط المتواتر

منها أن لا[1] يكون السّامع عالمًا بما أخبر بِهِ، لإستحالة تحصيل الحاصل. وأن لا يكون قد سبق شُبهة أو تقليد إلىٰ إعتقاد نفي موجب الخبر. وأن يكون المخبرون مضطرين إلىٰ ما أخبروا عنه، |لإستنادهم إلىٰ الحسّ. وشَرَطَ قومٌ العدد واختلفوا. 87b

فقال قوم اثنا عشر وقال أبو الهذيل عشرون وقيل أربعون وقيل سبعون وقيل ثلثمائة وبضعة عشر. والكلّ[2] ضعيف، بل المرجع فيه إلىٰ حصول اليقين وعدمه، فإن حصل فهو متواتر، وإلّا فلا.

البحْث الرّابع: [في الأقسام الدالة علىٰ صدق الخبر]

خبر الله تعالىٰ صِدق، وهو ظاهر علىٰ قولنا. لأنّه غنيّ عن الكذب، حكيم في أفعاله، عالم بكلّ معلوم، فاستحال وقوع الكذب منه. ولأنّ الرّسول ﷺ أخبر بصدقه، ولا دور هنا.

وخبر النبيّ ﷺ صدق، لدلالة المعجزة عليه. وخبر الإمام صدق، لأنّه معصوم. وخبر كل الأمّة صدق، لما بيَّنا أنّ الإجماع حجة.

البحْث الخامس: [في خبر الواحد]

خبر الواحد هو ما يفيد الظن، وإِنْ تعدَّدَ المخبر وهو حجّة في الشرع، خلافًا للسّيد المرتضىٰ وجماعة.

---

1 سقطت (لا) من "أ" وهي ثابتة في "ج" و"د" و"ه" و"ط". والصّواب ما أثبتناه. 2 في "ط": فالكل.

3 Discussion Three: On the Conditions of the Continuous Narration (*al-mutawātir*)

Among them are that the listener knows not what he is being informed of, due to the impossibility of the realisation of the realised (*taḥṣīl al-ḥāṣil*).

It should not be preceded by any uncertainty (*shubhah*), nor should there be an unquestioning acceptance of a belief that negates the necessarily concomitant knowledge arising from the narration.

The narrators (*al-mukhbirūn*) are compelled to [accept] what they have reported, due to their reliance upon sense perception.

A group of people has set the number [for the narrators] as a condition and they have differed on this matter. A group of people upholds that there should be twelve; Abū al-Hudhayl upholds that they are twenty; and it is also said that they are forty, seventy, three hundred, and ten and some.

All these are weak views; the referent regarding this is the realisation of certainty (*al-yaqīn*) or the lack thereof; thus, if certainty is realised, then it is continuous, otherwise not.

4 Discussion Four: On the Classifications which Signify the Truth (*ṣidq*) of a Narration (*al-khabar*)

A narration (*khabar*) from God, the Exalted, is true. This is evident according to our doctrine because He is needless of lying, He is wise in His actions, and He knows all that is known; therefore, the occurrence of a lie from Him is impossible. Furthermore, the Envoy, peace be upon him, informed us of His veracity, and there is no circular argument (*dawr*) regarding this issue.

A narration (*khabar*) from the Prophet, peace be upon him, is true because of the signification of the miracle regarding it; a narration (*khabar*) from the Imām is true because he is infallible (*maʿṣūm*); the narration (*khabar*) from the entire *ummah* is true, because, as we have elucidated, consensus (*ijmāʿ*) is a legal proof.

5 Discussion Five: On the Solitary Narration (*khabar al-wāḥid*)

The solitary narration is that which conveys probability (*al-ẓann*) even though its reporters are many. It is a legal proof (*ḥujjah*) regarding revealed law (*sharʿ*), contrary to the opinion of al-Sayyid al-Murtaḍā and a group.[3]

---

3 See al-Sharīf al-Murtaḍā, *al-Dharīʿah ilā uṣūl al-sharīʿah*, vol. II, pp. 517–19; Abū Jaʿfar

لنا قوله تعالىٰ: ﴿فَلَوْلَا نَفَرَ مِن كُلِّ فِرْقَةٍ مِّنْهُمْ طَآئِفَةٌ لِّيَتَفَقَّهُواْ فِي ٱلدِّينِ وَلِيُنذِرُواْ قَوْمَهُمْ إِذَا رَجَعُوٓاْ إِلَيْهِمْ لَعَلَّهُمْ يَحْذَرُونَ﴾ [سُورة التَّوْبَة:١٢٢]، أوجب الحذر بإخبار عددٍ لا يفيد قولهم العلم.

وأورد أبو الحسين اعتراضًا لازمًا، وهو دلالته علىٰ قبول[3] الفتوى لا الخبر. وأيضًا قوله تعالىٰ: ﴿إِن جَآءَكُمْ فَاسِقُۢ بِنَبَإٍ فَتَبَيَّنُوٓاْ﴾ [سُورة الحُجُرات:٦]، أوجب التثبت[4] عند إخبار الفاسق، فإذا أخبر العدل لم يخلُ، إمّا أن يجب القبول وهو المطلوب، أو الردّ فيكون أسوأ حالاً من الفاسق وهو باطل، أو يتوقف فينتفي فائدة الوصف بالكليّة.

وأيضًا، فإنَّ خبر الواحد مقبول في الفتوى والشّهادات مع إنتفاء العلم. وأيضًا، فإنّه يتضمَّن دفعَ ضرر مظنون، فيكون واجبًا. ولأنَّ جماعةً من الصّحابة عملوا بأخبارِ الآحاد، ولم ينكر عليهم أحد،[5] فكان إجماعًا.

البحْث السّادس: في شرائطه

88a يشترط[6] كون الرّاوي بالغًا عاقلاً مسلمًا عدلاً ضابطًا. فلا يُقبل[7] | رواية الصّبي، لأنّه إن لم يكن مميّزًا، لم يحصُل الظنّ بقوله، وإن كان مميّزًا، عَلِمَ نفي الحَرَج عنه مع الكذب فلا يمتنع منه. ويُقبل روايته لو كان صبيًّا وقت التّحمل بالغًا وقت الأداء.

---

3 في النسخة المطبوعة (قول) بدلاً من (قبول) وهو خطأ. والصّحيح ما أثبتناه. 4 في "هـ" و"ط": التبين. 5 لا توجد في "ب": أحد. 6 لا توجد في "ط": يشترط. 7 في "هـ": فلا تُقبل. ولعلّه الصّواب.

Our argument for this is due to His word, the Exalted: 'Why should not a party from every section of them go forth to understand the religion and to warn their people when they return to them so that they may be cautious'.[4] This verse obligates [the adoption of] caution (*al-ḥadhar*) with respect to the information presented by a number of people whose statement does not convey knowledge (*al-ʿilm*). Abū al-Ḥusayn brought forth a necessary objection, and this is that it is a signification for the statement of an edict (*al-fatwā*) and not [for] the narration (*al-khabar*).[5]

Also His word, the Exalted, 'If an ungodly man (*al-fāsiq*) comes to you with a tiding then clarify',[6] obligates the verification (*al-tathabut*) of information presented by an ungodly man. When a just person (*ʿadl*) presents information there are three possibilities, it would be obligatory: to accept it, which is what is sought; to reject it, which would mean that he is worse in state than an ungodly man and that is void; or to suspend judgement on it, which would negate the point of the qualification completely (*al-waṣf bi al-kulliyyah*).

In addition, the solitary narration is accepted regarding an edict (*al-fatwā*) and testimonies (*al-shahādāt*), despite the lack of knowledge (*al-ʿilm*).

Furthermore, if it encompasses the prevention of a probable (*maẓnūn*) harm, it would be obligatory (*wājib*) to accept it, because a group of the companions acted in accordance with the solitary narrations and no one disputed with them, thus there was a consensus (*ijmāʿ*).

6 Discussion Six: On the Qualifications (*sharāʾiṭ*) for a Transmitter of a Narration

It is a condition that the transmitter (*al-rāwī*) is of age (*bāligh*), sane (*ʿāqil*), a Muslim, just (*ʿadl*), and in possession of exactitude (*ḍābiṭ*). Thus, the transmission (*riwāyah*) of a child would not be accepted because he was not of discernment, then probability (*ẓann*) would not be realised by his word. However, if he were of discernment he could be aware that he was excluded from sin (*nafīal-ḥaraj*) in relation to lying, hence he might not hold himself back from doing so. The transmission of the child will be accepted if he was a child at the time of hearing it, but was of age at the time of conveying it.

Muḥammad b. Manṣūr b. Aḥmad b. Idrīs al-Ḥillī, *Kitāb al-sarāʾir al-ḥāwī li-taḥrīr al-fatāwī*, Qum, 1410, vol. I, p. 47; ʿIzz al-Dīn Ḥamzah b. ʿAlī b. Zuhrah al-Ḥalabī, *Ghunyat al-nuzūʿ*, in: *al-Jawāmiʿ al-fiqhiyyah*, Tehran, n.d., p. 537. Al-Mufīd does not permit abrogation of the Qurʾān by the *Sunnah*. See al-Mufīd, *al-Tadhkirah*, pp. 43–4.

4 Q. 9:122.

5 Abū al-Ḥusayn al-Baṣrī, *al-Muʿtamad fī uṣūl al-fiqh*, vol. II, pp. 110–11.

6 Q. 49:6.

والكافر لا يقبل[8] روايته سواء كان مذهبه جواز الكذب أو لا، لأنّه فاسق والفاسق مردود الرّواية، ولا يقبل[9] رواية الفاسق للآية.

ولا يقبل[10] رواية المجهول حاله، خلافًا لأبي حنيفة، لأنّ عدم الفسق شرط في الرواية، وهومجهول، والجهل بالشّرط يستلزم الجهل بالمشروط.

البحث السّابع: في ما ظن أنّه شرط وليس كذٰلك

الصّحيح أنّ الواحد إذاكان عدلاً قُبِلَت روايته، سواء عضده ظاهر أو عملُ[11] بعض الصحابة أو إجتهاد أو رواية عدل آخر خلافًا للجُبائي[12]. لأنَّ الصّحابة رجعوا إلىٰ أخبار العدل، وإن كان واحدًا ولأنَّ الأدلّة تتناوله.[13]

ولا يشترط كون الرّاوي فقيهًا، خلافًا لأبي حنيفة، فيما خالف القياس، لما تقدّم من الأدلّة العامّة. ولقوله عليه السلام: "نَضَّرَ اللّٰه إمرءًا سمع مقالتي فوعاها فأدّاها كما سمعها، فرُبَّ حاملِ فقهٍ[14] ليس بفقيه"[15]. ولا يُشترط عدم مخالفة الرّاوي له، لإحتمال صيرورة الرّاوي إلىٰ ما توهّمه[16] دليلاً وليس كذٰلك.[17]

والأقرب عدم اشتراط نقل اللفظ، مع الإتيان بالمعنىٰ كملاً، لأنّ الصّحابة لم ينقلوا الألفاظ كما هي، لأنّهم لم يكتبوها، ولاكرّروا عليها مع تطاول الأزمنة.

---

8 في "هـ": لا تقبل. ولعلّه الصّواب. 9 في "هـ": لا تقبل. ولعلّه الصّواب. 10 في "هـ": لا تقبل. ولعلّه الصّواب. 11 في "أ": عمل به. وفي "ج" و"د" و"هـ" و"ط": عمل بعض. ولعلّه الصّواب. 12 في "ط": للجبائين. 13 في "ب": يتناوله. 14 وفسره الناسخ في الهامش الأيمن مِن "أ": الى من هو أفقه منه. 15 الكافي ج ١ / ص ٤٠٣. 16 في "ط": توهم. 17 في "د": بدليل.

The transmission (*riwāyah*) of the disbeliever will not be accepted, regardless of whether his system of belief (*madhhab*) allows him to lie or not, because he is deemed an ungodly man (*fāsiq*) and the transmission of an ungodly man is rejected. The transmission of an ungodly man is not accepted on account of the Qur'ānic verse.[7]

The transmission of a person whose state is not known (*al-majhūl*) will not be accepted, contrary to the opinion of Abū Ḥanīfah, for the absence of ungodliness (*al-fisq*) is a condition for the acceptability of a transmission. Thus, his state is unknown and ignorance of a condition necessitates ignorance of the conditioned.

7 Discussion Seven: On that which is Considered a Condition (*sharṭ*) Whilst it is not

The correct opinion is that the transmission (*riwāyah*) of the single individual is accepted if he is just (*ʿadl*); regardless of whether he is supported ostensibly (*ẓāhir*), or by the action of one of the companions (*al-ṣaḥābah*), or by juristic reasoning (*ijtihād*), or by the transmission (*riwāyah*) of another just person, contrary to the opinion of Jubbā'ī, because the companions referred to the narrations (*akhbār*) of a just person even though he was a single individual because he is included in the pieces of evidence (*al-adillah*).

In cases that contradict analogical reasoning (*al-qiyās*), it is not a condition that the transmitter (*rāwī*) be a jurist (*faqīh*), contrary to the opinion of Abū Ḥanīfah, due to the general arguments which were presented earlier. And due to what he, peace be upon him, said, 'May God illuminate the face of a person who hears my sayings and commits them to his memory, and conveys them as he heard them, for there are many bearers of law (*fiqh*) who are not jurists (*faqīh*)'.

It is not a condition that there should be no opposition to a transmitter (*rāwī*) of a narration, due to the likelihood of a transmitter coming to the conclusion that what he imagined to be a piece of evidence, was not.

The most favoured opinion is that it is not a condition to convey the utterance with the meaning [being] brought forth in its entirety, since the companions did not convey the utterances as they were, and neither did they record them in writing, nor did they reiterate them with the passing of time.

7 Q. 49:6.

البحْث الثّامن: في الأخبار المردودة

خبر الواحد إذا اقتضىٰ علماً، ولم يوجد في الأدلّة القاطعة ما يدلّ عليه وجب ردّه، لأنّه اقتضىٰ التكليف بالعلم ولا يفيده فيلزم تكليف ما لا يطاق.

وإن اقتضىٰ العمل، وجب قبوله وإن عمَّت به البلوىٰ، خلافاً للحنفيّة لعموم الأدلّة، ولأنّ الصّحابة رجعوا | في أحكام الرّعاف والقيّ والقهقهة في الصّلاة، إلىٰ الآحاد 88b مع عموم البلوىٰ فيها.

والمُرسَل لا يُقبل، خلافاً لأبي حنيفة ومالك وجمهور المعتزلة، لأنّ عدالة الأصل مجهولة، والشّك في الشّرط يستلزم الشّك في المشروط.

وإذا جَزَمَ راوي الأصل، بكذب رواية الفرع عنه، لم تقبل رواية الفرع[18]. وإن توقَّف، قُبِلَ قول الفرع لعدم المنافي.

البحْث التّاسع: في الجرح والتعديل

العدد شرط في الجرح والتّعديل، في الشّهادة دون الرّواية، لأنّ الفرع لا يزيد عن[19] الأصل. ولا بدّ من ذكر سبب الجرح دون التّعديل.

ومع التّعارض يقدّم الجارح،[20] إلا إذا نفى المُعَدِّلُ ما أثبته الجارح قطعاً، فيتعارضان.

---

18 لا توجد في "ط": لم تقبل رواية الفرع. 19 في "ب" و"ج" و"ه": علىٰ. 20 في "ط": الجرح.

8 Discussion Eight: On Rejected Narrations (*al-akhbār al-mardūdah*)

When the solitary narration demands knowledge (*ʿilm*) and what signifies it, and the decisive [pieces of] evidence (*al-adillah al-qāṭiʿah*) are not to be found, then its rejection is obligatory, because it would demand an injunction (*al-taklīf*) on the basis of knowledge and yet would not convey it. Thus, it would necessitate an injunction of what is not feasible (*taklīf mā lā yuṭāq*).

If the solitary narration demands action (*al-ʿamal*), then its acceptance is obligatory if there is a general need—contrary to the opinion of the Ḥanafīs—due to the generality of the evidence (*al-adillah*), and because the companions referred to the solitary narration, with regard to the rulings for nosebleeds, vomiting, and coughing during prayer (*al-ṣalāt*), with the generality of need therein.

The narration that does not include the name of its original transmitter (*al-mursal*) is not acceptable—contrary to the opinion of Abū Ḥanīfah, Mālik, and the great majority of the Muʿtazilīs—because the justness (*ʿadālah*) of the original [transmitter] is unknown, and doubt with regard to the condition necessitates doubt with regard to the conditioned.

If the transmitter of the source (*rāwī al-aṣl*) is absolutely certain of the falsehood of the transmission of the second person from him, then the transmission of the second person will not be accepted, and if he suspends judgement, then the words of the second person will be accepted due to the absence of inconsistency.

9 Discussion Nine: On Invalidation (*al-jarḥ*) and Validation (*al-taʿdīl*)

Number (*al-ʿadad*) is a condition regarding invalidation (*al-jarḥ*) and validation (*al-taʿdīl*) in the matter of testimony (*al-shahādah*) and not with regard to the transmission (*al-riwāyah*) because the second [person] cannot add to the source.

It is a must to mention the reason for the invalidation, but not for the validation (*al-taʿdīl*).

In the case of contradiction, the invalidator takes precedence except when the validator denies what the invalidator has confirmed in definite terms, and thus they contradict one another.

وإذا[21] حكم بشهادته، أو عمل بروايته أو قال: "هو عدل لأني عرفت منه كذا"، أو أطلق مع عرفانه، فهو تزكية. ولو روى عنه لم يكن تزكيةً، إلا أن تكون عادته عدم الرواية عن غير العدل. وليس ترك الحكم بالشّهادة جرحًا.

21 توجد في "ط": قال المعدل احكم.

If judgement is passed on the basis of the [transmitter's] testimony, or action is performed on the basis of his transmission, or it is said, 'he is a just person because I know him to be so', or justness is applicable to him with knowledge thereof,[8] then that is an attestation of integrity (*tazkiyah*). However, if he has transmitted from him then that is not to be considered as an attestation of integrity (*tazkiyah*), except if it is his habit of only transmitting from just persons. Furthermore, abstaining from passing a judgement on the basis of testimony is not an invalidation (*jarḥ*).

8 For a complete understanding of this phrase, which is here concisely expressed by 'Allāmah, it is helpful to consult 'Allāmah's *Tahdhīb al-wuṣūl ilā 'ilm al-uṣūl* and *Nihāyat al-wuṣūl ilā 'ilm al–uṣūl*. From what is stated therein it becomes clear that the phrase 'knowledge thereof' is a reference to the knowledge of the conditions of justness. See pp. 79–80 in the former and vol. III, p. 429 of the latter, where he discusses the four stages of the attestation of integrity.

الفَصْلُ العَاشِر

فِي القِيَاس، وفيه مباحث

الأوّل: في تعريفه

القياس عبارة عن حمل الشيّء علىٰ غيره، في إثبات مثل حكمه له، لإشتراكهما في علّة الحكم.

وأركانه أربعة:[1] الأصل وهو المقيس عليه، والفرع هو المقيس،[2] والعلّة هي المعنىٰ المشترك، والحكم وهو المطلوب اثباته في الفرع.

البحْث الثاني: في أنّه ليس بحجّة

اختلف النّاس في ذٰلك، والذي نذهب إليه أنه ليس بحجة لوجوه.

أحَدها، قوله تعالىٰ:

﴿لَا تُقَدِّمُوا۟ بَيْنَ يَدَىِ ٱللَّهِ وَرَسُولِهِۦ﴾ [سُورة الحُجُرَات:١].

﴿وَأَن تَقُولُوا۟ عَلَى ٱللَّهِ مَا لَا تَعْلَمُونَ﴾ [سُورة الأَعْرَاف:٣٣].

﴿إِنَّ ٱلظَّنَّ لَا يُغْنِى مِنَ ٱلْحَقِّ شَيْـًٔا﴾ [سُورة النَّجْم:٢٨].

﴿وَأَنِ ٱحْكُم بَيْنَهُم بِمَآ أَنزَلَ ٱللَّهُ﴾ [سُورة المَائِدَة:٤٩].

---

1 لا توجد في "ط": أربعة. 2 لا توجد في "ط": عليه والفرع هو المقيس.

CHAPTER TEN

On Analogical Reasoning (*al-qiyās*)–Consisting of Five Discussions

1 Discussion One: On the Definition (*taʿrīf*) of Analogical Reasoning (*al-qiyās*)

Analogical reasoning (*al-qiyās*) is an expression given to the predication of one case to another, in order to confirm the likeness of its judgement for it, because of both cases sharing the cause of the judgment (*ʿillat al-ḥukm*).[1]

The foundations of analogical reasoning are fourfold: the principle case (*al-aṣl*), that from which analogy is drawn (*al-maqīs ʿalayhi*); the secondary case (*al-farʿ*), that which is analogically compared (*al-maqīs*); the cause (*al-ʿillah*), that is the common notion; and the ruling (*al-ḥukm*), the confirmation of which is sought regarding the secondary case.

2 Discussion Two: On Analogical Reasoning not being a Legal Proof (*ḥujjah*)

The people have differed regarding this issue. The view that we uphold is that it is not a legal proof (*ḥujjah*) due to the following reasons.

Firstly, His word, the Exalted:

> 'Be not forward in the presence of God and His Envoy'.[2]
> 'That you say concerning God such as you know not'.[3]
> 'Verily surmise avails naught against truth'.[4]
> 'And judge between them according to what God has revealed'.[5]

---

1 The word 'case', as a translation of *al-shay'*, is used in this context according to the sense of 1. b. as given by the OED—meaning 'a thing'.

2 Q. 49:1.

3 Q. 7:33.

4 Q. 53:28.

5 Q. 5:49.

الثّاني، قوله عليه السلام:

"وتعمل هٰذه الأمة برهةً بالكتاب وبرهةً بالسنَّة وبرهةً بالقياس فإذا فعلوا ذٰلك فقد ضلّوا وأضلّوا".[3]

وقوله عليه السلام:

89a "ستفترق أمّتي علىٰ بضع وسبعين فرقة | أعظمهم فتنةً قومٌ يُقِيسُون الأُمور برأيهم فيحرّمون الحلال ويحلّلون الحرام".[4]

الثالث، إجماع الصّحابة عليه. روي عن عليّ عليه السلام أنه قال: "من أرادَ أن يقتحمَ جراثيم جهنّم فليقل في الجَدّ برأيِه"[5] وقال: "لو كان الدين بالرأي لكان باطن الخُفّ أولىٰ[6] بالمسح من ظاهِرِه"[7]. وقال أبوبكر: "أيّ سماء تظلّني وأيّ أرض تُقلّني إذا قلت في كتاب الله برأيي".[8]

وقال عمر: "إياكم وأصحابُ الرأي فإنهم أعداءُ السنن، أعيَتْهم الأحاديث أن يحفظوها فقالوا بالرأي فَضَلّوا وأضلّوا".[9]

---

3 مُلخّص إبطال القياس والرأي والاستحسان والتقليد والتعليل، ابن حزم الأندلسي، دمشق: ١٣٧٩هـ/١٩٦٠م، ص٥٦. 4 الإِحكام في أصُول الأحكام، أبي محمد علي بن أحمد بن سعيد بن حزم الظاهري، ٢مجلدات، بيروت: ج ٢ / ص٥٣٦. مُلخّص إبطال القياس والرأي والاستحسان والتقليد والتعليل ص٦٩. 5 من لا يحضره الفقيه ج ٤ / ص٢٠٨.
6 لا توجد في "ط": أولىٰ. 7 سنن أبي داود، أبي داود سليمان بن الأشعث السجستاني الأزدي، ٥مجلدات، حمص: ١٣٨٨هـ / ١٩٦٩م، ج ١ / ص١١٤. 8 مُلخّص إبطال القياس والرأي والاستحسان والتقليد والتعليل ص٥٦–٥٧. 9 مُلخّص إبطال القياس والرأي والاستحسان والتقليد والتعليل ص٥٨.

Secondly, the statements of the Prophet, peace be upon him:

> This *ummah* will at times resort to the Book; at times to the *Sunnah*; at times to analogy (*al-qiyās*), and when they have done such they shall have gone astray and led others astray.
>
> My *ummah* shall be divided into seventy and some sects. The greatest of them in discord shall be those who make analogy with matters on the basis of their personal opinion (*ra'y*), thus forbidding the lawful and allowing the unlawful.

Thirdly, the consensus of the companions on this matter. It is reported from ʿAlī, peace be upon him, that he said, 'One who wishes to plunge into the pits of Hell, then let him speak in matters of seriousness according to his personal opinion'. Also he said, 'If religion is to be according to personal opinion, then the sole of the foot would be more appropriate for anointing [in ablution] than its back'.

Abū Bakr said: 'Which sky will shade me, which earth will raise me, if I give my personal opinion (*ra'y*) regarding the Book of God?'

ʿUmar said: 'Be warned about the people of personal opinion (*aṣḥāb al-ra'y*), for they are the enemies of the *Sunnah*. They could not memorise the traditions (*al-aḥādīth*) and so they gave their personal opinions and went astray and led others astray'.

ولم يزل[10] أهل البيت عليهم السلام ينكرون العمل بالقياس،[11] ويذمون العمل به، وإجماع العترة حجة.

الرّابع، إنّ العمل بالقياس يستلزم الإختلاف، لإستناده إلىٰ الإمارات المختلفة والإختلاف منهي عنه.

الخامس، مبني شرعنا علىٰ تساوي المختلفات في الأحكام، واختلاف المتماثلات فيها، وذٰلك يمنع من القياس قطعًا.

البحْث الثّالث: [في إلحاق المسكوت عنه بالمنطوق]

إلحاق المسكوت عنه بالمنطوق، قد يكون جليًا كتحريم الضّرب المستفاد من تحريم التأفيف، وذٰلك ليس من باب القياس. لأنّ شرط هٰذا كون المعنىٰ المسكوت عنه، أولىٰ بالحكم[12] من المنصوص[13] عليه، بخلاف القياس بل هو من باب المفهوم.

البحْث الرّابع: [في الحكم المنصوص علىٰ علته]

الأقرب عندي أنّ الحكم المنصوص علىٰ علّته متعدّ إلىٰ كلّ ما علم ثبوت تلك العلة فيه، بالنصّ لا بالقياس. لأنّ قوله: "حرّمت الخمر لكونه مسكراً" ينزّل منزلة قوله: "حرمت كل مسكر". لأنّ مجرّد الإسكار إن كان هو العلّة لزم وجود المعلول معه أينما[14] تحقق، وإلّا لم يكن[15] علة.

---

10 لا توجد في "ط": يزل. 11 لا توجد في "ط": بالقياس. 12 لا توجد في "ط": بالحكم.
13 في "ه" و"ط": بالنصوص. 14 في "أ" و"د" و"ه": أين. ولعلّه تصحيف. و في "ج" و"ط": أينما. ولعلّه الصّواب. 15 توجد في "ط": الاسكار.

The Folk of the House (*ahl al-bayt*), peace be upon them, continuously denounced actions on the basis of analogical reasoning (*al-qiyās*), and rebuked the practitioners thereof. The consensus (*ijmāʿ*) of the descendants of the Prophet (*al-ʿitrah*) is a legal proof (*ḥujjah*).

Fourthly, action on the basis of analogical reasoning (*al-qiyās*) necessitates discordance due to its reliance on different indications (*al-imārāt*), and discordance is not allowed.

Fifthly, the foundation of our law is the alikeness of the dissimilar (*al-mukhtalifāt*) in rulings and the difference (*ikhtilāf*) of the similar therein. This assuredly bars the use of analogical reasoning.

3 Discussion Three: On the Connection of the Unspoken (*al-maskūt*) to the Spoken (*al-manṭūq*)

The connection of the unspoken to the spoken is sometimes obvious (*jalī*), such as with the forbiddance of striking (*taḥrīm al-ḍarb*) which is understood (*al-mustafād*) from the forbiddance of the expression of anger and displeasure (*al-taʾfīf*).[6] This is not a form of analogical reasoning, because the condition for this is that the meaning that is unspoken is more appropriate for the ruling than what is explicitly designated (*al-manṣūṣ ʿalayhi*). This is contrary to analogical reasoning, rather, it comes under the category of the implicit (*al-mafhūm*).

4 Discussion Four: On the Ruling (*al-ḥukm*) in Which the Cause is Explicitly Designated (*al-manṣūṣ ʿalā ʿillatihi*)

The most favoured opinion, nigh myself, is that the ruling whose cause is explicitly designated will extend to every subject where it is known to have the same confirmable cause through an explicit designation (*al-naṣṣ*) and not through analogical reasoning (*al-qiyās*), because the Lawgiver saying, 'I have forbidden wine due to it's being an intoxicant'[7] is the same as him saying, 'I have forbidden every intoxicant'. If mere intoxication is the cause (*al-ʿillah*), it is necessary that the effect (*al-maʿlūl*) exist with it wherever the cause is realised, otherwise, it would not be the cause.

---

6 See Q. 17:23. This is the standard given example that the Qurʾānic prohibition on being verbally dismissive or rude towards one's parents naturally implies that physical violence towards them must also be prohibited.

7 This is not a Qurʾānic verse, rather it is a long-accepted principle among jurists based on various sources, including Q. 4:43.

وإن كانت العلّة إنّما هي[16] الإسكار المقيّد بالخمرية، لم يكن ما فرضنا علّة بل جزء العلّة، وهٰذا خُلْفٌ.[17]

والنصّ علىٰ العلّة قد يكون صريحًا، كقوله: "لعلّة كذا أو لأجل كذا أو لسبب[18] كذا".

وقد يكون ظاهرًا، كقوله: "لكذا | أو بكذا[19]"، أو يأتي بحرف "ان" كقوله: "إِنَّها مِنَ الطَّوَّافِينَ عليكم"[20]، أو بالباء كقوله تعالىٰ: ﴿فَبِظُلۡمٖ مِّنَ ٱلَّذِينَ هَادُواْ حَرَّمۡنَا عَلَيۡهِمۡ طَيِّبَٰتٍ أُحِلَّتۡ لَهُمۡ﴾ [سُورة النِّسَاء: ١٦٠]. 89b

البحث الخامس: [في العلة المستنبطة]

اعلم أنّا لمّا جوزنا تعدية الحكم بالعلّة المنصوصة، وجب علينا البحث عن العلة المستنبطة، وبيان امتناع تعدية الحكم بها كما يقوله[21] أصحاب القياس.

واعلم أنّ الطرق التي يُثبت القائسون التعليل بها ستة ونحن نبيّن في كلّ واحد منها، أنّه لا يصلح الإستدلال به[22] علىٰ عليّة الوصف.

الأوّل: المناسبة

وعرفوا المناسبة بأنّه الملائم لأفعال العقلاء في العادات، وهو غير دال علىٰ العلية.

---

16 لا توجد عبارة (إنّما هي) في "أ" وتوجد في "ج" و"د" و"هـ" و"ط" ولعلّ الصّواب ما أثبتناه.

17 لا توجد لفظة (خلف) في "هـ" و في "ط": (هف). وهو محرف.

18 في "ب": بسبب.

19 لا توجد في "ط": بكذا.

20 مسند أحمد بن حنبل، ٦ مجلدات، ج ٥ / ص ٣٠٣ و٣٠٩.

21 في "ط": يقول.

22 لا توجد (به) في "أ" و"ج" و"د" و"هـ" وتوجد في "ط" ولعلّه الصّواب.

However, if the cause is intoxication delimited to wine, then whatever we have assumed will not be the cause but will be a part of the cause and this is a contradiction (*khulf*).

Sometimes the explicit designation (*al-naṣṣ*) of the cause (*al-ʿillah*) is clear (*ṣarīḥ*), as when the Lawgiver says, 'Due to such a cause' or 'Because of such and such' or 'For such a reason'. Sometimes the cause is evident (*ẓāhir*), such as the Lawgiver saying, 'Due to this' or 'By this', or using the particle of *an*, like his statement, 'Verily it is of those that go round about waiting upon you', or of the *bāʾ*, such as the saying of God, the Exalted: 'And for the evildoing of those of Jewry, We have forbidden them certain good things that were permitted to them'.[8]

5 Discussion Five: On the Derived Cause (*al-ʿillah al-mustanbiṭah*)

Let it be known that since we permit the extension of the legal ruling (*taʿdiyat al-ḥukm*) through an explicitly designated cause (*al-ʿillah al-manṣūṣah*), it is a must that we discuss the derived cause (*al-ʿillah al-mustanbiṭah*) and elucidate the impossibility of the extension of the ruling through it, as is the view of the proponents of analogical reasoning (*aṣḥāb al-qiyās*).

Let it be known that there are six methods by which the practitioners of analogical reasoning have asserted the matter of causational inference (*al-taʿlīl*).

We shall elucidate all six and show the invalidity of inference by means of them in accordance with the causality of a quality (*ʿilliyyat al-waṣf*).

5.1 *The First: Suitability* (*al-munāsabah*)

The practitioners of analogical reasoning have defined suitability (*al-munāsabah*) as something appropriate for the actions of men of sound mind in customary practices, and this does not signify causality.

---

8 Q. 4:160.

إمّا اولاً، لما[23] بيّنا أنّ شرعنا مبني علىٰ الجمع بين المختلفات، والتفرقة بين المتماثلات، فلا ضابط في الحكم سوىٰ النصّ. وأمّا ثانيا، فلأن الوصف المناسب، قد يقترن مع الحكم وضدّه. وأما ثالثًا، فلأنّ الحكم لا يجوز استناده إلىٰ الحكمة، لكونها مضطربة غير مضبوطة، ومثل ذٰلك لا يجوز من الحكيم رد الأحكام إليه، ولا إلىٰ الوصف، لأنّه إن[24] لم يشتمل علىٰ الحكمة لم يصلح[25] للتعليل، وإن اشتمل كانت[26] الحكمة علة العلة وقد بينا بطلانه.

الثاني: المؤثر

وعرفوه بأنّه الوصف المؤثّر في جنس الحكم[27] في الأصول دون وصف آخر، فيكون أولىٰ[28] بالتعليل من الوصف الآخر. مثال ذٰلك، البلوغ المؤثّر في رفع الحجر عن[29] المال، فيؤثر في رفع الحجر عن النكاح[30] دون الثيبوبة. لأنّها لا تؤثر في جنس هٰذا الحكم وهو رفع [31] الحجر. وكقولهم، الأخ من الأبوين مقدم علىٰ الأخ من الأب في الميراث، فيكون مقدّمًا في ولاية النّكاح. ويعللون تقديمه في النّكاح، بسبب تقديمه في الإرث بالمناسبة. وهو راجع في الحقيقة إلىٰ الوصف المناسب، وإبطاله يقتضي إبطال هٰذا.

---

23 في "ب": فلما. 24 في "ط": لو. 25 في "ه" و"ط": يصح. 26 لا توجد في "ط": كانت. 27 توجد في "ط": المناسب. 28 لا توجد في "ط": اولى. 29 المتن من (البحث الخامس...) إلىٰ (...رفع الحجر عن) ناقص في "ج"، واعتمدنا علىٰ النسخة "د" لاستنساخ وقراءة وتصحيح النصّ. 30 لا توجد في "ط": عن النكاح. 31 توجد في "د": هٰذا.

Either: firstly, since we have elucidated that our law is based on the drawing together of the dissimilar (*al-mukhtalifāt*) and differentiation between the similar (*al-mutamāthilāt*), and since there is no exactitude (*ḍābiṭ*) regarding the ruling (*al-ḥukm*) except explicit designation (*al-naṣṣ*); or, secondly, because the suitable quality (*al-waṣf al-munāsib*) might be linked to the ruling (*al-ḥukm*) and its opposite; or, thirdly, because it is not permitted for the ruling to be based upon philosophising (*al-ḥikmah*), due to its being muddled (*muḍṭaribah*) and not exact (*ghayr maḍbūṭah*), and in suchlike it is not permissible for the wise to refer rulings to that nor to the quality (*al-waṣf*) since, if it does not include philosophising it would not be appropriate for causational inference (*al-taʿlīl*), and, if it does include it, then the philosophising would be the cause of the cause (*ʿillat al-ʿillah*), which we have elucidated the voidness thereof.

5.2 *The Second: The Effective* (*al-mu'aththir*)

The practitioners of analogical reasoning have defined this as the effective quality (*al-waṣf al-mu'aththir*) in the genus of the ruling, regarding the principles (*al-uṣūl*), excluding another quality (*waṣf*), and so it is more appropriate for causational inference (*al-taʿlīl*) than any other quality. The example given for this is [the issue of] maturity that is effective (*al-bulūgh al-mu'aththir*) in removing the interdiction on the use of goods [from an inherited estate], hence it is also effective in the removal of the interdiction regarding marriage (*nikāḥ*), other than the status of deflowering, for it is not effective in the genus of this ruling and that is the removal of the interdiction. Like their upholding the view, 'The brother from both parents takes precedence over the brother from the father in matters of inheritance, and hence he has precedence regarding legal guardianship in marriage'. They have inferred the cause of his precedence in marriage through the reason of his precedence in inheritance by suitability (*al-munāsabah*), and this refers in reality to the suitable quality (*al-waṣf al-munāsib*) and the voidness thereof demands the voidness of this.

الثـالث: الشبه 90a

وهو الوصف المستلزم للمناسب، وليس فيه مناسبة. وهو غير دالّ علىٰ العلية أيضًا، لأن المناسب أقوىٰ منه وقد أبطلناه، ولأنّ الصّحابة لم يعملوا بالوصف الشبهي، فيكون مردودًا.

الرابـع: الدّوران

وهو[32] غير دال علىٰ العلية، سواء كان ذٰلك في صورة واحدة أو صورتين، لتحققه فيما ليس بعلة. فإنّ المعلول دائر مع العلة وبالعكس، وليس المعلول علة وجزء العلة المساوي دائر مع المعلول وليس بعلة. وكذا الشّرط المساوي واحد المعلولين، دائر مع صاحبه ولا عليّة بينهما. والجوهر والعرض متلازمان. وكذا المضافان والحركة والزّمان، مع انتفاء العليّة في ذٰلك كلّه، إلى غير ذٰلك من الأمثلة التي لا تحصى كثرة.

الخـامس: طريقـة السّبر والتقسيم

بأن يقال لا بدّ للحكم من علّة، والوصف الفلاني لا يصلح لذٰلك، وكذٰلك الوصف الفلاني[33] فبقي الثالث. وهو غير دال علىٰ العلية أيضًا. أمّا أولا، فللمنع[34] من تعليل كل حكم. وأمّا ثانيًا، فللمنع من حصر الأوصاف،[35] وعدم الوجدان لا يدلّ علىٰ عدم الوجود. وأمّا ثالثًا، فللمنع من بطلان التعليل بأحد الأوصاف المذكورة. وأمّا رابعًا، فلجواز التعليل بمجموع وصفين من هٰذه أو ثلاثة. وأمّا خامسًا، فلجواز إنقسام أحد هٰذه الأقسام إلىٰ قسمين أحدهما صالح للعلية دون الثاني.

---

32 لا توجد (وهو) في "أ" و"ب" و"ج" و"د" و"ه". وتوجد في "ط": وهو. ولعلّه الصّواب.

33 لا توجد في "ط": لا يصلح لذٰلك وكذٰلك الوصف الفلاني.

34 في "د": فبالمنع.

35 لا توجد في "ط": المسكورة.

5.3 *The Third: Resemblance* (*al-shabah*)

This is the quality that is deemed necessary for suitability (*al-waṣf al-mustalzim li al-munāsib*), whilst therein is no suitability. It also does not signify the causality (*ʿilliyyah*), because suitability (*al-munāsib*) is stronger than it and we have proved that to be void. Furthermore, the companions did not act in accordance with the quality of resemblance (*al-waṣf al-shabhī*) and so it is rejected.

5.4 *The Fourth: Rotation* (*al-dawrān*)

This does not signify causality, regardless of whether it is in one form or two forms, because it is realised in that which is without a cause. The effect (*al-maʿlūl*) rotates with the cause (*al-ʿillah*) and *vice versa*, and the effect (*al-maʿlūl*) is not the cause, and part of the equal causality (*juzʾ al-ʿillah al-musāwī*) rotates with the effect (*al-maʿlūl*) whilst it is without a cause (*al-ʿillah*).

Likewise is the case regarding the equal condition (*al-sharṭ al-musāwī*), which is one of the two effects; it rotates with its companion, whilst there is no causality between the two.

Substance (*al-jawhar*) and accident (*al-ʿaraḍ*) implicate each other, as do the two correlatives (*muḍāfān*), and movement (*al-ḥarakah*) and time (*al-zamān*), despite the lack of causality regarding all of the above, and other such examples, which are too many to enumerate.

5.5 *The Fifth: The Method of Probing* (*al-sabr*) *and Division* (*al-taqsīm*)

This is to say, it is a must for a ruling to have a cause and such-and-such a quality is not appropriate for that, nor is such-and-such a quality, and so the third [quality] remains [which must be the cause]. This, also, does not signify causality (*al-ʿilliyyah*). Firstly, due to the impossibility of the causational inference (*taʿlīl*) of each ruling; secondly, due to the impossibility of exhaustively enumerating all qualities (*al-awṣāf*), and the lack of finding (*ʿadam al-wijdān*) something, does not signify the lack of its existence; thirdly, due to the impossibility of rendering void the causational inference (*al-taʿlīl*) by one of the mentioned qualities; fourthly, due to the possibility of the causational inference (*al-taʿlīl*) by bringing two of these qualities together, or all three; and fifthly, due to the possibility of any one of these divisions being further divided into two divisions, one of them appropriate for causality (*al-ʿilliyyah*) but not the other.

السّادس: الطـرد

وهو أن يكون الوصف الذي ليس بمناسب ولا مستلزم له، لا يتخلف الحكم عنه في جميع الصور المغايرة لمحل النزاع ولا يدل علىٰ التعليل، لأنّ الإطّراد إنما يتمّ لو كان الوصف لا يوجد إلا ويوجد[36] معه[37] الحكم، وهٰذا يتوقّف علىٰ وجود الحكم في الفرع.

فلو أثبت وجود | الحكم في الفرع، يكون الوصف علّة، وثبتت عليته بالإطّراد لزم الدور. 90b

وأيضًا فإن الطرد يوجد من دون العلية، كالحدّ مع المحدود والجوهر مع العرض.

ولأنّ فتح هٰذا الباب يفضي إلىٰ الهذيان، كما نقول في إزالة النجاسة بالخل، مائع[38] لا تبنى القنطرة[39] علىٰ جنسه، فلا يجوز إزالة النجاسة به كالدّهن.

---

36 لا توجد في "ط": إلا ويوجد. 37 في "د": له. 38 لا توجد في "ط": ما نقول في إزالة النجاسة بالخل مائع. 39 في "ه": (القطرة)، وكذٰلك في النسخة المطبوعة. وهو خطأ، والصّحيح ما أثبتناه.

5.6 *The Sixth: Co-Extension (al-ṭard)*

[Co-extension] is that the quality be that which is neither suitable nor necessitating suitability from which the ruling is not held-back, with regard to all of the differing cases in consideration of the object of dispute (*li maḥal al-nizāʿ*). It does not signify causational inference, because co-extension would only be complete if the quality were not to be found, except if the ruling were to be found with it, and this is dependent on the existence of the ruling in the secondary case, and if the existence of the ruling is confirmed in the secondary case then the quality would be its cause, and its causality would be confirmed through co-extension (*al-iṭṭirād*), [thus] necessitating a circular argument (*al-dawr*). Also, co-extension is to be found without causality (*al-ʿilliyyah*), such as the definition (*al-ḥadd*) with the *definiendum* (*al-maḥdūd*), and the substance (*al-jawhar*) with the accident (*al-ʿaraḍ*).

Furthermore, the opening of this discussion would lead to senseless jabber, as we say, regarding the removal of ritual impurity (*al-najāsah*) by means of vinegar, 'It is a liquid over whose kind a bridge cannot be built', and so it is not permissible to remove ritual impurity by it, as is the case with oil.

الفَصْلُ الحَادِي عَشَر

فِي الترجِيح، وفيه مباحث

الأوّل: [في تعارض الدليلين]

لا يتعارض دليلان قطعيّان. وهل يتعارض الظنيان. جوَّزه قوم لإمكان أن يخبرنا إثنان[1] عدلان بحكمين متنافيين، ولا يترجّ أحدهما علىٰ الآخر. ومنع منه آخرون، لأنّه لو تعارض دليلان، علىٰ كون هٰذا الفعل مباحًا أو محظورًا، فإن لم يُعمل بهما أو عمل بهما لزم المحال، وإن عمل بأحدهما علىٰ التعيين لزم الترجيح من غير مرجح، أو لا علىٰ[2] التعيين وهو باطل. لأنّا إذا خيّرنا بين الفعل والترك، فقد سوّغنا له الترك، فيكون ذٰلك ترجيحًا لدليل الإباحة، وقد تقدّم بطلانه.

والأوّل عندي أقوىٰ. والجواب عن الثاني، أن التّخيير ليس إباحة، لأنّه يجوز أن يقال له، إن أخذت بدليل الإباحة فقد أبحت لك، وإن أخذت بدليل الحظر فقد حرمته عليك. كمن عليه درهمان، فقال له صاحبهما، فقد تصدقت عليك بأحدهما إن قبلت، وإن لم تقبل وأتيت بالدرهمين قبلتهما عن الدين. فإن من عليه الدين مخيّر، إن شاء أتى بدرهم، وإن شاء دفع درهمين عن الواجب.

---

1 لا توجد في "ط": إثنان.　　2 لا توجد في "ط": علىٰ.

CHAPTER ELEVEN

On Preferment (*al-tarjīḥ*)–Consisting of Four Discussions

1 Discussion One: On the Contradiction of Two Pieces of Evidence (*al-dalīlayn*)

Two definite pieces of evidence cannot contradict each other. May two probable pieces of evidence (*al-ẓanniyān*) contradict each other? A group of people have deemed it possible, due to the possibility of two just persons informing us of two mutually exclusive rulings (*ḥukm*) whilst neither of the two outweighs the other. Others have deemed it impossible because if two pieces of evidence contradict each other regarding whether an action is indifferent or prohibited, and [furthermore] if an action is not performed or is performed in accordance with them, it would necessitate the impossible. And if action were performed according to one of them in a determined manner, that would necessitate preferment without a preferrer, or else not in a determined manner and that would be void; because if we choose between performance (*al-fiʿl*) and abstainment (*tark*), then we [would] have permitted the abstainment thereof, and that would be preferment for the argument of indifferency (*dalīl al-ibāḥah*), the voidness of which has already been presented.

The first argument is stronger according to me. The response to the second argument is that choice (*al-takhyīr*) is not [the same as] indifferency (*ibāḥah*), because it is possible to say to someone, 'If you adopt the argument of indifferency (*dalīl al-ibāḥah*) then I consider it indifferent for you, and if you adopt the argument of prohibition (*dalīl al-ḥaẓr*) then I forbid it for you'. As in the example of the debtor who owes two *dirhams* and the creditor says to him, 'If you accept, I give one *dirham* in alms to you, and if you do not accept then I give you the two *dirhams* and you accept them as a loan'. Now the debtor has a choice; if he wishes he could pay back one *dirham* or if he wishes he could pay back the two *dirhams* as an obligation.

وكذا نقول في المسافر، إذا حضر في أحد الأمكنة الأربعة التي يستحب فيها التمام، فإنّه مكلّف بركعتين إن شاء الترخص، وبأربع وجوبًا إن لم يرده.

إذا عرفت هٰذا فالتعادل إن[3] وقع للمجتهد في عمل نفسه كان حكمه[4] التخيير، وإن وقع للمفتي كان حكمه أن يخير[5] المستفتي، وإن وقع للحاكم كان حكمه العمل بأحدهما[6] ووجب عليه التعيين.

91a البحث الثاني: [في العمل عند وقوع التعادل]

إذا وقع التّعادل وجب الترجيح، وقيل بالتخيير أو التوقف. لنا أنّه لو لم يعمل بالرّاجح لعمل بالمرجوح، وهو خلاف المعقول، ولأنّ الإجماع من الصّحابة وقع علىٰ ترجيح بعض الأخبار علىٰ البعض.

ومن المرجّحات كثرة الأدلّة، كترجيح أحد الخبرين علىٰ الآخر بكثرة الرواة، لأنّ الظنّ أقوىٰ،[7] لأنّ تطرق تعمد الكذب إلىٰ[8] الجماعة أبعد من الواحد.

---

3 في "ط": قد. 4 في "ط": الحكم. 5 في "ط": يتخير. 6 أشير إليه بخط الناسخ في الهامش الأسفل مِن "أ": بأحدهما. 7 أشير إليه بخط الناسخ في الهامش الأيسر مِن "أ": أقوىٰ. 8 في "ط": علىٰ.

Similarly, we uphold the view regarding the case of the traveller (*al-musāfir*), that whenas he is present in one of the four places[1] wherein it is esteemed to offer full prayers, he will be charged (*mukallaf*) for either performing two inclinings [of prayer] if he wishes for a dispensation (*al-tarakhkhuṣ*), or the four by way of obligation if he does not wish for the dispensation.

If this were acknowledged, then when two equal pieces of evidence present themselves to the skilled practitioner of juristic reasoning (*al-mujtahid*) regarding his own action, then the ruling (*ḥukm*) for him would be to choose (*al-takhyīr*) [between the two]; when they present themselves to the one who makes edicts (*al-mufti*), then the ruling for him would be that the one who seeks the edict chooses; and when they present themselves to the judge (*al-ḥākim*) then the ruling for him would be to act in accordance with one of the two and the determination [thereof] would be obligatory upon him.

2 Discussion Two: On the Course of Action When Two Equal Pieces of Evidence Present Themselves (*al-taʿādul*)

Preferment is obligatory when two equal pieces of evidence present themselves (*al-taʿādul*), and it is said that [the course of action] is either by choice (*al-takhyīr*) or by the suspension of judgement (*al-tawaqquf*).

Our argument is that if action is not taken according to the preferable (*al-rajīḥ*), then action would be taken according to the outweighed (*al-marjūḥ*), and this is contrary to what is intellected (*al-maʿqūl*). Furthermore, the consensus (*al-ijmāʿ*) of the companions (*al-ṣaḥābah*) has occurred with regard to the preferment of some narrations (*al-akhbār*) over others.

From among the preferrers there is an abundance of evidence, such as the preferment of one of the two narrations over the other due to the abundance of transmitters (*al-ruwāt*). This is because probability (*al-ẓann*) is stronger, because deliberately arriving at the [attribution of] falsehood to a group of people is less likely than [the attribution of falsehood] to an individual.

1 These are the Grand Mosque of the Kaʿbah, the Grand Mosque of the Prophet, in Madīnah, the Grand Mosque in Kufa, and the Holy Shrine of Imām al-Ḥusayn in Karbala.

وأيضًا فإن مخالفة الدّليل علىٰ خلاف الأصل، فمخالفة الدليلين أشدّ محذورًا من مخالفة دليل واحد. وإذا أمكن العمل بكلّ واحد من الدليلين المتعارضين، من وجهٍ دون وجهٍ، كان أولىٰ من[9] إبطال أحدهما بالكلية.

البحْث الثالث: في حكم الأدلّة المتعارضة

إذا تعارض دليلان فإن كانا عامّين أو خاصّين وكانا معلومين كان المتأخر ناسخًا إن قَبِل المدلول النّسخ، وإلّا تساقطا ووجب الرّجوع إلىٰ غيرهما، وكذا لو لم يعلم التأريخ.

ولو كانا مظنونين، كان المتأخر ناسخًا. ولو تقارنا أو لم يعلم التأريخ وجب الترجيح، فإن تساويا وجب[10] التخيير. وإن كان أحدهما معلومًا دون الآخر، فإن كان المعلوم متأخرًا كان ناسخًا، وإلا تعيّن العمل بالمعلوم.

وإن كان أحدهما أعمّ من[11] الآخر مطلقًا وكانا معلومين أو مظنونين، كان الخاص المتأخر ناسخًا للعام المتقدم، والعام المتأخر ناسخًا للخاص المتقدم عند الحنفية، وعند الشافعية يبنى العامّ علىٰ الخاص.

---

9 لا توجد في "ط": (من مخالفة دليل واحد. وإذا أمكن العمل بكلّ واحد من الدليلين المتعارضين من وجه دون وجه كان أولىٰ من). 10 وردت لفظة (وجب) في كلّ من "أ" و"د" و"ه" و"ط". ولكن في الهامش الأيسر مِن"د": (ثبت). وأيضًا في "ب" و"ج": (ثبت). ولكن في الهامش الأيسر مِن "ج": (وجب). 11 ساقطة في "ط": من.

Furthermore, because the violation of the evidence (*mukhālafat al-dalīl*) is contrary to the principle (*al-aṣl*), the violation of two pieces of evidence is more severely cautioned than the violation of one piece of evidence. However, if it is possible to act in accordance with each of the two contradictory pieces of evidence (*dalīlān mutaʿāriḍān*) from one aspect but not the other, then that would be more appropriate than the invalidation of one of them in its entirety.

3 Discussion Three: On the Ruling of Contradictory Pieces of Evidence (*al-adillah al-mutaʿāriḍah*)

When two pieces of evidence contradict each other and if both are general (*ʿāmmān*), or specific (*khāṣṣān*), and both are known (*maʿlūmān*), in such a case the later one (*al-mutaʾakhkhir*) would be considered the abrogator (*nāsikh*), if the signified accepts abrogation (*al-naskh*), otherwise both pieces of evidence would be annulled and reference to other than them would be obligatory. Likewise is the case if the date is unknown.[2]

If both pieces of evidence are probable (*maẓnūnayn*), then the later one (*al-mutaʾakhkhir*) will be the abrogator. If both pieces of evidence are connected or the date is unknown, then preferment (*tarjīḥ*) is obligatory, and when both are equal then choice (*al-takhyīr*) is obligatory. If one of them is known (*maʿlūm*) but not the other, and if the known one is later (*mutaʾakhkhir*), then it would be the abrogator, otherwise action is determined according to the known one.

If one of them is more general (*aʿamm*) than the other, in absolute terms, and both are either known or probable, then the later specific one (*al-khāṣṣ al-mutaʾakhkhir*) would be the abrogator for the earlier general one (*al-ʿāmm al-mutaqaddim*). According to the opinion of the Ḥanafīs, the later general one (*al-ʿāmm al-mutaʾakhkhir*) would be the abrogator for the earlier specific one (*al-khāṣṣ al-mutaqaddim*). According to the opinion of the Shāfiʿīs, the general will be based upon the specific.

2 The date (*al-tārīkh*) appertains here to whichever piece of evidence is earlier or later.

وإن وردا معًا، خص العام بالخاص إجماعًا، وإن كان أحدهما معلومًا والآخر مظنونًا، قُدِّم المعلوم، إلّا إذا اقترنا وكان المظنون هو الخاص، فإنه يخصص العام عند جماعة، وقد تقدم.[12]

البحْث الرابع: في ترجيح الأخبار

الخبر الذي رُواته أكثر، أو أعلىٰ إسنادًا، أو كان رُواته أعلم أو أزكى أو أزهد أو أشهر، راجحٌ. 91b

والفقيه أرجح من غيره، والأفقه[13] أرجح. والعالم بالعربية أرجح، والأعلم بها أرجح من العالم.

وصاحب الواقعة أرجح.[14]

والأكثر مجالسة للعلماء أرجح، والمعلوم عدالته بالإختبار أرجح من المزكى، والمزكى بالأعلم أولىٰ.

والأشدّ ضبطًا أرجح، والجازم أرجح من الظّان.

والمشهور بالرياسة أرجح من غيره.

والمتحمل وقت البلوغ أرجح.

وذاكر السّبب أولىٰ.

---

12 لا توجد في "ط": وقد تقدم. 13 توجد في "د": من غيره. 14 لا توجد في "ط": والأعلم بها أرجح من العالم. وصاحب الواقعة أرجح.

If both pieces of evidence are set forth together, then the general will be specified by the specific in accordance with consensus (*ijmāʿ*). If one of them is known (*maʿlūm*)[3] and the other is probable (*maẓnūn*), then the known one takes precedence. Otherwise, when both are connected[4] and the probable (*al-maẓnūn*) is the specific one (*al-khāṣṣ*) then it would specify the general (*al-ʿāmm*), in accordance with the opinion of a party, as mentioned earlier.

4 Discussion Four: On the Preferment of the Narrations (*tarjīḥ al-akhbār*)

The narration whose transmitters (*ruwāt*) are numerous (*akthar*), or whose chain of transmission is superior (*aʿlā isnādan*), or whose transmitters are more learned (*aʿalam*), or possess more integrity (*azkā*), or lead a more ascetic life (*azhad*), or are better known (*ashhar*), is preferable (*rājiḥ*).

The jurist (*al-faqīh*) is more preferable than others, yet the master jurist (*al-afqah*) is the most preferable (*arjaḥ*). The scholar of Arabic is the most preferable (*arjaḥ*), whilst the most learned (*aʿlam*) in Arabic is more preferable (*arjaḥ*) than the one who is [merely] a scholar (*ʿālim*) [of Arabic].

The person involved in the incident (*ṣāḥib al-wāqiʿah*) is the most preferable (*arjaḥ*).

The one who frequently engages with scholars is most preferable (*arjaḥ*). The one who is known for his justness (*ʿadālah*) through empirical knowledge (*al-ikhtibār*) is more preferable (*arjaḥ*) than the one whose integrity has been attested. The one whose integrity has been attested by the most learned is more appropriate (*awlā*).

The one who is more exact is most preferable (*arjaḥ*). The one who is absolutely certain (*al-jāzim*) is more preferable (*arjaḥ*) than the one who puts forth an argument on the basis of probability (*al-ẓānn*).

The one whose authority is well known is more preferable (*arjaḥ*) than others.

The one who took upon the responsibility [of the narration] upon attaining adulthood is most preferable (*arjaḥ*).

The one who remembers the reason is most appropriate.

---

3 Namely, in respect to its time of issue.

4 In the time of their issuance.

وراوي اللّفظ أرجح من راوي المعنىٰ. والمُعتضَد بحديث غيره أرجح.

والمدني أرجح من المكّي، لقلّة المكي بعد المدني.

والوارد بعد ظهور النبي عليه السلام أرجح. وذو السّبب أولىٰ.

والفصيح أولىٰ من الركّيك، ولا يترجح الأفصح علىٰ الفصيح.

والخاصّ متقدم. والدّال بالوضع الشّرعي أو العرفي أولىٰ من اللّغوي.

والحقيقة أولىٰ من المجاز، والدّال بوجهين أولىٰ من الدّال بوجه واحد.

والمعلّل أولىٰ، والمؤكَّد أولىٰ، وما فيه تهديد أولىٰ.

والنّاقل عن حكم الأصل راجح علىٰ المقرِّر، وقيل بالعكس.

والمشتمل علىٰ الحظر راجح عند الكرخي علىٰ المشتمل علىٰ الإباحة ومستويان عند أبي هاشم.

والمثبِت للطلاق والعتاق مقدم علىٰ النّافي عند الكرخي لموافقته الأصل ومستويان عند آخرين.

والنّافي للحد راجح علىٰ المثبِت. والذي عمل به بعض العلماء، أرجح[15] من الذي تركه، إذا كان بحيث لا يخفى عليه.

15 لا توجد في "ط": علىٰ المثبِت. والذي عمل به بعض العلماء أرجح.

The transmitter of the utterance is more preferable (*arjaḥ*) than the transmitter of the meaning.

The one supported by another's tradition is most preferable (*arjaḥ*).

The Madanī is more preferable than the Makkī, due to the paucity of Makkī narrations compared to Madanī narrations.

What has been set forth (*al-wārid*) after the appearance of the Prophet, peace be upon him, is most preferable (*arjaḥ*).

The narration endowed with the reason (*dhu al-sabab*) is most appropriate.

The eloquent (*al-faṣīḥ*) is more appropriate than the ineloquent, and the most eloquent is not preferred over the eloquent.

The specific (*al-khāṣṣ*) takes precedence.[5]

The signifier through a legal or a customary assignation (*waḍʿ*) is more appropriate than [the signifier through a] linguistic [assignment].

The veritative (*al-ḥaqīqah*) is more appropriate than the figurative (*al-majāz*).

The signifier through two aspects is more appropriate than the signifier through one aspect.

The narration that gives the cause (*muʿallal*) is most appropriate.

The narration that is emphasised is most appropriate.

The narration in which there is a threat is most appropriate.

The narration that reports the ruling from the source is preferable over (*rājiḥ*) the one that affirms it (*al-muqarrir*) and, it is said, *vice versa* is the case.

Al-Karkhī is of the opinion that the narration that includes a prohibition (*al-ḥaẓr*) is preferable over the one that includes indifferency (*al-ibāḥah*), however, Abū Hāshim is of the opinion that both are equal.

The narration that confirms a divorce or manumission takes precedence over the one that excludes it, according to al-Karkhī, because of its agreement with the principle (*al-aṣl*); and according to others, both are equal.

The narration that excludes legal punishment (*al-ḥadd*) is preferable over the one that confirms it.

The narration upon which some of the scholars have based their action is more preferable (*arjaḥ*) than the narration from which they abstained, insofar as it was not concealed from them.

5 The implication here is that it takes precedence over the general.

الفَصْلُ الثَّانِي عَشَر

فِي الإِجْتِهَـاد وتَوابِعِـهِ، وفيـه مبـاحث

الأوّل: [في الاجتهاد]

الإجتهاد[1] استفراغ الوسع في النظر فيما هو من المسائل الظنّية الشرعية على وجه لا زيادة فيه.

ولا يصحّ في حق النبيّ ﷺ وبه قال الجبائيان لقوله تعالىٰ: ﴿وَمَا يَنطِقُ عَنِ ٱلْهَوَىٰٓ﴾ [سُورة النَّجم:٣]. ولأنّ الإجتهاد أنما يفيد | الظنّ وهو ﷺ قادر علىٰ تلقيه من 92a
الوحي. ولأنه[2] كان يتوقف في كثير من الأحكام حتىٰ يرد الوحي ولو ساغ له الإجتهاد لصار إليه لأنه أكثر ثوابًا. ولأنه لو جاز له لجاز لجبرئيل ﷺ. وذٰلك يسدّ باب الجزم بأنّ الشرع الذي جاء به محمّد ﷺ من الله تعالىٰ. ولأنّ الإجتهاد قد يخطي وقد يصيب فلا يجوز تعبّده ﷺ به لأنّه يرفع الثقة بقوله.

وكذٰلك لا يجوز لأحد من الأئمة عليهم السلام الإجتهاد عندنا لأنهم معصومون وإنما أخذوا الأحكام بتعليم الرّسول ﷺ أو بالإلهام من الله تعالىٰ.

وأما العلماء فيجوز لهم الإجتهاد بإستنباط الأحكام من العمومات في القرآن والسنّة وترجيح الأدلّة المتعارضة. أما بأخذ الحكم من القياس والإستحسان فلا.

---

1 تمّت إضافة ضمير الشأن (هو) هنا في النسخة المطبوعة بعد كلمة (الإجتهاد)، وإنّه لم يرد في "أ". 2 في "المطبوعة": وأنه. وهو خطأ.

CHAPTER TWELVE

On Juristic Reasoning (*al-ijtihād*) and its Dependents–Consisting of Nine Discussions

1 Discussion One: On Juristic Reasoning (*al-ijtihād*)

Juristic reasoning is the utmost exertion of one's ability in the theorisation (*al-naẓar*) of the probable legal problems (*al-masāʾil al-ẓanniyyah al-sharʿiyyah*), in a manner in which there is no addition therein.

Juristic reasoning is not correct with regard to the Prophet, peace be upon him—and that is the opinion that the two Jubbāʾīs upheld—due to His word, the Exalted, 'He does not speak of his own accord'.[1] For juristic reasoning conveys only probability (*al-ẓann*) and the Prophet, peace be upon him, is able to acquire knowledge from revelation (*al-waḥy*). The Prophet suspended judgement regarding many rulings (*al-aḥkām*) until the revelation came forth; if juristic reasoning were allowed for him then he would have practiced it, because it is greater in reward; and if juristic reasoning were permissible for him then it would be permissible for Gabriel, peace be upon him, and that would close the door of certainty (*al-jazm*), since the revealed law which Muḥammad, peace be upon him, brought forth is from God, the Exalted.

Moreover, juristic reasoning is sometimes incorrect and sometimes correct, hence it is not permissible for the Prophet, peace be upon him, to pursue it, for it would remove the trustworthiness of his word. Likewise, according to us, juristic reasoning is not permissible for any one of the Imāms, peace be upon them, because they are infallible (*maʿṣūmūn*), and they only adopted the rulings (*al-aḥkām*) through the instruction of the Envoy [of God], peace be upon him, or through inspiration (*al-ilhām*) from God, the Exalted.[2]

As for the scholars, for them juristic reasoning is permissible, through the derivation of the rulings from the generalities of the Qurʾān and the *Sunnah*, and through preferment of contradictory pieces of evidence. However, it is not permissible to adopt a ruling (*ḥukm*) through analogical reasoning (*qiyās*) or through the 'principle of juristic approbation' (*istiḥsān*).

---

1 Q. 53:3.

2 See al-ʿAllāmah al-Ḥillī, *Kashf al-murād fī sharḥ tajrīd al-iʿtiqād*, p. 365.

البحْث الثاني: في شرائط المجتهد

وينظمها شيء واحد وهو[3] أن يكون المكلف بحيث يمكنه الإستدلال بالدلائل[4] الشرعية علىٰ الأحكام.

وهٰذه المكنة أنما تحصل بأن يكون عارفًا بمقتضى اللّفظ ومعناه وبحكمة الله تعالىٰ وعصمة الرّسول عليه السلام ليحصل له الوثوق بإرادة ما يقتضيه ظاهر اللفظ إن تجرد وغير ظاهره مع القرينة. وعالمًا بتجرد اللفظ أو عدم تجرّده ليأمن[5] التخصيص والنسخ وبشرائط التواتر[6] والآحاد وبجهات الترجيح عند تعارض الأدلّة.

وهٰذا أنما يحصل بمعرفة الكتاب لا[7] بجميعه بل بما[8] يتعلق بالأحكام[9] منه وهو خمسمائة آية ومعرفة الأحاديث المتعلّقة بالأحكام لا بمعنىٰ أن يكون حافظًا لذٰلك بل يكون عالمًا بمواقع الآيات حتىٰ يطلب منها الآيةَ المحتاجَ إليها وعنده أصل محقَّق يشتمل علىٰ الأحاديث المتعلّقة بالأحكام. وأن يكون عالمًا بالإجماع لئلّا يفتي بما يخالفه. وأن يكون عارفًا[10] بالبراءة الأصلية.

ولابدّ أن يكون عالمًا[11]| بشرائط الحدّ والبرهان والنحو واللغة والتصريف ويعلم الناسخ 92b
والمنسوخ وأحوال الرّجال. إذا عرفت هٰذا فالحق أنّه يجوز أن يحصل الإجتهاد لشخص[12] في علم دون آخر[13] بل في مسئلة دون أخرىٰ. وانمّا يقع الإجتهاد في الأحكام الشرعية إذا خلت عن دليل قطعي.

---

3 لا توجد في "ط": هو. 4 في "ط": الدليل. 5 في "د": امّا من. وفي "ط": لبيان من.
6 في "أ" و"ط": المتواتر. ولعلّه تصحيف. وفي "ج" و"د" و"ه": التواتر. ولعلّه الصّواب.
7 لا توجد في "ط": لا. 8 لا توجد في "ط": بما. 9 توجد في "ط": حافظا. 10 في "د" و"ه" و"ط": عالمًا. 11 في "د" و"ط": عارفًا. 12 زيادة في "ه": واحد. 13 في "ط": علم.

2 Discussion Two: On the Qualifications of the Skilled Practitioner of Juristic Reasoning (*al-mujtahid*)

The qualifications are regulated by one thing, and that is that he is legally charged (*al-mukallaf*) insofar as it is possible for him to infer (*al-istidlāl*) rulings (*al-aḥkām*) through legal evidence.

This ability is only achieved through: his being cognisant of the demands of the utterance (*al-lafẓ*) and its meaning, and of the wisdom of God, the Exalted, and of the infallibility of the Envoy, peace be upon him, so that he may achieve assurance in what the evident (*ẓāhir*) intended meaning (*irādah*) of the utterance demands when it is in isolation and its non-evident intended meaning with the context; his being knowledgeable of the isolation of the utterance or the lack of its isolation so that he may corroborate specification and abrogation; and his being knowledgeable of the conditions of the continuous and solitary narrations and the directions of preferment whenas the pieces of evidence contradict one another.

This is only achieved through: the knowledge of the Book, not in its entirety, but of that which is related to the rulings thereof, and these are five hundred verses and the knowledge of the traditions (*al-aḥādīth*) related to the rulings, not in the sense that he knows the verses and traditions by heart, but that he is knowledgeable of where the verses occur, so that he can locate from it the verse that he is in need of and that he possesses a verified source (*aṣl muḥaqqaq*) that is comprised of traditions related to the rulings; that he is knowledgeable of consensus (*al-ijmāʿ*) so that he may not make an edict that violates it; and that he is cognisant of the 'principle of exemption' (*al-barāʾah al-aṣliyyah*).

It is a must that he is knowledgeable of the conditions of the definition (*al-ḥadd*), logical demonstration (*al-burhān*), syntax (*al-naḥw*), language (*al-lughah*), morphology (*al-taṣrīf*), and that he knows the abrogator (*al-nāsikh*), the abrogated (*al-mansūkh*), and the status of the transmitters (*al-rijāl*). If this is understood then the truth is that it is possible for a person to achieve juristic reasoning in a single science, even in a single legal problem, but not in another. Juristic reasoning only occurs in legal rulings (*al-aḥkām al-sharʿiyyah*) when they are devoid of definite evidence (*dalīl qaṭʿī*).

البحث الثالث: في تصويب المجتهد

الحق أنّ المصيب واحد وأنّ لِلّٰه تعالىٰ في كل واقعة حكمًا معينًا وأن عليه دليلاً ظاهرًا لا قطعيًا. والمخطيء بعد الإجتهاد غير مأثوم لأن كلّ واحدٍ من المجتهدين إذا اعتقد رجحان أمارته كان أحد هٰذين الإعتقادين خطأ. لأن إحدىٰ الأمارتين إما أن تكون راجحةً أولا وأياً ما كان يلزم الخطأ فيكون [14] منهيًا عنه.

وأيضًا القول بغير طريق باطل بالإجماع فذٰلك الطريق إن خلا عن المعارض تعين العمل به إجماعًا وإن كان له معارض[15] فإن كان أحدهما راجحًا تعين العمل [16] بالراجح إجماعًا وإلا كان الحكم إما التخيير أو التساقط. وعلىٰ التقديرين فالحكم معين[17] وكان تاركه مخطيئًا.

البحث الرابع: في تغيير[18] الإجتهاد

المجتهد إذا أدّاه إجتهاده[19] إلىٰ حكم ثم تغير إجتهاده وجب الرّجوع إلىٰ الإجتهاد الثاني. ويجب علىٰ المستفتي العمل بما أدّاه إجتهاده ثانيًا.

وإذا أفتى غيره عن أجتهاد ثم سئل ثانيًا عن تلك[20] الحادثة فله الفتوى بالأوّل إن كان ذاكرًا للإجتهاد الأوّل. وإن كان ناسيًا لزم الإجتهاد ثانيًا علىٰ[21] إشكال منشأه غلبة الظن بأن الطريق الذي أفتى به صالح لذٰلك الحكم.

---

14 توجد في "د": الخطأ. 15 لا توجد في "ط": تعين العمل به إجماعًا وإن كان له معارض.
16 لا توجد في "ط": العمل. 17 في "ط": متعيّن. 18 في النّسخة المطبوعة: (تغير) وهٰذا خطأ بيّن. 19 في "أ" و"ب" و"ج" و"د": اجتهاد. ولا توجد في "ه": اجتهاد. وفي "ط": اجتهاده. ولعلّه الصّواب. 20 لا توجد في "ط": تلك. 21 في "ط": بلا.

3 Discussion Three: On the Correctness (*taṣwīb*) of the Skilled Practitioner of Juristic Reasoning

The truth is that the correct is one, and that God, the Exalted, with regard to every incident, has a determined ruling (*ḥukm muʿayyan*), and for that there is an evident evidence (*dalīl ẓāhir*) not definite (*qaṭʿī*).

The one who is incorrect after practicing juristic reasoning is not considered a sinner, because if each one of two skilled practitioners of juristic reasoning firmly believed in the preponderance (*rujḥān*) of his indication (*amārah*), then one of these two firm beliefs would be incorrect, because one of the two indications (*amāratayn*) would either be preferable or not, and whichever one necessitates incorrectness would be prohibited.

Furthermore, a statement without a method is void in accordance with consensus (*al-ijmāʿ*), and if that method (*al-ṭarīq*) is devoid of obliquity (*al-muʿāriḍ*), then it will determine action, in accordance with consensus. However, if it possesses obliquity because one of the two is preferable, the one that is preferable will determine action, in accordance with consensus. Otherwise, the ruling would either be a matter of choice (*al-takhyīr*) or both will be annulled, and, in accordance with both assessments, the ruling is determined and the one who abstains from it is incorrect.

4 Discussion Four: On the Changing (*taghyīr*) of Juristic Reasoning

If the juristic reasoning of the skilled practitioner leads him to a ruling and thereafter his juristic reasoning undergoes a change, then it is obligatory to refer to the second [instance of] juristic reasoning; and it is obligatory for the one seeking an edict to act in accordance with what the skilled practitioner's second [instance of] juristic reasoning has concluded.

If he made an edict to others according to his juristic reasoning, and then he is questioned about that incident a second time, his edict should be according to the initial [instance of] juristic reasoning; that is, if he recollects his initial juristic reasoning. However, if he has forgotten it then it is necessary that he practices juristic reasoning anew; regarding this there is uncertainty, and it arises from [the] overwhelming probability that the method by which he made the [initial] edict was appropriate for that ruling.

البحْث الخامس: في جواز التقليد

المسألة إما أن تكون من باب الاصول أو من باب الفروع فالأول لا يجوز التقليد[22] فيه إجماعًا إذ يلزم من تقليد من اتفق اعتقاد النقيضين أو الترجيح من غير مرجح فلابد من تقليد المصيب | وهو يستلزم النظر فيدور. ولأنّ النبيّ صلّى الله عليه وآله كان 93a
مأمورًا بالعلم فيه[23] لقوله تعالىٰ: ﴿فَٱعۡلَمۡ أَنَّهُۥ لَآ إِلَٰهَ إِلَّا ٱللَّهُ﴾ [سُورة مُحَمَّد:١٩]، فيكون واجبًا علينا لقوله تعالىٰ: ﴿فَٱتَّبِعُوهُ﴾ [سُورة الأَنْعَام:١٥٥]. والثّاني يجوز التقليد فيه خلافًا لمعتزلة بغداد. وقال الجبائي يجوز في الإجتهاديّة.

لنا عدم إنكار العلماء في جميع الأوقات علىٰ الإستفتاء[24]. ولأنّ ذٰلك حرج ومشقّة إذ تكليف العوامّ للإجتهاد[25] في المسائل يقتضي إخلال نظام العالم واشتغال كلّ واحد منهم بالنظر في المسائل عن أمور معاشه. ولقوله تعالىٰ: ﴿فَلَوۡلَا نَفَرَ مِن كُلِّ فِرۡقَةٖ مِّنۡهُمۡ طَآئِفَةٞ﴾ [سُورة التَّوۡبَة:١٢٢]، أوجب النفور علىٰ بعض الفرقة ولوكان الإجتهاد واجبًا علىٰ الأعيان لأوجب علىٰ كلّ فرقة النفور.

---

22 لا توجد في "هـ": التقليد. 23 في "ط": به. 24 توجد في "ط": مطلقا. 25 في "ط": بالإجتهاد.

5 Discussion Five: On the Permissibility of Compliance with the Conclusions of the Skilled Practitioner of Juristic Reasoning (*taqlīd*)

This problem pertains either to the domain of faith (*al-uṣūl*) or to the domain of ritual (*al-furūʿ*). Regarding the former, compliance with the conclusions of the skilled practitioner of juristic reasoning is not permissible in accordance with consensus (*ijmāʿ*), as in doing so it would necessitate compliance with the conclusions of one who [may] agree with the belief of two opposites, or preferment without a preferrer, thus it is a must to comply with the conclusions of the one who is correct, and that would necessitate theorisation, and so the matter would became a circular argument. Furthermore, the Prophet, may the blessing of God be upon him and his descendants, was charged to have knowledge therein, due to His word, the Exalted: 'Know that verily there is no god save God'.[3] Therefore, it is obligatory upon us, due to His word, the Exalted, to: 'follow him'.[4] Regarding the latter, compliance with the conclusions of the skilled practitioner of juristic reasoning is permissible, contrary to the Muʿtazilīs of Baghdad. Al-Jubbāʾī was of the opinion that it is permissible only in matters that pertain to juristic reasoning.

Our argument is that at no point in time have the scholars disapproved the seeking of an edict. Furthermore, juristic reasoning is a difficulty and a hardship; since the charging (*taklīf*) of the laity with juristic reasoning regarding the problems of law (*al-masāʾil*) would demand the disturbance of the social order of the world, and the engagement of each one of them with theorisation (*al-naẓar*) concerning legal problems (*al-masāʾil*) rather than the matters of their livelihood; and also due to His word, the Exalted, 'Why should not a party from every section of them go forth…'[5] which obligates the going forth of some of the section, and if juristic reasoning were obligatory for all individuals, then the verse would have obligated the going forth of the entire section.

3 Q. 47:19.
4 Q. 6:155.
5 Q. 9:122.

البحْث السادس: في شرائط الإستفتاء

الإتفاق[26] علىٰ أنه لا يجوز أن يستفتي إلّا من غلب علىٰ ظنه أنه من أهل الإجتهاد والورع بأن يراه منتصبًا للفتوى بمشهد من الخلق. وعلىٰ أنّه لا يجوز أن يسأل من يظنه غير عالم ولا متديّن.

و يجب عليه الإجتهاد في معرفة الأعلم والأورع فإن استويا تخيّر في استفتاء من شاء منهما وإن ترجح أحدهما من كلّ وجه تعين العمل بالراجح وإن ترجح كلّ منهما علىٰ صاحبه بصفة[27] فالأقوىٰ الأخذ بقول الأعلم.[28]

البحْث السابع: [في افتاء غير المجتهد]

إذا افتى غير المجتهد بما يحكيه عن المجتهد فإن كان يحكي عن ميّت لم يجز الأخذ بقوله إذ لا قول للميّت فإن الإجماع لا ينعقد مع خلافه حيًّا وينعقد بعد موته. وإن كان يحكي عن حيّ مجتهد فإن سمعه مشافهة فالأقرب جواز العمل به وإن وجده مكتوبًا وكان موثوقًا به فالأقرب جواز العمل به[29] أيضًا وإلّا فلا.

البحْث الثامن: [في من لم يبلغ الاجتهاد]

العالم الذي لم يبلغ رتبة الإجتهاد إذا وقعت له واقعة فالأقرب جواز الإستفتاء.

---

26 في "ط": وقد وقع الاتّفاق. 27 لا توجد في "ط": بصفة. 28 في "ج": أعلم. وفي "ط": الأصل. وهو خطأ. 29 لا توجد في "ط": إن وجده مكتوبًا وكان موثوقًا به فالأقرب جواز العمل به.

6 Discussion Six: On the Conditions for Seeking an Edict (*al-istiftāʾ*)

There is agreement that: it is not permissible to seek an edict except from one about whom there is an overwhelming probability that he is one of the folk of juristic reasoning, and of God-fearingness, through the fact that he is seen as holding an office of ediction witnessed among mankind, and that it is not permissible to ask the opinion of one about whom there is probability that he is neither a scholar nor religious.

It is obligatory to endeavour to know of the most learned (*al-aʿlam*) and the most God-fearing (*al-awraʿ*). However, if there are two who are equal in these matters, then the seeker of an edict can choose whomsoever he wishes of the two; and if one of them is preferred in regard to all aspects, then action is determined through the one who is preferable; and if both of them are preferred due to their possession of a quality, then the strongest opinion is to adopt the statement of the most learned.

7 Discussion Seven: On the Ediction (*iftāʾ*) of One Who is not a Skilled Practitioner of Juristic Reasoning

If one who is not a skilled practitioner of juristic reasoning makes an edict, inasmuch as he is relating from the skilled practitioner of juristic reasoning, and if he is relating from the deceased, then it is not permissible to adopt his statement, since the deceased has no view—for consensus (*al-ijmāʿ*) cannot be established in disagreement with him while he is alive, but can be established after his death—and if he is relating from a living skilled practitioner of juristic reasoning, then if he heard it from him directly, the most favoured opinion is that it is permissible to act thereby, and if he finds it in a document, and it is a reliable source, then the most favoured opinion is that it is also permissible to act thereby, otherwise not.

8 Discussion Eight: On the One Who has not Attained the Degree of Juristic Reasoning (*al-ijtihād*)

The most favoured opinion is that it is permissible for the scholar who has not attained the degree of juristic reasoning to seek an edict when an incident occurs for him.

والمجتهد الذي لم يغلب علىٰ ظنه حكم فقال محمّد بن الحسن[30] يجوز للعالم تقليد 93b
الأعلم. وقيل يجوز فيما[31] يخصه إذا كان بحيث لو اشتغل بالإجتهاد فاته الوقت وهو جيّد لأنّه مأمور بالإجتهاد ولم يأت [32] فكان مأثومًا وإنما سوّغنا له التقليد مع ضيق الوقت للضرورة.

البحْث التاسع: في الاستصحاب

الأقرب أنّه حجّة. لأن الباقي حال بقائه مستغن عن المؤثر وإلّا لزم تحصيل الحاصل فيكون الوجود أولىٰ به وإلا إفتقر ولإجماع الفقهاء علىٰ أنّه متىٰ حصل حكم ثمّ وقع الشك في أنه هل طرأ ما يزيله أم[33] لا. وجب الحكم بالبقاء علىٰ ما كان أوّلا ولولا القول بالاستصحاب لكان ترجيحًا لأحد طرفي الممكن من غير مرجح.

إذا عرفت هٰذا فنقول اختلف الناس في أن النافي[34] هل عليه دليل أم لا. فقال قوم لا دليل عليه. فإن أرادوا به أن العلم بذٰلك العدم الأصلي يوجب ظنّ بقائه في المستقبل فهو حق. وإن أرادوا[35] غيره فهو باطل لأنّ العلم أو الظن بالنفي لا بدّ له من دليل.

30 والمراد بـ"محمد بن الحسن" هو: محمد بن الحسن بن فرقد الشيباني بالولاء. وهو من أصحاب أبي حنيفة رأس الحنفية. وروج الشيباني مذهب رئيسه. ولد بواسط سنة ١٣١هـ / ٧٤٨م. وانتقل إلىٰ بغداد فولّاه هارون الرشيد القضاء بالرقّة ثم عزله. ولما خرج هارون الرشيد إلىٰ خراسان، صحبه فمات في الريّ سنة ١٨٩هـ/٨٠٤م. ونعته الخطيب البغدادي بإمام أهل الرأي. وله تصانيف كثيرة في الفقه. لاحظ الأعلام للزركلي: ج ٦/ ص ٣٠٩. وفي هٰذا الموضع من الطبعة العراقية، إخراج وتعليق وتحقيق البقّال، ص ٢٤٩. لقد تورط البقّال بخطأ فاحش حيث قال أن المراد بـ" محمد بن الحسن" هنا: "محمد بن الحسن الطوسي"، الملقب بشيخ الطائفة، توفي ٤٦٠ هـ وتحقيقا هو ليس كذٰلك فافهم.

31 توجد في "ط": كان.

32 توجد في "ط": به.

33 لا توجد في "ط": أم.

34 كذا في "ج"، وفي "د" و"ه" و"ط": الباقي.

35 لا توجد في "ط": أن العلم بذٰلك العدم الأصلي يوجب ظن بقائه في المستقبل فهو حق. وإن أرادوا.

The skilled practitioner of juristic reasoning who has no overwhelming probability on a ruling, according to the opinion of Muḥammad b. al-Ḥasan, it is permissible for a scholar to comply with the conclusions of the most learned. It is said that it is permissible in the matter, which is specific to him, insofar as if he engaged with juristic reasoning the time would lapse for him. This is a very good opinion because he is charged to practice juristic reasoning, and if he should not [then] he would have sinned. We have allowed him to comply with the conclusions of the skilled practitioner of juristic reasoning only in the case of constrained time, due to necessity.

9 Discussion Nine: On the Presumption of Continuity (*al-istiṣḥāb*)

The most favoured opinion is that this is a legal proof, because: that which remains, in the state of its existence, is needless of the effective (*al-muʾaththir*), otherwise it would necessitate the realisation of the realised, and so its existence is more appropriate for it otherwise it would be in need; the consensus of the jurists (*al-fuqahāʾ*), that when a ruling has been realised and then a doubt (*al-shakk*) occurs [as to] whether something has happened that eliminates it or not, then [in such a case] it is obligatory that the ruling remain as it were foremost. If it were not for the doctrine on the presumption of continuity then there would be a preferment for one of the two possible sides without a preferrer.[6]

If this is understood, we can see why people have disputed whether or not there is evidence for the negation (*al-nāfī*);[7] some people are of the opinion that there is no evidence thereupon; if what they intend by this is the knowledge of the absence of the original then the probability of its remaining is obligated in the future, and that is right; and if what they intend is other than that, then that is void because knowledge (*al-ʿilm*), or probability (*al-ẓann*) about the negation (*al-nafī*), must have evidence.

6 For a thorough analysis of this, see al-Rāzī, Fakhr al-Dīn Muḥammad b. ʿUmar, *al-Maḥṣūl ilā ʿilm al-uṣūl*, vol. VI, pp. 121–22.

7 Here ʿAllāmah is alluding to the concept of *iṣtiṣḥāb al-ʿadam al-aṣlī*, which is presumption of the original absence. For further details see al-Rāzī, *al-Maḥṣūl ilā ʿilm al-uṣūl*, vol. VI, pp. 121–2.

[خَاتِمة]

وليكن هٰذا آخر ما نذكره في هٰذه المقدمة والحمد للهِ تعالىٰ علىٰ بلوغ ما قصدناه وحصول ما أردناه. والصّلاة والسّلام علىٰ أشرف الأنبياء محمد المصطفىٰ وعترته الأتقياء.[36]

فرغ من تسويد بياضه العبد الضعيف المحتاج إلىٰ رحمة ربّه اللطيف هارون بن الحسن بن علي الطبري يوم الاثنين حادي وعشرين من شهر المبارك شعبان سنة سبع مائة حامدا لله مصليا علىٰ نبيه محمد واله اجمعين.

---

36 في "ب" و"ج": وعترته الأتقياء محمد المصطفىٰ.

Epilogue

Therefore, let this be the last of what we have mentioned in this introduction. Praise be to God for bringing us to what we aimed and for the realisation of what we intended. Blessings and peace be upon the most noble of the prophets, Muḥammad, the Chosen One, and his pious descendants.

The humble servant in need of the mercy of his Kind Lord, Hārūn b. al-Ḥasan b. ʿAlī of Ṭabaristān concluded the application of ink onto the blank pages on Monday the twenty-first day of the blessed month of Shaʿbān in the year seven hundred, whilst praising God, and invoking blessings on His Prophet Muḥammad and all his descendants.

Appendix

نسخة مكتبة المرعشي، سنة ٧٠٠ هـ ق

الابتداء:

كتاب مبادى الوصول

إلىٰ علم الأصول

تصنيف مولانا الشيخ الإمام العلامة أوحد الزمان

المبرز في فنّي المعقول المنقول المطرّز للواء علمي الفروع

والأصول جمال الملة والحق والدين أبي منصور

حسن مطهر أدام الله أيامه

قَرَأَ هٰذا الكتاب الشيخ العالم الفاضل الكامل المحقق

المدقق ملك العلماء الفضلاء رئيس المتأخرين لسان المتقدمين

ضياء الملة والحق والدين هارون بن المولىٰ الإمام العلامة أفضل المتأخرين

رئيس الأفاضل عمدة العلماء نجم الملة والدين الحسن بن علي بن محمد الطبري أدام الله

أفاضله وأعز إقباله قراءةً مُهدية تشهد بفضله ويدل علىٰ علمه

وبينت له المسائل المشكلة فيه وأجزت له رواية هذا الكتاب

عني لمن شاء وأحب فهو أهل لذٰلك كتب حسن يوسف مطهر

مصنف الكتاب في أواخر شهر ربيع الأول سنة إحدىٰ وسبع مائة

حامدًا الله تعالىٰ ومصليًا علىٰ سيدنا محمد النبي وآله الطاهرين

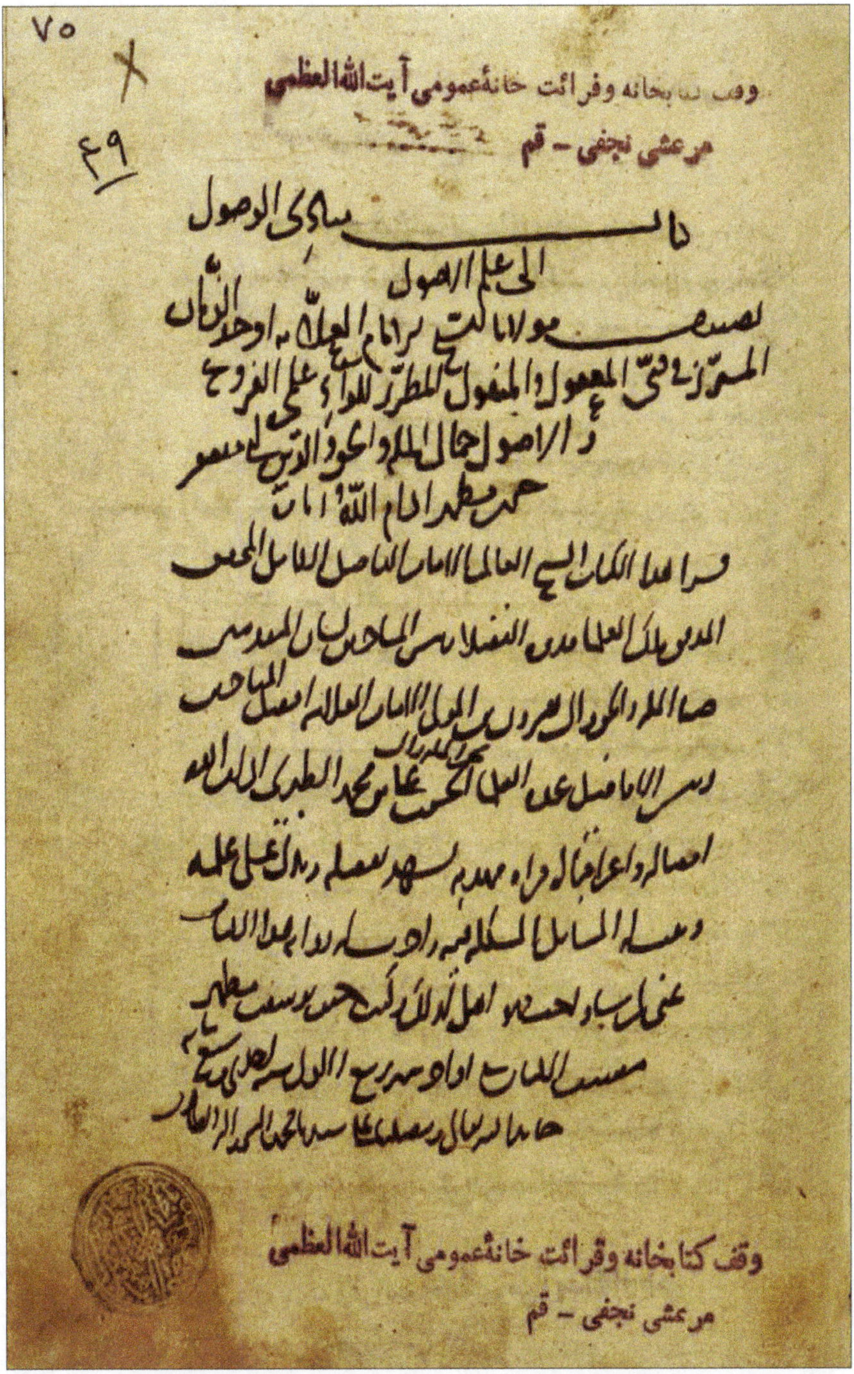

MS. 1 First colophon of *Mabādiʾ al-wuṣūl ilā ʿilm al-uṣūl*; Marʿashī Library, Qum, Iran, *fiqh*, *kalām*, *ʿarabī*, 49. 93 fols., 130 x 18 mm. Date of Completion: 21 Shaʿbān 700 AH/1301 CE. Symbol in app. crit.: أ

الاختتام:

إنها أيده الله تعالىٰ قراءةً وبحثًا
واستشراحًا وفقه الله تعالىٰ
بما يرضاه وكتب حسن مطهر
في شهر ربيع الأول سنة
إحدىٰ وسبع مائة

فرغ من تسويد بياضه العبد الضعيف
المحتاج إلىٰ رحمة ربه اللطيف هارون بن
الحسن بن علي الطبري يوم الإثنين حادي
وعشرين من الشهر المبارك شعبان سنة سبع
مائة
حامدًا لله ومصليًا علىٰ نبيه محمد وآله أجمعين

هٰذه النسخة محفوظة في مكتبة آية الله السيد مرعشي النجفي قدس سره الشريف
بعنوان «مختلف» في موضوع: فقه وكلام باللغة العربية
الرقم «٤٩» عدد الأوراق «٩٣» ورقة
١٨٠ مم x ١٣٠ مم

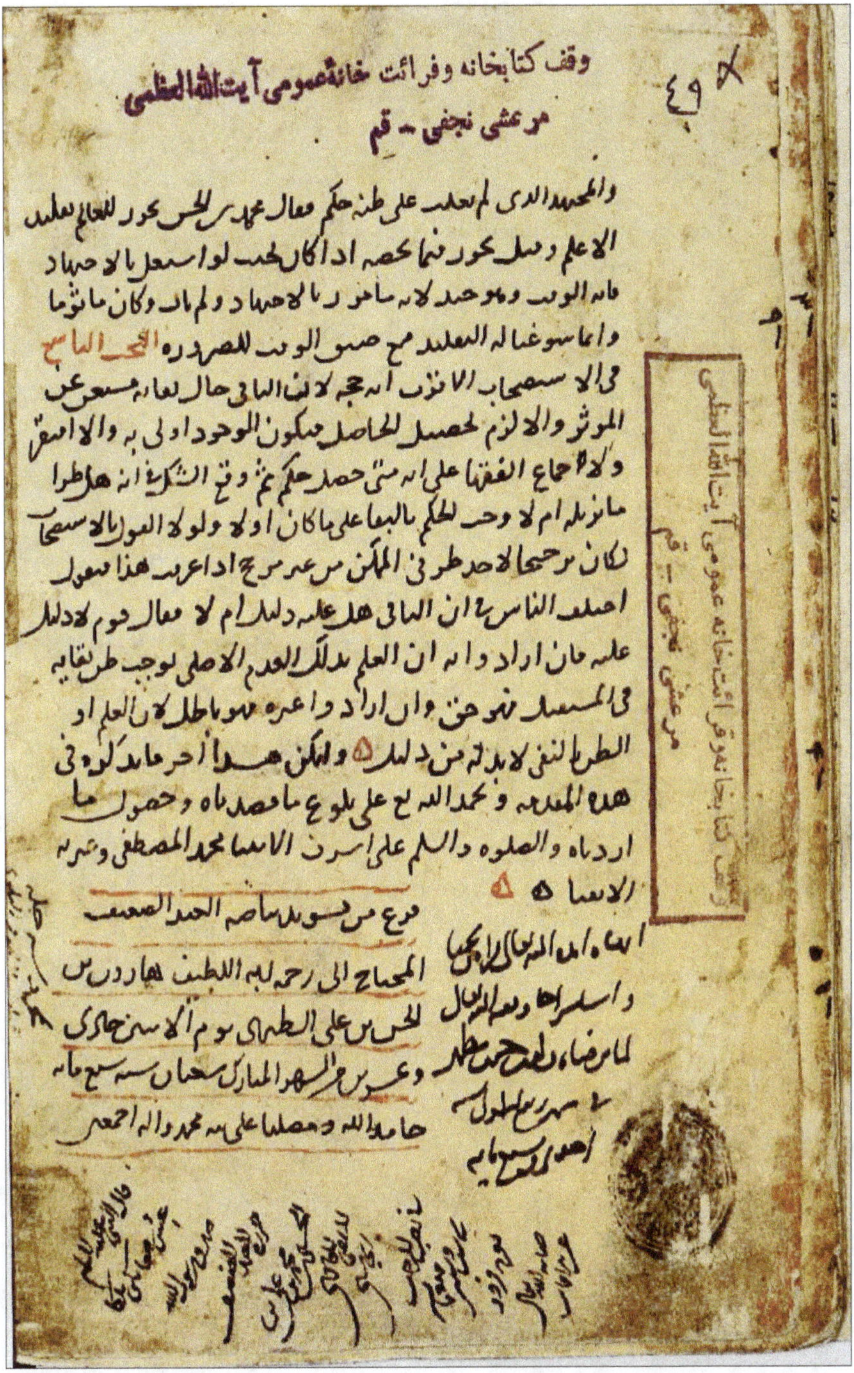

MS. 1 Last colophon of *Mabādiʾ al-wuṣūl ilā ʿilm al-uṣūl*; Marʿashī Library, Qum, Iran, *fiqh*, *kalām*, *ʿarabī*, 49. 93 fols., 130 x 18 mm. Date of Completion: 21 Shaʿbān 700 AH/1301 CE. Symbol in app. crit.: أ

نسخة مكتبة الآستانة المقدسة الرضوية، سنة ٧٠٢ ﻫ ق

الابتداء:

من ممتلكات العبد
محمد كاظم الموسوي المشهدي

حكيم محمود

من بركات عمدة أعيان الزمان وخلاصة أكابر
الدوران الذي أجرىٰ في بحار المحدرات
ألف ملك ملك شريف الملك دام عزه وإقباله
عند العبد الجاني محمد الشهير بابن خاتون
تحرير في أوساط سنة ١٠٣٩ ﻫ

كتاب المبادىء في أصول الفقه
من مصنفات مولانا وشيخنا الإمام العلامة الفاضل
الكامل المحقق المدقق أفضل المتقدمين والمتأخرين مكمل
علوم الأولين والآخرين ذي الفضائل والفواضل والمناقب
والمآثر جمال الحق والمتوالدين كمال الإسلام والمسلمين
أبي منصور الحسن بن يوسف بن مطهر الحلي متع الله كافة الناس

الواقف
أسد الله
المشتهر بابن
خاتون

قرأ علىٰ مولانا أفضل المتأخرين لسان
المتكلمين رئيس الأصحاب المتقدمين باسط أوصاف
فضائل الأخلاق الفائز بالسهم المعلى من طيب اللّواق
شمس الملة والحق والدين ابو يوسف محمد بن بهاء الله
أبي طالب الآوي أدام الله أيامه وحرس مجده وإنعامه
هٰذا الكتاب من أوله إلىٰ آخره قراءةً مُهديةً يشهد بفضله
ويدل علىٰ معرفته وعلمه وأجزت له روايته عني عن
والدي مصنف الكتاب أدام الله أيامه وكتب
محمد بن المطهر حامداً مصلياً في رجب سنة خمس وسبعمائة

MS. 2 First colophon, *Mabādiʾ al-wuṣūl ilā ʿilm al-uṣūl;* Astānah-yi Quds-i Raḍawī Library, Mashhad, Iran, *uṣūl*, 2947. 30 fols. Date of Completion: Ramaḍān 702 AH/1303 CE. Symbol in app. crit.: ب

الاختتام:

فرغ من تحرير ذلك صاحبه محمد بن أبي طالب بن الحاج محمد الآوي في شهر الله المبارك
رمضان الحجة اثني [هكذا] وسبعمائة بمقام بغداد
هجرية نبوية عليه
الصلواة
والسلم

أنهاه أيده الله تعالىٰ
قراةً وبحثًا
وفهمًا وضبطًا
واستشراحًا وفق الله لمراضيه
وذٰلك بمجالس متعددة آخرها
الحادي والعشرون من رجب سنة
خمس وسبعمائة وكتب
محمد بن المطهر والحمد الله
وحده

بلغت المقابله علىٰ حسب الجهد
والطاقة مع نسخة مقروءة علىٰ المصنف

وصلىٰ
الله علىٰ
سيدنا
محمد وآله الطاهرين

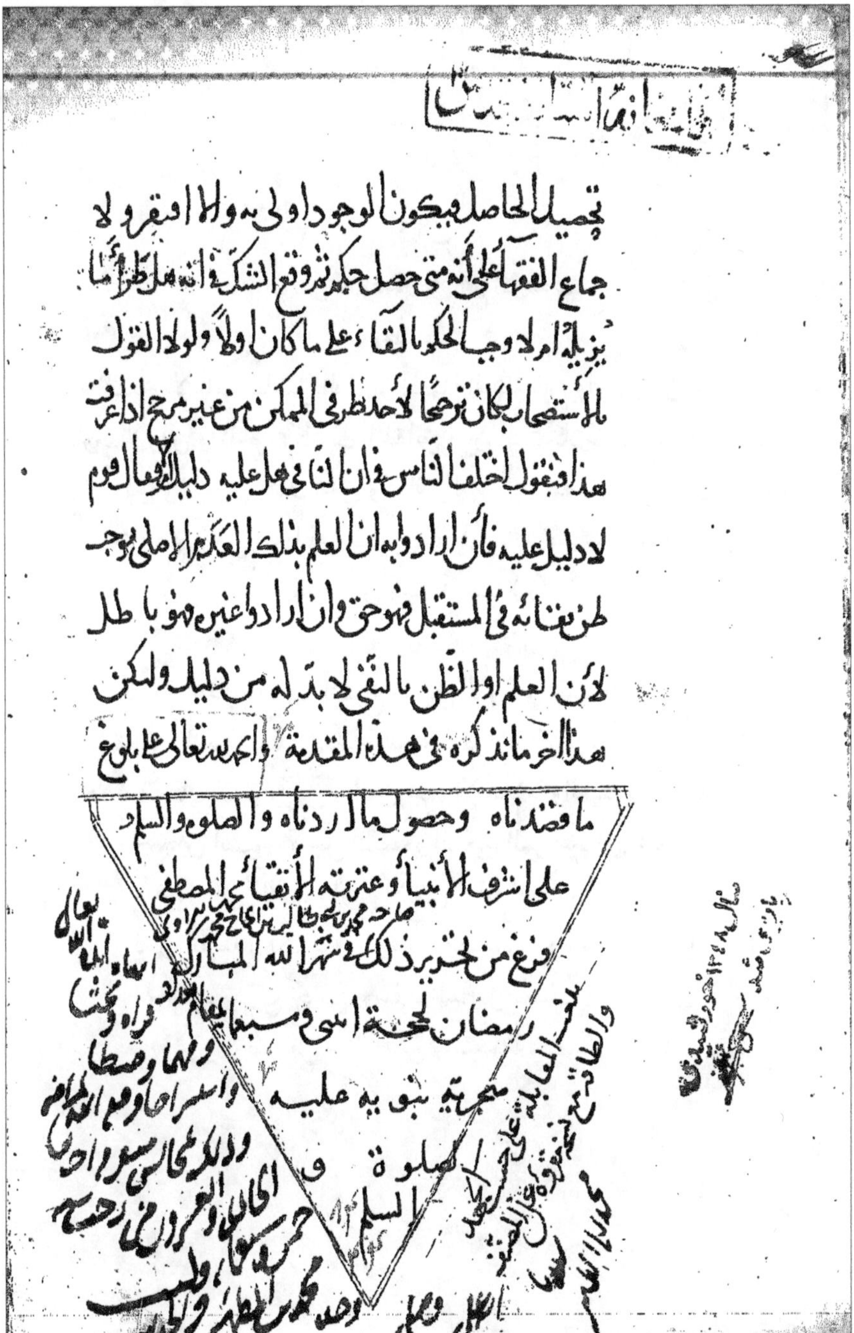
تحصيل الحاصل فيكون الوجود اولى به ولهذا اتفق الا
جماع الفقهاء على انه متى حصل حكم ثم وقع الشك في انه هل طرأ ما
يزيله ام لا وجب الحكم بالبقاء على ما كان اولا ولولا القول
بالاستصحاب لكان ترجيحا لاحد طرفي الممكن من غير مرجح اذا عرفت
هذا فنقول اختلف الناس في ان النافي هل عليه دليل ام لا فقال قوم
لا دليل عليه فان ارادوا به ان العلم بذلك العدم الاصلي يوجب
ظن بقائه في المستقبل فهو حق وان ارادوا غيره فهو باطل
لان العلم او الظن بالنفي لا بد له من دليل ولكن
هذا اخر ما نذكره في هذه المقدمة والحمد لله تعالى على بلوغ
ما قصدناه وحصول ما اردناه والصلوة والسلام
على اشرف الانبياء وعترته الاتقياء محمد المصطفى
وفرغ من تحرير ذلك في شهر الله المبارك
رمضان لسنة اثنى وسبعمائة
هجرية نبوية عليه
الصلوة
والسلام

MS. 2 Last colophon, *Mabādiʾ al-wuṣūl ilā ʿilm al-uṣūl;* Astānah-yi Quds-i Raḍawī Library, Mashhad, Iran, *uṣūl*, 2947. 30 fols. Date of Completion: Ramaḍān 702 AH/1303 CE. Symbol in app. crit.: ب

نسخة مكتبة المرعشي، سنة ٧٠٣ هـ ق

الابتداء:

كتاب

مبادىء الوصول في علم الأصول

مصنف

الشيخ الإمام الفاضل العلامة أفضل المتقدمين والمتاخرين مكمل علوم الأولين والآخرين كاشف الحقائق مبين المشكلات والدقائق وارث علم الأولين والآخرين جمال الحق والملة والدين أبي منصور الحسن بن يوسف ابن مطهر الحلي متع الله المسلمين بطول بقائه بحق محمد وآله الطيبين الطاهرين وسلم تسليمًا كثيرًا

قرأ علي هٰذا الكتاب الشيخ الأجل الأوحد الفقيه الكبير العالم المحقق المدقق ملك العلماء قدوة الفضلاء رئيس الأصحاب مُفخِرُ الأئمة جمال الملة والحق والدين نجم الإسلام والمسلمين أبو الفتوح أحمد بن الشيخ الأجل المغفور السعيد المرحوم أبي عبد الله بلكو بن أبي طالب بن علي الآوي أدام الله أيامه وقد أجزت له رواية هذا الكتاب وغيره من مصنفاتي ورواياتي لمن شاء وأحب وكتب حسن يوسف المطهر مصنف الكتاب في شهر رجب من سنة خمس وسبعمائة حامدًا ومصليًا

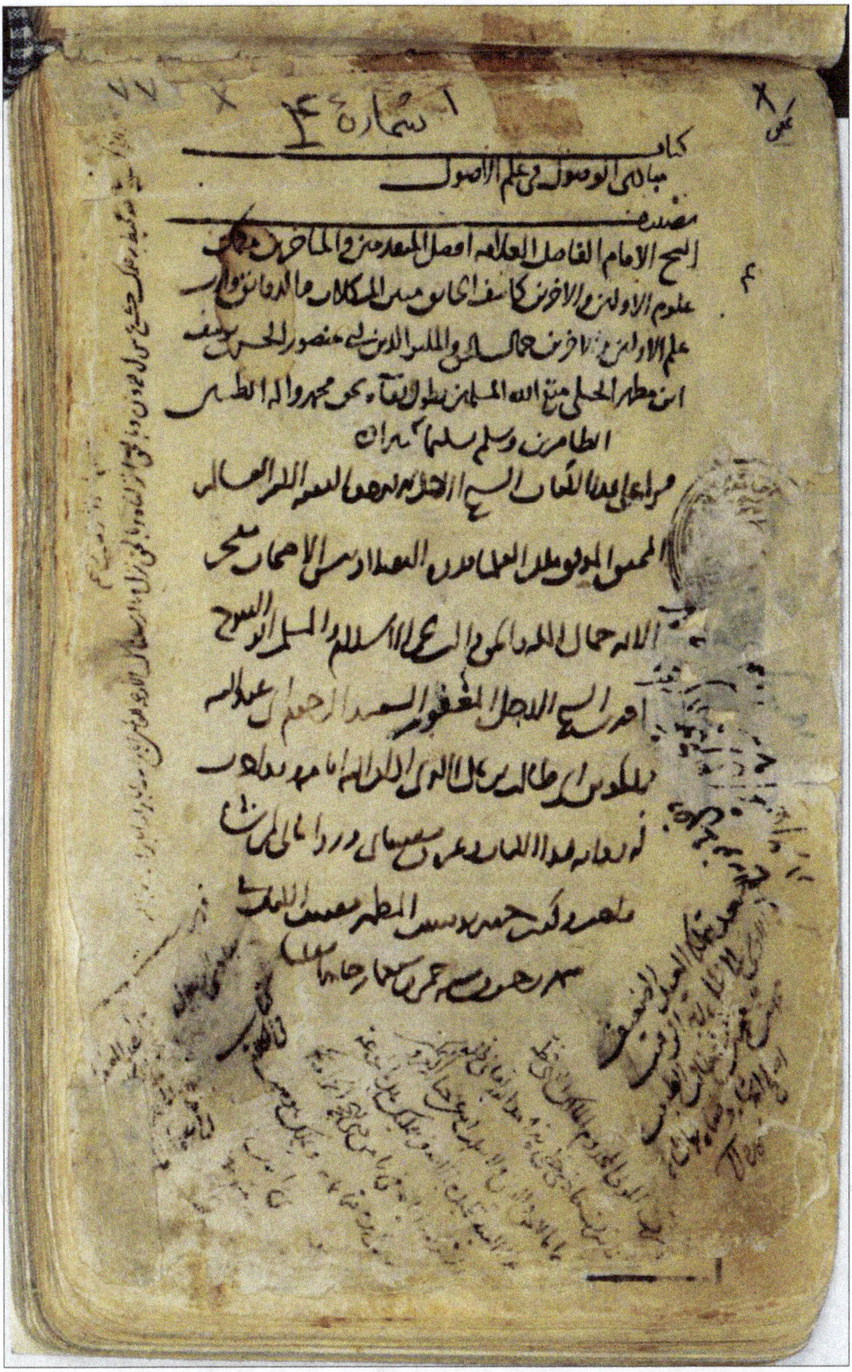

MS. 3 First colophon, *Mabādiʾ al-wuṣūl ilā ʿilm al-uṣūl,* Marʿashī Library, Qum, Iran, *kalām, uṣūl, ʿarabī,* 4. 144 fols., 110 x 183 mm. Date of Completion: 21 Ramaḍān 703 AH/1304 CE. Symbol in app. crit.: ج

الاختتام:

أنهاه أيده الله
تعالىٰ قراءةً وبحثًا
وفهمًا وضبطًا
واستشراحًا وفقه الله
لمراضيه وذٰلك في
مجالس آخرها الحادي
والعشرون من رجب سنة
خمس وسبعمائة وكتب محمد بن المطهر
حامدًا لله تعالىٰ مصليًا علىٰ نبيه
صلىٰ الله عليه وآله

فرغ من تحرير
ذٰلك أضعف عباد الله جرمًا وأقواهم
جزمًا أحمد بن أبي عبد الله بلكو بن أبي
طالب الآوي ظهيرة يوم الحادي
والعشرين من شهر الله
المبارك رمضان حجة
ثلاث وسبعمائة
هجرية نبوية
عليه
السلم

هذه النسخة محفوظة في مكتبة آية الله السيد مرعشي النجفي (قدس سره الشريف)
بعنوان «مجموعة» في موضوع: كلام واصول باللغة العربية
عدد رقم «٤» وتعداد اوراقة «١٤٤» عدد
وطول اوراقها ١٨٣ مم وعرضها ١١٠ مم

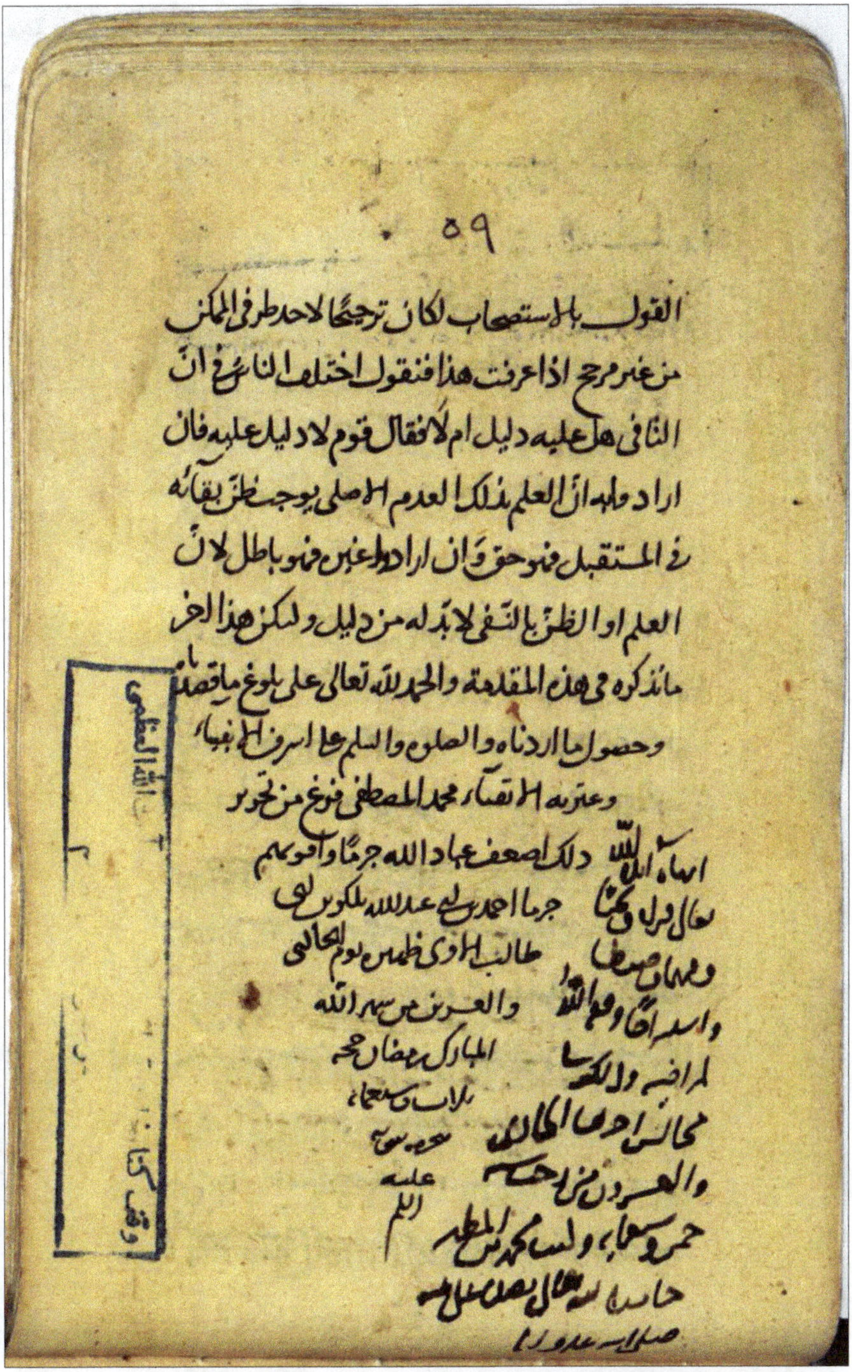

MS. 3 Last colophon, *Mabādiʾ al-wuṣūl ilā ʿilm al-uṣūl*, Marʿashī Library, Qum, Iran, *kalām*, *uṣūl*, *ʿarabī*, 4. 144 fols., 110 x 183 mm. Date of Completion: 21 Ramaḍān 703 AH/1304 CE. Symbol in app. crit.: ج

نسخة المكتبة البريطانية بلندن، سنة ٧١٥ هـ
الابتداء:

كتاب مبادىء الوصول إلىٰ علم الأصول
من تصانيف الشيخ الإمام العلامة أفضل المتقدمين وأعلم المتاخرين
قطب الشيعة ناصر الشريعة مفتي الفريقين جمال الملة والحق والدين
سديد الإسلام والمسلمين أبو منصور الحسن يوسف المطهر الحلي أدام الله أيامه

قرأ علي المولىٰ السيد المعظم الحبيب النسيب
شرف آل أبي طالب العالم الفاضل الزاهد
العابد الورع زين الدين علي بن الحسن الرضي العلوي الحسيني
[كلمة مبهمة] كتاب مبادي الوصول إلى علم الأصول قراءةً تشهد
بفضله ويدل علىٰ علمه وقد أجزت له رواية هٰذا
الكتاب عني عن والدي المصنف أدام الله أيامه
وكذٰلك أجزت له رواية جميع ما قرأته ورويته وأجيز
لي روايته فليروذٰلك علىٰ الشرائط المعتبرة وكتب
محمد بن الحسن يوسف المطهر في غرّة جمادىٰ الأولىٰ سنة
خمس وعشرين وسبعمائة والحمد لله وحده وصلىٰ الله علىٰ نبينا محمد وآله
وسلم تسليما كثيرا

هذا خط بن المصنف
الشيخ فخر الدين محمد
رحمهما الله

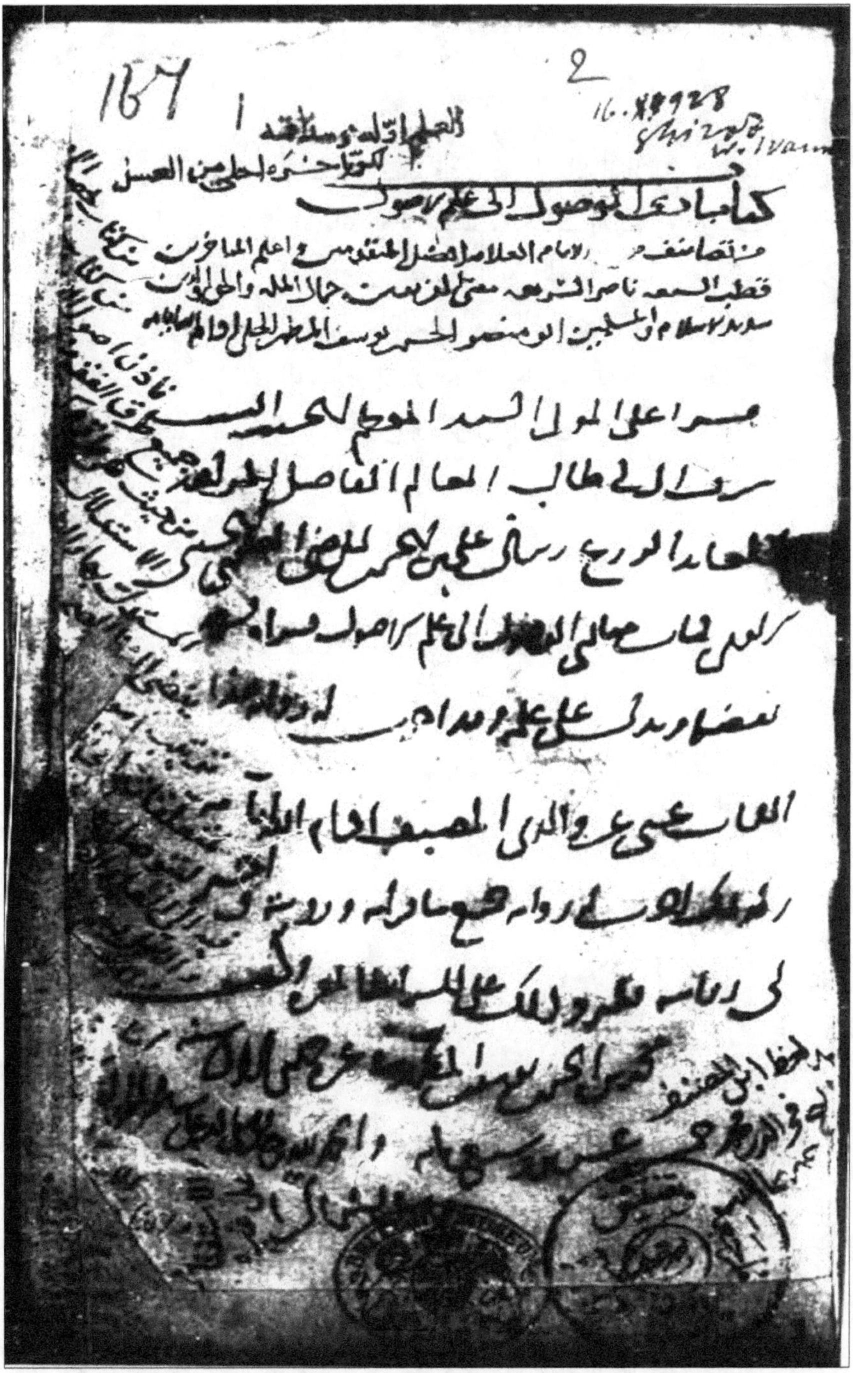

MS. 4 First colophon, *Mabādiʾ al-wuṣūl ilā ʿilm al-uṣūl*, British Library, London, Or. 10963, Date of Completion 1 Rajab 715 AH/1315 CE. Symbol in app. crit.: د

الاختتام:

تمت المقابلة مع نسخة قرئت علىٰ الإمام العالم فخر الملة والدين ابن
الإمام العالم مصنف الكتاب الحسن بن يوسف
المطهر أدام الله ظلالهما
حرر الكتاب علىٰ يدي العبد الضعيف
المحتاج إلىٰ رحمة الله تعالىٰ
علي بن الحسن بن الرضي العلوي
الحسيني الرضوي [؟]
في سلخ رجب
سنة خمس عشر
وسبعمائة
حامدًا
مصليًا

هٰذه النسخة محفوظة في المكتبة البريطانية بلندن
بعنوان: مبادي الوصول
مؤلف: الحلي
الرقم: OR ١٠٩٦٣

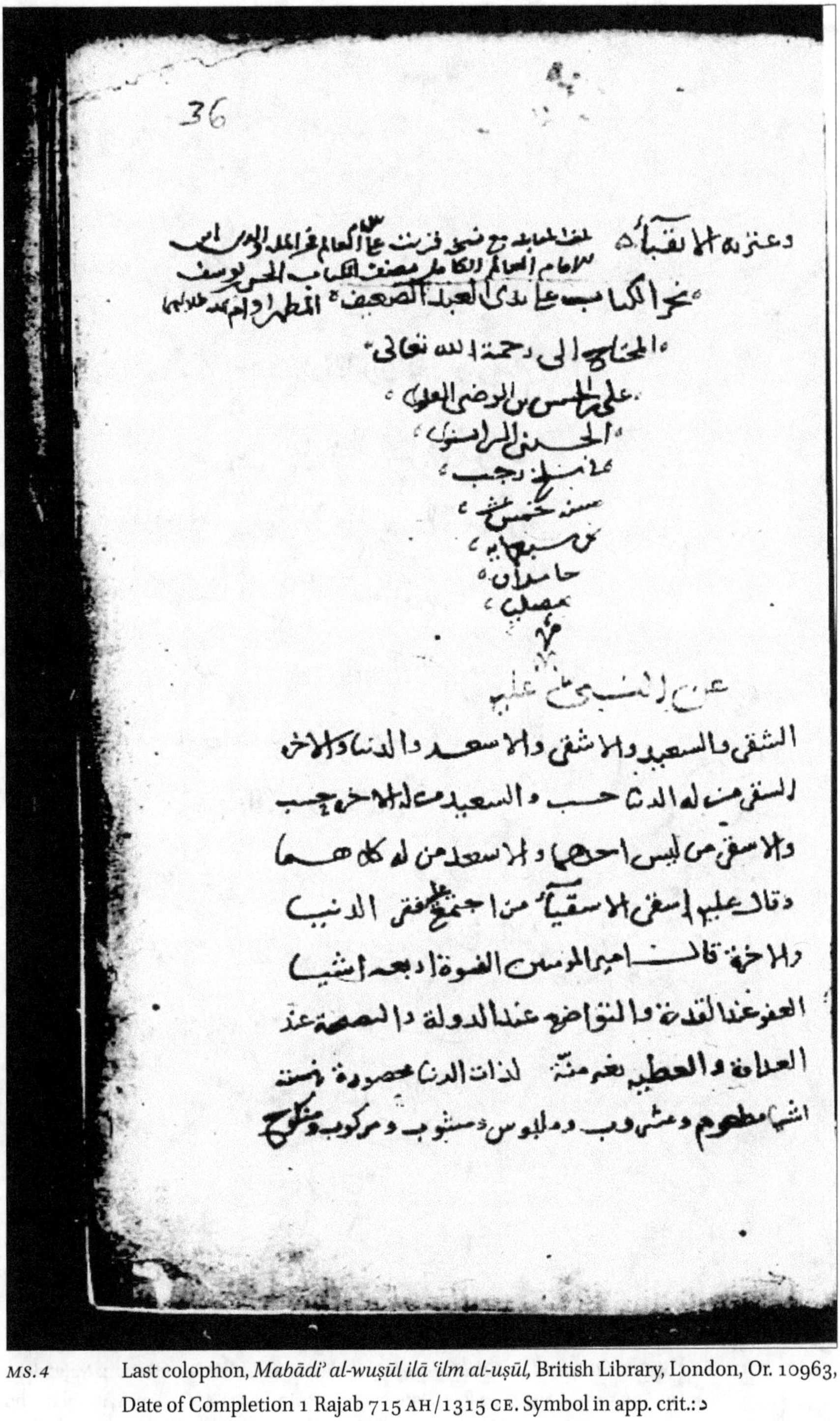

MS. 4 Last colophon, *Mabādiʾ al-wuṣūl ilā ʿilm al-uṣūl*, British Library, London, Or. 10963, Date of Completion 1 Rajab 715 AH/1315 CE. Symbol in app. crit.: د

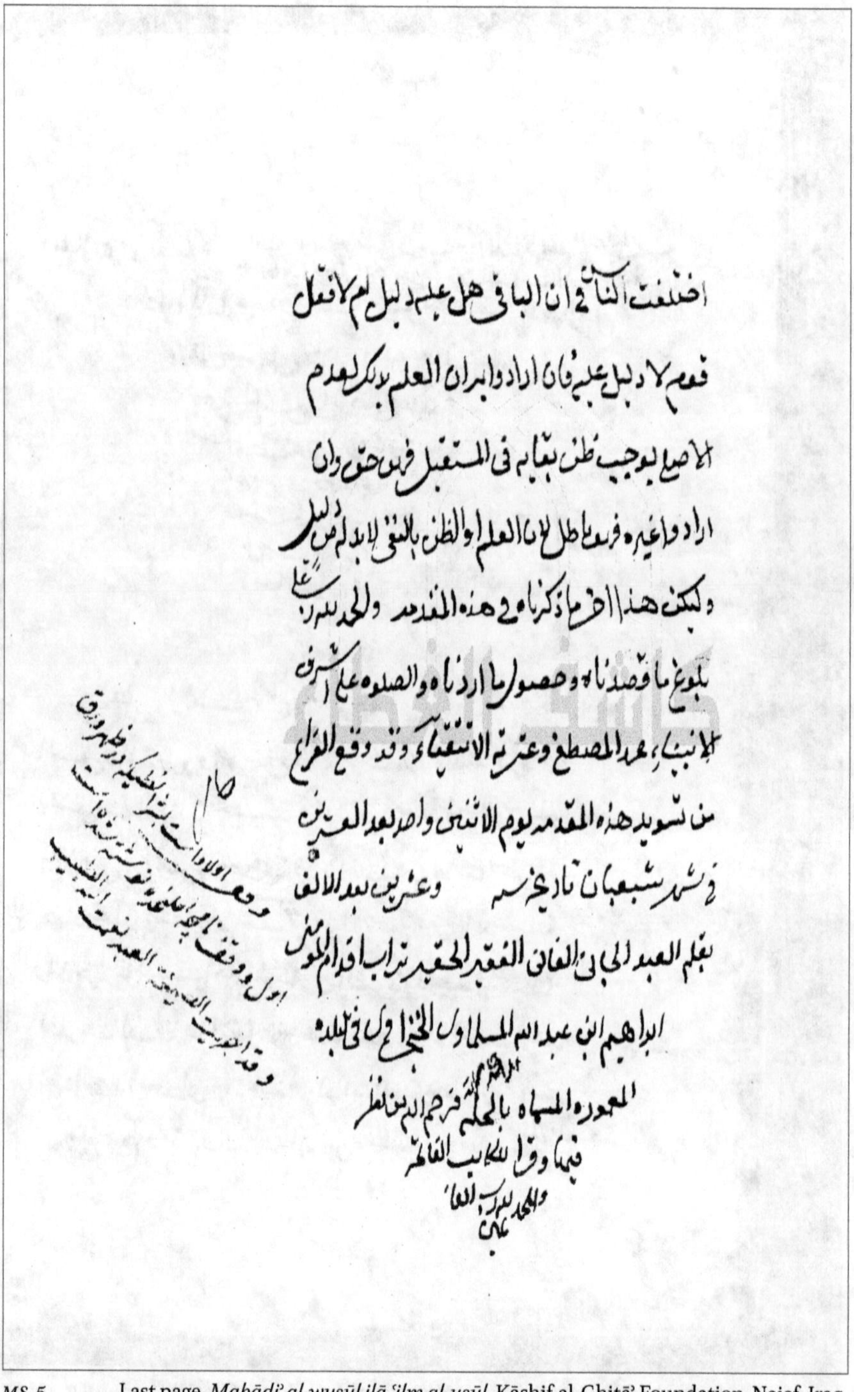

MS. 5 Last page, *Mabādiʾ al-wuṣūl ilā ʿilm al-uṣūl,* Kāshif al-Ghiṭāʾ Foundation, Najaf, Iraq, *uṣūl al-fiqh, ʿarabī,* 7954. 80 fols. Date of completion 1021 AH/1612. Symbol in app. crit.: ه

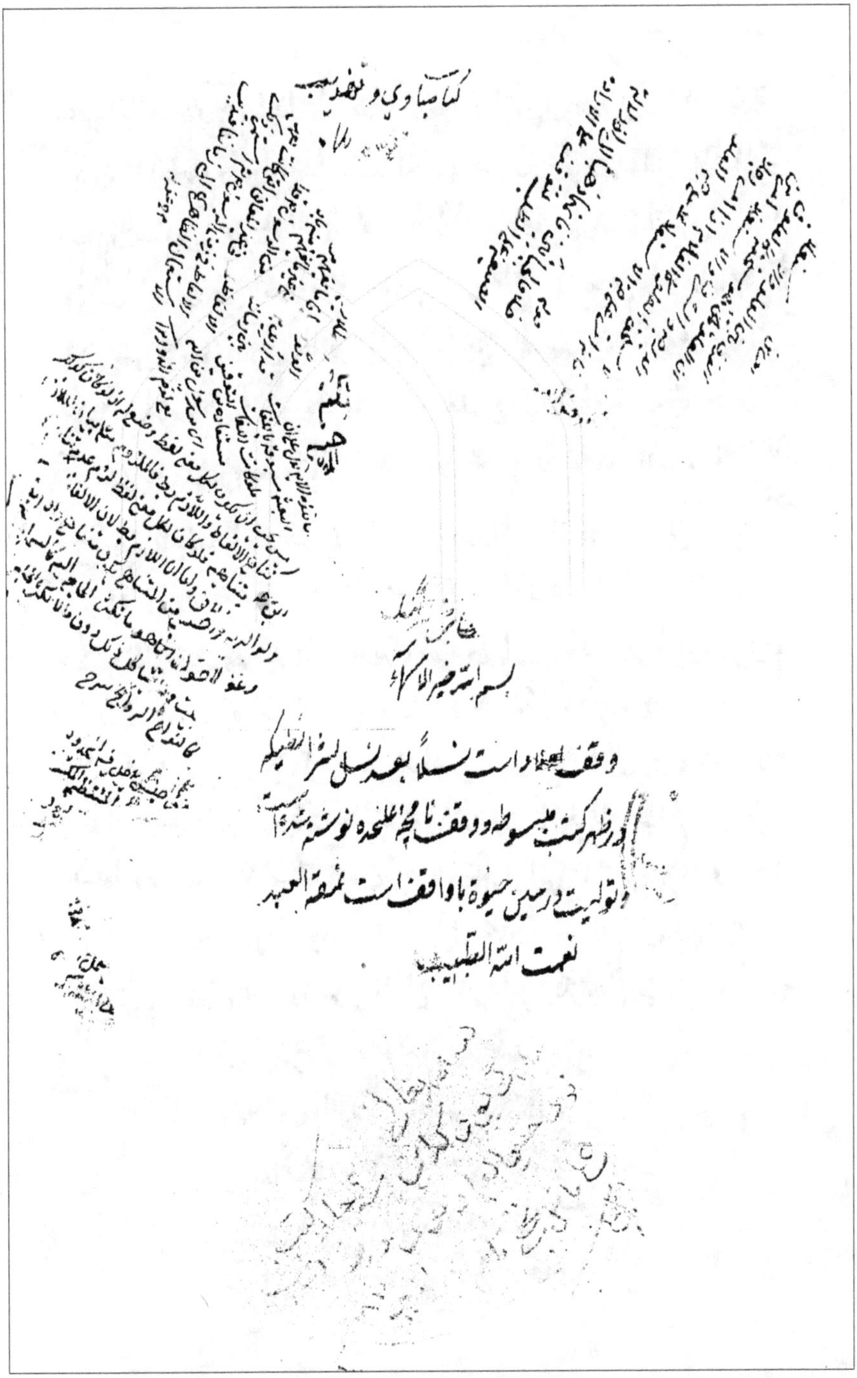

MS. 5 First page, *Mabādiʾ al-wuṣūl ilā ʿilm al-uṣūl*, Kāshif al-Ghiṭāʾ Foundation, Najaf, Iraq, *uṣūl al-fiqh, ʿarabī*, 7954. 80 fols. Date of completion 1021 AH/1612. Symbol in app. crit.: ه

هي كل فرقة النفور الى اتبح في شرائط الاستفتاء وقد وقع الاتفاق على انه لا يجوز ان يستفتي الا من غلب على ظنه
انه من اهل الاجتهاد والورع بان يراه منتصبا للفتوى متشهدا بين الخلق وعلى انه لا يجوز ان يسأل من يظنه
غير عالم ولا متدين ويجب عليه الاجتهاد في معرفة الاعلم والاورع فان استويا تخير في استفتاء
من شاء منهما وان ترجح احدهما من كل وجه تعين العمل بالراجح وان ترجح كل منهما على صاحبه فالاقوى
الاخذ بقول الاعلم الاصل الخامس اذا افتى غير المجتهد بما يحكيه عن المجتهد فان كان يحكي عن ميت لم يجز
الاخذ بقوله اذ لا قول للميت فان الاجماع لا ينعقد مع خلافه لو كان حيا وينعقد بعد موته وان كان
يحكي عن حي مجتهد فان سمعه مشافهة فالاقرب جواز العمل بما يقوله والا فلا السادس العامي الذي
لم يبلغ رتبة الاجتهاد اذا وقعت له واقعة فالاقرب جواز الاستفتاء والمجتهد الذي لم يبلغ على ظنه
حكم فقال الجبائي ابن الحسن يجوز تقليد العالم الاعلم وقيل يجوز فيما كان يخصه اذا كان بحيث لو اشتغل با
لاجتهاد فاته الوقت وهو حسن لانه مامور بالاجتهاد ولم يات به فكان ماثوما وانما سوغنا
له التقليد مع ضيق الوقت للضرورة السابع في الاستصحاب الاقرب انه حجة لان الباقي حال
بقائه مستغن عن المؤثر والا لزم تحصيل الحاصل فيكون الوجود اولى به والا لافتقر ولاجماع
الفقهاء على انه متى حصل حكم ثم وقع الشك في انه هل طرأ ما يزيله لا وجب الحكم بالبقاء على ما
كان اولا ولولا القول بالاستصحاب لكان ترجيحا لاحد طرفي الممكن من غير مرجح اذا عرفت هذا
فنقول اختلف الناس في ان النافي هل عليه دليل ام لا فقال قوم لا دليل عليه فان ارادوا
به غيره فهو باطل لان العلم او الظن بالنفي لا بد له من دليل ولكن هذا اخر ما نذكره في هذه
المقدمة والحمد لله تعالى على بلوغ ما قصدناه
وحصول ما اردناه والصلوة والسلام
على اشرف الانبياء محمد المصطفى صلى الله عليه وآله
وعلى عترته البررة الاتقياء تمت الكتاب
المبادي الاصول من العلامة الحلي سنة ١٢٥١

MS. 6 Last page, *Mabādi' al-wuṣūl ilā 'ilm al-uṣūl,* Kāshif al-Ghiṭā' Foundation, Najaf, Iraq, *uṣūl al-fiqh, 'arabī,* 797. 24 fols.Date of completion 1251 AH/1835. Symbol in app. crit.: ط

هذا كتاب مبادي الاصول

بسم الله الرحمن الرحيم

الحمد لله المتفرد بالأزلية والدوام الموحد بالجلال والإكرام المتفضل بسوابغ الأنعام المتقدس عن مشابهة الأعراض والأجسام وصلى الله على سيدنا محمد المصطفى وعترته الأماجد الكرام ما تعاقبت الليالي والأيام أما بعد فهذا كتاب مبادي الوصول إلى علم الأصول قد اشتمل في أصول الفقه على ما لا بد منه ويحتوي على ما لا يستغني عنه نرجو به ضعف التقرب إلى الله تعالى وهو حسبنا ونعم الوكيل ورتبت على فصول الفصل الأول في اللغات وفيه مباحث البحث الأول في أحكام كلية ذهب قوم إلى أن اللغات توقيفية لقوله تعالى وعلم آدم الأسماء كلها وقوله تعالى واختلاف ألسنتكم والمراد به اللغات وقال أبو هاشم إنها اصطلاحية لقوله تعالى وما أرسلنا من رسول إلا بلسان قومه والحق أن يكون لكل معنى لفظ وإلا لزم عدم تناهي الألفاظ بل الواجب وضع اللفظ لما يكثر الحاجة إلى التعبير عنه والعلم باللغة واجب لوجوب معرفة الشرع المتوقف عليها والكلام عند المعتزلة هو المنتظم من الحروف المسموعة المتميزة المتواضع عليها إذا صدرت عن قادر واحد ويطلق على الجملة المفيدة البحث الثاني في تقسيم الألفاظ وهو من وجوه أحدها أن اللفظ إن دل على الزمان المعين بصيغته فهو الفعل وإلا فهو الاسم إن استقل بالدلالة وإلا فهو حرف والثاني أن اللفظ إما مفرد وإما مركب فالأول ما لا يدل جزؤه على جزء معناه حين هو جزؤه والثاني ما يدل الثالث أن اللفظ والمعنى إن اتحدا فإن منع نفس تصور المعنى من وقوع الشركة فهو العلم والمضمر وإلا فهو المتواطي إن تساوت أفراده فيه والمشكك إن اختلفت وإن تكثرا فهي الألفاظ المتباينة وإن نقل لمناسبة فهو المنقول اللغوي والعرفي أو الشرعي إن غلب المنقول إليه وإلا فهو حقيقة بالنسبة إلى الأول ومجاز بالنسبة إلى الثاني وإن وضع لهما فهو المشترك بالنسبة

إليهما

MS.6 First page, *Mabādiʾ al-wuṣūl ilā ʿilm al-uṣūl,* Kāshif al-Ghiṭāʾ Foundation, Najaf, Iraq, *uṣūl al-fiqh, ʿarabī,* 797. 24 fols.Date of completion 1251 AH/1835. Symbol in app. crit.: ط

Bibliography of Primary Sources

Abī Dāwūd, Sulaymān b. al-Ashʿath al-Sijistānī al-Azdī, *Sunan Abī Dāwūd,* Ḥamd b. Muḥammad Khaṭṭābī, and ʿIzzat ʿUbayd Daʿās (eds.), 5 vols., Homs, 1388 AH/1969

Abū al-Maʿālī, *Ḥujjiyyat al-ẓann*, lithograph, n.p., 1316 AH/1898

al-Āmidī, Sayf al-Dīn Abū al-Ḥasan ʿAlī b. Abī ʿAlī b. Muḥammad, *al-Iḥkām fī uṣūl al-aḥkām*, 4 vols., Beirut, 1403 AH/1983

al-ʿĀmilī, Muḥammad b. ʿAlī b. Abī al-Ḥasan, *Madārik al-aḥkām fī sharḥ sharāʾiʿ al-islām*, Qum, 1410 AH/1990

al-Amīn, al-Sayyid Muḥsin, *Aʿyān al-shīʿah*, 15 vols., ed. al-Sayyid Ḥasan al-Amīn, Beirut, 1420 AH/2000

al-Anṣārī, al-Shaykh Murtaḍā b. Muḥammad Amīn, *Faraʾid al-uṣūl*, 2 vols., Qum, 1416 AH/1995

al-Asadābādī, Abū al-Ḥasan ʿAbd al-Jabbār al-Hamadhānī, *al-Mughnī fī abwāb al-tawḥīd wa al-ʿadl*, in: *Kitāb al-tanabuwwāt wa al-muʿjizāt*, Cairo, 1388 AH/1968

al-Astarabādī, Muḥammad Amīn, *al-Fawāʾid al-madaniyyah*, lithograph, Tehran, 1321 AH/1904

al-Baghdādī, al-Khaṭīb, *al-Fiqh wa al-mutafaqqih*, n.p., n.d.

al-Bahāʾī al-Shaykh, al-Bahāʾ al-Dīn Muḥammad b. Ḥusayn al-Ḥarithī al-Hamdānī al-ʿĀmilī al-Jabaʿī, *Zubdat al-uṣūl*, lithograph, Tehran, 1319 AH/1901

al-Baḥrānī, Yūsuf, *al-Ḥadāʾiq al-nāḍirah*,24 vols., Qum, 3rd ed., 1434 AH/2012

al-Baṣrī, Abū al-Ḥusayn, Muḥammad b. ʿAlī b. al-Tayyib, *al-Muʿtamad fī uṣūl al-fiqh*, 2 vols., Damascus, 1964–5

———, *al-Muʿtamad fī uṣūl al-fiqh*, Beirut, 1407 AH/ 1987, vol. 1

al-Bayḍāwī, ʿAbd Allāh b. ʿUmar b. Muḥammad, *Minhāj al-wuṣūl ilā ʿilm al-uṣūl*, Damascus, 1989

al-Bihbahānī, al-Waḥīd Muḥammad Bāqir b. Muḥammad Akmal, *al-Rasāʾil al-uṣūliyyah*, Qum, 1416 AH/1995

al-Burujurdī, Ḥusayn al-Ṭabāṭabāʾī, *Nihāyat al-uṣūl*, ed. Ḥusayn ʿAlī al-Muntaẓarī, 2 vols., Qum, 1415 AH/ 1994

al-Firūzabādī, al-Sayyid Murtaḍā al-Ḥusaynī al-Yazdī, *ʿInāyat al-uṣūl fī sharḥ kifāyat al-uṣūl*, Qum, 1410 AH/1990

al-Ghazālī, Abū Ḥāmid Muḥammad b. Muḥammad b. Muḥammad, *al-Mustaṣfa fī ʿilm al-uṣūl*, Beirut, 1993

al-Ḥalabī, ʿIzz al-Dīn Ḥamzah b. ʿAlī b. Zuhrah, *Ghunyat al-nuzūʿ*, in: *al-Jawāmiʿ al-fiqhiyyah*, Tehran, 1362 SH/1982, p. 537

al-Ḥarrānī, Abū Muḥammad al-Ḥasan b. ʿAlī b. al-Ḥusayn b. Shuʿbah, *Tuḥaf al-ʿuqūl ʿan āl al-rasūl* Qum, 1404 AH/1984

al-Ḥillī, Abū Jaʿfar Muḥammad b. Manṣūr b. Aḥmad b. Idrīs, *Kitāb al-sarāʾir al-ḥāwī li-taḥrīr al-fatāwī*, 3 vols., Qum, 1993

al-Ḥillī, al-ʿAllāmah, Jamāl al-Dīn Abū Manṣūr b. Yūsuf, *Ghāyat al-wuṣūl wa īḍāḥ al-subul fī sharḥ mukhtaṣar al-suʾāl wa al-amal,* Ms., British Library, Or. 3970

———, *Īḍāḥ al-Ishtibāh,* ed. al-Shaykh Muḥammad al-Ḥassūn, Qum, 1411 AH/1990-91

———, *Irshād al-adhhān ilā aḥkām al-īmān,* ed. al-Shaykh Fāris al-Ḥassūn, 2 vols., Qum, 1410 AH/ 1989-90, vol. I

———, *Kashf al-fawāʾid fī sharḥ qawāʾid al-ʿaqāʾid,* Beirut, 1993

———, *Kashf al-murād fī sharḥ tajrīd al-iʿtiqād,* Qum, 1416 AH/1995

———, *Mabādiʾ al-wuṣūl ilā ʿilm al-uṣūl,* ed. ʿAbd al-Ḥusayn Muḥammad ʿAlī al-Baqqāl, Najaf, 1348 SH/1969

———,*Mabādiʾ al-wuṣūl ilā ʿilm al-uṣūl,* ed. Sayyid Amjad H. Shah Naqavi, London, 2016

———,*Mukhtalaf al-shīʿah,* 9 vols. Qum, 1433 AH/2011

———, *Nahj al-ḥaqq wa kashf al-ṣidq,* Beirut, 1982

———,*Nihāyat al-wuṣūl ilā ʿilm al-uṣūl,* 5 vols., ed. Ibrāhīm al-Bahādurī, Qum, 1425 AH/2004

———, *Tahdhīb al-wuṣūl ilā ʿilm al-uṣūl,* lithograph Tehran., 1308 AH/1890-1891

al-Ḥillī, Miqsād b. ʿAbd Allāh al-Sayurī, *Naḍd al-qawāʿid al-fiqiyyah ʿalā madhhab al-imāmiyyah,* Qum, 1403 AH/1983

al-Ḥillī, al-Muḥaqqiq, Najm al-Dīn Abū al-Qāsim Jaʿfār b. al-Ḥasan, *Maʿārij al-uṣūl,* ed. Muḥammad Ḥusayn al-Raḍawī, Qum, 1403 AH/1983

———, *al-Muʿtabar fī sharḥ al-mukhtaṣar,* lithograph, Qum, n.d.

———, and al-Ṭūsī, Shaykh al-Ṭāʾifah, *al-Nihāyah wa nukatuhā,* 3 vols, Qum, 1417 AH/ 1996

———, *Nukat al-nihāyah,* n.p., n.d.

al-Ḥumayrī, Nashwān Abū Saʿīd, *al-Ḥūr al-ʿayn,* ed. Kamāl Muṣṭafā, Cairo, 1368 AH/1948

Ḥusayn, al-Shaykh Muḥammad, *al-Fuṣūl al-garawiyyah fī al-uṣūl al-fiqhiyyah,* lithograph, n.p., n.d.

Ibn Ḥanbal Abū ʿAbd Allāh al-Shaybānī, Aḥmad b. Muḥammad, *Musnad al-Imām Aḥmad Ibn Ḥanbal,* 6 vols., n.p., n.d.

———, *Kitāb faḍāʾil al-ṣaḥābah,* n.p., n.d.

Ibn Ḥazm al-Ẓāhirī al-Andalusī, ʿAlī b. Aḥmad b. Saʿīd, *al-Iḥkām fī uṣūl al-aḥkām,* 2 vols., Beirut, n.d.

———, *Mulakhkhas ibṭāl al-qiyās wa al-raʾy wa al-istiḥsān wa al-taqlīd wa al-taʿlīl,* ed. Saʿīd al-Afghānī, Damascus, 1379 AH/1960

Ibn Idrīs al-Ḥillī, Abū Jaʿfar Muḥammad b. Manṣūr b. Aḥmad, *Kitāb al-saraʾīr al-ḥāwī li taḥrīr al-fatāwī,* 3 vols., Qum, 1410 AH/1990

Ibn Mājah, Abū ʿAbd Allāh Muḥammad b. Yazīd, *Kitāb al-diyyāt,* in: *Sunan Ibn Mājah,* n.p., n.d.

al-Iṣbahānī, al-Mīrza ʿAbd Allāh Afandī, *Riyāḍ al-ʿulamāʾ wa ḥiyāḍ al-fuḍalāʾ,* Qum, 1403 AH/1982

al-Jaṣṣāṣ, Aḥmad b. ʿAlī al-Rāzī, *al-Fuṣūl fī al-uṣūl*, Kuwait City, 1410 AH/1990

al-Jabaʿī, al-Shaykh Ḥasan b. Zayn al-Dīn al-ʿĀmilī, *Maʿālim al-uṣūl*, Tehran, 1983

al-Juwaynī, ʿAbd al-Malik b. ʿAbd Allāh, *Kitāb al-talkhīṣ fī uṣūl al-fiqh*, Beirut, 1983

Kalāntar, al-Sayyid Muḥammad, *Dirāsāt fī uṣūl al-fiqh*, 2 vols., Najaf, 1388 AH/1968

al-Karājikī, Abū al-Fatḥ Muḥammad b. ʿAlī b. ʿUthmān, *Kanz al-fawāʾid*, 2 vols., Beirut, 1412 AH/ 1992

al-Karakī, Ḥusayn b. Shihāb al-Dīn, *Hidāyat al-abrār*, Baghdad, 1977

al-Kāẓimī, al-Muḥaqqiq, al-Shaykh ʿAsad Allāh al-Tustarī, *Kashf al-qināʿ ʿan wujūh ḥujjiyyat al-ijmāʿ*, lithograph, reprint, Qum, 1317 AH/ 1899

al-Khumaynī, al-Sayyid Ruḥ Allāh al-Musawī, *Manāhij al-wuṣūl ilā ʿilm al-uṣūl*, 2 vols., Qum, 1414 AH/1993

———, *Anwār al-hidāyah fī al-taʿliqah ʿalā al-kifāyah*, Tehran, 1415 AH/1994

———, *The Mystery of Prayer*, trans. Amjad H. Shah Naqavi, Leiden, 2015

al-Khuʾī, al-Sayyid Abū al-Qāsim, *Miṣbah al-uṣūl*, Najaf, 1989

———, *Muḥāḍarāt fī uṣūl al-fiqh*, 5 vols., Qum, 1410 AH/1990

———, *Muʿjam rijāl al-ḥadīth*, 3rd edition, 25 vols., Beirut, 1983

Khwānsārī, Muḥammad Bāqir al-Mūsawī, *Rawḍāt al-jannāt fī aḥwāl al-ʿulamāʾ wa al-sādāt*, 8 vols., Beirut, 1431 AH/2010

al-Kulaynī, Abū Jaʿfar Muḥammad b. Yaʿqūb b. Ishāq, *al-kāfī*, 8 vols., Tehran, 1388 AH/1968

Madrasat al-Imām Bāqir al-ʿUlūm, *Mawsūʿat kitāb Allāh wa ahl al-bayt fī ḥadīth al-thaqalayn*, 4 vols., Qum, 1429 AH/ 1387 SH

Majlisī, Muḥammad Bāqir, *Biḥār al-anwār*, Beirut, 1403 AH/1983

Mālik b. Anas, Abū ʿAbd Allāh, *Muwaṭṭaʾ Imām Mālik*, n.p., n.d.

al-Marʿashī, Ismāʿīl b. Aḥmad al-Husaynī, *Ijmāʿiyyāt fiqh al-shīʿah*, Qum, 1994

al-Mufīd, al-Shaykh Abū ʿAbd Allāh Muḥammad b. Muḥammad b. Nuʿmān, *Awāʾil al-maqālat*, in: *Muṣannafāt, al-Shaykh al-Mufīd,* 14 vols., Qum, 1993, vol. IV

———, *al-Fuṣūl al-ʿasharah fī al-ghaybah*, in: *Muṣannafāt, al-Shaykh al-Mufīd*, 14 vols., Qum, 1993, vol. III

———, *al-Fuṣūl al-mukhtārah min al-ʿuyūn wa al-maḥāsin*, in: *Muṣannafāt, al-Shaykh al-Mufīd,* 14 vols., Qum, 1993, vol. II

———, *al-Irshād fī maʿrifat ḥujaj allāh ʿalā al-ʿibād*, in: *Muṣannafāt, al-Shaykh al-Mufīd,* 14 vols., Qum, 1993, vol. 11

———, *al-Iʿlām*, in: *Muṣannafāt, al-Shaykh al-Mufīd,* 14 vols., Qum, 1993, vol. IX

———, *al-Tadhkirah bi-uṣūl al-fiqh*, in: *Muṣannafāt, al-Shaykh al-Mufīd,* 14 vols., Qum, 1414 AH/1993, vol. IX

Muḥammadī, ʿAlī, *Sharḥ rasāʾil*, Qum, 1372 SH/1993

al-Murawwij, al-Sayyid Muḥammad al-Jazāiʾrī, *Muntahā al-dirāyah fī tawḍīḥ al-kifāyah*, 4 vols., Qum, n.d.

al-Murtaḍā, al-Sharīf Abū al-Qāsim ʿAlī b. Ḥusayn al-Mūsawī, *al-Dharīʿah ilā uṣūl al-sharīʿah,* ed. Abū al-Qāsim Gurjī, Tehran, 1363 SH/ 1984

———, *al-Intiṣār*, Najaf, 1971

———, *Mawsūʿat al-Sharīf al-Murtaḍā*, 22 vols., Beirut, 1433 AH/2012

———, *al-Rasāʾil*, 4 vols., Qum, 1405 AH/1984-5

———, *al-Shāfī fī al-imāmah*, 4 vols., Qum, 1410 AH/1990

al-Muẓaffar, Muḥammad Riḍā, *al-Manṭiq*, 3 vols., Beirut, 1980

———, *Uṣūl al-fiqh*, 2 vols., Qum, 1405 AH/1985

al-Najafī, Ākhūnd Muḥammad Kāẓim b. Ḥusayn al-Harawī al-Khurāsānī, *Kifayat al-uṣūl*, Qum, 1413 AH/1992

al-Najāshī, Abū al-ʿAbbās Aḥmad b. ʿAlī, *Kitāb al-rijāl*, ed. Ḥasan Muṣṭafawī, Tehran, n.d.

al-Narāqī al-Fāḍil, Aḥmad b. Muḥammad Mahdī, *Manāhij al-aḥkām wa al-uṣūl*, lithograph, Tehran, 1299 AH/1882

al-Nasafī, ʿAbd Allāh b. Aḥmad, *al-Manār fī uṣūl al-fiqh*, Istanbul, 1308 AH/1891

———, *Manār al-anwār*, Istanbul, 1390 AH/1970

al-Naysābūrī, Faḍl b. Shādhān, *al-Īḍāḥ*, ed. al-Muḥaddith al-Urmawī, Tehran, 1976

al-Pazdawī, ʿAlī b. Muḥammad, *Kanz al-wuṣūl ilā maʿrifat al-uṣūl*, Karachi, n.d.

al-Qāḍī ʿAbd Jabbār, *al-Mughnī, Kitāb al-sharʿīyāt*, n.p., n.d.

al-Qazwīnī, al-Sayyid Ibrāhīm b. Muḥammad Bāqir, *Ḍawābiṭ al-uṣūl*, lithograph, Najaf, 1271 AH/1855

al-Qummī, al-Mīrzā Abū al-Qāsim al-Jilānī, *al-Qawanīn al-muḥkamah fī al-uṣūl*, lithograph, Tehran, 1275 AH/1859

al-Rashtī, Mīrzā Habīb Allāh, *Badāʾiʿ al-afkār*, Najaf, n.d.

al-Rāzī, Fakhr al-Dīn Muḥammad b. ʿUmar, *al-Maḥṣūl ilā ʿilm al-uṣūl*, 6 vols., ed. Ṭaha Jābir Fayyāḍ al-ʿAlawānī, Beirut, 1416 AH/1996

———, *al-Maṭālib al-ʿāliyyah fī al-ʿilm al-ilāhiyyah*, Beirut, 1983, vol. III

al-Sabzawārī, al-Sayyid ʿAbd al-ʿAlā al-Mūsawī, *Tahdhīb al-uṣūl*, 2 vols., Beirut, 1996

al-Ṣadr, al-Sayyid Muḥammad Bāqir, *Durūs fī ʿilm al uṣūl*, 2 vols., Qum, 1415 AH/1994

al-Ṣadr, Muḥammad Ṣādiq, *al-Ijmāʿ fī al-tashrīʿ al-islāmī*, Beirut, 1969

Ṣadūq, al-Shaykh Muḥammad b. ʿAlī b. al-Ḥusayn b. Bābawayh, *al-Khiṣāl*, Najaf, 1389 AH/1970

———, *Man la yaḥḍuruhu al-faqīh*, 4 vols., Tehran, 1390 AH/1970

———, *al-Tawḥīd*, Tehran, 1387 AH/1967

al-Sarakhsī, Abū Bakr Muḥammad b. Aḥmad b. Abī Sahl, *Uṣūl al-sarkhisī*, 2 vols., Beirut, 1410 AH/1990

al-Shahrastānī, Muḥammad Ḥusayn, *Ghāyat al-masʾūl fī ʿilm al-uṣūl*, lithograph, Qum, n.d.

al-Shahīd al-Awwal, Shams al-Dīn Abū ʿAbd Allāh Muḥammad b. Makkī al-ʿĀmilī al-Jizzīnī, *Dhikrā al-shīʿah fī aḥkām al-sharīʿah*, lithograph, n.p., 1274 AH/1858

———, *al-Qawāʾid wa al-fawāʾid*, Najaf, 1980

al-Shahīd al-Thānī, Zayn al-Dīn b. ʿAlī al-ʿĀmilī al-Jubaʿī, *Munyat al-murīd*, Beirut, n.d.

———, *Tamhīd al-qawāʾid*, lithograph, n.p., 1271 AH/1855

al-Shāwkānī, Muḥammad b. ʿAlī b. Muḥammad, *Irshād al-fuḥūl ilā taḥqīq al-ḥaqq min ʿilm al-Uṣūl*, Beirut, 1994
Shaykh al-Ṭāʾifah; al-Ṭūsī, Abū Jaʿfar Muḥammad b. al-Ḥasan b.ʿAlī, *al-Fihrist*, Mashhad, 1351 SH/1972
———, *Ikhtiyār maʿrifat al-rijāl*, Mashhad, 1348 SH/1969
———, *al-Istibṣār*, 4 vols., Tehran, 1390 AH/1970
———, *al-Khilāf*, 4 vols., Qum, n.d.
———, *Kitāb al-ghaybah*, Qum, 1411 AH/1991
———, *al-Nihāyah fī mujarrad al-fiqh wa al-fatāwā*, n.p., n.d.
———, *al-Rasāʾil al-ʿashr*, Qum, 1414 AH/1993
———, *Tafsīr al-tibyān*, 10 vols., Najaf, n.d.
———, *Tahdhīb al-aḥkām*, ed. Sayyid Ḥasan al-Mūsawī al-Kharsān, Tehran, 1983, vol. x
———, *Tahdhīb al-aḥkām*, 10 vols., Tehran, 1390 AH/1970
———, *al-Talkhīṣ al-shāfī*, 4 vols., Qum, 1974
———, *al-ʿUddah fī uṣūl al-fiqh*, lithograph, Bombay, 1312 AH/1894
———, *al-ʿUddah fī uṣūl al-fiqh*, lithograph, Tehran, 1314 AH/1896
———, *al-ʿUddah fī uṣūl al-fiqh*, ed. Muḥammad Mahdī Najaf, Qum, 1983, vol. I
———, *al-ʿUddah fī uṣūl al-fiqh*, 2 vols., ed. Muḥammad Riḍā al-Anṣārī al-Qummī, Qum, 1417 AH/1997
al-Shīrāzī, Abū Isḥāq Ibrāhīm , *Sharḥ al-lumaʿ*, ed. ʿAbd al-Majīd Turkī, Beirut, 1988
al-Shirāzī, Nāṣir Makārim, *Anwār al-uṣūl*, 3 vols., Qum, 1415 AH/1994
al-Shirāzī, al-Sayyid Muḥammad, *al-Waṣāʾil ilā al-rasāʾil*, Qum, n.d.
Shubbar, ʿAbd Allāh, *al-Uṣūl al-aṣliyyah wa al-qawāʿid al-sharʿiyyah*, Qum, 1404 AH/1984
al-Suyūṭī, Jalāl al-Dīn Abū al-Faḍl ʿAbd al-Raḥmān b. Abī Bakr, *al-Bahjat al-marḍiyyah fī sharḥ al-afiyyah*, lithograph, n.p., 1414 AH/1994
———, *al-Muzhir fī ʿulūm al-lughah wa anwāʿihā*, 2 vols., Cairo, n.d., vol. 1
al-Ṭabāṭabāʾī, al-Sayyid Muḥammad, *Mafātīḥ al-uṣūl*, lithograph, Najaf, 1229 AH/1814
Taqī, Muḥammad, *Hidāyat al-mustarshidīn fī sharḥ uṣūl maʿālim al-dīn*, lithograph, n.p., 1310 AH/1893
Thānvī, *Muḥammad b. ʿAlī, Kashāf iṣtilāḥāt al-funūn*, Istanbul, 1899
al-Ṭihrānī, Āqā Buzurgh Muḥammad Muḥsin, *al-Dharīʿah ilā taṣānīf al-shīʿah*, Beirut, 1983–1988
———, *Ṭabaqāt aʿlām al-shīʿah al-nābis fī al qarn al-khāmis*, Beirut, 1391 AH/1971
al-Tirmidhī, Abū ʿĪsā Muḥammad b. ʿĪsā b. Sawrah, *Sunan al-Tirmidhī*, 5 vols., ed. Aḥmad Muḥammad Shākir, Beirut, 1937
al-Ṭiqṭaqā, Muḥammad b. ʿAlī b., *al-Fakhrī fī al-ādāb al-sulṭāniyyah wa al-duwal al-islāmiyyah*, n.p., 1927
Ziriklī, Khayr al-Dīn, *al-Aʿlām*, 11 vols., supplement, Beirut, 1389 AH/1969
al-Zuḥaylī, Wahbah, *Uṣūl al-fiqh al-islāmī*, 2 vols., Damascus, 1986

Bibliography of Secondary Sources

Aghnides, N.P, *An Introduction to Mohammedan Law and a Bibliography*, Lahore, 1981

Ameer Ali, Syed, *Muhammadan Law*, New Delhi, 1986

al-Amīn, Sharīf Yaḥyā, *Muʿjam al-firaq al-Islāmiyyah,* Beirut, 1406 AH

Arabi, Oussama, David S. Powers, and Susan A. Spectorsky (eds.), *Islamic Legal Thought: A Compendium of Muslim Jurists*, Leiden, 2013

ʿArifin, Muhammad b., *The Principles of ʿUmūm and Takhṣīṣ in Islamic Jurisprudence,* PhD thesis, University of Edinburgh, 1988

al-Bahādilī, Aḥmad Kāẓim, *Miftaḥ al-wuṣūl ilā ʿilm al-uṣūl*, Baghdad, 1995

Bearman, Peri, and Rudolph Peters (eds.), *The Ashgate Research Companion to Islamic Law*, Farnham, 2014

———, Rudolph Peters, and Frank E. Vogel (eds.), *The Islamic School of Law: Evolution, Devolution, and Progress*, Cambridge, Mass., 2005

———, Bernard G. Weiss, and Wolfhart Heinrichs (eds.), *The Law Applied: Contextualizing the Islamic Sharīʿah*, London, 2008

Belhaj, ʿAbd Essamad, ʻLegal Knowledge by Application: Sufism as Islamic Legal Hermeneutics in the 10th/12th Centuries', *Studia Islamica*, 108, 1, (2013), pp. 82–107

Bedir, Murtaza, ʻAn Early response to Shāfiʿī: Īsā b. Abān on the Prophetic Report (Khabar)', *Islamic Law and Society*, 9, 3, (2002), pp. 285–311

Burton, John, *The Sources of Islamic Law*, Edinburgh, 1990

———, *An Introduction to the Ḥadīth*, Edinburgh, 1994

Calder, Norman, *Classical Islam: A Sourcebook of Religious Literature*, London, 2012

———, ʻDoubt and Prerogative: The Emergence of an Imāmi Shīʿī Theory of Ijtihād', *Studia Islamica*, 70, (1989), pp. 57–78

———, *Interpretation and Jurisprudence in Medieval Islam*, Farnham, 2006

———, *Islamic Jurisprudence in the Classical Era*, Cambridge, 2010

———, *Studies in Early Muslim Jurisprudence*, Oxford, 1993

———, *The Structure of Authority in Imāmī Shīʿī Jurisprudence*, PhD thesis, SOAS, University of London, 1979

Coulson, N. J., *A History of Islamic Law*, reprint, Edinburgh, 1990

Dahlén, Ashk P., *Islamic Law, Epistemology and Modernity: Legal Philosophy in contemporary Iran*, London, 2003

Ezzati, Abu'l-Fadl, *Shīʿī Islamic Law and Jurisprudence*, Lahore, 1976

al-Faḍlī, ʿAbd al-Hādī, *Mabādiʾ uṣūl al-fiqh*, Qum, 1374 SH/1995

Fayḍ, ʿAlī Riḍā, *Mabādiʾ fiqh wa uṣūl*, Tehran, 1374 SH/1995

Fyzee, Asaf Ali Asghar, *A Shiite Creed*, Oxford, 1942

———, *Outlines of Muhammadan Law*, Oxford, 1949

Gleave, Robert, ʻAkhbari Shi'i *usul al-fiqh* and the juristic theory of Yusuf al-Bahrani', in: R. Gleave and E. Kermeli (eds.), *Islamic Law: Theory and Practice*, London, 2001,

Part 1: Legal theory, pp. 24–45
———, *Books and Bibliophiles: Studies in Honour of Paul Auchterlonie on the Bio-Bibliography of the Muslim World*, Oxford, 2014
———, 'Imāmī Shīʿī Refutations of *Qiyās*', in *Studies in Islamic Legal Theory*, Leiden, 2002, Part 3: Controversies Within and Between Schools, pp. 267–292
———, *Inevitable Doubt: Two Theories of Shi'i Jurisprudence*, Leiden, 2000
———, *Islam and Literalism: Literal Meaning and Interpretation in Islamic Legal Theory*, Edinburgh, 2012
———, and A. Kevin Reinhart (eds.), *Islamic Law in Theory: Studies on Jurisprudence in Honor of Bernard Weiss*, Leiden, 2014
———, and Eugenia Kermeli (eds.), *Islamic Law: Theory and Practice*, London, 2001
———, *Scripturalist Islam: The History and Doctrines of the Akhbari School of Shīʿī Thought*, Leiden, 2007
———, 'Shi'i Jurisprudence During the Seljuq Period: Rebellion and Public Order in an Illegitimate State', in: Lange, Christian and Songül Mecit (eds.), *The Seljuqs: Politics, Society and Culture*, Edinburgh, 2011, pp. 205–28
———, and Andreas Christmann (eds.), *Studies in Islamic Law: a Festschrift for Colin Imber*, Oxford, 2007
———, 'Questions and Answers on Akhbari Jurisprudence: *The Jawabat al-Masa'il al-Zahiriyya* of Muhammad Amin al-Astarabadi', in: *Studies in Islamic Law: a Festschrift for Colin Imber*, Oxford, 2008
Goldziher, Ignaz, *The Zahiris: Their Doctrine and Their History*, trans. Wolfgang Behn, Leiden, 1971
Guraya, Muḥammad Yūsuf, *Islamic Jurisprudence in the Modern World*, Lahore, 1992
———, *Origins of Islamic Jurisprudence*, Delhi, 1992
Hallaq, Wael B., *A History of Islamic Legal Theories: An Introduction to Sunni Usul al-Fiqh*, New York, 1997
———, *An Introduction to Islamic Law*, Cambridge, 2009
———, *Authority, Continuity, and Change in Islamic Law*, Cambridge, 2001
———, *Law and Legal Theory in Classical and Medieval Islam*, Aldershot, 1995
———, 'On the Authoritativeness of Sunni Consensus', *IJMES*, 18, 4, (1986), pp. 427–54
———, *Shari'ah: Theory, Practice, Transformations*, Cambridge, 2009
———, *The Impossible State: Islam, Politics, and Modernity's Moral Predicament*, New York, 2012
———, *The Origins and Evolution of Islamic Law*, Cambridge, 2005
———, *Was the Gate of Ijtihad Closed? The Early Essays on the History of Islamic Legal Theories*, Tokyo, 2003
Halm, Heinz, *Shi'a Islam: From Religion to Revolution*, Princeton, 1997
———, *Shiism*, Edinburgh, 1991
Ḥasan, Aḥmad, *Analogical Reasoning in Islamic Jurisprudence*, Delhi, 1994

———, *The Doctrine of Ijmāʿ in Islam: A Study of the Juridicial Principle of Consensus*, Islamabad, 1978

Hascall, Susan.C, 'Restorative Justice in Islam: Should *Qisas* Be Considered a Form of Restorative Justice?', *Berkeley Journal of Middle Eastern & Islamic Law*, 4, 18, (2011)

Hourani, G. F., 'The Basis of Authority of Consensus in Sunnite Islam', *Studia Islamica*, 21, (1964), pp. 13–60

Howard, I. K. A.,'The Early Imāmī Shīʿī School of Islamic Law', *al-Serat*, London, 1976, vol. II, no. I, pp. 6–11

Kamali, Mohammad Hashim, *Principles of Islamic Jurisprudence*, 3rd ed., Cambridge, 1991

———, 'Legal Maxims and Other Genres of Literature in Islamic Jurisprudence', *Arab Law Quarterly*, 20, 1, (2006), pp. 77–101

Khadduri, Majid, *al-Shāfiʿī's Risāla: Treatise on the Foundations of Islamic Jurisprudence*, repr., Cambridge, 1987

Khan, Mahdī ʿAlī, *The Elements of Islamic Philosophy*, repr., Lahore, 1992

Kohlberg, Etan, 'Aspects of Ahkbārī Thought in the Seventeenth and Eighteenth Centuries', in: Levtzion, Nehemia and John O. Boll (eds.), *Eighteenth-Century Renewal and Reform in Islam*, New York, 1987, pp. 133–66

al-Madan, ʿAlī, *Taṭawwur ʿilm al-kalām al-imāmī*, Baghdad, 1431 AH/2010

Madelung, Wilferd, 'al-Akhbāriyya', *Encyclopaedia of Islam*, 2nd edn., Leiden, 1954–2005, supplement

———, *Religious and Ethnic Movements in Medieval Islam*, London, 1992

———, *The Succession to Muḥammad: A Study of the Early Caliphate*, Cambridge, 1997

McDermott, Martin J., *The Theology of al-Shaikh al-Mufīd*, Beirut, 1978

Mielziner, Moses, 'The Abrogation of Laws', *Jewish Encyclopaedia*, 12 vols., New York, 1901-1906

Miller, William McElwee, *A Treatise on the Principles of Shiʿite Theology*, London, 1928

Moezzi, Amir, *The Divine Guide in Early Shiʿism*, Albany, NY, 1994

———, Mohammad Ali, and Christian Jambet, *Qu'est-ce que le shīʿisme?*, Paris, 2004

Moussavi, Ahmad Kazemi, *Religious Authority in Shiʿite Islam: From the Office of the Muftī to the Institution of Marjaʿ*, Kuala Lumpur, 1996

Mughniyyah, Muḥammad Jawād, *ʿIlm uṣūl al-fiqh fī thawbihī al-jadīd*, Beirut, 1975

Mulder, Stephennie, 'Abdūlhamid and the ʿAlids: Ottoman patronage of "Shiʿi" shrines in the Cemetery of Bāb al-Ṣaghīr in Damascus', *Studia Islamica*, 108, 1, (2013), pp. 16–47

Munir, Muḥammad, 'Triple Ṭalāq in One Session: An Analysis of the Opinions of Classical, Medieval, and Modern Muslim Jurists under Islamic Law', *Arab Law Quarterly*, 27, (2013), pp. 29–49

Najafiyān, Saʿīd, 'Imām Khumaynī: Life and Works', pt. 1, in: *al-Tawḥīd*, 7, 4, Tehran, 1990, pp. 117–35

———, 'Imām Khumaynī: Life and Works', pt. 2, in: *al-Tawḥīd*, 8, 1, Tehran, 1990, pp. 95–125

Naqavi, Sayyid Amjad H. Shah, *The Jurisprudence of al-ʿAllāmah al-Ḥillī*, Forthcoming

———, *The History of Imāmī Shīʿī Uṣūl al-Fiqh Without Any Gaps*, Forthcoming

Nyberg, H.S. 'Abu 'l-Hudhayl al-ʿAllāf', *Encyclopaedia of Islam*, 2nd edn, (eds.) P. Bearman, Th. Bianquis, C.E. Bosworth, E. van Donzel, and W.P. Heinrichs, Leiden, 2014

Omotosho, ʿAbd al-Rāfaʿī Oyewumī, *The Problem of al-Amr in Uṣūl al-Fiqh*, PhD thesis, University of Edinburgh, 1984

Pill, Shlomo, C.,'Law as Faith, Faith as Law: The Legalization of Theology in Islam and Judaism in the Thought of Al-Ghazali and Maimonides', *Berkeley Journal of Middle Eastern & Islamic Law*, 6 (2014), pp. 1–26

Powell, Russell, 'Forgiveness in Islamic Ethics and Jurisprudence', *Berkeley Journal of Middle Eastern & Islamic Law*, 4, 17, (2011), pp. 17–34

Rāmyār, Maḥmūd, *Shaykh Ṭūsī: The Life and Works of a Shīʿite Leader*, PhD thesis, University of Edinburgh, 1977

Ryding Karin C., 'Aspects of the Genitive:Taxonomy in *al-Jumal fi al-naḥw*' in Ryding, Karin.C (ed.), *Early Medieval Arabic: Studies on Al-Khalīl Ibn Ahmad*, Washington, DC, 1998, pp .92–142

Schacht, Joseph, *The Origins of Muhammadan Jurisprudence*, repr., Oxford, 1979

Schmidtke, Sabine, *The Theology of al-ʿAllāma al-Ḥillī (d. 726/1325)*, Berlin, 1991

Shalakany, Amr. A., 'Islamic Legal Histories', *Berkeley Journal of Middle Eastern & Islamic Law*, 1, 1, (2008), pp. 1–83

Shukri, Murād, *Tāḥqīq al-wuṣūl ilā ʿilm al-uṣūl*, Amman, 1991

Stewart, Devin J., *Islamic Legal Orthodoxy: Twelver Shiite Responses to the Sunni Legal System*, Utah, 1998

———, 'Ḥusayn b. ʿAbd al-Ṣamad al-ʿĀmilī's Treatise for Sultan Suleiman and the Shīʿī Shāfiʿī Legal Tradition', *Islamic Law and Society*, 4, 2, (1997), pp. 156–199

———, 'al-Sharīf al-Murtaḍā (d. 436/1044)', in: Powers, David, Susan A. Spectorsky, and Oussama Arabi (eds.), *Islamic Legal Thought: A Compendium of Muslim Jurists*, Leiden, 2013, pp. 167–210

Ṭabāṭabāʾī, Hossein Modarressi, *An Introduction to Shīʿi Law: A Bibliographical Study*, London, 1984, p. 48

———, *Tradition and Survival: A Bibliographical Survey of Early Shīʿite Literature*, Oxford, 2003

al-Ṭabāṭabāʾī, Sayyid ʿAbd al-ʿAzīz, *Maktabat al-ʿAllāmah al-Ḥillī*, Qum, 1416 AH/1995

Tomeh, Mamoud Munes 'Persuasion and Authority in Islamic Law', *Berkeley Journal of Middle Eastern & Islamic Law*, 3 (2010), pp. 141–171

Tyabji, Faiz Hassan Badrudin, *Muslim Law*, Mumbai, 1968

Ullman, Stephen, *Semantics: An Introduction to the Science of Meaning*, Oxford, 2nd edn., 1964 al-Wāsiṭī, Aḥmad, *Sīrah wa ḥayāt al-imām al-khū'i*, Beirut, 1998

Weiss, Bernard G., *The Search for God's Law: Islamic Jurisprudence in the Writings of Sayf al-Din al-Amidi*, Utah, 1992

———, *The Spirit of Islamic Law*, Athens, GA, 1998

———, *Studies in Islamic Legal Theory*, Leiden, 2002

Zilio-Grandi, Ida, 'Ḥilm or "Judiciousness": A Contribution to the Study of Islamic Ethics', *Studia Islamica*, 101, 1 (2015), pp. 81–100

Index

Index of Qur'ānic Verses